Essentials of HRM

Essentials of HRM

Fourth edition

Shaun Tyson and Alfred York

OXFORD AUCKLAND BOSTON JOHANNESBURG MELBOURNE NEW DELHI

Butterworth-Heinemann
Linacre House, Jordan Hill, Oxford OX2 8DP
225 Wildwood Avenue, Woburn, MA 01801-2041
A division of Reed Educational and Professional Publishing Ltd

℞ A member of the Reed Elsevier plc group

First published as *Personnel Management* 1982
Second edition 1989
Third edition 1996
Fourth edition 2000

British Library Cataloguing in Publication Data
A catalogue record for this book is available from the British Library

ISBN 0 7506 4715 9

Typeset by Avocet Typeset, Brill, Aylesbury, Bucks
Printed and bound in Great Britain

Contents

Figures

Tables

Acknowledgements

We wish to acknowledge with thanks the permissions to reproduce the material from the following works, granted by the publishers and authors:

The model of strategic change and human resource management, granted by Chris Hendry and Andrew Pettigrew, and by Routledge and John Wiley, originally published in the *International Journal of Human Resource Management* (1990) **1** (1) 17–44, and in the *British Journal of Management* (1992) **3** (3), 137–56.

The model of HRM reprinted with the permission of the Free Press, a Division of Simon and Schuster, from *Human Resource Management: A General Managers Perspective* by Michael Beer, Bert Spector, Paul R. Lawrence, D. Quinn Mills and Richard E. Walton, copyright ©1985 by the Free Press.

The cohort analysis from *Manpower Planning in the Civil Service* (1976), Table 5.1, Crown Copyright, which is reproduced with the permission of the Controller of Her Majesty's Stationery Office.

Keith Cameron for permission to quote his chart on commission schemes and to publish his format of a flexible reward system.

To use a portion of Table 3.6 from Appendix III of *Policy and Practice in European Human Resource Management* by (1994) Chris Brewster and Ariane Hegewisch, reproduced with the permission of International Thomson Publishing Services Limited and the authors.

We also wish to thank the numerous people and organizations whose ideas have contributed in so many ways to this book, including best practice examples from Air Products (for an earlier version of their organization structure) British Aerospace (for a description of their BEST management development programme objectives) and Standard Life (for a description of their contribution management system).

We wish to express our gratitude in particular to Nicola Kerr, Partner and Head of the Employment and Pensions Group and Rhodri McDonald her assistant, at SJ Berwin and Co. Solicitors of 222 Grays Inn Road, London, for their helpful comments and advice on our employment law chapter.

Finally, we wish to thank Jayne Ashley and Victoria Grigg for their tireless enthusiasm and considerable skills in preparing a manuscript that grows in length with every new edition.

Any errors and omissions in the text remain our own.

Shaun Tyson
Cranfield, Bedford
Alfred York
Poole, Dorset
January 2000

The behavioural bases of human resource management

The behavioural bases of human resource management

This part of the book is intended to provide a general background for all the subsequent chapters on specific aspects of human resource management (HRM). Since work and its management are human activities set in motion, carried out, continuously super-vised, monitored and assessed by people who are constantly interacting with each other, human factors are crucially important. Nevertheless, managers do not always act as though they fully understand and acknowledge that success in management has to be based on an awareness and at least a broad knowledge of human behaviour, including, of course, their own.

For the last 100 years there have been studies of the behaviour of people, and in par-ticular of the special kinds of problems that modern working life creates. These studies are described collectively as the behavioural sciences and include contributions from specialists trained in a variety of disciplines, particularly in the different branches of psychology and sociology. In times of increasing academic specialization we need to remind ourselves that the situations themselves have no such specialized distinctions. The value of the various specialisms lies in the difference of emphasis and perspective that they give in looking at the same situations, and hence in providing a broader under-standing of their nature.

The behavioural sciences have sometimes been the subject of criticism for an appar-ently disappointing level of achievement in terms of the very considerable amount of time and money spent on research in this field. But criticism on these grounds is a mis-understanding of their purpose, which is certainly not to dispense prescriptions and solutions for the problems of managing people at work, but rather to provide a frame-work for analysis and to indicate possible courses of action and possible consequences. The opportunity costs of decisions, to use the language of economics, have to be eval-uated by individual managers for themselves. In fact, there is tangible evidence that the research data accumulated over the years have had a considerable influence upon present-day managerial thinking and behaviour: for example, the significant growth globally in courses and literature concerned with management education; the general direction of much recent legislation in Europe; the growth of consultancy in manage-ment; the recognition accorded to people management in economics and social policy; and the significance of people management for organizational performance.

In this preliminary phase of the book we are setting out to make a systematic survey of the important areas covered by research into the behaviour of people at work, which is, of necessity, no more than an outline. Apart from providing a necessary background for the main subjects of the book it will also, hopefully, indicate areas where further study may usefully be made.

Chapter 1

Individuals

Individual differences

Human beings share certain common features, such as physical and mental characteristics. These attributes which link all the members of the species produce common patterns of behaviour. Thus, all humans have physiological and basic needs mainly concerned with survival, that is, needs for food, shelter, security, reproduction, affection, group membership and, unlike animals, they also reveal a higher range of needs, concerned with making sense of what might otherwise be a meaningless world. These needs show themselves in the form of exploratory, creative and self-fulfilling activities of many and varied forms. In consequence, a common feature of all human behaviour is that it is goal directed, as the members of the species are driven to satisfy these needs. At the same time every individual is the product of a unique combination of genetic and environmental factors. Apart from the exceptional circumstance of identical twins, every human is physically distinct from all other humans at birth. Thereafter, everyone is subjected to a unique pattern of environmental influences, produced by the accumulative and distinctive features of a particular family, sex, region, race, education, religion, epoch, etc. This is a constantly changing process with the result that all of us are being continuously shaped and modified by new experiences and new relationships.

The differing factors of heredity and environment produce an individual uniqueness that has important consequences.

As we grow physically and develop mentally, and join in, so to speak, the general human process of satisfying needs and making sense of the world, we are subjected to the socializing influences of other people with whom we have most contact, in the family, at school, at church, for example, and in the larger society to which we belong. During this time we are also developing emotionally, getting in touch with our feelings and learning how to control them. As a result of these influences we acquire attitudes, values and expectations which shape our behaviour towards other people and strongly affect judgements and decisions about goals to pursue. When our beliefs have no rational basis, they may also be described as prejudices.

The condition of common, human similarity and individual dissimilarity has a significance for the problems of interpersonal relationships and hence for human resource management. Information received by individuals from the external environment is processed in terms of their personal backgrounds, and the results are used as a basis for judgements, decisions and actions. In the course of everyday relationships there is a general tendency either to assume that other people see and interpret the world as we do or to expect that they should do so.

The importance of understanding the effects of individual differences on interpersonal relationships is not so much that assumptions and expectations about the behaviour of others will be eliminated or modified – although the possibilities of this will, no doubt, be increased. It is, rather, that we should have a framework for making as objective an analysis as possible of our own and other people's behaviour. This will lead to a greater insight into people management issues, and hence may improve the quality of our interpersonal relationships, because we understand that reality is not absolute but is determined by individual perception and interpretation. In practical terms, this means that we may be less likely to become confused, frustrated or angry when the behaviour of others does not appear to match our own assumptions or expectations of what it should be. We are also correspondingly less likely to be impelled to explain apparently odd or unreasonable behaviour of other people by ascribing our own reasons and motives, for example, stupidity, spite, jealousy, obstinacy, lack of interest, etc. This kind of insight and understanding is most important as a basis for studying specific areas such as communication, motivation, group and organizational behaviour, and leadership.

Self-awareness

The need for and importance of self-awareness has been recognized since the earliest times. The injunction 'Know thyself' was apparently written in gold above the portico of the Temple of Apollo in ancient Greece. Robert Burns addressed the same theme when writing 'O wad some power the gift tae gie us, to see oursels as ithers see us'.

An understanding of one's own capabilities and limitations in terms of knowledge, skills and personal traits is especially important in work. The more insight managers have into their own behavioural traits and the effects on the members of their groups, the more effective they are likely to be, and the less likely they are to alienate the very people they should be motivating. As managerial styles have become more democratic or participative and less authoritarian so employees are encouraged more than ever before to assess themselves in terms of employment suitability, career paths, work performance and developmental and training needs.

There are two views of individuals. There is the view that individuals have of themselves, and there is the view that other people, who have seen them in various situations, have of them. Obviously there may often be some divergence in these views. The view of self may conflict with the views others have of us. There may be differences among the external assessors. The main possible variants in assessing individual behaviour have been summarized in the model known as the Johari window (Figure 1.1), named after its psychologist authors, Joe Luft and Harry Ingham.

The window in Figure 1.1 has four panes, described as follows:

1 Known to self and to others (public), e.g., I know that I am lazy and other people think so too.

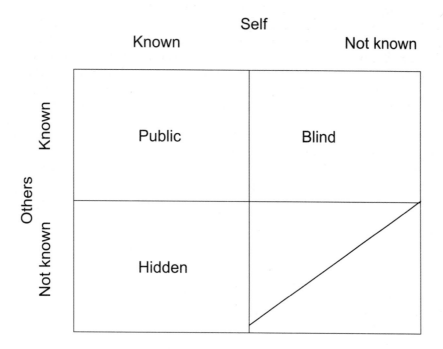

Figure 1.1 The Johari window

2 Known to others, but not to self (blind), e.g., I think that I am a caring, sensitive person. Others do not see me in this way. I am not aware that others hold a different view.
3 Known to self, but not to others (hidden), e.g., I know that my lack of moral courage is a major weakness. Apparently others are not so aware of this problem.
4 Not known to self and not known to others, e.g., I am a poor judge of people. I do not realize this and neither do others who know me.

How should self-aware people be described?

- They realize that their behaviour affects others and that they may need to change in order to achieve effectiveness in performance and human relationships.
- They take active steps to obtain feedback about their behaviour and performance.
- They take particular note of any consensus of external views, especially when these diverge significantly from their views of self.
- They have reached as honest and balanced a view of themselves as is humanly possible.

All this, of course, is very much easier said than done. In real life we find it much easier to list our perceived strengths than our weak points. We do not like unpalatable home truths. We generally prefer to judge other people rather than ourselves. Paradoxically, the achievement of self-awareness depends on awareness of the need for, and importance of, self-awareness in the first place. The person who occupies windowpane number three in the Johari window may find it very difficult to move to windowpane number one for the very reasons that placed him or her in pane number three.

When we are dealing with questions concerning individual differences it is useful to consider whether we are discussing differences in personality. In HRM, questions about the appropriateness of 'specific traits' or attributes are frequently raised in selection and assessment decisions. We discuss psychometric tests later in the book, but we should note here that researchers have identified a variety of personality traits. There is evidence that the many individual-specific traits, such as 'warmth' or 'unreliability', can be subsumed under what are known as the 'Big Five' dimensions of personality these being extroversion, neuroticism, agreeableness, conscientiousness and openness to experience.

These dimensions can be defined as follows:

1 *Extroversion*: extroverts tend to be sociable, relate themselves readily to the world around them.
2 *Neuroticism*: view the world as a frightening place. Neurotics have anxieties and are self-conscious.
3 *Agreebleness*: the ability to care, to be affectionate.
4 *Conscientiousness*: careful, scrupulous, persevering behaviour.
5 *Openness to experience*: these people have broad interests, are willing to take risks.

These attributes are scales in themselves, for example, extroversion–introversion, neuroticism–stability, and the balance will be a mixture of positions for any individual, along the five continua.

The answers to the questions that an analysis of self should provide can only come from the evidence of past and present behaviour. Actions speak louder than words. An analysis of the individual for purposes of self-awareness requires an investigation that is much the same as that which takes place during the effective selection interview or performance appraisal discussion. It requires discipline and a system. The evidence of the individual's abilities, potential, strengths, weaknesses, values, attitudes, motivation, likes, dislikes, personality traits, etc., is likely to be provided from the following sources:

- major influences in life such as family, education, religion, work, social life, study and reading, spare-time interests and pursuits, travel
- life history in terms of achievements and decisions.

Individuals can carry out this investigation for themselves, but the process is considerably enhanced with the help of another person, who has the counselling and investigative skills needed to ask relevant, probing and at times awkward questions in a friendly, helpful, but firm manner.

Communication

The problems that human individuality poses for interpersonal relationships lead logically to a study of communication. This may be seen as an extension of the study of the nature of individuals and their relationships with each other, the problems that human individuality creates and the extent to which these barriers can be reduced. Communication is a flow of information which humans use to pass messages and intentions to each other, therefore it follows that no collaborative human action can take place without it.

Since pleas for improved communication are constantly voiced, it would be useful to pause for a moment to discuss its essential nature. Although the process is subtle and not easy to simplify, it is useful to think of communication as it is applied to telegraphy, where a message is encoded by one person, transmitted over a certain wavelength and received and decoded by another. For the message to be received and understood as the transmitter intended, a number of conditions have to be fulfilled.

1 Both sender and receiver have to know the code.
2 They have to use the same wavelength.
3 There has to be the minimum of interference.

This simple analogy emphasizes its essential nature – it is a two-way process and to be effective the intended meaning of the sender has to be received in as near an uncontaminated state as possible by the receiver. This basic prerequisite is not always understood in practice. Sometimes when managers speak about improved communication, they really mean turning the volume up, or sending more or different kinds of messages without any thought for the receiver.

It is common to think at first of human communication as taking three forms, that is, spoken face to face, or written or e-mailed messages from a distance, or spoken messages from a distance. In all these situations there is an emphasis on the use of words and their meanings. Of course, language is the basic form of human communication and here the slant of the message will be affected by the choice of words and their juxtaposition, and the tone of voice when the language is spoken. However, communication may involve all the senses. As most of us are aware, there has been a marked growth of interest in non-verbal behaviour. The significance of non-verbal messages can be readily illustrated if we think of a telephone conversation and the difference between a situation where only the voice can be heard and another where both people are speaking face to face. We usually have to be much more careful when speaking on the telephone, where there is no opportunity to show by a twinkle in the eye or a smile that a remark is not meant to be taken too seriously.

The encoded communication signal is a combination of elements, comprising words used in particular ways, accompanied by expressions in the eyes, facial expressions, gestures and body postures, all of which contribute to the total meaning and the complexity of the message. It is most important, therefore, to realize that when we send messages to other people the code, so to speak, is very much determined by the influences of the individual's heredity and environment. Our attitudes, value systems and expectations all contribute not only to the way a message is sent, but also to the way in which it is received. Receivers will decode information in the light of their individual perceptions of the world. Short of being able by some miraculous means to change identities with another person, there is no way that we can accurately check how other people receive our meanings. Nevertheless, we have to make the best of an imperfect world, and since communication is vital to effective management we need to seek every possible way to ensure that it is as sound as we can make it.

Despite the continued attention that the subject receives, the basic problems seem to remain as intractable as ever. Any newspaper on any day will provide a catalogue of a wide range of human problems which all stem from a central problem in communication. Since the problem is inherent in the human condition, there can be no easy solutions. The best hopes for making any progress seem to lie, first, in acquiring a better understanding of the nature of communication, its inherent problems and their causes and, second, in making use of this insight to create the most favourable conditions for the highest possible level of communication that can be achieved. We can now consider what these conditions are.

1 There has to be a genuine desire to communicate. In other words, the sender of a message must be truly concerned to help the receiver as much as possible to understand the intended meaning. A seemingly overt message sometimes hides a covert intention. Sometimes the sender even seems to be making more effort to obscure than to reveal a meaning. Bureaucratic correspondence regularly provides examples of this.

2 A climate of trust and openness is a very important factor in establishing effective communication. This style of management is much more likely to create a sense of security and an absence of threat, and hence to encourage the upward communication which managers need as a basis for sound decisions.

3 There has to be awareness of the problems inherent in the individual's uniqueness of perception. We need to deal with others not on the basis of our assumptions that their meanings are or should be the same as our own, but as far as possible in terms of their experience and possible expectations. For example, when communicating with young children most of us recognize that we are dealing with people who have a very limited experience of the world and have a distinctive kind of perceptual framework. We naturally adapt our vocabulary and the way we present ideas to accommodate this limited experience and particular perception. The insight and sensitivity commonly shown in this situation is no different in principle from what is required in dealing with other adults. It seems that it can be achieved, but we frequently do not recognize that it is necessary. In our comments upon 'emotional intelligence' in the next section, we expand upon this point.

4 The more experience is shared, the better the chances of communication are likely to be. Obviously the patterns of general experience are often shaped by forces outside our control. Nevertheless, the point is very relevant to working life, where the more varied the managers' experience can be the easier it is likely to be for them to communicate with the different kinds of employee with whom they come into contact. A real-life example of this principle is seen in the insistence by police forces in the UK that everyone should begin on the bottom rung of the ladder as a police constable. In this way, the Commissioner of Police knows from personal experience what it is like to pound the beat and to deal with the drunk and disorderly. The Commissioner will therefore speak the same language as his or her subordinates, and is unlikely to have problems of credibility.

5 We need to check regularly the understanding of our messages and intentions. In particular, we need to know specifically what others have understood, rather than

whether they have understood. This is why a climate of openness and trust is especially important so that subordinates will not feel threatened or inhibited from saying what they actually think and feel, rather than what they imagine the manager might like to hear, nor be afraid to admit that they have not understood the manager's messages.

6 Finally, sound communication also means listening. This is a skill that does not come naturally. It requires much concentration and practice. Too often we become occupied with our own thoughts and seek opportunities to interject. The bore is an extreme case of deficiency in this skill. Real listening is an important skill that all managers need to acquire if they are to be successful. It is especially important for human resource managers who necessarily spend much of their time listening to the views, proposals, problems and complaints from line managers and their subordinate staff.

Emotional intelligence

In recent years, authors have become more convinced that feelings and emotions are not so well recognized as they ought to be as legitimate sources for skills. Intelligence quotient (IQ) and technical competencies are not enough to produce high performance; increasingly work also requires emotional competencies. This is especially significant due to the expansion of the service sector of the economy. 'Emotional intelligence refers to the capacity for recognising our own feelings, and those for motivating ourselves and for managing emotions well in ourselves and in our relationships' (Goleman, 1998: 317).

Intelligence quotient and emotional intelligence (EI) are not in opposition, but are different sets of competencies. Emotional intelligence requires knowing one's own emotions, managing emotions, motivating oneself, recognizing emotions in others and handling relationships successfully (Goleman, 1996: 43). Emotional intelligence skills can be developed and those who possess such skills are more likely to be effective, having 'mastered the habits of mind that foster productivity' (Goleman, 1996: 36).

Motivation

Motivation may be defined as an inner force that impels human beings to behave in a variety of ways and is, therefore, a very important part of the study of human individuality. Because of the extreme complexity of human individuals and their differences, motivation is very difficult to understand both in oneself and in others. Nevertheless, there are certain features of motivation that may be regarded as generally applicable:

1 The motivational force is aroused as a result of needs which have to be satisfied. Thus, a state of tension or disequilibrium occurs that stimulates action to obtain satisfaction.
2 The satisfaction of a need may stimulate a desire to satisfy further needs (for example, 'The more they have, the more they want').
3 Failure to satisfy needs may lead to a reduction or a redirection of the motivational force towards other goals seen as more obtainable.

4 The motivational force has three basic elements – direction, intensity and duration – that is, it is directed towards goals, its force may vary considerably depending on the strength of individual desires and it may last for long or short periods or be intermittently recurring.

5 There are two main sources of human needs:
   (a) inherited, i.e. all humans share primary physiological needs that must be satisfied for survival
   (b) environmental, i.e. through the main socializing influences in their lives people acquire attitudes, values and expectations, which lead to learned needs such as status, fame, wealth, power.

Some authorities claim that needs for affiliation with others, creativity and achievement are also inherent in human beings.

Because of its central importance to the study of people at work, motivation has been a subject of continued research for the greater part of this century. Many theories have already been proposed and continue to appear. In very broad terms, these theories are of two kinds: they may be based on assumptions by practising managers, resulting from experience and direct observation, or they may be the result of methodical research, usually by psychologists and similar specialists.

Managerial theories

Traditionally, assumptions made by managers about motivation have largely reflected a 'carrot and stick' approach. Ample evidence of the prevalence of this approach may be seen in the systems of rewards and punishments, applied in both direct and subtle ways, that are characteristic of very many work organizations. Sometimes described as a Rational-Economic Theory, it is exemplified in the ideas of F. W. Taylor and his followers in the so-called 'Scientific Management School', which introduced methods of time and motion study into work organizations at the beginning of the twentieth century. This theory is based on assumptions that workers are motivated mainly by material incentives. Such assumptions inevitably have a fundamental effect upon the organizational environment, managerial styles, working arrangements and methods. In Taylor's system, for example, time and motion studies were used to maximize efficiency and productivity. Workers were regarded as a factor of production. Little heed was paid to the potential influence or importance of human factors upon work performance.

Research studies

Because of their variety it is not easy to classify theories of motivation without oversimplification. However, for the convenience of a general survey, two very broad categories may be distinguished. In one group of studies the emphasis is directed mainly towards the importance of needs as an influence on motivation. Because most of these studies are concerned with higher human needs for creativity and self-fulfilment, they represent a form of reaction to managerial assumptions about the dominance of economic motives. The main authors in this category are Abraham Maslow, Elton Mayo and colleagues, Fred Herzberg, David McLelland and Douglas McGregor.

Maslow's hierarchy of needs

Based on the premise that humans are wanting beings whose behaviour is goal directed, Maslow postulates a catalogue of needs at different levels ranging from the basic physiological and biological needs to the higher, cultural, intellectual and spiritual needs:

1 *Physiological*: these are essential to survival, e.g., food, drink, sleep, reproduction, etc.
2 *Security or safety*: these refer to needs to be free from danger and to live in a stable, non-hostile environment.
3 *Affiliation*: as social beings, people need the company of other humans.
4 *Esteem*: these include self-respect and value in the opinion of others.
5 *Self-actualization*: these are needs at the highest level, which are satisfied by opportunities to develop talents to the full and to achieve personal goals.

Two important assumptions are fundamental to Maslow's theory: first, higher needs do not become operative until lower needs have been met (for example, the hungry professor in prison is likely to be more interested in food than philosophy); second, a need that has been satisfied is no longer a motivating force. Research into the applicability of this system to real situations has indicated that it is an over-simplification. Nevertheless, the classification of needs into categories has provided a very useful basis for subsequent research.

Mayo's theory of social needs

Between 1927 and 1939, on-site experiments were carried out by Mayo, Roethligsberger and Dickson at the Hawthorne Plant of the Western Electric Co., Chicago, which have assumed a classical status in the study of human relations. The initial objective was to study the effect of illumination on productivity, but the experiments revealed some unexpected data on human relations which had very significant consequences for subsequent research in the behavioural sciences. Very briefly, the main conclusions of the experiments were these:

1 Industrial life has taken much of the meaning out of work so that workers are driven to fulfil their human needs in other directions, especially in human relationships.
2 Workers are not solely concerned with economic needs and material comfort.
3 Human factors play a very significant part in motivation, and in this respect the research work emphasized the importance of social needs and the influence of the work group.
4 Workers are likely to be more responsive to the influence of colleagues than to attempts of management to control them by material incentives.
5 If management styles produce a threatened, frustrated, alienated workforce, worker groups will tend to form, with their own norms and strategies designed to counter the goals of management.

The main lessons for managers which emerge from the Hawthorne data are that the personal and social needs of employees are very important in determining behaviour and that concentration by management exclusively on productivity, material and environmental issues will prove to be a self-defeating aim. There are also lessons for management about group behaviour, discussed in Chapter 2.

Herzberg's two-factor theory

The two-factor theory is a development of Maslow's system. Herzberg classified two categories of needs corresponding to the lower and higher levels of human goals. He calls one group 'hygiene factors' and the other group 'motivators'. The 'hygiene factors' are the environmental factors in the work situation which need constant attention in order to prevent dissatisfaction. These factors include pay and other rewards, working conditions, security, supervisory styles, etc. They are essentially negative factors in that neglect leads to dissatisfaction, but they cannot actively promote satisfaction or motivate workers. Motivation and satisfaction, says Herzberg, can only come from internal sources and the opportunities afforded by the job for self-fulfilment. According to this theory, a worker who finds work meaningless may react apathetically, even though all the environmental factors are well looked after. Thus, managers have a special responsibility for creating a motivating climate and for making every effort to enrich work. Herzberg's ideas have provoked much controversy, because they imply a general applicability and do not seem to take enough account of individual differences. His insistence that motivation comes from within each individual and that managers cannot truly motivate but can stimulate or stifle motivation is, nevertheless, an important contribution to the study.

Job satisfaction and motivation

Herzberg and others have advocated job redesign to make the work itself inherently motivating, through designing the content and nature of the tasks in the job. According to Hackman and Oldham's theory, the five core characteristics that produce psychological states that can produce job satisfaction, motivation and improved performance are in any one job:

- skill variety (range of different skills demanded)
- task identity (whether work is the whole process or part of the process)
- task significance (impact the job has on others) which together produce the degree of meaningfulness experienced in the job by the job holder
- autonomy (degree of choice, control over the work) which produces experiences of responsibility
- feedback (whether the results of the work itself show clearly the performance level achieved).

The feedback is motivational from the employee's perspective according to the strength of the need for 'growth' required by the employee. All five characteristics combine to produce the 'scope' or complexity of the job.

McLelland's power affiliation achievement model

McLelland's research has identified three basic categories of motivation needs, that is, power, affiliation and achievement, into which people could be grouped according to which need appears to be the main motivator in their lives. Those most interested in power seek positions of control and influence; those for whom affiliation is most important seek pleasant relationships and enjoy helping others; achievement seekers want success, fear failure, are task oriented and self-reliant. These three needs are not mutually exclusive. Many people are well motivated by all three, but invariably one area is predominant. McLelland's research has also indicated that motivational patterns can be modified by specially designed training programmes. The achievement drive, in particular, can apparently be increased by this means. The implications of the theory in practice are that managers can identify employees who are self-motivated, those who rely more on internal incentives and those who could increase their achievement drive through training.

McGregor's Theory X and Theory Y

McGregor proposed that management makes two kinds of assumptions about people, which he calls Theory X and Theory Y. Theory X is seen as a set of traditional beliefs that people are inherently lazy and unambitious, and will avoid responsibility. The main incentives to work are provided by the carrot or the stick and constant supervision is necessary. Theory X attitudes, in McGregor's view, are the main reasons why workers adopt defensive postures and group together to beat the system whenever they can. Management expects them to behave in this way and they fulfil the prophecy. Theory Y, on the other hand, takes a benevolent view of human nature. It assumes that work is a natural human activity, which is capable of providing enjoyment and self-fulfilment. According to Theory Y, the chief task of the manager is to create a favourable climate for growth, for the development of self-reliance, self-confidence and self-actualization through trust and by reducing supervision to a minimum.

The second category of studies is more concerned with the dynamics of the motivational process. In this group there is much more emphasis on the importance of individual differences, of individual expectancy as a function of motivation, and of the contingencies of different situations.

Lewin's field theory

Believing that behaviour is the result of an individual's reaction with his or her environment (that is, B, Behaviour, is a function of P, Person, and E, Environment), Lewin reached the following conclusions about motivation:

1 Motivation depends upon the individual's subjective perceptions of his or her relationships with his or her environment.
2 Behaviour is determined by the interaction of variables, i.e., tension in the individual, the valency of a goal and the psychological distance of a goal (in other words, the existence of a need, the perception of the possibility of fulfilment and the reality of this possibility)

3 Human beings operate in a field of forces influencing behaviour like the forces in a magnetic field, so that people have different motivational drives at different times
4 In the context of work some forces inhibit (e.g., fatigue, restrictive group norms, ineffective management) whilst others motivate (e.g., job satisfaction, effective supervision, rewards).

Vroom's valency expectancy theory

Vroom proposes that motivation is a product of the worth or value that individuals place on the possible results of their actions and the expectation that their goals will be achieved. The theory is expressed by the formula: Force *(F)* = Valency *(V)* × Expectancy *(E)*. The importance of this approach is the emphasis that it places on the individuality and variability of motivational forces, as distinct from the generalizations implied in the theories of Maslow and Herzberg.

Porter and Lawler's model

This model is in the same genre as the theories of Lewin and Vroom in its concern with the influence of perception and expectancy on motivation. However, it is a more comprehensive account than the other theories. The model is based on the following propositions:

1 The motivational force of an individual depends on how he or she perceives the value of the goal, the energy required to achieve the goal and the probability that the goal will be achieved.
2 This perception is, in turn, influenced by the individual's past experience of similar situations, because this will enable a better self-assessment of the required effort, the ability to perform as required and the probability of achieving the goal.
3 Performance achievement is mainly determined by the effort expended, the individual's understanding of the task requirements and self-assessment of ability.
4 Performance is seen by the individual as leading to both intrinsic and extrinsic rewards, which produce satisfaction if the individual perceives the reward as fair.

This progress model is probably the most comprehensive and adequate description of the motivational process in its potential practical application. It underlines the need for a system of management by objectives, performance appraisal and very careful attention to the organization's system of intrinsic and extrinsic rewards.

Schein's theory of 'complex man'

Schein's thesis is an appropriate conclusion for a survey of motivational 'complex man' theories. His view is that whilst all theories contain some truths about human behaviour, no single theory is adequate by itself. His position may be summarized as follows:

1 People are driven by nature to fulfil a variety of needs, some basic and some on a higher plane

2 Needs once satisfied may reoccur (e.g., basic needs); others (e.g., higher needs) are constantly changing and being replaced by new needs.

3 Needs vary, therefore, not only from one person to the next, but also within the same person according to differences of time and circumstances.

4 Effective managers are aware of this complexity and will be as flexible as possible in their approach to their subordinate staff. Above all, they will learn to avoid generalized assumptions about the motivation of others based on projections of their own views and expectations.

Because of the complexity of motivation, managers cannot expect to be able precisely to gauge the various motivational forces that influence their individual subordinates. They can, however, use the available data to broaden their understanding and to provide a framework for analysing the general influences (Figure 1.2) that may interrelate to produce a variety of individual motivational patterns:

1 *Forces within individuals themselves*: attitudes, beliefs, values, assumptions, expectations and needs.

2 *The nature of the job*: extrinsic and intrinsic rewards, component tasks, responsibilities, work arrangements, feedback on performance.

3 *The environment of work*: senior managers and their styles; other colleagues and relationships with them; organizational climate and practices.

Questions

1 Why is it important to be aware of individual differences? What are they and what effects may they have in behaviour and relationships?
2 What is the Johari Window?
3 How may self-awareness be described and how may it be achieved?
4 Briefly describe the essential nature of human communication.
5 What are its inherent problems, and what conditions are necessary for communication to be effective?
6 Give a brief definition of motivation.
7 What are the distinctive features of the theories of the following authorities: Maslow, Herzberg, McGregor, McLelland, Porter and Lawler?
8 Describe a simple framework for a systematic analysis by managers of motivational factors.

References

Goleman, D. (1996). *Emotional Intelligence*. Bloomsbury.
Goleman, D. (1998). *Working with Emotional Intelligence*. Bloomsbury.

INDIVIDUALS

Uniqueness of each individual derives from inherited and environmental factors. Individuals develop unique systems of attitudes, assumptions, values, expectations, etc. These fundamentally influence personal motivation and interpersonal relationships.

SELF-AWARENESS

Important to managers and employees alike. Johari window describes four states (panes). Requires concord between views of individual and others. Plus and minus points are revealed by systematic review of life history.

COMMUNICATION

Its essence is a two-way process of transmission-reception. Each message is a complex of signals, e.g. spoken messages comprise words, tone, expressions, gestures, postures, etc.

Encoding and decoding are filtered through each individual's personal system of assumptions, expectations, values, needs, etc. This process is the fundamental cause of communication barriers. The problem may be mitigated by:

1. A genuine desire to communicate
2. Trust and openness
3. Awareness of the nature and problems of the process
4. Sharing experience
5. Checking understanding

MOTIVATION

In essence it is an inner force driving humans to satisfy needs inherited and environmentally acquired. The force has three elements: direction, intensity, duration. There are three main groups of theories:

Managerial assumptions (e.g. Taylor's Rational-Economic Theory);

Human needs (e.g. Maslow, Mayo, Herzberg, McLelland, and McGregor);

Expectancy/contingency (e.g. Lewin, Vroom, and Porter and Lawler).

Schein's 'complex man' summarizes the complexity of motivation.

A general analysis model:

1. Forces within individuals
2. Nature of the job
3. Work environment

Figure 1.2 Summary of studies of individuals, communication and motivation

Chapter 2

Groups and leadership

Groups

The behaviour of groups has important consequences for management. Research into this subject has produced data from which has emerged the main conclusion that a variety of behaviour takes place in working groups that is often not apparent on the surface. These studies have revealed the importance of research into groups because of the potential impact of group behaviour on organizational performance. Studies that have been made throughout the past fifty years have indicated the existence of phenomena of group behaviour, and in particular of informal patterns, which are not taken into account in formal, official prescriptions about work, issued by management. These revelations are especially significant because of the implications for leadership. If managers are unaware of these phenomena and their causes, they will make unwarranted assumptions based on their own perspectives, and will establish goals, structures, plans and work arrangements that are inappropriate to the groups that they lead. In fact, some of these phenomena may be a reaction to inappropriate, insensitive behaviour on the part of management, so that a vicious circle of negative behaviour may be set in motion, which is virtually self-perpetuating.

The main concern of managers about their work-groups is that they should work cohesively in order to achieve the required results. Their interest in group behaviour is centred, therefore, on basic questions such as what factors make groups work cohesively and what factors cause disruption. In order to find likely answers to these questions we need to examine a series of related questions: what are the characteristics of work groups? Why and with what expectations do people join them? How in general do they operate? What kinds of problems may arise within the group, between groups and managers, and between different groups? These questions will provide a useful framework for a systematic analysis of the subject.

Reasons for and expectations from group members

The reasons why individuals join groups, and the expectations that each person has, will naturally cover a very wide range. The main identifiable group membership reasons closely match the categories of Maslow's hierarchy: material or economic; social; self-esteem or status; self-development of fulfilment. Evidently, the satisfaction of material needs is only one of a number of possibilities.

When people join work groups a contract is formally drawn up which makes precise statements about what employers require and what they will give in return. These terms and conditions are invariably expressed in material language. They do not say, for example, that the firm will undertake to satisfy the employees' needs for self-esteem or self-fulfilment. Nevertheless, behind the formal language of the official contract there is always implied what has been described as a 'psychological contract', this being the 'deal' between employer and employee resting upon reciprocal obligations and understandings. This means employers assume that employees' decisions to join organizations indicate a willingness to accept the principle of subordination and to recognize the authority of the organization as legitimate. The employees' perception, on the other hand, is that, since the relationship is voluntary, they have some freedom for the exercise of influential behaviour, which could, if necessary, lead to changes in the work situation.

Interaction within and between groups

Before the particular manifestations of group behaviour revealed by specialized studies are examined, it would be useful to consider the subject in general terms. Tuckman, for example, has proposed a four-stage model as a general description of the chronology of a group's progress towards cohesive collaboration:

Stage 1 – Forming: the initial stage, when members are tentative about the task, about each other and the group leadership. Extremes of view are usually restrained. Members test each other and draw up rules of conduct. In a leaderless group, leaders may be chosen or begin to emerge. These may be changed in later stages.
Stage 2 – Storming: the members are getting to know each other better and are prepared to put forward their views more vigorously. This leads to conflict between individuals, leaders or subgroups that may have formed.
Stage 3 – Norming: the conflicts begin to be controlled as the members realize the need to co-operate in order to perform the task. The group produces norms of behaviour, i.e. an accepted code of attitudes and conduct that all the members accept.
Stage 4 – Performing: the group has now developed the required degree of cohesion to work as a team and to concentrate on the problems it has to overcome to attain its goal.

This is only a very generalized model and it may not apply to all types of groups. Nevertheless, the basic principles have a wider application and give a useful insight into the behaviour of groups with a continuous existence and an ongoing task.

Another useful general model of group behaviour is the result of specific studies carried out by R. F. Bales and colleagues at Harvard University. These data are based on the observation of small discussion groups, and like Tuckman's model, these conclusions would be directly applicable to work groups of a similar nature, such as committees. However, some general principles may be derived to describe the behaviour of people in working groups whose relationship extends over much longer periods. Briefly to summarize Bales's data, he found that behaviour fell into two main categories:

- task oriented
- socioemotional oriented.

His observations showed that, apart from efforts directed towards the task, there was another type of behaviour that concerned the human aspects of the group and its individual members. Bales further distinguished two subcategories of socio-emotional behaviour:

- emotionally positive
- emotionally negative.

Emotionally positive behaviour is directed towards enhancing the cohesiveness of the team, and expresses itself in tension-releasing humour, action to support of other members of the team, etc. Emotionally negative behaviour is egocentric, and expresses itself in the form of antagonism, signs of tension, appeals for help, withdrawal of co-operation, etc. This study also indicated that some people tend to give a lead either in the task-oriented or socioemotional roles, for example, one person would be primarily concerned with the task and another would be more interested in maintaining group cohesiveness. Occasionally, the two functions might be combined in the same person.

These two general models are not only helpful for providing a broad understanding of group behaviour, but particularly for emphasizing two basic orientations, namely task fulfilment and group cohesiveness. On this basis, we can now look in rather more detail at particular phenomena of group behaviour and associated problems with which managers have to contend. Certain factors have been identified as fundamental in their influence on the behaviour of groups:

1 *The task*: its nature and the arrangements imposed by management in terms of methods and work conditions.
2 *The group*: its size, composition, relationships and norms.
3 *The leadership function*: styles and their appropriateness to the task and the group.
4 *The environment*: relationships with other groups and the main organization.

The influences of these factors are described below and are illustrated with examples from work situations and data from various research studies.

The task

The nature of the work and the way it is arranged can have a very important influence on either stimulating or impeding group cohesiveness. For example, where the tasks of the group involve prestige and esteem, such as the public display or special service units of the armed forces, there is seldom much difficulty in obtaining recruits to the group, retaining members or developing a high level of group cohesiveness. Similar cohesiveness is found among groups who share dangerous or hard conditions, e.g. miners. On the other hand, where the technology of the task reduces social interaction to a minimum, as, for example, in the production lines of the motor industry, then the problem of creating a spirit of group unity may become virtually impossible.

Some well-known and valuable studies have been conducted on the effects of the task upon the group. A team from the Tavistock Institute of Human Relations studied the effects on groups of coal miners of a technological change from traditional short-wall to long-wall methods of mining. Traditional methods had been based on small, highly autonomous, cohesive teams. When new mechanical equipment was introduced, which revolutionized the working arrangements, the traditional small groups were replaced with much larger groups under a supervisor, and divided into three shifts, each performing different stages of the total task. Although the new arrangements were very sound in technical terms, the human consequences were very serious: the former cohesiveness of the small group was destroyed; workers developed feelings of social disorientation; and low productivity became an accepted norm.

Data that underlined the findings of the Tavistock Institute were produced in a classic study of a gypsum factory in the USA by Alvin Gouldner. Here, management introduced a series of new working arrangements into a factory that had a long tradition of highly autonomous working groups and well-established group norms. The new-broom methods were intended to produce greater efficiency, but, in fact, they created much tension, countermeasures and a series of bitter disputes.

Both of the examples quoted above illustrate the possibly serious consequences of management's lack of awareness of the general nature of group behaviour and of the particular influence of the task and working arrangements.

The group

Relationships within the group are affected by factors such as size, composition, individual personalities of group members and their roles, group norms, etc. Managers need to understand these factors and their influence as a basis for analysing possible sources of unity or disunity inside a group. All the evidence suggests that highly cohesive groups are generally more productive than groups that are less cohesive. At the same time, it would be wrong to assume that group cohesiveness necessarily correlates with high levels of productivity. A group may become cohesive as a reaction to and a defence against the tactics of management of which it disapproves, or because of perceived threats from other groups.

The size of a group may influence possible patterns of behaviour, and it has an obvious relevance to questions of communication. No hard and fast rules can be laid down because of the varying requirements of different situations. However, if the group is too large, it may divide into subgroups that may collaborate for reasons other than productive work. In large groups, leaders have problems of the span of control. It is difficult for them to know their subordinates well, and communication barriers are more likely to occur.

The composition of the group will also influence patterns of interaction. Managers cannot normally be expected to plan or manipulate the composition of their groups to take care of all possible subtle influential factors of personality, experience, social class, age, etc. In theory, the greater the homogeneity a group has, the more cohesive it is likely to be. Except for circumstances where there are too many dominant personalities, a blend of personality traits could be as much an advantage as a disadvantage.

A brief reference has already been made to group norms. They occupy such a prominent role in the general behaviour of all groups that more needs to be said about them. Norms are to a group what the individual perspective is to each separate human being. Thus, a group will develop an identity of its own in terms of common patterns of behaviour and attitudes, as in clubs, gangs, societies, etc., which attract people of a like mind. Work groups develop norms about work, e.g. standards, quantity of output and attitudes to management. They may also develop other norms which act, as it were, as the unwritten 'rules of the club', e.g. members of this work group will dislike certain other groups, will read certain kinds of newspapers, will hold certain kinds of political views and so on. Newcomers to the group are expected to comply initially whilst they pass through what is termed the socializing process of learning the expected behaviour. Eventually they will find that they have unconsciously made the group's behaviour and attitudes their own, that is, they have internalized the norms of the group, or else the group will reject them and they will remain outside the group.

Closely linked with the phenomena of norms is the pressure exerted by the group on members to conform. Non-conformists may well be rejected by the group. In extreme cases, this means being totally ignored. A number of authors, especially in the USA, for example, Millgram, Asch and Janis, have made special studies of conformity which have produced some rather disturbing conclusions about the degree to which people may succumb to social pressures to 'toe the line 'and to suppress their real beliefs. Applied to working situations, these data indicate that group decisions, for example those made by committees, are often not nearly as sound as is popularly supposed. Strong pressures within a group to reach consensus may well result in the suppression of wiser counsels.

The Hawthorne studies discussed in the previous chapter showed how group solidarity – the face-to-face relationships with group members – were more significant to them than their relationship with managers.

Leadership

This has a crucially important bearing on group behaviour. As an influential factor we are especially concerned with different styles of leadership and their possible effects upon groups. Because of its special importance, leadership will be discussed in detail later in this chapter. For now, it is enough to say that the effective performance of a group is obviously greatly determined by the skill of the leader in co-ordinating the efforts of the individual members, and also by the degree to which the style of leadership is appropriate to the task and the nature of the group. Studies of group behaviour have revealed the importance of informal leaders. In the work situation most leaders are appointed by the organization, but there are very often other unofficial and influential group leaders, who emerge from the informal behaviour of groups.

The environment

Work groups operate mainly in the environment of the organization to which they belong. The significance of the group's environment lies chiefly in its relationship with the organization as a whole and with the other groups that comprise the organization. At best there might be what could be termed friendly rivalry or healthy competition between different groups, but in the work situation, where there is often competition for limited or scarce resources, intergroup feelings may well extend to hostility.

Paradoxically, such negative feelings can arise from the very force of cohesiveness that gives an individual group its strength. Some valuable experiments to study intergroup relationships were carried out by Sherif in the USA with groups of boys at a camp. Situations were deliberately contrived to stimulate intergroup hostility, in which one group could only win at the expense of another. The results were markedly increased intragroup solidarity and intergroup hostility. Tensions were reduced or removed by giving common goals to all groups and deliberately increasing social contacts in non-competitive situations.

Finally, it has to be emphasized that although we have been considering the task, the group itself, its leadership and environment as separate factors of possible influence, in practice the influences of these factors interrelate and overlap in a variety of subtle and complicated forms.

Conclusions

To achieve cohesiveness within individual groups, collaboration between different groups and hence total effectiveness, certain basic requirements need to be met:

1 An equilibrium has to be maintained within a group between the energies directed towards the achievement of tasks and maintaining the team as a cohesive unit.
2 Conditions have to be established which make membership of the group worthwhile and meaningful to the individuals in the group.
3 The effectiveness of the organization as a whole rather than the effectiveness of individual groups needs to be emphasized. Measures need to be taken to develop collaboration between groups and to establish sound communication links.
4 Exchanges between members of groups should be encouraged to reduce insularity and to promote mutual understanding of problems.
5 Situations that produce winners and losers should be avoided.
6 Leaders of groups need to meet regularly to discuss common problems and to concentrate on total effectiveness rather than the interests of individual groups.
7 Group leaders need to be aware of the significance of the informal behaviour of groups, of group norms and of the possible existence of leaders other than those officially appointed.

Leadership

Leadership is obviously a subject of extreme importance in management. As modern research has clearly shown, leadership is a part of the study of group behaviour. Leaders cannot operate in isolation, and groups with tasks to perform cannot perform these tasks without leaders. Leaders are members of groups, influencing them and being influenced by them. They are especially concerned with the cohesive development of the group as a prerequisite for the ultimate achievement of the group's goals. If management is defined as a process of making the most effective use of available human and material resources for the achievement of specified goals, then leadership may be described as the component of management that is most concerned with the use of human resources. Until recently, nearly all the emphasis of leadership study had been concentrated on leaders themselves, usually by examining the careers of well-known leaders of history in an attempt to analyse the secrets of their apparent success. Thus, a belief predominated for centuries that leadership was dependent on the circumstances of one's birth. Some became leaders because they had the good fortune to be born into noble, naturally ruling classes, others because they were endowed with certain innate qualities. The idea that leadership is a facet of group behaviour has only emerged in recent times from studies of the human problems of industrial society. It has led to some profoundly important conclusions:

1 Leadership has no meaning outside the context of tasks to be performed and groups to perform these tasks.
2 Studies of leaders as isolated individuals provide little useful insight into the nature of leadership.
3 A deeper understanding can only come by analysing what leaders and groups do in a variety of specific situations.

Studies on leadership published in earlier times invariably included lists of what their authors regarded as the essential traits of a good leader. Whilst these lists naturally coincide in a number of important respects, at the same time they inevitably vary in their total contents, their priorities and their emphases. These variations clearly illustrate the fundamental limitations of attempts to study leadership on a basis of personal qualities. Such an approach has been shown to provide no means for answering some of the fundamental questions that need to be asked, for example, if there is no consensus on what makes effective leaders, by what criteria are they to be identified, developed and assessed? Even if a consensus on essential qualities did exist, and some kind of valid test could be devised to identify those who measure up to these requirements, are we then to believe that such people could perform with equal effectiveness as leaders in any circumstances? The very wide variety of possible work situations immediately suggests that this cannot be so.

The functional approach to leadership as an element of group behaviour has dispelled much of the mystique that formerly surrounded the subject. Above all, it has provided a framework for meaningful analysis and for the systematic selection, training and assessment of leaders. The emphasis has shifted from the study of leaders to leadership as a function of co-ordinating the efforts of a group to achieve specified tasks. At the same time, it is apparent that there is considerable variation in the nature of tasks and in the composition of groups. From this, certain conclusions may logically be deduced. People can be trained to gain insight into the nature of group behaviour and to develop the interpersonal skills required to accomplish a productive co-ordination of human efforts; the very wide variety of situations means that certain styles of leadership will be more appropriate to some situations than to others. Therefore, leaders should be trained to be as flexible and adaptable as possible or if, in fact, people cannot significantly vary their leadership styles, then particular types of leaders should be matched with particular situations.

After the Hawthorne experiments had aroused the initial interest in group behaviour, serious research into leadership soon followed and has continued ever since. The change of emphasis from the personality of leaders to leadership as a function in a collaborating group had a profound effect during the postwar years, first on the selection and training of military leaders and, subsequently, of managers in general. However, the innovation of the functional approach caused some problems of misunderstanding, because traditionalists interpreted this approach to mean that personal qualities are not important – a view that misrepresents this theory. The personal qualities for effective leadership are not in question. The message of the functional approach is simply that an analysis of personal qualities gives little help in understanding what leadership means in action.

The quantity and variety of research is so extensive that a comprehensive summary cannot be attempted in this brief survey. Nevertheless, the findings and conclusions of some of the most important works merit a brief description because of what they have to say about effectiveness in the management of people. Many of the studies of leadership have been carried out by direct observation of people at work. Others have taken the form of 'armchair philosophy', based on personal experience or the reorientation of previous works. Some of the research has been carried out by university teams and some by particular individuals.

University of Iowa

This was the first serious attempt to study leadership in groups in action. It was based on the activities of boys who were members of a model-making club and were quite unaware that they were being observed for experimental purposes. They were divided into three groups and subjected in turn to three quite different styles of leadership:

1 Autocratic, whereby they were given no scope for initiative and were tightly disciplined.
2 Democratic, whereby the leadership was positive and firm, but allowed participation and freedom of expression.
3 Laissez-faire, whereby the boys were allowed to do as they pleased.

The results clearly indicated the superiority of the democratic style for all three groups in terms of general contentment, group cohesiveness and productivity. The other styles produced apathy, disunity and low productivity. It would be dangerous to seek correlations between the behaviour of juveniles in leisure activities and adults at work, but the data of the experiments at least emphasized for the first time the importance of leadership styles.

Harvard Department of Social Relations

The work of R. F. Bales and his colleagues has already been mentioned in connection with group behaviour. Since there is a very close link between the study of groups and leadership, it is not surprising that this research has important messages for managers in their leadership roles, which are:

1 They need to be aware of the equilibrium problem, to balance the demands of the task against those of personal and interpersonal feelings.
2 They need to recognize the main kinds of contributions to a group's work, i.e., task-oriented behaviour and socio-emotional behaviour, and especially to distinguish

between the positive (group maintenance-directed) and negative (individually oriented) aspects of this behaviour.

3 The leader's constant task is to move the group in a co-ordinated way and towards the achievement of its goals, but at the same time to keep relationships harmonious and personal outcomes at a high level (to motivate people who want to retain membership).

4 The two facets are interdependent. In practice, there could sometimes be high-quality work but a rapid turnover of staff, which reduces total efficiency.

Ohio State University

A team from this university carried out an extensive on-site study with employees of the International Harvester Company to study the effects of leadership, which covered a very wide range of different types of behaviour that leaders use in their dealings with subordinates. A statistical analysis of results revealed two broad categories of behaviour: one directed towards fulfilling tasks and goals, the other concerned with group reactions and individual feelings. Applying these categories to different levels of managers, the team found that some managers showed clear preferences for one of the two styles, whilst others exhibited both in fairly equal measure. It was also found that, in general, extremes in task-oriented styles correlated with high grievance rates and that the subordinates of leaders who strongly favoured people-oriented styles had lower grievance rates.

University of Michigan

These experiments took place at the offices of the Prudential Insurance Company and looked at the correlation between work performance and leadership styles. Taking sections engaged in similar work, the team identified those with high productivity and those with low productivity. Next, they established that there were no significant differences in the supervisors of the sections in terms of variables such as age, sex and experience. A study of the supervisory styles produced most interesting results. The supervisors of high-performance groups revealed similar behaviour. In particular, they exhibited concern for their employees, allowed them to share in decisions affecting work and generally established an atmosphere of trust. The supervisors of low-performance groups exhibited opposite types of behaviour and in general were much more concerned with productivity than their subordinates.

Likert's four-systems model

Rensis Likert, also of the University of Michigan, has made a prolonged study of management and, in particular, the effect of leadership styles upon people at work and in consequence upon group cohesiveness, effective performance and productivity. His research has led him to propose four main identifiable styles, which he calls Systems 1–4, described as follows:

System 1 – Exploitive-authoritative: managers are very autocratic, do not trust subordinates, motivate mainly by fear and punishment, attempt to communicate only in a downward direction and make all decisions unilaterally.

System 2 – Benevolent-authoritative: managers have a less harsh attitude, but still keep a tight control, especially in decision-making. They motivate with rewards and sometimes punishment and allow a limited measure of upward communication.

System 3 – Consultative: managers are much more employee oriented than those of Systems 1 and 2. They motivate with rewards, participation and occasional punishment. They allow fairly unrestricted two-way communication. They tend to keep decision-making on major issues mainly to themselves.

System 4 – Participative-group: managers show complete trust and confidence in subordinates, who share in communication and decision-making at all levels. They operate with themselves and their subordinates as a group.

Likert's research into actual work situations indicated a clear correlation between the four systems and the managers' success as leaders and the groups' achievement of goals and productivity. System 4, needless to say, was found to be superior to the others, a conclusion that closely matched the research data at the Prudential Insurance Company.

F. E. Fiedler's contingency model

Fiedler has made a unique contribution to the study of leadership. He has proposed that there are three critical dimensions for classifying leadership in situations:

1   The leader/group relationship.
2   The ease or difficulty of the task (e.g., structured or unstructured).
3   The leader's vested authority.

He further proposes that in these three dimensions the situation may be favourable or unfavourable for the leader (for example, he or she may not have enough authority to deal with a particular kind of group). Matching favourability and unfavourability with the three basic dimensions, he then produces eight possible combinations, ranging from dimensions 1, 2, 3 all favourable, to dimensions 1, 2, 3 all unfavourable. This is the model for determining the nature of the situation.

Next, he produces a model for categorizing leadership styles. An individual leader's style is determined by scoring a questionnaire designed to reveal the individual's attitudes towards persons that they themselves choose as the work colleague with whom they have had most difficulty in working (designated by Fiedler as 'the least preferred co-worker' – LPC). Each tested subject is then given an LPC rating, in which high scores indicate leaders who are people oriented and low scores those who are task oriented. The essence of Fiedler's Contingency Theory is that in practice we need to identify the nature of the situation and then select leaders most likely to be suited to a particular situation. Thus, for some situations, a people-oriented leader (that is, high LPC) will be more effective, whilst other situations call for the task-oriented style (that is, low LPC). This theory differs from other as theories on leadership in that Fiedler inclines to the view that individuals tend to have preferred styles and that these need to be adapted to situations. Most other authors urge the need for developing flexibility in leaders to meet the needs of varying situations.

Tannenbaum and Schmidt

These authors are concerned with problems of leadership style and with questions such as whether managers can be democratic towards subordinates and yet maintain the necessary authority and control. For purposes of analysis they have produced a 'continuum of leadership behaviour' ranging from authoritarian styles at one extreme to democratic styles at the other, which they call 'boss-centred' and 'subordinate-centred' leadership. Unlike other models that advocate a preferred style, this model attempts to provide a framework for analysis and individual choice. The authors propose three key factors on which choice of leadership pattern depends:

1 Forces in the manager (e.g., attitudes, beliefs, values).
2 Forces in the subordinates (e.g., their attitudes, beliefs, values and expectations of the leader).
3 Forces in the situation (e.g., pressures and constraints produced by the tasks, organizational climate and other extraneous factors).

In summary, their conclusions are:

1 When deciding which point along the continuum represents the appropriate style, leaders need to begin with an analysis of these three factors, but in particular they need to clarify their own objectives.
2 Leaders need to develop skills in reading situations in these terms and then should be able to behave appropriately in the light of their perceptions.
3 No single style of leadership is always right and another always wrong. Successful leaders are neither assertive nor permissive, but are consistently accurate in their assessment and application of where on the continuum they should be.

The Blake–Mouton managerial grid

This is a well-publicized system for identifying leadership styles as a basis of training. Following the data of other authors, Blake and Mouton identify two critical basic dimensions: concern for the task and concern for the people. To find the precise location of a leader's style they have produced a grid, with 'concern for people' along one axis and 'concern for the task' along the other. Each dimension ranges from 1 (low) to 9 (high) so that a grid of eighty-one squares is produced. The extremes are found in each corner:

1 Highest concern for people, lowest for task = 1.9.
2 Lowest concern for people and task = 1.1.
3 Highest concern for task, lowest for people = 9.1.
4 Highest concern for people and task = 9.9.

A moderate concern for both is in the middle of the grid and scores 5.5. The ideal which leaders should aim to achieve is 9.9.

John Adair's functional leadership model

This model was developed whilst the author was lecturing at the Royal Military Academy, Sandhurst. It is based on the research data of studies of leadership and groups, and the author's own experience at Sandhurst. The model is three-dimensional, and proposes that in all leadership situations there are three crucial areas to which the leader must attend:

- the task
- the maintenance of team cohesiveness
- the needs of the individuals.

All three areas require constant attention, but effective leadership depends upon the leader's skill in giving appropriate emphasis to particular areas at particular times. The special importance of this model is its usefulness for training purposes, since activities can be meaningfully analysed and assessed in these terms. It has had a marked influence on military training and is now widely used in many other organizations.

Conclusion

The broad conclusions that emerge from research on group behaviour and leadership (Figure 2.1) are these:

1 Democratic-participative styles are generally likely to be more effective in creating group cohesiveness and productivity than strongly task styles.
2 At the same time, varying situations require different leadership styles, which have to be adapted or selected to suit these different circumstances.
3 Effective leadership depends upon awareness of the nature of the task, the group and its individual members, the environment, and particularly – the self-awareness of the leaders themselves.

Questions

1 What are the main features of Tuckman's and Bales's methods for analysing group behaviour?
2 What are the main factors that influence group behaviour?
3 What are the group norms and why are they important in the study of group behaviour?
4 Summarize the main conclusions that have emerged from studies of group behaviour.
5 What are the significant differences between the former and current approaches to the study of leadership?
6 Briefly summarize the main features and conclusions of the studies of leadership carried out by the universities of Iowa, Michigan and Ohio.
7 What are the distinctive features of Fiedler's theory?

8 Summarize the main conclusions that have emerged recently from research into leadership.

NATURE OF GROUP BEHAVIOUR

Tuckman's model proposed four stages:

1. Forming   2. Storming
3. Norming   4. Performing

Bale's data includes two areas:

Task oriented; socio-emotional (positive and negative).

Fundamental influential factors are:

Task nature and work arrangements
Group size, composition, relationships and norms
Leadership – styles and appropriateness
Environment relationships with other groups and the organization

---

CONCLUSIONS

1. Balance between task requirements and team maintenance is essential.
2. Membership of group must be worthwhile.
3. Total organization harmony is paramount; positive steps are needed to reduce intergroup rivalry.

NATURE OF LEADERSHIP

Modern studies emphasize superiority of a functional analysis of leadership in action rather than leaders' personal qualities. Main contributions are:

University of Iowa: study of leadership styles at boys club (autocratic; democratic; laissez-faire)

Harvard (Bales): theory of task-oriented and socio-emotional axes.

Ohio State University: data on effects of task-oriented and people-orientated styles at International Harvester Co.

University of Michigan: similar data from studies at Prudential Assurance Co.

Likert's four systems: exploitive-authoritative; benevolent-authoritative; consultative, participative-group.

Fiedler: Contingency Theory, i.e. matching leaders' LPC ratings with a three-dimensional model (leader/group relationship; nature of task; leaders' vested authority).

Tannenbaum and Schmidt: continuum of leadership behaviour ('boss-centred'–'subordinate-centred').

Blake and Mouton: 9 – 9 managerial grid (concern for task/concern for people).

Adair: functional leadership model (needs of task, team, individuals).

CONCLUSIONS

In general, democratic-participative styles are more effective.

However, much depends on situational variables. Styles have to be adapted to suit these.

Effective leadership requires awareness of task, group, individual and self.

Figure 2.1 Summary of studies of group behaviour and leadership

Chapter 3

Organizations

Theory and practice

Individuals and groups operate within the framework of larger groups, which are loosely described as organizations. Although much of what has already been said about the behaviour of individuals and groups makes assumptions about the organizational context, we need to study them because of the complexity of their structure, the inter-relationships of their component groups and their relationships with the external environment. The importance to managers of organizational studies is this: first, when we reach the organizational level of study, we are considering the total effectiveness of the system; second, having considered how an organization does and should control its component elements, we are still left with the very difficult question – how is the organization itself to be controlled? Is it capable of controlling itself? Northcote Parkinson, for example, acquired a special fame for his comments about the uncontrolled ways in which organizations behave and expand.

The basic problem of size and complexity in organizations is something that everyone experiences sooner or later. It is seen in everyday working life in the difficulties that employees find in describing the organization where they work or in relating to it. Employees usually find themselves identifying more with smaller groups. When they try to relate to organizations it is as though individual employees are dealing with a mystical, unseen, indefinable force that controls their working lives, but with whom, like God, they can never come face to face.

In the last ten years there has emerged a more radical critique of 'rational' approaches to the study of organizations. *Postmodernism* rejects the 'objective' positivist way organizations are researched, and with this rejection comes a denial of the scientific basis of knowledge accumulation. The postmodernist critique owes much to philosophers such as Foucault and Derrida. Postmodernism is a valuable antidote to the over-confidence found amongst consultants and managers who have lost sight of their own part in perceiving and constructing reality, but it does not propose a coherent theoretical alternative. Postmodernism values diversity, symbolism and reinterpretations of old into new ways of working: a view of knowledge as fragmented, rejecting ideas of 'grand narrative', which involve simplifying assumptions and appeals to universal models, or universal laws (Hatch, 1997). We should note the following aspects to postmodernism. Organizations are not necessarily rational – they only exist in the perceptions of their members and those who wish to deal with them. Reality is socially constructed. Our understanding is based on a number of distinct discourses that frequently are in opposition to each other. Language use and power are linked, and power and control are inherent within language structure and use. Words carry a history; there are different meanings that are part of the language games we play as we define meanings in use. Therefore human resource management could be understood as a mechanism for creating taken for granted power relations (Legge, 1995).

Like the other aspects of the study of people at work, there has been considerable research into organizations and a vast quantity of literature has now accumulated. These works could be classified in various ways, but there is a common thread running through the diversity of particular themes, which is the implicit assumption that organizations as a phenomenon of modern industrial life need to be studied and analysed to provide a basis for designing structures that are as effective as possible both in terms of productivity and human contentment.

In addition to postmodernism, it is possible to distinguish four broad categories of approach, which reflect different emphases in studying the subject:

1 *Structural approach*: this group includes authors who form the so-called classical or traditional school. They are mainly concerned with formal organizations and related questions such as structural design, the definition of responsibilities and the legitimacy of authority.
2 *Human relations approach*: those who follow this approach stress the importance of individuals, their needs and reactions to organizational life, and the existence of an informal system which needs to be taken into account when organizations are designed.
3 *Systems approach*: authors included in this category are interested mainly in the significance of the interaction and interrelationships between the component elements of organizations and between organizations and their environments.
4 *Contingency approach*: this has links with the structural and systems approaches, but emphasizes the need for on-site, comparative studies to find out what organizations are really like, to analyse the interactions of all the internal and external variables, and on this basis to design organizations to take account of the contingencies of differing situations.

This categorization is a simplification of a very complex field of study, but is adequate as a basic framework for a broad analysis of the subject. For the purpose of this review, it would be useful briefly to examine some of the important contributions in each group as samples of the main trends of thought about problems that typically occur, their causes and possible remedies.

Studies of organizational structure

The first major study of organizations was made by Max Weber. This work was doubly important because it laid a foundation for subsequent studies and raised the question of authority types:

1 *Charismatic*: authority stems from the personality of the leaders of the organization and is typified in religious, political and industrial organizations by people like Gandhi, Churchill, Ford, etc.

2 *Traditional*: the basis is precedent and custom. The commonest example is a monarchy. In industry, examples are found in family firms, where the leadership is passed from parent to son or daughter, even though initially at least the son or daughter may derive no authority from experience.

3 *Rational-legal*: this is described as a normal basis for democratic society and formal work organizations. The main requirement is a hierarchy of levels of authority, which is based on the assumed ability of managers to perform better than their subordinates either through superior professional or superior administrative experience, knowledge and skills, or a combination of both. This authority is then incorporated into a set of rules and codes governing the arrangements for work and the conduct of employees.

Weber described the rational-legal organization as a bureaucracy, which he considered to be the predominant and most effective form of organization. Its particular virtue, in Weber's view, and hence its name is that once the roles of office at various levels have been defined, the organization continues to function independently of individuals. A simple analogy would be a long-running play, where different actors join and leave the cast over the years, but the play continues. Weber was not so concerned with what later authors have described as the dysfunctions of bureaucracy, for example, the potential for the misuse of authority by the substitution of power by certain individuals who seek to pursue personal ends by means of coercion or manipulation; conflicts which arise from personal interpretations of the meanings of organizational rules, etc. Furthermore, whilst the basic model of the typical bureaucracy is useful for general analysis, it does not take account of the importance of role interpretation. Employees interpret their work roles in the light of their own attitudes, values, beliefs, needs and expectations. Weber has adequately described the formal pattern of organizational behaviour, but beneath the surface there is an informal pattern that is just as important, as the 'Human Relations School' has shown. People interact socially at work and take part in activities not prescribed in the formal system. Nevertheless, the introduction of the idea of authority and legitimacy has made a most important contribution to the study of organizations, especially in terms of the psychological contract, discussed earlier.

Another significant contribution to the theme of organizational authority has been made by Amitai Etzioni. This author was interested in the idea of matching individuals' attitudes and expectations with types of organizations. He identifies three main types of organization, according to their authority base, and three types of individual involvement:

1 Organization types
   (a) *Coercive*: used in prisons, mental hospitals and sometimes in military units.
   (b) *Utilitarian*: used mainly in industry, related to Weber's rational-legal type and relying mainly on economic rewards.
   (c) *Normative*: used mainly in organizations where voluntary service predominates, e.g. religious, welfare, and political and professional associations.
2 Individual types of involvement

(a) *Alienative*: members are forced to join and have no psychological involvement.
(b) *Calculative*: members join mainly to satisfy economic and similar needs.
(c) *Moral*: members place a high personal value on the objectives of the organization.

There is a general correlation between the organizational type and the type of involvement. This model may also be useful when related to the idea of the psychological contract between employer and employee and possible problems of misperception. For example, if an organization that is expected to be essentially utilitarian tries to introduce patterns of authority that are coercive in nature, then an alienative response is likely to be produced. Similarly, if this type of organization expects a moral involvement, such as a heart and soul commitment from employees to the firm and its products, it could be making a psychological miscalculation in asking for more from its employees than it is really prepared to give in return.

The human relations approach

This approach to organizational life is concerned with the effects that the dispositions of management, as expressed in the form of organizational structures, rules of conduct, hierarchical systems of authority, working arrangements, etc., may have upon the individual employees. Amongst the contributors to the school of thought that emphasizes the importance of the individual are Mayo, Maslow, McGregor, Herzberg and Argyris whose theories we have already examined in discussions of motivation and group behaviour. Their value has been to draw attention to the existence and significance of the informal systems of behaviour and relationships that are not considered in the traditional approach to organizational structure.

The systems approach

Chronologically, the theories that belong to this group are more recent in origin. The emphasis of the approach is concentrated upon the interactions between the different elements of an organization – the people, the structure, the technology and the environment – which could be seen as a response to the greatly increased pressures upon organizations and their employees in recent years as a result of the very rapid changes in political, technological, economic and social environments.

The studies of coal-mining made by the social scientists of the Tavistock Institute and the conclusions that they reached about the impact of the task upon group behaviour have already been mentioned. Strongly advocating the view that an organization is a complex of interacting variables, this group has produced two important ideas:

1 The concept of the *sociotechnical system*: this implies that an organization is a combination of two systems: the technology (the tasks, the equipment and working arrangements) and the social system (the interpersonal relationships of employees). The two systems are in constant interaction and each influences the other.
2 The *open-system model*: the essence of this idea is that organizations import

resources and information from the environment, which are processed within the organization and then exported to the environment in the form of products or services.

The significance of these ideas lies in their emphasis on the organization's dependence on its environment and on the need to design organizations that take full account of the sociotechnical system. A well-known example of the systems approach to organizational studies is Likert's theory of overlapping groups and linking pins, the main theses of which are:

- The significant environment for a group is composed of other groups.
- Groups are linked to their environment by people holding key positions and being members of more than one group (e.g. the Head of Department who is also a member of the Organizational Management Committee).

The total system comprises three levels – society as a whole, organizations of similar function, and subgroups within a larger system – which are connected by people in key positions, acting as linking pins. Likert's model emphasizes the importance and the possibly far-reaching consequences of relationships and dependencies.

A theory that is very similar to Likert's in concept, but adds a further important idea, has been developed by Kahn and colleagues. On the basis of Weber's view that organizations should be regarded as a hierarchy of offices and the behaviour of office holders as roles, Kahn proposes that all those with whom office holders have contacts can be described as their role sets. In this way an organization can be regarded as a complex of overlapping role sets. The model is useful for analysing organizational problems of relationships and integration. For example, there may be role conflict because members of the role set have different views about the ways role holders should behave; role ambiguity may arise if office holders are not given adequate information to perform their roles; office holders may experience role stress when members of their role set have different expectations of their behaviour, as often happens to supervisors when dealing with the expectations of management on the one hand and those of their subordinates on the other.

The systems approach to organizational study has made a particularly valuable contribution in emphasizing the possible extents of influence, what Rosemary Stewart (1972) has called 'the concept of boundaries'. For example, in studying an organization, we need to think beyond the internal confines of the organization's immediate environment and consider the clientele that it exists to serve and its general social environment. This idea is closely related to the model developed by Blau and Scott, who proposed that an organization's survival and growth depends on its ability to clarify its purpose and to be aware of its beneficiaries. On this basis they propose four categories of organizations:

1 *Mutual benefit* associations – serving their own members (e.g. unions, political, professional and religious groups).
2 *Businesses* – serving their owners, shareholders and the general public.
3 *Services* – serving particular clients (e.g. hospitals, schools, etc.).
4 *Commonweal organizations* – serving the public at large (e.g. police, fire, welfare services, governmental departments).

Contingency studies

In recent times, there have been developments in organizational research which are different in approach from, but related to, the structural and systems approaches. The authors of these studies have in common that they are especially concerned with current problems faced by organizations, such as the suitability of structures for different organizational purposes, their capacity to adapt to their environment in times of considerable instability and the organizational designs likely to be most effective for various situations. Unlike traditional structural theories, this research has usually been very practical and carried out at work sites over long periods of time by means of direct observation and questioning. The authors are concerned with what organizations are really like and what they need to do to be effective, rather than what they seem superficially to be.

In the 1950s, Joan Woodward carried out detailed research of a wide variety of firms in Essex with reference to certain characteristics, for example, the number of levels of authority, the span of control, definitions of responsibilities, communication patterns and divisions of labour, and the effects that environmental variables such as technology have upon them. Three types of production technologies were distinguished:

- Unit and small batch, including self-contained units making products for customer specifications.
- Large batch and mass, where the technology is characterized by mass production.
- Process, in which the technology is directed towards an intermittent or continuous flow production for example of chemicals or food production.

When the types of internal organizational variables mentioned above were examined, relative to the three categories of factories, it was found that there was a direct relationship between these and the technological processes employed. The main conclusions drawn from these studies were:

- Variables in the environment, and especially technology, should be a fundamental factor in organizational design.
- It is inadvisable to think of organization design in terms of universally applicable principles.

A sociologist, Burns, collaborated with a psychologist, Stalker, in a similarly important on-site study of manufacturing firms in Scotland. They were particularly interested in problems of introducing modern electronic technology into traditional organizations. As a result of these studies, the authors have produced a well-known model based on the difficulties that different firms experienced in adapting to change. They propose a continuum of organizational structures, with what they describe as 'mechanistic' and 'organic' types of organization at the extremes. The 'mechanistic' organization is typical of Weber's bureaucracy in structure, and works satisfactorily in stable conditions. In unstable conditions, such as those of rapid technological change, the 'organic' type of organization has much more flexibility. Its significant differences compared with the traditional organization are these:

- Functions and duties are not enshrined in organizational charts.
- Interactions and communication are not restricted by a hierarchical structure of authority, but depend on the specialist requirements of the situation.
- There is continuous readjustment to meet changing circumstances.

The impact of technology on organizations has produced opportunities to change the nature of the employment relationship. Changes to size, reporting relationships and contractual relationships are well summarized by the idea of 'post-Fordism' – a post assembly-line, lean production approach, which provides a modern version of Woodward's theory (Table 3.1).

Table 3.1 Changes resulting from the impact of technology

From	To
Technology:	
Fixed dedicated machines	Microelectronically controlled multipurpose
Vertically integrated operation	Subcontracting
Mass production	Batch production
Products:	
For a mass consumer market	Diverse production
Relatively cheap	High quality
Labour process:	
Fragmented	Task flexible
Little discretion	Some autonomy
Hierarchical authority and technical control	Group control
Contracts:	
Collectively negotiated rate for job	Individual pay for performance
Relatively secure	Secure for core workers not for contingent workforce

Source: Ward (1990).

A major study typical of the contingency approach has been produced by Lawrence and Lorsch, based on the work of Woodward, Burns and Stalker. These authors studied ten firms from three different industries in terms of different rates of technological change and the influence of different elements in the environment. They analysed the internal structures of these firms according to two dimensions:

- The differentiation of different functional departments (differences in objectives, time allocation, interpersonal relationships, etc.).
- Integration (the degree of interdepartmental co-ordination, collaboration and relationships).

Then they analysed the relationships between differences in external environments and differences in internal environments. They found that the internal variables have a complex relationship with each other and with the external variables. In contingency terms, their findings may be summarized as follows:

- In an unstable and varied environment, the organization needs to be relatively unstructured.
- In a stable and uniform environment, a more rigid structure is appropriate.
- If the external environment is very varied and the internal structure is highly differentiated, positive measures need to be taken to ensure integration.

There is a clear similarity in the data from all these contingency studies. These show that organizational effectiveness is greatly influenced by the degree of harmony between the internal and external environments of organizations, and this is a fundamental factor to be taken into account in their design.

A great deal of contemporary research into organizations is concerned to explain the variety of new organization forms, caused by moves away from large bureaucracy, as the most common type, towards federal structures, matrix forms, smaller collegiate structures, flatter organizations and structures which change rapidly in response to market demands.

Postmodernist explanations are partly a consequence of new technologies which can offer customers flexible specialization (customizing products from a standard range) and stronger lateral rather than hierarchical relationships for organization members, who network and who work in many different teams. The organization subunits now often have considerable autonomy, and there is a return to semi-autonomous work groups as the centre of customer relations or product output. Taking these trends, together with cost-conscious delayered organizations, we have what Peters and Waterman (1982) described as simultaneous 'tight-loose' properties of organizations.

There is a realization that earlier attempts to explain organizations as simply an outcome of rational economic design decisions were inadequate. The effects of a variety of institutional and power pressures clearly affect organization behaviour and structure. Agency theory takes the perspective of the stakeholders which acknowledges that, for example, managers do not always behave in the interests of the owners, but have their own agendas and power relationships.

The degree of change experienced by modern organizations has also been seen as a consequence of the impact of economic and social forces on organizations. This 'institutional' perspective sees behaviour and organizational choice from a somewhat deterministic viewpoint. For example, Oliver Williamson, an economist, argues that there are two alternative ways in which activities can be organized: as hierarchies (bureaucracies), or as markets. Using transaction costs as the basic unit of analysis he demonstrated that with the additional behavioural assumptions that managers act with bounded rationality, and try to minimize opportunism among organization members, all forms of organization action could be viewed as contractual relations. The notion of the 'internal market' is well illustrated by the reorganized National Health Service, which was changed from a bureaucracy into a market-driven range of transactions, with consequences for organization structures (greater autonomy for general practitioners, 'supplier' status for hospitals and the like).

Case study

The relationship between strategy and structure can be illustrated by the way the organization of today has to move beyond the old bureaucratic formula, to be adaptive and to serve many different markets, whilst maintaining systems of integration which permit economies of scale, and an organization direction and control over marketing in an increasingly global context.

The US company, Air Products, created in Europe a three-dimensional matrix structure, under the responsibility of a European President who reported to the USA. The matrix in Figure 3.1 shows the picture in 1998.

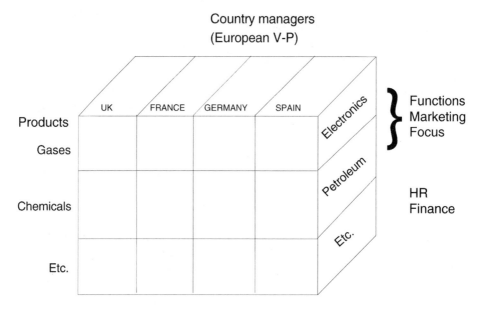

Figure 3.1 Air Products matrix, 1998

The matrix consisted of the products × specific marketing focus, which was industry based across the whole of Europe. Employees could thus be located in France, specializing in gases for the electronics or the petroleum markets, for example. Country managers were responsible for activities within their own country, such as contractual relations, relations with government, etc. There were functional managers responsible across all countries for human resource (HR), finance etc., although with local counterparts who reported to a functional manager, in Europe, as well as to a country manager. These are expressed in a complex matrix structure in which the organization becomes more like a network than a hierarchy.

In this case the leader should think about how Lawrence and Lorsch's ideas on integration and differentiation are useful in explaining the structure, and also the ideas of Oliver Williamson.

Conclusion

Research data have produced the following general conclusions about organizational behaviour and management's responsibilities (see also Figure 3.2):

1 Managers need to be aware of the general nature of organizations, and especially of the complexity of the interactions between the organization's component elements and between an organization and elements in the external environment.
2 Managers need to be aware of the existence and significance of informal systems and their relationships with formal systems in the organization.
3 No universal principles should be assumed in the design of organizations, which should be tailor-made to take account of interactions between internal and external variables. The predominant technology is a fundamentally important factor affecting design.
4 The design should encourage the maximum possible integration of groups and prevent intragroup and intergroup conflict as far as possible.
5 A general atmosphere of trust and openness has to be established, whereby clearly defined objectives are communicated to all employees, and the psychological contract (what the organization can give and what it expects) should be clarified.
6 Finally, in order to survive and grow, organizations need to develop a capacity for self-analysis, whereby diagnosis is possible, and solutions may be proposed. In this connection, the emergence and application in recent years of the idea of organization development (OD) is particularly promising. The essential objectives of OD are:
   (a) to help organizations to become much more aware of their own structures and of their internal and external relationships
   (b) to become more adaptive to change, often in combination with management development strategies
   (c) to programme a process of continued self-analysis as an integral element of organizational life and to use appropriate knowledge and techniques from the social sciences to create new cultures, structures and styles of working.

Organization development requires the employment of external or internal consultants on a long-term basis to fulfil a catalytic function in helping managers at all levels to achieve the objectives described above.

Questions

1 What different kinds of categories of organizational theory can be distinguished and what are the distinctive features of each?
2 Describe briefly the essential features of the theories of the following authors: Weber, Etzioni, Likert, Kahn, Burns and Stalker.
3 Summarize the main conclusions about organization design and behaviour that have emerged from studies of organizations.
4 What is organization development and what are its principal objectives?

STRUCTURAL STUDIES	HUMAN RELATIONS SCHOOL	SYSTEMS APPROACH	CONTINGENCY APPROACH	POST-MODERNIST AND INSTITUTIONAL APPROACHES (OPPOSITE APPROACHES)
This group is concerned with types and rationale of organizational structures and raises important questions of authority-legitimacy, e.g. Weber's three authority-categories	This group emphasizes the effects of managerial behaviour on working life and especially on motivation: the importance of informal systems of behaviour below the surface of the formal organizational system.	This group emphasizes the importance of interaction between organizational variables: people, structure, technology, external environment.	This group is concerned with the suitability of structures for organizational functions and technology, and with capacity to adapt to the environment and change. Data are derived from on-site study.	Institutional ideas deal with the questions of whether new organization forms are a result of economic and social changes. 'Post-modernist' approaches stress the move from rational towards other criteria for organization structures. Institutional theorists see specific forms of rationality underlying action, caused by economic forces.
Charismatic. Traditional. Rational-legal.	The main influences are Mayo, Maslow, Herzberg, McGregor and Argyris	Important contributors are:	Important contributors are:	
Etzioni's three types of organization and corresponding individual involvement:		Tavistock Institute: Socio-technical theory Likert: Link-pin theory	Woodward Burns and Stalker Lawrence and Lorsch	Post-modern theory: Kenneth Gergen, Gareth Morgan
Coercive – alienative Utilitarian – calculative Normative – moral		Kahn: Role-set theory		Institutional theory: Oliver Williamson

CONCLUSIONS

- Awareness of organizational complexity, the inter-relationship of component elements and the existence and influence of informal system is fundamentally important
- Organizations must be specially designed to suit particular functions.
- Design should facilitate integration of component groups.
- A general atmosphere of trust needs to be established for organizations to function effectively.
- Organizations need to develop a capacity for self-analysis (e.g. Organizational development).
- Organizations form changes rapidly and in response to non-rational dynamics.
- Organizations are determined by economic and social conditions.
- Action in organizations can be measured in terms of transaction costs

Figure 3.2 Summary of studies of organizations

References

Hatch, M. J. (1997). *Organizations Theory*. Oxford University Press.
Legge, K. (1995). *Human Resource Management Rhetorics and Realities*. Macmillan.
Peters, T. and Waterman, R. H. (1982). *In Search of Excellence*. Harper and Row.
Stewart, R. (1972). *The Reality of Organizations*. Penguin.
Ward, A. (1990). The future of work. In *Society and Social Science* (Anderson, J. and Ricci, M. eds.). Open University Press.

Further reading for Part One

Argyle, M. (1967). *The Psychology of Interpersonal Behaviour*. Penguin.
Argyle, M., (1974). *The Social Psychology of Work*. Penguin.
Child, J. (1977). *Organizations*. Harper and Row.
Dawson, S. (1986). *Analysing Organizations*. Macmillan.
De Board, R. (1978). *The Psychoanalysis of Organizations*. Tavistock Publications.
Evans, P. (1975). *Motivation*. Methuen.
Gahagan, J. (1975). *Interpersonal and Group Behaviour*. Methuen.
Gibb, C. 91969). *Leadership*. Penguin.
Handy, C. (1985). *Understanding Organizations*. Penguin.
Hatch, M. J. (1997). *Organizations Theory*. Oxford University Press.
Kirby, R. and Radford, J. (1976). *Individual Differences*. Methuen.
Lassey, W. (1973). *Leadership and Social Change*. University Associates.
Legge, K. (1995). *Human Resource Management Rhetorics and Realities*. Macmillan.
Murrell, H. (1976). *Motivation at Work*. Methuen.
Porter, L. and Roberts, K. (1977). *Communication in Organizations*. Penguin.
Pugh, D. (1971). *Organization Theory*. Penguin.
Radford, J. and Kirby, R. (1975). *The Person in Psychology*. Methuen.
Reed, M. and Hughes, M. (1992). *Rethinking Organisations*. Sage.
Reich, B. and Adcock, C. (1976). *Values, Attitudes and Behaviour Change*. Methuen.
Schein, E. (1970). *Organization Psychology*. Prentice-Hall.
Silverman, D. (1970). *The Theory of Organizations*. Heinemann.
Stewart, R. (1972). *The Reality of Organizations*. Penguin.
Vernon, M. D. (1971). *The Psychology of Perception*. Penguin.
Vroom, V. and Deci, E. (1974). *Management and Motivation*. Penguin.

Human resource management as a system

Human resource management as a system

Managers are expected to organize and to be accountable for the work of other people. In this process, managers act as employers and as such they create and sustain the employment relationships of their organizations. The occupation of human resource management specializes in the technical skills of managing this employment relationship. As we defined specialist human resource management in the Introduction, it is the occupation that exercises a responsibility throughout the organization for creating, maintaining and adjusting the policies that form the employer's part of the employment contract. In this section, we shall look at how specialist human resource management has emerged. After we have seen how different models of human resource management have developed, we shall explore the interdependence between the activities that make human resource management by looking at how these activities interlock as a 'system'.

Chapter 4

From personnel management to human resource management: how did this field of work develop?

When we come to consider the essential nature of personnel management we immediately encounter the question: what are the goals of specialists in this field, and how do these specialists assist in the achievement of the organization's goals?

Since the early years of the last century, writers such as Fayol and, later, Urwick and Brech have classified the activities of managers under the headings 'planning', 'co-ordinating', 'controlling' and 'motivating'. These headings demonstrate an awareness of the primary managerial task of pushing work forward, adapting to changes in the environment and overcoming obstacles. Although this classification is helpful as an analysis of management deploying economic resources, when we observe managers at work it is difficult to see their actions in this simple way. For example, all their work involves co-ordination and control. Management work is better described as part of the continuous social processes that apply in organizational life.

The actions of managers are usually very much concerned with achieving results through other people, and therefore the interpersonal skills they demonstrate – notably their capacity to communicate and to receive information, the climate of trust they establish, the degree of enthusiasm they generate, their sense of fairness and their own humanity – will be more significant than a grasp of techniques such as how to discount cash flow or to prepare a critical path analysis.

We can now venture a description of what lies at the heart of managerial work. The essential characteristics seem to be that managers exercise their authority in such a way that it is regarded as legitimate, they maintain the adherence of subordinates to the organization's goals, and build teams which are capable of achieving these goals. Human resource management in its specialized sense is concerned to help in the widest possible way with these managerial tasks. The human resource function has organization-wide responsibilities for HR policy, and should be considered as quite separate from the function which all managers carry out when managing people.

From the 1960s up to the mid-1980s, the term most commonly used to describe the specialist occupation concerned with managing people was 'personnel management'. In the last twenty years, the title 'human resource management', an import from the USA, has become more frequently used. An academic debate has grown around the question of whether this signals a change in the nature of the work performed, with one school of thought arguing that there are strong normative factors driving HRM, in contrast to the administrative and industrial relations concerns of earlier periods.

Storey sets out a definition of HRM that emphasizes the strategic role. He sets out a twenty-five item checklist, differentiating personnel and industrial relations from HRM. The gist of these differences rests on the more individual contract between employer and employee found in HRM, the accent on managing by values and mission, and the strong business orientation of HRM. We discuss the 'fit' between human resource and business strategy in the final chapter.

However, definitions of the field of work have always described it in the broadest terms. For example, 'Personnel Management is the recruitment, selection, development, utilisation of, and accommodation to, human resources by organizations' (French, 1978: 3). British definitions tended to grant it a professional status in its own right. In summary, whilst there is some controversy still about the significance of the change to HRM, there have always been many different definitions of the work and many different job titles. This change of terminology, according to some commentators, signals a new way of undertaking the personnel management role: 'human resource management' is a term which stresses the development of people as assets rather than their control as costs, and places people management at the strategic heart of business planning. This view has been challenged by some academics who see the opposite trend, towards cost reduction, work intensification and a diminution of the power of the specialist personnel department. One way to interpret these contrary trends is to appreciate that organizations adopt different HRM strategies according to the threats and opportunities they face in their planning environments. There are also those who regard the term 'human resource management' as merely a glossy label which attempts to market the same personnel departments as before. Whether or not there is now a new dominant 'paradigm', the degree of change and the effects of the varying personnel traditions help to explain how different models of personnel management have emerged. For the sake of consistency, we will use the term 'human resource management', or 'HRM', throughout this text.

There are a number of different traditions in HRM. It can be perceived as a kind of social conscience, reminding the senior management of their social responsibilities. Human resource departments can spend much of their time operating on personal welfare problems. If control of personnel is the main consideration, the role of HRM will be principally concerned with issues such as the reduction of absenteeism, labour budgeting, headcount, etc. Other traditions in HRM include organization development, in which HRM helps the company to adapt to change, and strives to have a beneficial influence on relationships through the application of the social sciences to people management problems by using job redesign and job satisfaction schemes and communication techniques. In some organizations, HR departments perform a kind of low-level administration, dealing with routine requests from managers for recruitment, transfers and termination, whereas in other organizations they are concerned with strategic planning, developing long-term personnel plans and industrial relations strategy.

How the work is conducted will depend on the particular organization, and there is no common standard applicable throughout the public sector, industry and commerce. The way the company is organized and its size – whether, for example, it is broken down into divisions, profit centres or parts of a group – will also influence the way specialist HR departments fit into the policy-making and decision-making arrangements of the organization.

Different emphases are sometimes given to parts of the specialism, such as planning, selection, industrial relations, training and management development. In some cases, HR directors sit on company boards, advising their fellow directors on the influence of decisions on personnel policy. There is, therefore, a multiplicity of types of relationships between HR and line managers.

The HR manager is often depicted as an adviser to senior line managers. The amount of executive power he or she possesses to carry out decisions without referring them to others will be dependent on what the chief executive has delegated but, unlike some other managers, the amount of power HR staff possess to carry out policies is usually limited. If, for example, the HR manager wanted to introduce a new pension scheme, or to change the remuneration policy, it is extremely unlikely that this could be done unilaterally. Yet, as we have suggested, HR managers are sometimes given a general remit to improve relationships. The reason for this paradox can readily be found in the accountability that line managers have for the achievement of the organization's objectives. To illustrate this point, we may consider the case of the sales manager who is given a sales target to achieve, but no say over the number, quality or deployment of the sales force. In such circumstances, the sales manager could hardly be accountable for the attainment of the target. In their 'staff' role, HR managers act as advisers to management on policy and strategy, whilst the conduct of the policy is often left in the hands of their line manager colleagues.

As we have said, there are different models of HRM, and we can see these developing from a basic administrative role through to a 'business manager' or 'consultancy' role' as shown in Figure 4.1.

The shift to the right brings a number of problems for HRM. For example, the consultancy model of HRM can be performed either externally or internally to the business. The growth of a variety of specialist consultants, in areas such as rewards, development, communications and selection, threatens to 'Balkanize' the HR role. The need to 'fit' the HR strategy to the business strategy might best be achieved under the business manager model, but if we are also expecting HR to provide some kind of social conscience, and

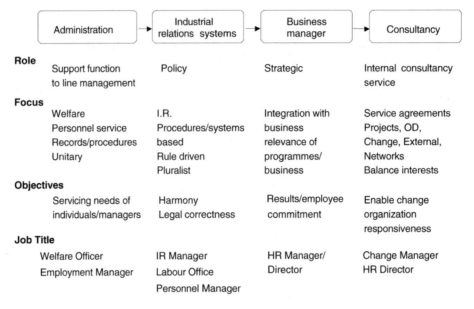

Figure 4.1 Models of personnel/HRM

to champion certain values (as those who see HRM as representing a normative position would) then the conflict within the business manager model can only be avoided if the business adopts these values – a difficult position for managers to adopt given frequent restructuring, redundancies, and cost pressures generated by a highly competitive marketplace.

So far we have outlined the complexities of line manager–HR manager relations, and we have mentioned some of the various traditions in HR work that exist. The history and development of personnel and HR work is a good starting point for understanding how different conceptions of HR management have emerged.

The early history of personnel management, up to 1914

The industrial revolution that spread throughout Britain during the middle of the nineteenth century was brought about by the application of the principle of the division of labour combined with the harnessing of steam and other power sources. Concentrations of working people in factories and the related growth of towns led to the helter-skelter existence that we associate with modern industrial life. The rapid increases in population, new markets, new technology and expansion by vertical integration were conditions that helped to create the need for a large-scale organization of resources.

During the first half of the nineteenth century, a groundswell of criticism appeared against what seemed the unchecked greed and exploitation of workers by their fellows. Movements for democracy, agitation for the repeal of anti-trade union legislation and for some minimal controls on employers found their expression through the Chartists, the Ten-Hour movement and the Anti-Corn Law League and in sporadic riots and petitions.

In the works of Dickens and the later social investigations of Mayhew, Booth and Rowntree, the worst abuses of sweating (excessive hours), child mistreatment and oppression by employers were revealed, and a working-class counterculture was described.

Even among enlightened liberal opinion, public acknowledgement of the reasons for poverty had usually supported the beliefs underlying the 1834 Poor Law. There was no understanding of structural unemployment or the effects of a downturn in the trade cycle. The general image of the pauper was of a lazy profligate brought down by his or her own failings, notably excessive drinking. Such a vision was congruent with the middle-class ideology that was a celebration of capitalist economics. Management and the owners of business were drawn from the upper middle class, where a high value was placed on individualism, competition and the survival of the fittest. Artisans, supervisors and shopkeepers would also have subscribed to such views. Little had changed for working people in the nineteenth century. Their conditions and life chances had always been poor. As John Clare, the Northamptonshire poet, wrote: 'the poor man's lot seems to have been so long remembered as to be entirely forgotten'.

Pressures for reform and for the protection of working people came towards the end of the nineteenth century, mostly from trade union leaders and members of the labour movement. The extension of the franchise added to these pressures in the last quarter of the century. Active campaigning by individuals such as Rowntree was also effective, and the large Quaker employers set out to provide an example of how good working conditions and profitability could be compatible. What has been called the movement towards 'industrial betterment' came on the fringes of a wider claim for improvement in living conditions. Out of this movement emerged the earliest attempts at welfare policies. One interpretation of the industrial betterment movement is that it was a response by employers to the demand for change in society.

Early welfare workers belonged to the property-owning classes, and at first were concerned only with women. The protection of women was seen as a worthy objective, and even the harshest employer would have found it difficult to oppose these aims openly. Extramural welfare workers visited sick employees and helped to arrange accommodation for women and girls, often including the supervision of moral welfare as part of their work. Welfare workers were usually employed in the newer industries, where women were engaged on light machine work, packing, assembly and similar routine jobs, and it was in these factories that full-time welfare staff were first in service.

The scope of welfare officers (sometimes called 'welfare secretaries') was allowed to grow in those companies where she could demonstrate a successful integration of welfare and managerial objectives, so that she became concerned with the recruitment, training and transfer of hourly paid women factory hands.

Up to 1900 there were still only a dozen or so full-time welfare secretaries, but their number had grown sufficiently by 1913 for them to seek a recognizable identity by forming the Welfare Workers' Association, this being the forerunner to the Institute of Personnel Management (now the Institute of Personnel and Development). They often found that managers and supervisors were suspicious of their work, and they were also attacked by the unions as a management device for controlling employees. The problems of being the 'person in the middle' were not unlike the difficulties faced by first-line supervisors. Workers were not sure whether the aims of welfare were altruistic, and felt that there was an element of hypocrisy in the welfare secretaries' actions. Managers saw the possibility of another standard besides economic efficiency being applied, and were antagonized by the thought of any restriction on their power.

The reasons for the development of a welfare movement can best be seen as a response to the wider trend of greater interest and concern for general living conditions. Although it has been argued that Quaker employers such as Cadbury may have been expiating their guilt feelings by becoming leaders of the welfare movement at a time when they had not yet reconciled the profit motive with Christian ethics, it is more accurate to see in their sponsorship of the welfare movement a belief in good organization, good health, hygiene and a broad mission of pastoral care for their workers. Individual welfare workers probably had mixed motives, but there is no doubt that most of them wanted to help improve conditions for working people.

What was the purpose of welfare work?

1 It was an assertion of a paternalistic relationship between employers and their work-force. This outlook was in the spirit of the old guild masters, which meant that employers might expect a reciprocal sense of service from their workers.
2 To grant some form of moral protection over women and children just as the Factory Acts sought to provide a form of physical protection.
3 To achieve higher output by control of sickness and absenteeism, and by the early resolution of grievances and problems.
4 To provide sanitary and acceptable working conditions. Much of the early welfare work was in food factories where cleanliness also benefited the consumer.
5 To make the organization of women by trade unions unnecessary through removing the employees' grievances.

From these early days some of the conflict and confusion about personnel work has persisted. In fact, welfare work was always undertaken to meet the interests of management, since ultimately it was a cost met by management. To some degree, the areas of welfare covered by welfare officers, or welfare secretaries, were on behalf of society as a whole, at a time when there was no help from the state.

The First World War

The First World War occasioned a 'step change' in the development of personnel management. There was a large increase in the number of welfare officers (to about 1300), largely in munitions and war factories, where men were also recruited to oversee boys' welfare. State regulation of employment was instituted through the Munitions of War Act 1915 which, together with its amendments, sought to control the supply of labour to war factories and made welfare services obligatory in these factories.

The extension of controls into such matters as timekeeping, attendance and 'diligence' gave the state an unprecedented impact on working life. However, there were initially a number of different approaches adopted towards personnel problems, and it was not until towards the end of the war that the controls became well organized and effective. Welfare work was performed on an impersonal, bureaucratic basis.

The government gave direct encouragement to welfare development through the Health of Munitions Workers' Committee, which was the precursor to the National

Institute of Industrial Psychology, and which continued the research into the psychological problems of working – boredom, fatigue, monotony, etc.

Women were recruited in large numbers to fill the staffing gap caused by the demand for war materials and the expansion of the armed services. In 1915 one man was expected to do the work of two. The employment of women necessitated agreement with the trade unions on what was termed 'dilution' – that is, accepting unskilled women into craftsmen's work, the abandonment of formal apprenticeship schemes, and changed manning levels. Although compulsory arbitration was introduced, there were many bitter wrangles. Lloyd George, as Minister of Munitions, was obliged to go to the Clydeside shipyards to try to resolve a dispute over 'dilutees' and discharge certificates, for example.

After 1918 various forms of joint consultation were proposed. The only enduring form was the Whitley Joint Consultative Committee in the Civil Service, which is still in existence. However, for the first time the state had to open up a dialogue with the trade unions, and a recognizable policy on industrial relations was evidenced in this period.

Growth of employment management

Employment management accented labour control, recruitment and discharge of labour and had separate origins from welfare. Labour managers came into being in the engineering industry and in large factories – for example, in process industries – and in some cases developed from more routine jobs such as 'timekeepers' or record-keeping assistants on the works office manager's staff. Often, wages clerks saw job applicants and came to deal with queries over absences, bonuses, piece rates, etc. The employers' federations had industrial relations responsibilities, and employed officials to help settle disputes. In engineering and shipbuilding there were national negotiations of rates, but districts 'plussed up' on these rates according to tradition and the supply of skilled labour. Records of grievances and disputes were kept by engineering employers because of the need to follow procedures within the employers' federation, and therefore specialists in the procedures evolved in some companies.

Early personnel departments, 1920–39

In the 1920s and 1930s employment managers with various job titles such as 'Labour Officer', 'Men's Employment Officer', etc., were increasingly common. The number of employers' associations that had traditionally fulfilled the major industrial relations role fell from 2403 to 1550 between 1925 and 1936. This was partly due to employers wanting to follow an independent tack, and because, with the growth in complexity of their businesses, they created their own personnel departments with industrial relations policies. In the large organizations, such as ICI, Courtaulds, Pilkingtons, London Transport and Marks & Spencer, the first specialist personnel departments were formed between the wars.

Specialist personnel management in organizations such as these was a response to the problem of control. Complex organization structures resulted in differing standards and divergent policies unless a central controlling influence was exercised. Mergers, acquisitions and expansions led to the establishment of personnel departments. These were usually in the newer industries, such as plastics, chemicals, mass-produced consumer goods and in multiple retail, whereas there was no attempt to develop employment management as a specialism in industries such as shipbuilding, textiles or mining, which were hit by the slump. This was because employment management addressed itself to the question of staffing control in matters like absenteeism and recruitment with the intention of improving output. In the older industries, the pressing problems were those of structural unemployment, and no techniques such as retraining adult workers, redeployment or work-sharing were considered by managements. The size of the problem (for most of the 1920s and 1930s there was never less than 10 per cent of the working population unemployed), and the worldwide recession, made it unlikely that solutions would be sought by the application of new techniques.

As trade began to pick up, and rearmament began in the late 1930s, the larger companies in the new industries showed an interest in management development and training. Management trainees were recruited, who followed a central training scheme, and in this way the latent purpose of spreading a common managerial philosophy throughout diverse organization structures was ensured when the trainees moved between divisions. Since the First World War the National Institute of Industrial Psychology had begun to develop selection tests and to contribute to the solution of training problems. In the larger modern companies, the welfare and employment management sections were merged in the later 1930s. Personnel management in all but these few enterprises was a low-level affair until after 1945. The employees covered were usually hourly paid operatives and junior clerical staff. In retail distribution, some moves towards including sales staff and buyers took place in the 1930s, and the Staff Management Association was set up in 1934 specifically to cover the difficult personnel problems of managing staff scattered in small units. Industrial relations was not regarded as the mainstay of personnel work, and was frequently the main responsibility of senior line managers.

The effects of large-scale unemployment retarded advances in techniques. With a cheap supply of labour available, and uncertainty about future demand, there was no pressure for sophisticated staffing planning, and the threat of unemployment averted attention from questions of motivation. Similarly, after the General Strike in 1926, and the weakening effect of structural unemployment, power was passing from the hands of trade union leaders. However, from 1937 onwards, rearmament and the prospect of war caused a change. There were also social pressures emanating from the Depression, for security and a better life. This was the period of improvements in suburban housing, of a national movement for holidays with pay, and it was a time when big corporations saw the value in improving employee benefits such as pension schemes as a way of ensuring a stable, tractable workforce.

The Second World War

In the Second World War, personnel management was expanded in its staffing control aspects to virtually all factories, and the designation of welfare and personnel occupations as 'reserved' (that is, those occupying them were exempt from conscription into the forces) shows the importance that was attached to the personnel role. The growth in numbers of personnel officers was again a feature of wartime, as had been the case with the First World War, there being around 5700 by 1943.

The three instruments of labour regulation were 'protected establishments' (engaged in war work), the registration of all employment, and 'essential work orders'. These gave an expanded Ministry of Labour and National Service considerable power to direct labour, to prevent the call-up of those with special skills, and to influence conditions of employment.

Welfare and personnel work were inaugurated on a full-time basis at all establishments producing war materials, and the concept of a total war carried with it the belief that no effort should be spared to ensure high productivity. In addition to the administration of the rules, all aspects of the management of people came under scrutiny, and the government saw specialist personnel management as an integral part of the drive for greater efficiency. For example, the Ministry of Aircraft Production stipulated that specialist personnel management was mandatory in aircraft factories.

The evacuation of large numbers of civilians, the extension of shift working and the problems of training large numbers of women and young people gave welfare and personnel departments the same central place in the organization of production as had emerged during the First World War. Welfare was again part of the rule-governed environment created for large-scale production. The pervasive aspects of the role were resented by workers, but less so in the Second World War than in the First World War. The acceptance of the vital importance of the struggle and the feeling of involvement by ordinary people in view of the Blitz were perhaps the main reasons for this different response. Nevertheless, personnel and welfare officers were seen as part of the operations of management, and the two world wars helped to create the image of the personnel officer as a bureaucrat.

To achieve wartime production targets, strikes were made illegal and compulsory arbitration was introduced. In 1940 three men were expected to cover the work of four, and once again the staffing gap necessitated the employment of women in unfamiliar jobs, such as crane drivers, and in war factories. Of necessity, restrictive practices had to be suspended by the unions, and the state entered into a dialogue with the unions to try to maintain harmony. The relationship was more intentionally fostered in the Second World War, when Ernest Bevin, as Minister of Labour (and an important prewar trade union leader), and a coalition government were able to persuade the unions that the suspension of normal practices was not a surrender. The linking of productivity improvements with joint consultation made a lasting impression on management thought, and the principles of joint consultation have come to be regarded as important in the training of personnel managers. After 1945, successive governments have found various forms of consultation with the Trades Union Congress (TUC) necessary, continuing the tradition.

Three significant tendencies deriving from both world wars can be summarized as follows:

1 The belief amongst managers, sustained by research, that output and employment conditions are related, and the development by personnel managers of specific personnel techniques.
2 The integration of employment management and welfare work into the broad function,

under the umbrella of personnel management, and the massive increase in the number of people in the occupation.

3 The wars demonstrated that the regulation of employment by the state could produce the desired outcomes in the short term at least, but that this required large-scale controls and could only succeed with the agreement of the workers, who needed a commitment to victory if they were to be convinced of the necessity to relinquish their freedoms.

1945–68

Industrial relations and personnel management

An understanding of the different facets of personnel management is not possible without an appreciation of what role personnel managers have played in employee relationships. The term 'industrial relations' is frequently used to describe only formal, institutional arrangements for management relationships between the mass of the workforce and managers as representatives of those in whose interests the organization is controlled.

However, the differences between 'formal' and 'informal' relationships have never been so strictly drawn for an analysis on that basis to be sufficient. Power relationships are central to our understanding of industrial relations, and these have fluctuated.

A brief account of the development of trade unionism is given in Chapter 16, so in this section we shall confine ourselves to the development of industrial relations (IR) responsibilities in HRM. The broader view of 'industrial relations' as the whole spectrum of relationships and the negotiation processes between power groups in an organization reveals at once the cardinal place that HR management occupies.

Trade unions were suspicious and hostile towards the early welfare workers. They felt that welfare workers were extending the employers' control into the private lives of the workers. The welfare movement had sprung up in non-unionized companies. Shipbuilding, engineering, mining and transport, for example, were industries where trade union traditions were strong, and regulation of labour was largely in the hands of both district and local trade union officials and the employers' federations.

Although large companies began to establish their own personnel departments from the late 1920s onwards, it was difficult for personnel officers to gain credibility quickly. This is a problem that has dogged the occupation to the present day. Institutional arrangements in the engineering industry militated against importance being granted to personnel management. The 'procedure' for settling disputes tended to favour the involvement of senior executives at the later stage rather than local personnel officers. Union negotiators, although now reconciled to personnel work as part of management, typically preferred to negotiate with the more senior members of companies, recognizing then, as now, the value of dealing with those who had the power to grant their case. Post-1945 industrial relations witnessed an enormous growth in the number and power of shop stewards, and the breakdown of national-level bargaining through employers' federations. Local-level bargaining gave greater scope for personnel staff, and the larger companies preferred to develop their own industrial relations policies that were in tune with their investment plans and their overall corporate strategy. There was a growth in productivity bargaining in the 1960s as employers and unions negotiated about shares in wealth that were to be found from improvements in technology, for example, agreements such as those made at ESSO's Fawley Refinery. The involvement of line managers in productivity bargaining was essential, both because of their technical knowledge and because they were the managers who had to make the bargain work.

The Donovan Report of 1968 on trade unions and employers was a Royal Commission report that examined British industrial relations in the light of the large number of unofficial strikes which were taking place. Donovan was particularly critical of what the Commission's members saw as the failure of personnel managers either to cope with the changes that were taking place, to be skilled in negotiation or to plan industrial relations strategy. The immediate *ad hoc* responses that were typical of management's reaction to the disagreements which so often led to unofficial action were seen as a failure on management's part to give personnel management a high priority. This was one of a series of criticisms against management, and the HR occupation seems destined to have periodic crises of confidence, although there may be some justification for the view that personnel staff had not been sufficiently innovative in their responses to the changing industrial relations scene. Donovan failed, however, to offer a solution or a range of techniques which would resolve the problems.

All kinds of organizations (local authorities, hospitals, service industries, for example, as well as manufacturing) were starting to employ full-time personnel staff by the mid-1960s, and the spread of ideas and of specialization within the field began to establish personnel management as an occupation in its own right. The 'consultant problem-solver' role is often the most acceptable one in an organization's authority structure, so there may be greater involvement for line managers in day-to-day negotiation. The research, co-ordination and backup activities of personnel officers were often an essential part of the management's control and direction of relationships, however.

The most significant contribution of personnel management to industrial relations was through the creation of conditions under which certain industrial relations policies came to be accepted. Wage payment systems, and conditions of service that created different status groupings, were examples of how personnel systems came to create relationships.

Industrial relations strategies are rarely explicit at any time. Examples of personnel managers operating latent strategies could be found in motor manufacturing, for example, in the 1960s and 1970s. The issues over which negotiation with the unions was accepted had widened to include pension schemes, training, working procedures, safety, discipline and even individual appointments, in some industries. This was noticeable in the public sector, where the growth in white-collar unionization had brought staff associations into the arena of collective bargaining.

Union leaders were heard to call for better personnel management since personnel managers brought order and were often able to promote good relationships, for instance, through organization development schemes, which started to be prescribed as solutions to difficulties in relationships in the later 1960s. Attention to personnel management might be expected to ensure some minimum standards and to curb the rogue employer.

National economic policy, legislation and personnel techniques, 1968–79

In postwar Britain there was a boom-slump cycle in which both Labour and Conservative governments tried fiscal and monetary policies to control the economy. Following the Second World War came a period of low unemployment for twenty-five years. During this period the stability of sterling and the rate of price inflation dominated economic thinking.

State legislation on prices and incomes ranged from voluntary regulations by individual employers to statutory controls maintained by special commissions and boards. Whatever form was used, the regulation of wages in accordance with national economic policies entailed the control of wage policies by personnel managers and other senior staff on a company-wide basis. This encouraged the use of job evaluation schemes and incremental scales.

Entry to the European Economic Community (EEC) came at a time when multinational companies were expanding, which gave some personnel departments an international dimension. In these circumstances, compensation planning became more complex since different payment systems had to be reconciled within a single status hierarchy.

In addition to prices and incomes policies, the state was extremely active in formulating new employment legislation during the early 1960s. The Contracts of Employment Act 1963, Industrial Training Act 1964 and Redundancy Payments Act 1965 were the forerunners of comprehensive legislation on job security, equal opportunity and the position of trade unions. Various state agencies were also set up during this time to encourage good employment practice. One of the major consequences of all this activity was the enhancement in formal authority of personnel departments, and these changes were also a factor in the spread of personnel functions into small organizations. The burst of legislation coincided with the development of personnel techniques. Management training courses with both educational and vocational aspects expanded, and theories drawn from the social sciences became popular in the late 1960s to explain motivation to work and organizational behaviour. Communication techniques such as briefing groups were emphasized and greater attention was paid to the social and technical environment of work, largely due to the influence of the Tavistock Institute and the 'sociotechnical systems' school. The Institute of Personnel Management (IPM) drew heavily on sociology and psychology when restructuring its examination scheme, and the IPM was active in the move to 'professionalize' personnel management.

In the 1970s manpower planning became more sophisticated with the advent of computer models which could predict future requirements by manipulating the many variables of labour supply and demand. Similarly, record-keeping for large concerns was aided by microfilm and computer storage. Selection tests had been available since the early 1920s, but they began to be used more frequently, often by specialized agencies.

1979 onwards

The election of a Conservative government with Mrs Thatcher as Prime Minister ushered in a new era for people management. The 1980s were characterized by a move to the right ideologically and the reassertion of managerial prerogatives. Elected with a mandate to reduce trade union power, the new government embarked on a legislative programme which outlawed sympathetic and 'political' strikes, increased the liability of trade unions to legal actions in the courts as a consequence of strikes or other forms of protest, increased the power of individual trade union members and sought to reduce the influence of trade unions nationally.

Following the recession of the early 1980s, organizations drove through new approaches to quality improvement and efficiency. Productivity improvements were achieved by new investments and by introducing more flexible working practices: flexibility of time, task and contract. Employers retained a shrinking core of full-time permanent employees while expanding in the secondary labour market of part-time, subcontract, temporary, casual and short-term contract employees, these people on non-standard contracts now being the majority of the employed.

During the boom period in the mid-1980s, the shortage skills attracted premium rates. There were 'golden hellos' and signing-on fees for recent graduates. This was a time when deregulation in financial services, and the privatization of companies such as British Telecom, British Airways and British Gas, gave a considerable boost to HR management in its resourcing and developmental activities. This was the time when the strategic role of HRM was beginning to be recognized. The management of change was seen as the key role, with considerable interest in creating new organization cultures and in organization development techniques. Following the Handy, Constable and McCormick reports on management education, British lack of competitiveness was identified with inadequate systems for management education – one consequence was a stimulus to new Master of Business Administration (MBA) programmes and to various forms of postexperience programmes, provided in-house or through university business schools.

At the start of the 1990s a new, deeper recession was experienced. Affecting the south-east of England as much as the north, in service industries as much as manufacturing, substantial redundancies occurred. 'Delayering', restructuring and outsourcing some of the functions previously conducted within the company were organization structure changes that affected HRM, with outplacement as a solution to help the change. These changes have brought about a collapse of the career concept and, even in the public sector, the end to 'jobs for life'. Divisional structures and empowerment policies have moved the day-to-day decision-making away from large corporate headquarters, which can concentrate on strategic issues. Many of the improvements to performance, such as total quality management (TQM) and business process redesign (BPR), originated outside the HR function, but nevertheless increased the focus on people management issues as the likely source of competitive advantage.

The demographic changes are potentially the most significant influences on HRM. The large reduction in the number of young people coming onto the labour market in Western Europe, and increasing longevity, mean that organizations must gear their employment policies towards the middle-aged and towards women. Similarly, Britain's multiracial society requires HR management techniques that manage diversity. This stimulated interest in equal opportunity policies. The major demographic changes are described in relation to HR strategy, in Chapter 22, but we should note here that the mixture of social, demographic and global business pressure has produced a highly unstable environment in which HRM is conducted.

Routine personnel administration is now often performed under the direction of a senior line manager (for example, at divisional or local company level) and a strategic, human resource manager role is performed at or near board level. In this latter position, human resource managers have been active in managing fundamental changes within their companies.

Summary

This chapter has shown that there are various traditions in personnel management, and that each has its own historical pedigree. A brief summary of the traditions of personnel management we have touched on is given in Table 4.1.

Table 4.1 Traditions in personnel management

Traditions	Period	Description
Welfare	Up to 1920s	Personnel management as a personal service to employees, who are the 'clients' of the personnel or welfare officer. Major concerns were the provisions of canteens, sick visiting, the supervision of moral welfare in anticipation of a reciprocal sense of service from the employee
Employment management	Up to 1930s	Emphasized the control of numbers and budgets and placed stress on economic efficiency plus a high value on performance investigation by organization and method type studies. Employees have not always shared these beliefs, thus leading to a 'Theory X' view of workers by managers.
Bureaucratic	1914 to present	The 'personnel administrator' typical of many large organizations operates a comprehensive set of rules based on a belief in order and rationality, and on the intrinsic merit of the organization's internal status system, to which employees are expected to subscribe
Professional personnel manager	1945 to present	A belief in specialization is sustained by the application of personnel techniques applied for the benefit of the 'client', who is the line manager, and is supported by a general social acceptance of 'experts'.
Liberal radical present	1930s to present	This personnel manager sees the role as that of improving communications and leadership. Approach is that of a radical liberal, a belief in individualism and in the need to participate with employees, anticipating agreement and enthusiasm from those at work.

Human resource manager	1980s to present	Accent on development and utilization of people resources as assets. Employment costs and the return on these costs are central concerns – leading to desire for adaptability, flexibility of people and to the use of outsourcing arrangements to reduce costs

No generalization about HR management is possible, therefore, at the level of description, and different models may be appropriate in different organizations. The ability to switch between models as required is one of the most important requisites for those working in this field. In the next chapter we shall see how the interdependence between line managers and HR managers is indicative of successful personnel work, by showing that the way the HR function is discharged is as important as what is done for the achievement of the organization's objectives.

Questions

1 Define personnel management, showing the distinction that should be made between the personnel department and the personnel function of management.
2 What are the main trends in the history of personnel management?
3 What impact does personnel management have on industrial relations?
4 To what extent is human resource management representative of a new paradigm in people management?

References

French, W. (1978). *The Personnel Management Process: Human Resources Administration and Development.* Houghton Mifflin.

Chapter 5

The elements of a system and their interrelationship

This chapter sets out a systematic way of conducting the HR function of management, and shows the respective spheres of line and HR managers.

As we have seen, specialized HR departments were frequently established by organizations responding to change, often as a consequence of acquisitions and mergers, or due to the increased size and complexity of their businesses.

Specialization in HR management has contributed to the success of famous companies, and through such companies has played a part in advancing the cause of civilization. The improvement of working conditions, the creation of job satisfaction, the development and training of employees, the maintenance of harmonious relationships and the fairness of rewards, for example, exist in organizational life because managements have seen the importance of a professional approach to HR management. However, there is evidence of failure in some organizations. The problems of low productivity, unfair dismissals, absenteeism, accidents and social abuses such as sexual and racial discrimination are still with us as we move forward in the twenty-first century.

In the previous chapter we described how some of the different traditions of personnel management developed. The variability of organization cultures and the changing environment in which people are managed would lead us to believe that there is no regular trend in the development of personnel management that applies to all organizations. No single model of HR management can meet all requirements. The problems arise when there is insufficient flexibility by managers in their response to the changing demands of their role. The co-ordination of this kind of variable, responsive attitude towards HR problems does require senior management to possess an outward-looking philosophy which questions the assumptions on which decisions are predicated. The approach advocated looks towards changing values in society, to the impact of market and technical changes on the workforce so that a comprehensive, sensitive and accurate response is made.

By operating a comprehensive, systematic coverage of the employment relationship in all the activities of HR management, and by following the appropriate process, HR managers can help to adapt their organizations to the changing environment and can

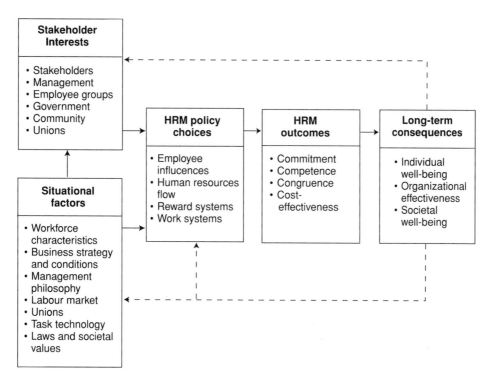

Figure 5.1 The Harvard analytical framework for HRM
Source: Beer *et al.* (1985).

contribute to the success of their organization's goals. In the remainder of this chapter we wish to describe in detail the interrelationship between all the activities that go to make up the HR function.

Human resources and business strategies

There have been a number of attempts to describe the interlinkages between human resource management and organizational goals. The Harvard model of Beer et al. (see Figure 5.1) characterizes human resource management as a system which links corporate objectives into societal needs and back into human resource activities. This framework, therefore, describes the integration between business and society. Perhaps the main weakness of this framework is its failure to show corporate or business strategy as a key determinant of human resource strategies and policies.

Other authors, such as Hendry and Pettigrew, have attempted to show human resource management as a process where there are interconnected decisions deriving from the corporate or business strategy, often, for example, originating in the product life cycle stage, or in decisions to move into new markets (see Figure 5.2).

Research has shown how complex are the relationships between corporate and human resource strategies. We discuss the 'fit' between HR and business strategy in

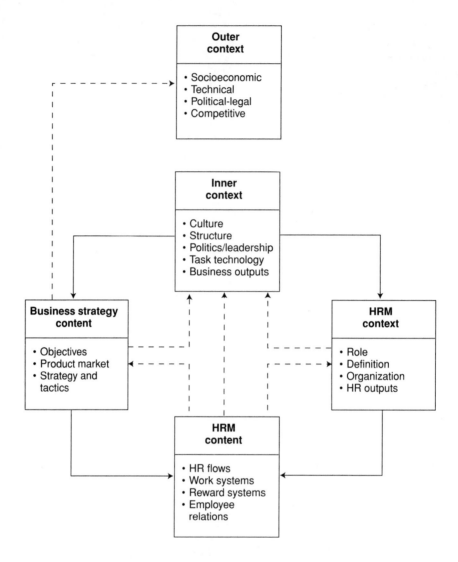

Figure 5.2 Strategic change and human resource management
Source: Hendry and Pettigrew (1990).

detail in Chapter 22. Definitions in this field of study are not always as clear as they should be. The term 'corporate strategy' is taken to mean the strategy pursued by a corporate board, which includes the portfolio of interests they wish to acquire or retain, together with the financial ratios (such as return on total assets) they use to measure the corporate performance of their various businesses. Business strategy is the strategy of a particular business unit (a strategic business unit – SBU), measured usually by the sales, product launches, return on investment and other measures of efficiency.

Human resource strategies should not be confused with human resource or personnel policies. Human resource strategies are typically a series of policies and programmes (such as change programmes) designed to achieve a people management objective. Similarly, there are sometimes express 'human resource philosophies' – these are usually value statements which set out the corporate values towards the employees, including minimum standards, and the overall vision for managing people.

Research by Purcell has shown how human resource strategies follow business strategies – these are 'downstream', second- or third-order strategies that are mostly concerned with implementing business strategies. However, there are recorded cases where the mix of skills of the workforce has influenced the decisions about the type of business to be developed.

Organization structure is also a deciding factor in the influence of the HR department over strategic issues. Highly divisionalized structures, now so common in industry and commerce, result in strong divisional HR functions, sometimes at the expense of the corporate HR role. The devolution of responsibility for profit or cost control to divisional managers can only be successful if they also have control over HR policies that have a major influence on employment costs. There is, therefore, often tension between corporate head office HR policies, for example, in areas such as fast-track recruitment, management development and benefits programmes and local company or divisional desires. Increasingly, HR departments have to 'sell' their policies to sceptical line managers or invoke the authority of the board to gain acceptance of their initiatives.

There are many variables that influence the range of HR policies chosen in support of particular business strategies. For example, size and the technology used in the production or service determines the occupational groups to be employed; how they will be organized and the labour intensity of the firm determines the nature of the work; the industrial relations traditions determine the procedures used for deciding pay rates, for introducing changes and the decision-making style to be adopted. At the organization level of analysis, therefore, HR departments perform a variety of functions according to these variables, and reinterpret management strategies into people management strategies.

The HR role is now often that of an internal consultant. This may lead to various projects, as exemplified by the co-operation between HR manager and line manager in organization development programmes. There is also a need for HR managers to be able to analyse and dispose of problems, and propose solutions to a management that may be unaware of the facts. These could be what Legge (1978) describes as 'convergent innovation' solutions – that is, working within the management's mind-set, values and assumptions – or 'divergent innovation' approaches – proposing original methods outside the experience of the management team, challenging their assumptions. The human resource strategy will thus be likely to contain some elements of ongoing activity where HR is working towards the solution of long-standing problems.

David Ulrich has suggested eight HR roles that seek to show the relationship between HRM as a specialism, and the rest of the business. These are listed as:

1 Employment brand champion: managing the image of the company in the various labour markets.
2 Observant engineer: working the efficiency and effectiveness level in the organization, and diagnosing any problems.
3 Partner in strategic thinking: acting as strategic partner to senior management.
4 Agent of change: helping to keep the organization competitive by anticipating and facilitating change.

5 Champion of the talent bank: ensuring short-term measures do not overtake the long-term need for attracting, retaining and developing talent.
6 Faultless administrator: handling all the basic administration efficiently.
7 Uncomfortable companion: challenging occasionally the received wisdom of the organization in order to improve effectiveness.
8 Corporate conscience: whilst not the preserve of HR the function should be prepared to deal with any ethical issues in the employment relationship.

The activities of the human resource function

The labels we give to these activities are rough descriptions of a collection of related events and tasks that make up the work of managing the employment relationship.

In this section we shall try to examine the relationship between the activities, using the notion of a 'system', that is, a set of interdependent parts each providing an input to another. This helps to explain the activities of the HR function as logically related, and adjustable to meet the changing needs of the organization. It is another feature of a system that feedback is possible to adjust the system to change. The system of activities we will be describing is therefore a related set of activities which adjusts to circumstances and which provides a comprehensive coverage of the employment relationship.

At the heart of all HR activities is the HR plan or strategy. This is the centrepiece, where corporate staffing objectives are set out, in numbers of people within each area of production, sales and administration, the skills required and the costs. The plan may cover any period, but most typically it will be for the period of one to five years, and will be a part of the company's budgetary programme. Corporate planning is often undertaken on a three- to five-year rolling cycle, with each successive year being brought up to date as it comes closer to the current year, and it would be usual for the HR plan to be part of this procedure. In the HR plan the organization's demand for labour is set out, and this results in an examination by the HR manager of the internal labour supply. Where possible, posts are filled from within as the most efficient source of labour, but it would be unusual for the right mix of skills and experience to be available for every vacancy, and so recruitment into the organization is necessary. The transfer of employees, their promotion and recruitment result in the establishment of training schemes.

Training is also an adjunct to appraisal. Appraisal is an activity designed either formally or informally to measure the performance of subordinates against the achievement of agreed objectives. Welfare policies are available to help individuals who have personal problems that inhibit their performance. Along with the activities of appraising and training, there is concurrent attention to staffing control, by the application of reporting and discipline procedures.

Throughout all these actions there may be a requirement to consult and/or negotiate with the appropriate trade unions. The stage at which negotiations take place will obviously vary with the practice of the industry, but in view of the crucial importance of wage costs for determining prices, and thus sales revenue and net profit, the earlier the negotiation the greater the certainty that costs will be as predicted.

The chart in Figure 5.3 is a simplified version of this scheme, and there may be more

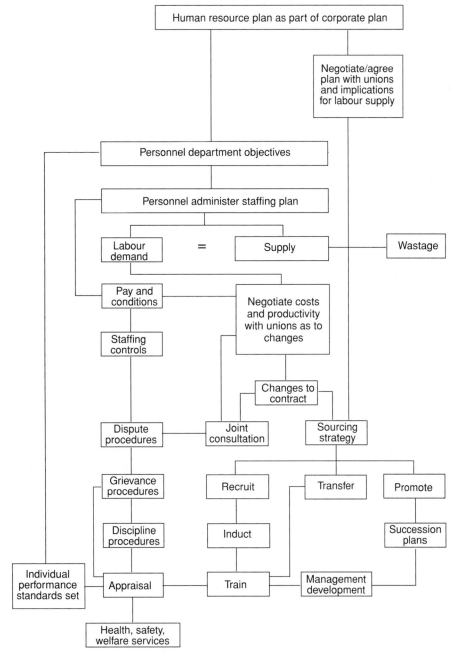

Figure 5.3 Personnel activities

complex links that could be made – for example, joint consultative committees are often concerned with training matters, and in areas such as fast-track management recruitment schemes the recruitment is for long-term demand for labour rather than for meeting an immediate (or next year) demand. Some of the links in the chart may also not be applicable in particular companies. There are some who would dispute the notion that performance appraisal, although linked to the setting of individual standards which unquestionably should fit into the corporate objectives, should necessarily be linked with pay. These kinds of issues we will explore fully as we consider each of the items mentioned in the succeeding chapters.

The essential message here is that each HR activity is linked to another and therefore failures in any one part of this system may result in the breakdown of the whole. As a system, there are links between corporate and individual objectives, joint agreement on the approach to be taken between management and work people, a monitored and flexible HR plan which allows for the development of individuals who are appraised and rewarded in accordance with their contribution to the organization's objectives.

We mentioned earlier the importance attached to integrating the human resources plan into the corporate or business plan. Taking our view of HR policies, there should also be integration between the policies, so that they are experienced as a coherent means of attaining management's objectives.

The activities we have outlined are not the exclusive province of the HR manager, but are activities which managers in all parts of the organization share. The HR plan must be integrated with the corporate plan, and we would anticipate that all senior managers would make an input to this planning activity, just as managers are originators of job descriptions, appraisers are initiators of salary increases for their staff and of action within the discipline procedure. In other words, managers have the major role to play in the day-to-day management of people.

Without the advice and support of specialist staff, however, managers would find their tasks difficult to achieve. It is worth remembering that when Great Britain faced its most difficult struggles, in the First and Second World Wars, the way to victory on the home front included the expansion of specialist welfare and personnel management. In the list of managerial contributions to the HR function outlined in the paragraph above, we can note that the appraisal systems, the salary administration policies, the discipline procedures and the policies within which managers manage their subordinates are created and monitored by specialists in HR management. The responsibilities of management are shared, and in addition to their central 'resourcing' role, of specializing in finding, deploying and developing employees, HR managers must co-ordinate and administer the whole range of personnel policies.

The ways in which HR managers interlink their work with line managers is often a source of difficulty, but conflict is not inevitable. The relationships between HR and line managers are crucial to the success of both parties.

Summary

This chapter has described human resource management analytically as a system and as a process by which activities for the management of people are performed. The benefits in describing human resource management as a system are that the logical relationships between the elements are revealed, showing how each part contributes to the whole and how any failure of one part would result in further problems in other parts of the system.

The integration between business strategy and human resource strategy has also been discussed. This form of integration is achieved when human resource management is discussed within the corporate planning process, an issue to which we will turn in Chapter 6. Human resource strategies are frequently designed to implement business strategies. There are, however, fundamental human resource strategies in organization design, organization development and in the creation of particular organization cultures which go beyond a mechanistic implementation plan – in a sense, they are so integral to the business strategies that the whole business improvement plan is based on them. The second form of integration discussed here is the integration between policies – that is, the coherent set of activities which represent management's intentions. The interrelationship between these different activities must always be borne in mind when we discuss them in subsequent chapters. Within organizational activity itself, work is not necessarily divided up into these neat boxes, with clear labels. Management addresses itself to problem-solving. To conduct the HR process successfully, the HR manager will require a range of interpersonal skills. Interpersonal skills are the 'cement' that joins together the process of managing people with all the activities described.

A glossary of terms used

Appraisal Formal techniques for assessing individuals, with a view to advising them of their progress, improving their performance, identifying potential and helping with any personal difficulties.

Business strategy The attempt by those who control an organization to find ways to position their business/organization objectives so that they can exploit the planning environment and make the optimum use of capital and human assets.

Corporate plan A plan devised by the board, showing *inter alia* marketing changes anticipated, the net profit projected and the investment decisions that are necessary. The return on total assets, on capital employed, are the measures often used. The corporate plan in diversified corporations includes the portfolio of interests desired.

Discipline procedures Formal procedures for improving performance/behaviour which is judged inadequate for the job. These result in a series of warnings, verbal and written, to ensure compliance with the organization's rules, and penalties for misconduct and poor performance, including dismissal.

Disputes procedures Procedures agreed between management and employee representatives concerning the methods adopted in resolving disputes. Should there be a disagreement over the authorization of overtime, control of sickness absence, etc., this would be resolved through the disputes procedure, which may contain a clause allowing for arbitration.

Grievance procedures Procedures whereby individual employees may take up grievances which are of concern to them, such as complaints about their own managers. These procedures would involve other senior managers, and ultimately the personnel department.

Health/safety welfare services The services provided by the company to ensure that acceptable standards are maintained in respect of the health and safety of their employees (such as regular medical checks) and that, where the company can prevent personal difficulties from inhibiting performance, the welfare of the individual is taken into account.

Human resource strategy A set of programmes and policies which management adopt in order to achieve the people management objectives which form part of the business strategy.

Human resources plan A plan showing the demand for labour over a period of time, which incorporates assumptions about productivity and labour costs. The supply of labour available within the company, and the shortfall that will need to be made good, will be revealed. There will also be a narrative account of key human resource issues and how the company should resolve them, with a time frame and performance standards.

Individual performance standards These are the performance standards which derive from the objectives of the department where the employee works. They may be expressed as 'key tasks' or 'objectives' that have to be achieved in a given period of time. It is against these that the individual's performance is appraised. Where there is provision, merit or commission payments may be made to reward good performance.

Induction Induction is a formal programme, designed and partly carried out by personnel to introduce new employees to the organization, in all its social as well as work aspects.

Joint consultation Arrangements for management to discuss any proposals affecting the organization with employee representatives on a regular basis. Differences that emerge would be subject to a negotiated agreement.

Management development A term used to cover a series of arrangements by which organizations help to ensure that individuals with potential for managerial work are given experience and training to fit them for the likely opportunities that will become available.

Negotiation of pay and benefits This is now frequently undertaken on an annual cycle, and it would be sensible to phase the negotiations to fit the planning sequence, as the assumptions about costs and output that are built into the plan may need adjustment. Negotiation throughout the year may be necessary as contentious issues arise out of joint consultation.

Promotion Promotion, as part of the succession arrangements to fill vacancies as they occur, by which time the person promoted should have completed the necessary experience and should have been trained through the management development programme.

Recruitment Undertaken as an activity by personnel to fill vacancies from external sources to comply with the staffing plan.

Rewards and conditions of service The management of rewards and associated benefits such as company cars are the responsibility of the HR department.

Sourcing strategy The strategy by which the organization will fulfil its labour requirements, including utilization strategies, outsourcing and changes to working hours, shifts, and contracts and labour flexibility arrangements.

Staffing controls Controls on attendance, overtime, commission or bonus payments, as well as monitoring of line management requests for labour to ensure that any alterations to the staffing plan are authorized.

Succession plans These are the plans made between senior management for succession to managerial posts which best fulfil both the organization's needs and the needs of the management development programme.

Training Formal and informal instruction designed to improve the individual's performance at work, so that he or she can achieve from appraisal reports or be assessed on all new entrants to the posts in question.

Transfer Where a vacancy can be filled by level transfer, this may be done as part of the development of the individual, or it could be a fortuitous circumstance. Transfers are sometimes arranged also to resolve interpersonal disharmony.

Questions

1 Why is it helpful to think of the activities of human resource management as a 'system'?
2 What should be the relationship between human resource strategy and business strategy?
3 Why is it necessary to ensure that there is an explicit relationship between the HR policies?

References

Beer, M., Spector, B., Lawrence, P. R., Quinn Mills, D. and Walton, R. E. (1985). *Human Resource Management: A General Manager's Perspective*. Walton. Free Press.

Hendry, C. and Pettigrew, A. (1990). HRM: an agenda for the 1990s. *International Journal of Human Resource Management*, **1**(1), 3–8.

Legge, K. (1978). *Power, Innovation and Problem Solving in Personnel Management*. McGraw-Hill.

Further reading for Part Two

Legge, K. (1978). *Power, Innovation and Problem Solving in Personnel Management*. McGraw-Hill.

Marks, W. (1978). *Politics and Personnel Management. An Outline History 1960–76*. IPM.

Mintzberg, H. (1973). *The Nature of Managerial Work*. Harper and Row.

Niven, M. M. (1967). *Personnel Management 1913–1963*. IPM.

Sisson, K. (ed.) (1994). *Personnel Management: A Comprehensive Guide to Theory and Practice in Britain*. Blackwell.

Storey, J. (ed.) (1995). *Human Resource Management: A Critical Text*. Routledge.

Torrington, D. and Hall, L. (1987). *Personnel Management: A New Approach*. Prentice-Hall.

Tyson, S. (1995). *Human Resource Strategy: Towards a General Theory of Human Resource Management*. Pitman.

Tyson, S. and Fell, A., (1992). *Evaluating the Personnel Function*. 2nd edition. Stanley Thornes.

Watson, T. J. (1977). *The Personnel Managers*. Routledge and Kegan Paul.

Obtaining suitable human resources

Obtaining suitable human resources

The task of finding people who either possess or have the potential to develop the knowledge, skills and attitudes that will enable a work organization to carry out the tasks necessary for the achievement of its aim and objectives is obviously of fundamental importance. However, the whole process from start to finish is complex, and to be effectively accomplished it requires an understanding of the nature of the process, of the interrelationship of its component stages and a systematic application in practice. As with all systems, apart from the importance of each individual element the neglect or omission of any stage will inevitably adversely affect the total system.

The main elements of this system and their interrelationship are the subject of this part. These are:

1 The definition of the missions and strategic objectives of the organization as the basis for any assessment of the human resources needed to meet the organization's needs.
2 Human resource planning, which is the process whereby the quantity and quality of the required human resources are assessed and planned in the light of their availability in the appropriate labour markets.
3 Job analysis, which provides essential information about jobs as a basis for the recruitment and selection processes.
4 Recruitment, which is the positive action following the staffing plan to find the human resources in the number and quality that the organization needs.
5 Selection, the final stage in the system, when the organization examines the suitability of applicants that the recruitment process has produced.

Chapter 6

Human resource planning

Human resource planning must have been applied in a general sense ever since people have collaborated in working groups to undertake tasks. The idea itself is, therefore, certainly not new. The modern version of HR planning as we know it developed from studies carried out shortly after the last war by the Tavistock Institute of Human Relationships in subjects connected with labour wastage and turnover, and from operational research, which was initially concerned with the application of scientific and mathematical principles to solving the operational problems of military and industrial organizations. Inevitably it was realized that the human resource component of these problems could not be ignored. Thus, in 1967 the Manpower Study Group emerged from the Operational Research Society to become the Manpower Society in 1970. At about the same time, in 1969, the Institute of Manpower Studies, now the Institute of Employment Studies, was formed as a research unit.

The importance of planning the material resources of an enterprise has never been in question, and much effort has been devoted to optimizing financial and capital resources. Paradoxically, the human resource, which is ultimately the most important and least predictable asset, has not attracted the same level of attention. Despite significant developments and recent changes of attitudes towards HR planning, it continues to arouse some scepticism, apparently because the sceptics feel either that a process that ought to be largely common sense has become unnecessarily complicated, or that the many variable factors in an uncertain future make the returns on the investment of effort of very doubtful worth. Such views, however, indicate a misunderstanding of the nature and purpose of human resource planning, which has become a specialized field in which statisticians, economists and others have a disciplinary interest. However, it is also very much the concern of every manager in an organization, and especially of the senior staff responsible for policy, commitment of resources and accountability for achievement.

All management is about decision-making in an environment of risk and uncertainty. Effective management aims to reduce the risk and uncertainty as far as this is possible in an imperfect world by the acquisition of the best available information and the use of a system.

Human resource planning is an expression of this philosophy in the most important area of all, the effective employment of people. The changes and pressures brought about by economic, technological and social factors compel organizations of all kinds to study the costs and human aspects of labour much more seriously and carefully than ever before. For the same reason, it is a subject to which central government will continue to attach great importance and in which it will, of necessity, play a major influential role.

The general purpose of human resource planning has been described, but there are specific purposes in crucial areas of management which HR planning serves:

1 *Balancing the cost between the utilization of plant and workforce*: this involves comparing costs of these two resources in different combinations and selecting the optimum. This is especially important when costing projects.
2 *Determining recruitment needs*: an essential prerequisite to the process of recruitment is to avoid problems of unexpected shortages, wastage, blockages in the promotion flow and needless redundancies.
3 *Determining training needs*: this is fundamentally important to planning training programmes, for which it is necessary to assess not only quantity but also quality in terms of the skills required by the organization.
4 *Management development*: a succession of trained and experienced managers is essential to the effectiveness of the organization, and this depends on accurate information about present and future requirements in all management posts.
5 *Industrial relations*: the business plan will, of necessity, make assumptions about productivity, and the human resource implications of merger, acquisition and divestment decisions will have an impact on the organization's industrial relations strategies.

In practice, HR planning is concerned with the demand and supply of labour and problems arising from the process of reconciling these factors. Any system has to be based on analyses of demand and supply and the plans and decisions which follow these analyses.

A system of human resource planning

The main elements of a system are:

1 Defining or redefining organizational objectives.
2 Determining and implementing the basic requirements for sound planning.
3 Assessing future requirements to meet objectives (demand).
4 Assessing current resources and availability of resources in the future (supply).
5 Producing and implementing the plan in detail, i.e. balancing forecasts for demand and supply, related to short-term and/or long-term timescales.
6 Monitoring the system and amending as indicated.

The first two of these stages are preparatory; the last three are directed towards the detailed production and implementation of the plan itself.

Definition or redefinition of organizational objectives

The effectiveness of the plan will depend on how soundly the organization has considered and planned its corporate strategy and integrated the objectives of its component departments. Once these fundamental details have been thoroughly examined and decided, the senior directing staff of the organization can consider the implications in terms of human resources. Because of the constantly changing environment in which all work organizations operate, whether they manufacture a product or provide a service, the corporate strategy and objectives will necessarily require continuous monitoring and revision from time to time. This will entail a corresponding, regular review of the system.

Figure 6.1 shows how strategic planning and human resource strategies can be devised. Strategic planning requires the planners to assess the national/international political, economic, social and technological trends (a PEST analysis), and to look at how their own organization is responding. The planners will also wish to assess the likely challenges and opportunities available – perhaps through using a SWOT analysis – looking at the strengths, weaknesses, opportunities and threats to the organization. Strengths and weaknesses are usually internal, whilst threats and opportunities are external. Discussions of human resources strategies are also often to the fore when a new 'mission statement', or a 'value statement' (describing the underlying values to be adopted with regard to customers, employees and suppliers), is created. We discuss the creation of HR strategies in more detail in Chapter 22.

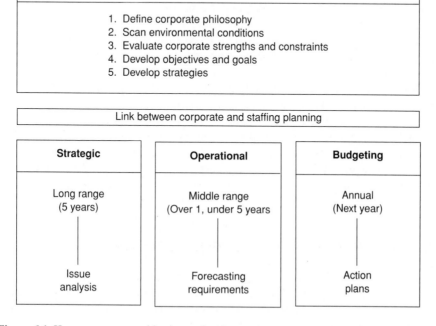

Figure 6.1 Human resource and business planning process

Determining and implementing basic requirements for human resource planning

Sound planning needs to be based on the following principles and actions:

1 It has to be fully integrated into the other areas of the organization's strategy and planning.
2 Senior management must give a lead in stressing its importance throughout the organization.
3 In larger organizations a central human resource planning unit responsible to senior management needs to be established. The main objectives of this unit are to co-ordinate and reconcile the demands for human resources from different departments, to standardize and supervise departmental assessments of requirements and to produce a comprehensive organizational plan. In practice, the personnel department would normally play a leading role in the task. In smaller organizations these responsibilities would probably be carried out by a senior member of staff, e.g. the HR manager or even the managing director.
4 The time span to be covered by the plan needs to be defined. Because of the abiding problem of making forecasts involving imponderable factors, a compromise is often adopted in which a general plan is produced to cover a period of several years, and a detailed plan produced for the first year. If the system is operated as a continuous, overlapping plan, the five-year period of general forecasting is maintained and each first year is used in turn for purposes of review and revision for the future. For example, 2000–5, 2001–6, 2002–7, 2003–8, 2004–9, 2005–10 is a series of five-year rolling plans covering a total of ten years.
5 The scope and details of the plan have to be determined. For large organizations separate plans and forecasts may well be needed for various subsidiary units and functions. In smaller organizations one comprehensive plan will probably suffice for all employees. Where particular skills or occupations may pose future problems in recruitment or training, special provisions will be required in the planning.
6 Human resource planning must be based on the most comprehensive and accurate information that is possible. Such personnel information is essential in any case for the effective management of the organization. Details of format and contents will naturally vary, but they will normally need to include details of age, sex, qualifications and experience and of trends likely to affect future forecasts, such as labour wastage, changes in jobs, salaries, etc. Apart from the routine collection of data for personnel records, special analyses may sometimes be necessary to provide particular information.

The assessment of future requirements (demand)

This task is concerned with estimating the quantity and quality of human resources needed to meet the objectives of the organization. Several methods of forecasting are in regular use, some of them simple and non-technical, others sophisticated and involving specialist statistical knowledge and skills. These include:

- estimates based on managers' experience, opinions and calculations
- statistical methods
- work-study methods
- forecasts based on measures of productivity.

In practice, these methods are often used in combination, especially in larger organizations. The essential features of each type are briefly summarized below:

1 *Estimates made by management*: this is the simplest method of assessment and is, therefore, the commonest method in use, especially in small organizations. Assessments of this kind are provided from two main sources: the estimates submitted by individual line managers and the corporate estimates produced by senior management, advised by the HR department. Since these forecasts rely entirely on personal judgements, they have an obvious potential weakness of subjectivity. However, this can be mitigated in the following ways: first, in submitting assessments, managers should include explanations and reasons to support their claims; second, these assessments 'from the bottom up', should be compared with those prepared by senior management, perhaps by an *ad hoc* staffing committee with the purpose of discussing and reconciling discrepancies.

2 *Statistical methods*: a number of statistical methods are now used for forecasting, which vary in their degree of sophistication. This is a task for specially qualified staff, and such methods are used, therefore, mainly by large organizations for which HR planning poses complex problems. Some of the techniques most often used are: simple extrapolation, which attempts to predict growth or decline of a variable or set of variables for a period of time; regression analysis, based on assumptions about the stability of certain relationships; and econometric models, in which past statistical data are studied on the assumption that relationships between a number of variables will continue in the future.

3 *Work-study methods*: work study is a systematic analysis of work in terms of people, skills, materials and machines, and in particular the work hours needed per output unit to achieve maximum productivity. Work-study data may be used for forecasts of productivity, for detailed production schedules for specific periods of time within the plan, and for estimating the total numbers needed to achieve production targets within a specific period. The production schedules may comprise the following details: product quantities; production methods; machinery needed and available; times for individual operations; and quantity and quality of labour needed and available. Work-study techniques are particularly appropriate for estimating human resource requirements for work that is directed towards end products. Where the product mix and the forecast changes are too complex to use this approach, a simple added value method can be adopted (Example 6.1).

Example 6.1

Using an added value approach where the added value (at constant prices) has to be increased from £10 million per annum to £12 million per annum, what is the effect on the demand for employees?

Clearly a number of assumptions are made, about existing working practices etc., but we can build in changes to our calculation:

Year 2000
Added value for the year = £10 000 000
Average no. of employees = 400 people
No. of weeks worked per annum = 47 weeks
Average hours per week = 35 hours
Total hours, per worker per week

$$35 \times 47 = 1645 \text{ work hours} \tag{6.1}$$

Total work hours per annum

$$400 \times 1645 = 658\,000 \text{ work hours} \tag{6.2}$$

Productivity

$$\frac{£10\,000\,000}{658\,000} = £15.197 \text{ per work hour} \tag{6.3}$$

Year 2004
Planned added value = £12 000 000
Productivity increase 5% = £15.957 per work hour
Required work hours

$$\frac{12\,000\,000}{15.957} = 752\,021.05 \text{ work hours} \tag{6.4}$$

No. of people required

$$\frac{752\,021.05}{1645} = 457 \text{ people} \tag{6.5}$$

However, if working hours are reduced further by one hour per week, and holidays increased by one week per year the work hour change is

$$34 \times 46 = 1564$$
$$\frac{752021.05}{1564} = 480 \text{ people} \tag{6.6}$$

Assessment of current resources and availability of resources in the future (supply)

Current resources

As a basis for estimating the future supply of people, a detailed and accurate account of the current situation is needed. Although accurate and comprehensive information is vitally important in planning, there is a danger of producing records in excessive detail, which may make it difficult to see the bigger picture, waste valuable resources and increase the possibility that information may not be kept up to date. In the end, each organization has to decide for itself the quantity and quality of information it needs, but some broad bases can be established for analysing existing resources, namely, operational functions, occupations, status and skill levels, and other specific categories (for example, qualifications, trainees, age distribution).

Examples of three different age profiles, for an organization or for an occupational group, are given in Figure 6.2. These profiles help to inform decisions about recruitment, development, succession planning, and the potential consequences for organization culture.

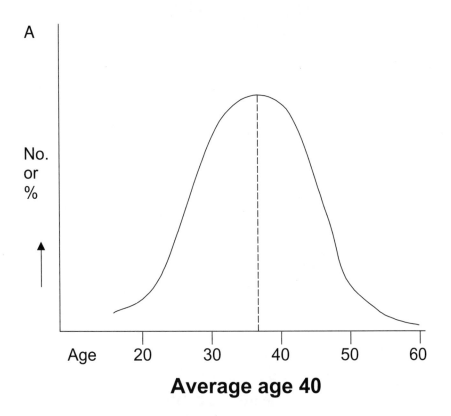

Figure 6.2 Age profiles

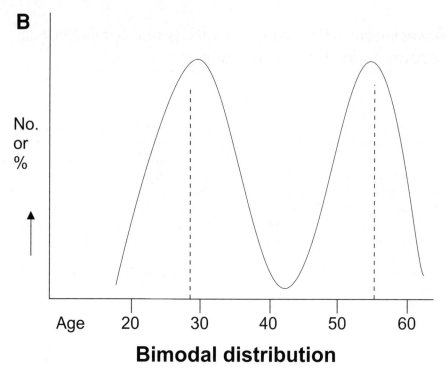

Bimodal distribution

Figure 6.2 Age profiles (*continued*)

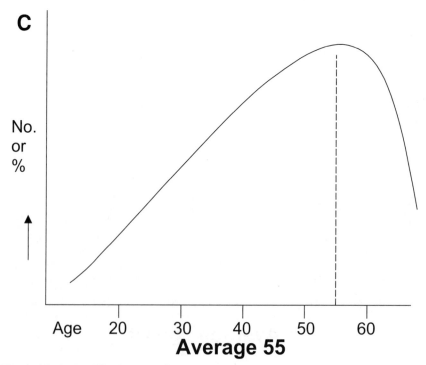

Average 55

Figure 6.2 Age profiles (*continued*)

Operational functions

An initial tally of all employees is made, based on divisions into functional units (for example, sales department, store's branch, repair workshop, etc.). Specific categories produced by subsequent analyses may be related to these units, if desired.

Occupations

Employees are categorized according to occupational groups. These categories may be particularly related to strategically significant occupations and anticipated recruitment problems in terms of detail required. Although broad homogeneous groupings will normally suffice, for certain key occupations detailed and specific categorizations may well be needed. In order to facilitate and standardize the task of occupational analysis and definition, the Office of Population and Censuses publishes the *Standard Occupation Classification* (*SOC*). The broad groupings conventionally used for occupational analysis are managers, supervisors, professional staff, technical staff, clerical staff, manual and other staff (skilled, semi-skilled and unskilled).

Status and skill levels

To a certain extent, the categorization of employees by occupation also implies a categorization by status and level of skills. Nevertheless, it may also be necessary to make a further distinction between, for example, senior, middle and junior managers, senior and junior clerical staff, administrative and technical supervisors, etc. This kind of analysis is especially relevant to the task of producing data for planning succession to senior levels.

Other specific categories

In addition to the basic kinds of analysis described above, it is normally necessary to produce other particular types of information, especially for critical groups and occupations, such as the qualifications of employees, records of employees under training and age group distribution.

Apart from for the purposes of human resources planning, an organization will need to have detailed records, usually computerized, of its employees, showing their qualifications, experience, particular skills and aptitudes, which are relevant to its functions and objectives. On this basis the organization can assess the strengths and weaknesses in its general pools of skills and experience and in particular areas, and will be in a better position than it might otherwise have been to plan for recruitment and selection, transfer or promotion, training, retirements, etc.

Training is systematically integrated with, and dependent upon, other important areas such as job analysis, recruitment and selection and performance appraisal. It is an extremely costly and time-consuming activity and must be taken into account when the supply of staff is being analysed. For the period to be covered by the plan, the analysis will project the flow of numbers of employees passing through all forms of training programmes, both internal and external.

The age distribution of employees in an organization has a strong influence on questions of promotion, retirement and, especially, wastage. It is most important that an organization should always be aware of the current and future age structure of its employees. It is essential information if employers are to take timely measures to anticipate and remedy the effects of any imbalance in experience, excessive losses of all kinds of employees or those in key occupations because of simultaneous retirements.

Labour turnover

As human resource planning is basically an exercise in projecting likely future situations based on past trends, it is important to obtain information about those which indicate any significant changes. These data are invaluable as a background against which the forecasts produced by other methods already described may be finally assessed. The changes which are likely to be significant and worth analysis are those that affect shifts in the relative numbers of employees in the various categories represented in the personnel record system. A well-known example in organizations with high-cost operational goals is the tendency for administrative and supporting staffs to grow disproportionately to the relatively small number of operational staff.

One of the commonest factors which complicates the task of human resource planning is unforeseen wastage. In making forecasts over a future period it is a fairly straightforward task to allow for employees whose retirement dates are known. However, there will always be unplanned losses of employees for a variety of reasons. The most significant source of loss is through voluntary wastage, that is, when employees leave of their own accord. In very large organizations it may also be necessary to include transfers or promotion of staff across divisions, departments or branches in these calculations.

Labour turnover (wastage) has traditionally been calculated by the following formula:

$$\frac{\text{Number leaving in a year}}{\text{Average number of employees}} \times 100 = x\% \qquad (6.7)$$

This index can be considerably distorted, however, by untypical features in the organization's employment pattern. For example, the significant element of wastage may be limited to a particular category, which may give a false impression of movement in an otherwise stable labour force. A commonly used guide to predict labour turnover in one part of the labour force is the Labour Stability Index which is deduced by the formula:

$$\frac{\text{Number of employees exceeding one year's service}}{\text{Number of employees employed one year ago}} \times 100 = x\% \qquad (6.8)$$

Even more sophisticated results can be obtained by the use of the actuarial/statistical techniques known as cohort and census analysis. In the same way that life expectancy for age groups can be actuarially assessed, a so-called survival curve can be graphically plotted to enable predictions to be made about the relationships between employees' length of service or age and rates of wastage.

Labour turnover is service and age specific. Hence we would expect a higher amount of wastage amongst new starters, than within a stable workforce.

Table 6.1 gives an example of a cohort analysis, drawn from the Civil Service, using the 'Markovian' wastage rate, which is calculated as follows:

Table 6.1 An example of cohort analysis

Length of service (completed years)	Survivors at start of period (I)	Leavers	Central wastage rate (M)	Markovian wastage rate (Q)	Mean strength
0	1000	113	0.120	0.113	943
1	887	161	0.200	0.182	806
2	726	144	0.220	0.198	654
3	582	55	0.100	0.095	554
4	527	31	0.060	0.059	511
5	496	24	0.050	0.048	484
6	472	18	0.040	0.038	462
7	454	13	0.030	0.029	446
8	441	13	0.030	0.029	433
9	428	13	0.030	0.030	420
10	415	12	0.030	0.029	408
11	403	12	0.030	0.030	396
12	391	391	(2.00)	1.00	195
13	0				0
Total		1000			6712

Expectation of service = 6712 ÷ 1000 = 6.7 years
Half life = 5 years (approx.)
Population surviving for 2 years: 73 per cent
Population surviving for 5 years: 50 per cent
Population surviving for 10 years: 42 per cent
Source: Smith et al. (1976: 58).

$$\frac{\text{Number of leavers during the year}}{\text{Number of staff present at start of year}} \times 100 = \begin{cases} \text{probability that staff will} \\ \text{not be present at year end} \end{cases} \quad (6.9)$$

Apart from wastage as a factor complicating human resource planning, any internal variations in working conditions, such as a reduction or increase in working hours or retirement age, will affect the situation.

Finally, there are external factors that also need to be taken into account when the availability of human resources is being considered. They may be categorized as macro- (national) or micro- (local) influences. At the macro level the commonly significant factors are:

1 The intervention by the state in the field of employment as a user and protector of the labour force in the form of employment legislation, regional development schemes, governmental and related agencies.
2 National trends affecting the working population such as, for example:
   (a) the higher percentage of older people
   (b) the percentage of people pursuing courses of higher education.
   (c) the variety of contractual arrangements available (part time, job sharing,

etc.) is a reflection of the needs for part time and flexible working arrangements.

3 International recruitment possibilities (e.g., the recruitment of nurses for hospitals in the UK from the Philippines and from mainland European countries).

The important factors at micro level are:

1 The nature of the local population in terms of numbers, growth or decrease, reserves of skills, availability of part-time labour, etc.
2 The level of unemployment.
3 The competition from other employers.
4 Costs of labour, local premia, and the ease of travel to the locations.
5 The degree of development of the area, accessibility and transport facilities.
6 Plans of central and local government and other organizations that may significantly affect the area.

The possible influences of these factors can never be easily assessed. Those responsible for planning should be aware of possible effects and should take them into account when making human resource plans.

The planning stage

The last stage, in which the plan is produced, is based on the information that the preceding stages have provided. This involves:

- matching the forecasts for supply and demand
- identifying key areas essential to the achievement of objectives
- making plans to minimize the effects of possible shortages or excesses of staffing
- considering whether the best use is currently being made of the organization's human resources.

Scenario planning is a technique that helps senior management to understand the various alternative scenarios by looking at the consequences of following different policy options.

There are now a number of computer-based approaches with software available to represent the options graphically, such as those developed by the Institute for Employment Studies, which examine staffing systems – building in the variables that influence the numbers employed in any given hierarchy of positions and showing how variations, for example in labour turnover or in recruitment rates, influence the numbers employed in the different grades. The rates of change are sometimes called 'flows' and the numbers employed in the grades or jobs 'stocks'.

The simplified example of a bank's system shown in Figure 6.3 illustrates this. (In practice, there may be many different levels, not just three, and also crossovers to other systems. The computer models can handle much greater complexity than is shown here.)

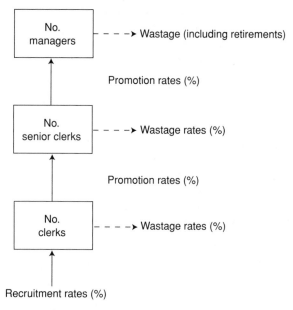

Figure 6.3 Manpower systems

The flows (or rates) can be varied to show the effect on stock sizes or the stock sizes may be held constant to show the effect on the flows (rates) over the planning period. By varying such factors as these, and by introducing proposed policy changes within the planning exercise, such as age at retirement, the likely consequences in terms of the main policy options can be discovered before the organization is committed to any change.

Until the preliminary analyses have been made and the final plans formulated, no meaningful plans can subsequently be made for recruitment and training of staff. Finally, it is worth emphasizing once again that planning cannot guarantee any particular levels of success in ensuring that the right number of employees of the necessary quality will be provided to meet an organization's requirements. The most important benefits from HR planning are that any staffing restrictions on future operations can be avoided, and the strength of the organization's capabilities can be taken into account in the strategy (Figure 6.4). There should be a regular review at various periods throughout the life span of the plan. This review could be incorporated into an annual general review of corporate objectives, achievement, budget planning, etc., in accordance with the system for a running, overlapping plan, as already discussed.

Questions

1 Refer back to the age profiles in Figure 6.2. Assume these are the profiles for whole management groups. What are the likely consequences of each of these profiles (a, b, c) for HR policies and for succession planning, and what kind of labour turnover would you anticipate for each profile?

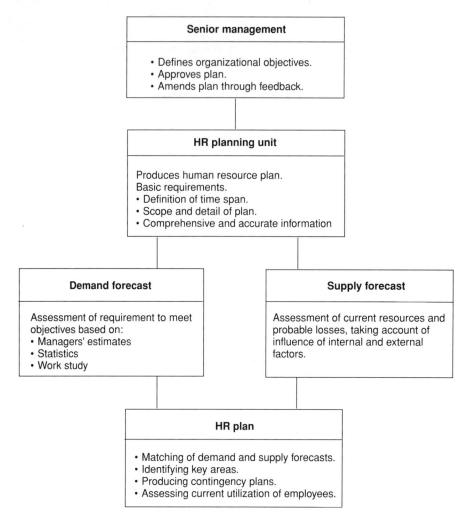

Figure 6.4 Summary of the main elements of a system of human resource planning

2 The wastage (turnover) rate for a group of your sales representatives is high (25 per cent) whilst the stability index is low (5 per cent). What conclusions do you draw about this group of sales representatives – do you have a major problem or not?
3 Name the methods of forecasting demand commonly used, and comment on the advantages and disadvantages of each one described.
4 What are the main stages in producing the HR plan, comment upon how these plans are integrated with the overall business strategy?

Reference

Smith, A. R. et al. (1976). *Manpower Planning in the Civil Service*. HMSO.

Chapter 7

Job analysis: defining effective performance

Defining what employees have to do in order to perform their work effectively, and hence to make a collective contribution to the achievement of organizational aims and objectives, is a foundation for the whole system for managing human resources. The definition of the requirements for effective performance of work provides the criteria or standards, which are an essential basis for finding answers to the main questions for this function, for example:

- What are the competences needed now and in the future?
- How should the requirements for effective performance be expressed in job advertisements?
- Which applicants appear to meet these requirements?
- Which applicants, chosen for assessment in the selection procedures, indicate the potential to meet these requirements?
- What help do newly appointed employees need in the induction stage to meet these requirements?
- What does the evidence of performance appraisal indicate about effectiveness or ineffectiveness of work performance?
- If any help is indicated by performance appraisal (e.g. career development, training, etc.), what form should it take to meet identified needs?
- How should jobs be evaluated for purposes of pay?
- How do the requirements for the effective performance of work affect the working environment and provisions for health and safety?

The competency approach

The term 'competences' has come to be used to describe the attributes necessary for effective performance. Competencies can be purely role related, or be a mix of personal and job attributes. Competences can be highly specific – as we suggest here for use in a person specification, or they can be generic, that is, general for certain types of work (for example, managerial work at different levels) for an organization. Many companies use competences as the touchstone for the whole human resources system so that recruitment, appraisal and training and development are all based on a common standard of effective performance.

In a recent series of fifty-one HRM audits, Tyson and Doherty (1999) found that 95 per cent of organizations used competency systems for their managerial staff, around 80 per cent for clerical level staff and 75 per cent for manual staff. These schemes were in all cases used for development and training, in around 88 per cent of cases for performance appraisal, 80 per cent for recruitment and in 58 per cent of cases for rewards. Managerial competencies usually consist of lists of competencies (sometimes devised from research within the organization, sometimes from a focus group or from the executive) with accompanying definitions. The following list, drawn from a large retail bank, illustrates managerial competencies:

- achievement motivation
- complex thinking
- customer-service orientation
- developmental ability
- delegation
- technical expertise
- flexibility
- initiative
- interpersonal sensitivity
- organizational awareness
- relationship-building
- self-confidence
- self-control
- team leadership.

Competencies can be defined at different levels. Taking the competency 'delegation' from the above list, there were four levels defined (1 low to 4 high), as in the following example.

Example 7.1: Delegation

Definition: Allocates tasks to others, making full use of resources and skills available. Knows to whom can delegate and how best to delegate, to ensure delivery to expectation. Makes objectives and expectations clear to others.
Levels:

1 Delegates discrete tasks with clear rules on how they should be completed. Gives clear instructions, telling the individual exactly what to do. Sets a specific deadline and reviews process at regular intervals when the task has to be completed over time.
2 Delegates discrete tasks with some discretion over how they are completed. Sets achievable short-term objectives for others, clarifying the standards required and

setting the time parameters for the work. Makes occasional checks on progress and formally reviews at key milestones.

3 Delegates complex tasks that need further delegation. Defines the problem for others, and explains the context and surrounding issues. Sets the priorities to attend and be attended to and then leaves the individual to complete the task as appropriate.

4 Delegates complex and problematic issues to be resolved by others first having agreed the issues to be tackled through discussion and consultancy. Delegates some accountability, keeping an overview through management information.

Competencies can be used to produce different role profiles. For example, a large pharmaceutical company produced a job profile and a spidergram (Figure 7.1) for sales management roles, showing where the individual's competencies matched those required and where they were deficient.

There are software systems that produce the competency clusters and plot a spidergram for each individual, based on appraisal and other data stored about each person's competencies.

If any job, no matter how simple or complex, is analysed, it will become apparent that the requirements for effective performance can be described in four interdependent, overlapping categories – knowledge, skills, attitudes and personal attributes. Whilst skill and knowledge are necessary, they are not sufficient for success. High performance that is sustainable requires appropriate attitudes, traits and motives. For example, the effectively performing lawyer could be said to need knowledge of the law and court procedures and customs, skills in relating to a variety of people, particular skills in advocacy; together with attitudes and personal attributes such as honesty, integrity, conscientiousness, care, patience, calm temperament, etc. Competence in performance

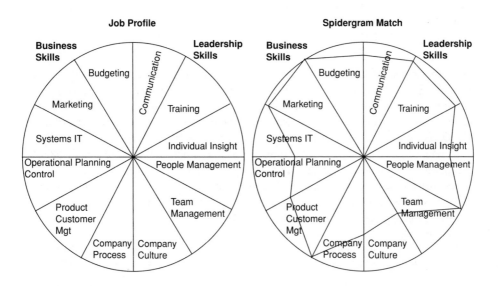

Figure 7.1 Job profile showing competencies for a sales manager in pharmaceuticals

sometimes tends to be considered mainly in terms of professional aspects, that is, knowledge and skills. But the personal qualities that an employee brings to a job may make all the difference between success and failure as we discussed in regard to emotional intelligence. Of what use to an employer, for example, is the employee who is professionally the most proficient member of the work group, but at the same time has a disruptive influence because of an uncooperative attitude and surly demeanour, and is a constant source of friction with colleagues and clients? In researching within the organization to establish the competencies, and the definition, the best practice is to examine low, average and high performers' behaviour, to show precisely what succeeds in the organizational context. For example, team leadership could be taken from the bank's list above, as follows in Example 7.2.

Example 7.2: Team leadership

Definition: The desire and ability to take on responsibility and role of leader. Values team-working as a means of achieving objectives; the ability to develop team effectiveness by encouraging team members' participation, creating an environment of integrity and professionalism; communicating and being supportive; setting an open climate and engendering pride.

Average performer	*Star performer*
Clearly communicates goals	Identifies sources of conflict and facilitates resolution
Gives clear accountabilities and empowers them	Sets an example by actions as well as words
Invites all team members to contribute ideas	Congratulates and publicly takes pride in team achievements
Gives specific feedback	
Gives praise to individuals and team as a whole	Creates open climate which encourages change

---

The criteria for effective performance are established by the process known as job analysis. Sometimes the same definition is known by different names. Semantic distinctions are unimportant, however. In practice, two specifications are required: one to describe the job, its component tasks and competencies; the other to describe the requirements for effective performance in the kind of personal terms mentioned above (this may well be a combination of competencies/personal attributes). We shall call one the job description and the other the person specification.

For managerial-level work, the role requirements are likely to be mostly personal. For lower-level jobs the tasks are more likely to be significant (as in the National Vocational Qualification approach), which means a more person-centred approach for senior roles, and a more task-centred one for others.

The lists below are intended to give a general guide to indicate the kind of information that job analysis needs to provide as a basis for the various functions of HR management.

Job description

1 *Basic data* Exact title and grade (if applicable). Numbers engaged in the job. Location(s).
2 *Purpose* Objectives and relationship to the aim of the organization.
3 *Tasks* Main tasks and key areas. Occasional tasks. Secondary duties. Hours of work.
4 *Competencies* These combine standards for effective performance of tasks, the criteria indicating that tasks have been effectively performed with levels of knowledge, skills to perform the tasks.
5 *Responsibilities* Position of job in organization structure. Managers/supervisors to whom job holder is accountable. Subordinate staff for whom job holder is responsible. Responsibilities for:
  (a) finance.
  (b) materials, equipment, etc.
  (c) information.
6 *Physical and social environment* Particular features of work environment (e.g., sedentary, static, indoor-outdoor, mobile, dirty, hazardous, etc.). Contacts with others (e.g. small/large groups, isolated, external contacts, etc.).
7 *Training/education* Training planned to bring new job holders to required levels of performance (e.g. induction programme, job rotation, visits, external courses, etc.). In-job training and educational courses normally associated with the job.
8 *Advancement opportunities* Opportunities open to job holders for promotion and career development.
9 *Conditions of employment* Salary and other emoluments and benefits. Possible overtime requirements. Sickness and pension schemes. Welfare, social and other facilities. Leave entitlement. Special employment conditions applying to the job.
10 *Trade union/associations* Appropriate unions/staff associations.
11 *Job circumstances* Aspects of the job commonly accepted as pleasant or unpleasant, easy/demanding.

Person specification

1 Competencies required, including knowledge, skills, attitudes and personal attributes.
2 Specific qualifications (if any are needed).
3 Previous experience (if any is needed).
4 Age range (if this is significant).
5 Health (general and specific requirements).
6 Special conditions (e.g. travel, unsocial hours, etc.).

The person specification may sometimes include 'appearance', although we must be cautious about the discriminatory overtones from such a subjective heading. There are, however, some occupations where the perceptions of customers and clients about employees' appearance, however biased and old-fashioned, still need to be considered because of possible adverse effects on business and relationships. Any requirements included under the heading 'health' may vary considerably from one organization to another. In some occupations, such as the armed forces and the police, the standards of health required are necessarily stringent and high.

The job description and the person specification are both necessary and comple-mentary definitions. Of the two, however, the person specification is especially impor-tant, since it provides the criteria for assessing effective performance affecting, as we have already seen, the main functions involved in the management of people at work, and in particular is the basis for job advertisements and candidate details. The job description has a wider applicability and can be used, in various formats, for appraisal and objective-setting, development reviews, etc.

Because all jobs in various ways require knowledge, skills, appropriate attitudes and personal attributes, it is sound practice to use these headings as the initial basis for analysing the job in terms of the person specification. The information that this analy-sis reveals can then be adapted to suit preferred formats. Starting the analysis on this basis is systematic and logical and has the following advantages:

1 Attention is focused immediately on the essential requirements for effective per-formance.
2 This approach provides the criteria for defining and assessing standards of potential and actual performance. For example, a candidate for employment may reveal during the selection procedures an insufficient level of knowledge defined as necessary for effective performance, but may be accepted nevertheless, because the deficiency could be remedied by training. An employee whose performance is being appraised may reveal attitudes that hinder effective performance and require counselling as a possible remedy.
3 It helps to review whether the formal qualifications and experience often associated with a particular role are, in fact, required. In some jobs specific qualifications are obviously essential, e.g. medicine, law, accountancy, etc. In others they may not be essential
4 Now that managers are asked to guard increasingly against unfair and discriminatory practice, it is especially important to produce person specifications that truly and fairly state what the job requires.

An illustration of how job analysis based on these lines has been applied to an actual job is provided in Figure 7.2. The job description and person specification refer to a training administrator, employed at a training centre which provides courses and consultancy work, in the UK and overseas, in management and related subjects. This job is demand-ing not only on account of the responsibilities implied in the job description, but espe-cially because of the crucial importance of human relationships. Effective performance of the job depends greatly on the job holder's ability to communicate successfully with a very diverse range of people – the various levels of staff at the centre, external spon-sors and agencies, external tutors, speakers and consultants, course members from the UK, Europe and other countries, covering a very wide variety of cultures and customs.

Before we leave the subject of the contents of the job description and person speci-fication, it is worth mentioning two particular frameworks that have been influential for many years in shaping the formats of job descriptions and person specifications. They are the seven-point plan (Rodger, 1973) and the fivefold grading system (Munro Fraser, 1966), as described below.

JOB DESCRIPTION
Training Administrator
Training International

Location: 9–10 Sheffield St, London WC2A

Purpose of job: To provide all supporting services necessary for effectively
                 organized courses.

Responsible to: Course Director.

Responsible for: Clerical staff allocated to courses.

Tasks

Before courses
- Corresponding (letter, telephone, e-mail, fax, etc.) with:
  1. Sponsoring agencies, overseas nominating authorities, course applicants.
  2. External course tutors.
  3. Centres to be visited.
- Preparing of nominal rolls.
- Arranging for any visits during courses (travel, accommodation, special
  diets, etc.).
- Arranging for training accommodation (class and syndicate rooms), training
  aids and materials (e.g. books, hand-out articles, etc.).
- Preparing of course statement of accounts (income and expenditure).

During courses
- Working in close collaboration with Programme Consultant and Course
  Director to meet their requirements.
- Confirming and checking arrangements made above.
- Meeting, liaising and collaborating with external contributors.
- Attending to various needs and welfare of course members (liaising with
  British Council, sponsors, embassies, etc.).
- Maintaining course statement of accounts and keeping Programme
  Consultant informed.

After courses
- Collating final report on course provided by Course Director and course
  members' individual assessment reports.
- Finalizing statement of course accounts for Programme Consultant.
- Ensuring that accounts of expenditure on the programme, and income are
  recorded, invoices are authorized.

Figure 7.2 A training administrator's job description and person specification

Standards
See person specification and schedule for performance appraisal.

Working environment
The training centre is located in a completely modernized eighteenth-century listed building characteristic of the area. Offices and classrooms are very large, well lit and equipped with modern equipment.

Training and development
Induction training; on-job training as required; external training as appropriate; development by job rotation.

Advancement opportunities
Opportunities may occur for suitably qualified and experienced staff to be promoted to senior administrative posts or occasionally, to be appointed as Programme Consultant or Course Director.

Conditions of employment
- Salary £20,000–£25,000, subject to annual review.
- Contributory pension scheme available.
- Interest-free travel loan available.
- Subsidized restaurant available.
- Leave: 25 days per annum plus public holidays.
- Working day: Monday to Friday, normally 0900–1700. Unsocial hours occasionally required.

Person specification
General requirements

Knowledge
- Work and organization of the training centre and associated agencies.
- Contacts in regular collaboration with external tutors, centre, etc.
- Purpose and contents of courses and consultancy projects.
- Computing packages, office procedures and equipment.
- Training methods, resources and materials.

Skills
- Office administration, organization and procedures.
- Use of office equipment (word processors, copiers, etc.).
- Interpersonal communicational.

Figure 7.2 A training administrator's job description and person specification (*continued*)

Attitudes and attributes
- Sympathetic to nature of the work of the organization.
- Conscientious.
- Able to stand pressure.
- Equable and calm in temperament.
- Patient and tolerant.
- Cheerful, co-operative, willing.
- Able to relate effectively with very wide variety of people.
- Able to use initiative.

Specific requirements

Age range	Probably about 22 to 50 years (flexible).
Appearance	Smart and tidy.
Health	No history of recurring illness likely to affect performance.
Qualifications	(1) Education to GCE A level or equivalent.
	(2) Recognized certificate/diploma in Business Studies, Office Administration, etc. (not essential but desirable).
Experience	Previous employment relevant to this job, e.g. office administration, training support (flexible).
Special conditions	Occasionally required to work away from home (e.g. during residential courses away from the training centre or for overseas projects).

Figure 7.2 A training administrator's job description and person specification (*continued*)

The seven-point plan

1 *Physical health*: physique, age, appearance, bearing, speech.
2 *Attainments*: academic attainments, training received, experience and skills and knowledge already acquired.
3 *Intelligence*: general intelligence, specific abilities and means for assessing these.
4 *Special aptitudes*: special aptitudes (e.g. manual, mechanical, verbal, numerical, artistic, etc.).
5 *Interests*: personal interests as possible indicators of aptitudes, abilities or personal traits (e.g. intellectual, practical/constructional, physically active, social, artistic).
6 *Disposition*: personality characteristics needed (e.g. equability, dependability, self-reliance, assertiveness, drive, energy, perseverance, initiative, motivation).
7 *Circumstances*: personal and domestic circumstances (e.g. mobility, commitments, family circumstances and occupations).

As we discussed in Part One of this book, there is an increased awareness of emotional intelligence as a quality which is as important as IQ or general intelligence mentioned in these early person specification frameworks. The significance of customer relationships in all jobs has put a premium on qualities needed to sustain such relationships.

The fivefold grading system

1 *Impact on others*: general demeanour, appearance, speech.
2 *Qualifications*: education, training, work experience.
3 *Innate abilities*: mental alertness, aptitude for learning.
4 *Motivation*: consistency, persistency, success in achieving goals.
5 *Adjustment*: stability, reaction to stress, relationships with others.

Job analysis in practice

Job analysis may be carried out in two ways. It may be a task for managers and job holders to discuss and agree among themselves, or it may be carried out by HR staff of the employing organization or by external consultants. Whether it is carried out by managers and job holders or others will depend on the nature of the organization, the jobs in question and the preferences of individual organizations.

Cost-effectiveness is a major consideration. For a large organization, in which there are groups of identical jobs, it may be worth while to employ the personnel staff or external consultants to carry out a comprehensive analysis. For other organizations, which are small or where a number of jobs are unique, it would probably be impracticable to incur the time and expense of a comprehensive, in-depth analysis. There is another important consideration: jobs are changing all the time, affected by technological and by economic and social factors. Therefore, they need constant revision and amendment.

Job analysis carried out through discussions between managers and job holders, can be an important part of the appraisal review. Before considering the performance of the person and what future action may be needed, it is obviously necessary to enquire whether the tasks of the job and criteria for effective performance are the same before drawing any conclusions about performance. When the task is carried out by HR staff or outside consultants, the following methods are often used:

1 *Direct observation*: here the analyst observes actual work in progress and makes notes as necessary under the various headings of the job description. These notes can be used as a basis for subsequent questions that the analyst may wish to ask. The advantages of seeing a job performed for oneself are obvious, but the method has the following limitations:
   (a) It is very time-consuming. A great deal of time would be needed adequately to observe a number of jobs. All jobs need to be observed with very close concentration over a period of time in order to appreciate the fluctuations between, for example, the quieter and busier periods. A brief observation can very easily produce a distorted view.
   (b) There is no subsitute for personal experience of the job and the evidence of observations can be very misleading. Special skills expertly applied may make jobs seem easier. Skilled workers could make jobs seem more difficult if they

chose to do so.

(c) Behaviour that is formally observed is inevitably influenced by the act of observation, unless this is done without the knowledge of those being observed. All the research data confirm this phenomenon (often described as the 'Hawthorne effect' from the studies carried out at the Hawthorne plant described earlier).

(d) There is a great difference between observation of manual and managerial jobs. It is unlikely that an observer can obtain any kind of accurate picture or evaluation of the mental energy expended, personal pressures, contemplative and planning activities or the subtleties of interpersonal relationships, which form a large part of the managers' and supervisors' work.

2 *Interviews*: these should be carried out with the job holders themselves, their immediate managers and any others who can give useful information. The interview is a necessary and potentially useful method in job analysis, enabling the job analyst to raise questions to elucidate the evidence of observation and to compare the perception of one job holder with others. The caveats that need to be made about the use of the interview in job analysis are these:

(a) As in all other interview situations considerable skill is needed. The interview has to be systematic and purposeful, and conducted with particular sympathy, tact and sensitivity.

(b) Job analyst has always to deal with personal biases and perceptions of jobs.

(c) The interviewer needs to be careful to distinguish fact from opinion.

3 *Diaries*: using this method, the job analyst provides job holders with the areas of the job description about which information is required. Job holders then analyse their own work over a period of time, recording information systematically in diary form under the required headings and the time spent on each item. The advantages and disadvantages of the diary method are these:

(a) Self-recorded data of this kind can be made over a longer period and thus provide a more reliable picture of the nature of the job.

(b) The data can be used as valuable bases on which to conduct interviews.

(c) The data are an obvious means of saving some of the time that prolonged direct observation of jobs requires.

(d) Like the other methods, diaries are inevitably affected by factors of subjectivity. Moreover, because the information is self-recorded there is no means of verifying accuracy.

(e) To be of real value the diary has to be kept accurately, conscientiously and regularly, if it is to be of any real value. The task can soon become a chore, especially if job holders are not in sympathy with the job in which case it might be perfunctorily fulfilled or neglected.

4 *Questionnaires*: here the job analyst compiles a series of questions designed to elicit the maximum possible useful information about the jobs under analysis, and distributes these with careful instructions about the completion of the form. The advantages and disadvantages of questionnaires are:

(a) They enable the job analyst to put standard questions to all the job holders taking part in the survey.

(b) Specialized skill is needed in devising the questionnaire and framing the questions. For example, attractive as the prospect of open questions may seem to be, it is probably better to require the respondent to choose from a range of answers that best fit particular situations. Skill is also required in the analysis of reponses.

5 *Critical incident review*: as the term implies, this method uses examples of real events at work as a means of eliciting what the criteria for effective performance should be. The component tasks of a job are systematically analysed with job holders, who are asked to cite actual examples of incidents from their experience of the job and how they dealt with them.

It is unlikely that any one of these methods will be adequate by itself. In practice, therefore, a combination of techniques is usually employed and adapted to meet the needs of particular situations.

A summary of the main elements of job analysis is shown in Figure 7.3.

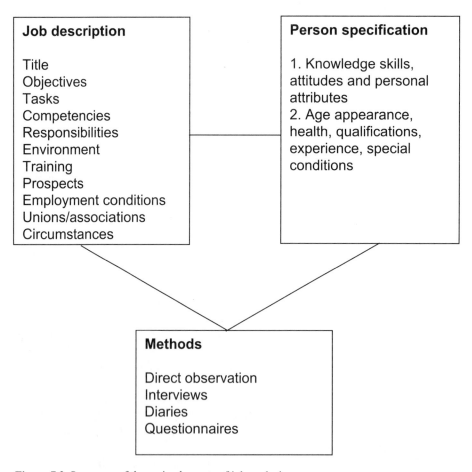

Figure 7.3 Summary of the main elements of job analysis

Questions

1 Why is the definition of effective performance fundamentally important to the whole system of HR management?
2 How would you define competencies? Are there fundamental attributes that are important for high performance?
3 What are the seven-point plan and fivefold grading system? What headings do they include?
4 Name and describe the methods commonly used in job analysis.

References

Munro Fraser, J. (1966). *Employment Interviewing*. Macdonald and Evans.
Rodger, A. (1973). *The Seven-Point Plan*. Paper No. 5. National Institute of Industrial Psychology.
Tyson, S. and Doherty, N. (1999). *Human Resource Excellence Report*. Cranfield/ Financial Times.

Chapter 8

Recruitment

Recruitment is the phase that immediately precedes selection. Its purpose is to pave the way for the selection procedures by producing, ideally, the smallest number of candidates who appear to be capable either of performing the required tasks of the job from the outset, or of developing the ability to do so within a period of time acceptable to the employing organization.

The smallest number of potentially suitable candidates can in theory, of course, be any number. The main point that needs to be made about the recruitment task is that the employing organization should not waste time and money examining the credentials of people whose qualifications do not match the requirements of the job. A primary task of the recruitment phase is to help would-be applicants to decide whether they are likely to be suitable to fill the job vacancy. This is clearly in the interests of both the employing organization and the applicants. But no matter how efficient an organization may be in the preparation of advertisements or in the general administration of its recruitment procedures, it still has no control over applicants' perceptions of their own suitability to fill jobs. Thus, Manchester United Football Club can do nothing to prevent any number of cranks or eccentrics who see themselves as a potential team manager from applying for the post when it falls vacant and wasting some of the employing organization's time. But apart from such extreme or bizarre examples, all advertised vacancies may regularly attract some applicants whose potential suitability is much more apparent to themselves than it is to the employing organization. In practice, then, the objective of a recruitment procedure is to attract genuinely suitable candidates and carefully examine their credentials in order to produce a short list for further investigation in the selection procedures. Apart from the methods used and the general administration of the task, the achievement of the objective will depend very much on how efficiently human resource planning and job analysis have been carried out and applied.

In short, efficient recruitment of staff may be described as knowing what resources you want, what resources are available, and where and how they may be found. For purposes of studying the main details and requirements of an efficient and systematic recruitment process, the task may conveniently be examined under the following headings:

1 Determining the vacancies.
2 Sourcing strategy.

3 Preparing and publishing information.
4 Processing and assessing applications.
5 Notifying applicants.

A flow chart showing the sequence of the recruitment process is shown in Figure 8.1.

Determining the vacancies

The first stage in the procedure is concerned with the question of what resources are needed, that is, the demand. Details of requirements will emerge from the compilation and regular revision of the human resource plan. In practice, job vacancies may occur when an organization or work unit is set up *ab initio*, when any reorganization takes place through changes of policy, technology, location, mergers, acquisitions, demergers or, most commonly, when employees leave the organization and need to be replaced. Because of the subtle changes that are continuously taking place in work organizations, the existence and nature of job vacancies should not be accepted without question. Sound human resource planning and job analysis, regularly and systematically reviewed, should ensure that this does not happen.

Considering the sources

This stage is concerned with general questions about the supply and availability of resources and the particular avenues through which these are likely to be obtained. The human resource plan is designed to provide general information about the types of factor that influence the supply of labour at macro and micro levels. Here the situation is similar to that which the manufacturer has to face in ascertaining in advance what the limits of the available market are, what competition and other constraints obtain and what, therefore, the share of the market is likely to be. In considering possible sources of recruiting employees, it is easy to assume that these are inevitably external. Even when it is possible and feasible to fill job vacancies from within the organization, the transfers and promotions which this usually involves will more often than not produce a vacancy at the end of a chain reaction, necessitating external recruitment. Nevertheless, the possibility of filling vacancies internally should always be given very careful consideration for the following reasons:

1 Existing employees are known to the organization and are generally familiar with its customs and practices.
2 The costs and the time that external recruitment, selection and induction procedures consume can be significantly reduced.
3 Internal recruitment to fill vacancies may be used as a means of career development, widening opportunities and stimulating motivation among existing employees.

When the organization has to use external sources, there are two main means of conducting the search for employees:

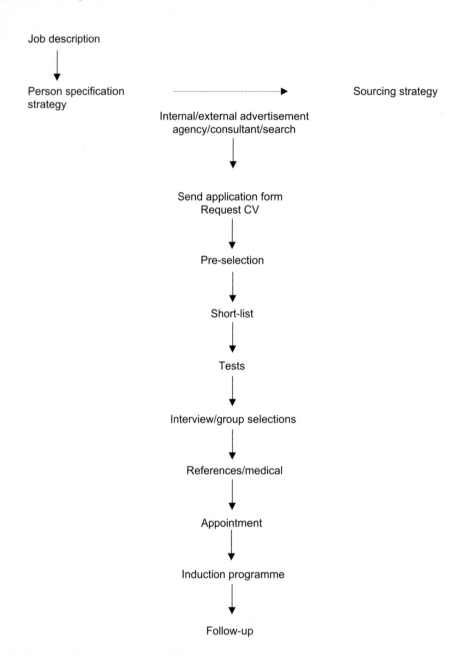

Figure 8.1 Flow chart of recruitment process

1 Through employment consultancies and agencies. These include specialist agencies and 'head-hunters' as well as governmental and institutional, and private commercial agencies of varying kinds.
2 By contacting the public directly through advertisements in newspapers journals, posters, on radio, on television and on the Internet.

A combination of these media may be used. The three main avenues available are described and evaluated below.

Institutional agencies

Several different kinds of agencies are included under this heading. The features they have in common are that they are all agencies set up by particular organizations to help their own members or ex-members find employment and that they are generally non-profit-making. The agencies of this kind that employers are likely to need and use most regularly are:

1 *Career services of academic institutions*: universities and similar institutions maintain a full-time careers advisory service. They serve as an employment agency for graduating or recently graduated students and are centres of information for graduates about employment opportunities and for employers who are seeking potential managers or professional specialists.
2 *Employment services of professional institutions and trade unions*: a number of professional institutions, such as those representing lawyers, doctors, accountants, engineers, linguists, etc. and a number of trade unions, have an employment advisory service whereby a register is kept of members seeking employment and information is collected from employers seeking staff in particular professions and trades.
3 *Resettlement services of the armed forces*: all three services have full-time officer and non-commissioned officer staffs with a specialized knowledge of employment opportunities liaising with government agencies, professional institutions, trade unions or directly with organizations to arrange employment for men and women who are returning to civilian occupations after periods of service of varying length.
4 *Job centres and careers advice provided by the state*: the latter service, for young people aged under 18 and especially for school leavers, provides a regular liaison between employers and schools.

Private employment agencies

These agencies have the largest share of the market and are now quite well known to most people from personal experience of local offices and advertisements in the press. Local employment agencies deal mainly with clerical, typing, junior administrative, shop staff, etc. The other type of agency concentrates on recruitment and, sometimes, the initial stages of selection of middle and senior managers or of professional and specialist staff in fields such as medicine, law, accountancy, engineering, etc. Private agencies provide at times a very valuable service, especially in recruiting staff in situations where there is a shortage of the particular types of employees required. However, since they exist to make a profit, employers have to pay for any employees they may recruit in this way.

There are also pros and cons that have to be carefully weighed, especially when these agencies are used to assist in the selection of managerial or professional staff. The advantages are the specialist knowledge that an agency can acquire of the employment conditions and requirements in particular fields, objectivity of view, and skill in conducting the selection procedure. The main possible disadvantage in using external assistance for recruitment and selection purposes is the agent's lack of first-hand experience of the cultural and environmental aspects of the organization's work and life.

There has been a growth of so-called 'head-hunters' or recruitment consultants. As the term suggests, these are private firms and agencies of recruitment consultants who earn fees by meeting the needs of organizations for specialist and senior managerial staff. Much of their work is carried on by means of an informal network of contacts, whereby they keep records of career profiles of people likely to be in constant demand, and obtain information about the needs of employers for appointments to be filled. This method has proved its value to the employer and employee clientele of these agencies.

Advertisements in the press or other media

This is the most common method by which employers carry out their search for suitable staff. Apart from the use of the national and local press and, to a limited extent, television and radio, professional and trade journals are an important source of recruitment by this means. When specialist staff are needed this is a very convenient and appropriate method for attracting the attention of those most likely to be suitable. The same basic information about the job has to be produced for publication whether the organization uses an agency or places its own advertisements.

The Internet

There has been a growth in the use of the Internet to attract applicants. Surveys by the Institute of Personnel and Development (IPD) showed 14 per cent of organizations used the Internet in 1997, 19 per cent in 1998 and 32 per cent in 1999. Benefits from this method are the speed by which applicants can obtain information about the organization, and application documents may be downloaded from the Internet. Responses by e-mail to the organization can, of course, be made whatever the advertising method. Whilst the Internet was initially suitable for professional and technical vacancies, one suspects that the spread of personal computing to all potential applicant groups will see this tool develop further.

The task of recruitment is likely to benefit greatly from regular personal contacts with recruitment agencies and sections of the population in which employees are most likely to be found. There are a number of ways in which contacts may be developed, for example, by:

- regular meetings between the recruitment representatives of the work organization and the employment agencies
- regular visits by representatives of the employment agencies or potential applicants to the work organization to acquire first-hand knowledge about the nature of jobs, facilities and working environment
- conventions designed to bring employers, agencies and potential employees together to explain, discuss and ascertain employment opportunities.

Meetings of this kind are especially useful for people entering full-time employment for the first time either from school or from university and similar institutions. There is a growing awareness by employers of the value of the employer 'brand'. Employers are engaged in marketing themselves to future recruits as much as to future customers. Brand image, and brand values – the organization's values – are important, and there is a benefit to ensuring consistency between product and organizational brand values.

Preparing and publishing information

This aspect of the recruitment process requires very special attention and skill. Its objective is to publish information that fulfils the following conditions:

1 It is succinct and yet gives a comprehensive and accurate description of the job and its requirements.
2 It is likely to attract the attention of the maximum number of potentially suitable candidates (i.e., is published through the right media).
3 It gives a favourable image of the organization in terms of efficiency and its attitudes towards people – including the values of the organization, its products or services.
4 It does not contravene employment laws concerning sex and racial discrimination (see Chapter 22).

The preparation and publication of this information is based on two simple questions that any applicant would normally ask:

1 What are the details of the job in terms of duties, opportunities, rewards, conditions and special circumstances?
2 How should applications be presented?

The preparation of the information needed to answer the first question is based on the data produced by the job analysis. There is not much point in waxing eloquently, as some job advertisements do, about the personal qualities needed. This is best left to the assessment of the personnel selectors. To ask job applicants whether they possess intelligence, drive and initiative, in other words to make an assessment of themselves, is a futile exercise. On the other hand, it could well be relevant to mention any special features, such as aptitudes or personal circumstances that are important to the job, for example, 'ability to read music at sight is desirable', or 'extensive travel throughout the UK and some evening or weekend work are an essential part of the job'.

Figure 8.2 is an advertisement for the job of training administrator based on the job description and person specification for this post described in Chapter 7.

The part of the advertisement advising applicants on the presentation of their applications varies in practice. Sometimes a personal letter covering the applicant's curriculum vitae (CV) is the only form of application required. More frequently, the employer provides an application form together with information on requirements for testimonials and referees' reports.

A letter of application or a CV is sometimes used as a kind of selection device. In France especially, personal applications of this kind may even be passed to graphologists for a personality assessment. In effect, with this method applicants are being invited to sell themselves on paper, that is, to argue their claims for appointment to the advertised post. There is certainly something to be said for giving applicants a free hand

---

Training International
Training Administrator

- Training International is a training and consultancy organization providing courses and consultancy services mainly for public sector employees from overseas, and especially developing countries.

- The training centre is located in central London.

- The particular requirements for this post are:
* good education – at least to A level standard or equivalent.
* skills in office administration and organization, and computer literacy with one of the commonly used packages, e.g. latest version of Word.
* ability to relate and communicate effectively in written and spoken language with a wide range of people from the UK and overseas.
* pleasant personality and equable temperament.
* sympathetic attitude towards the aims and work of the organization.

- The following qualifications are not essential but could be an advantage:
* previous employment in training or educational work.

- The rewards and conditions of service of the post are:
* Starting salary £20,000 p.a.
* Holiday 25 days per annum plus public holidays.
* Interest-free travel loan.
* Subsidized restaurant facilities.
* Optional contributory pension scheme/membership.

For further details and application form, please apply to
Human Resources Department (Ref. 1A)
Training International
9–10 Sheffield St
London WC2A 2E2
(Tel: 0171 242 3007)

Closing date for applications:

Figure 8.2 Specimen advertisement

to state their own cases without inhibition, especially for more senior roles, but there are some important caveats that have to be made about this method:

1 There is a great deal of evidence from those who work professionally in the field of careers advice and employment consultancy that many people are unable systematically and concisely to prepare a relevant account of their general and employment records. Employers using this method must be prepared, therefore, to receive a

number of lengthy, irrelevant and perhaps boring self-reports which protracts the recruitment process.

2 A strong case can be made against the use of personally planned applications as a form of suitability test. The assessment of suitability for employment is difficult enough during the selection procedures. It certainly cannot be carried out either effectively or with justice on paper based or written evidence alone. Further, if the employer relies on the applicant's CV the information provided suits the applicant, not the employer. Problems, gaps in employment or negative information are more easily concealed by applicants.

The use of an application form has the particular advantage that employers can ensure that the information provided by applicants is, on the whole, relevant to the job requirements. At the same time, some flexibility and common sense are needed in the use of the form. No form, however carefully designed, can cover every possible contingency. Ample space should be included, therefore, for any additional special points that applicants may wish to make.

The job advertisement

The advertisement needs to cover information derived from the job description and person specification in seven broad areas:

1 *The work organization*: its main occupation and location.
2 *The job*: its title; main duties, location.
3 *Qualifications and experience* (both necessary and desirable): personal requirements; specifically professional qualifications, experience, aptitudes, etc.
4 *Rewards and opportunities*: basic salary and other emoluments; any other benefits; opportunities for personal development.
5 *Training given*.
6 *Conditions*: any special factors and circumstances affecting the job.
7 *Applications*: form of application; closing date; address for forwarding.

The application form

The design of an appropriate application form will clearly depend on particular situations and needs, but there are some basic principles that are universally relevant. Different forms may be necessary for different kinds of work. If economy or any other reasons require the use of a general form for all appointments, then the form has to be sufficiently comprehensive and flexible to cover all possible situations. For all appointments the same general background details will be needed, for which a standard format is possible. Additional sections can be added, specifically designed to cover the whole range of jobs. Furthermore, there is no reason why these have necessarily to incur the expense of commercial printing. A form prepared on a word processor, carefully designed and adapted to cover the job vacancy in question, providing adequate space for the information required, is surely much better than a beautifully and expensively printed form which attempts unsuccessfully to serve a variety of purposes. The items that will normally need to be included in application forms are:

- job title
- applicant's full names
- date of birth
- address and telephone number
- nationality
- education (full-time, part-time training courses)
- academic qualifications
- professional qualifications
- present employment – details of present post, duties, accountabilities, skills used, numbers supervised
- previous employment in chronological order, with details of achievement in each post, name, address of employers, dates of employment
- main current interests, pursuits and achievements outside work
- health (including any serious illness or disability, past or present)
- court convictions (other than for spent convictions, see Chapter 21)
- additional information (any information not covered in the form, which the applicant considers significant to the application)
- referees
- source of information about the vacancy.

Processing and assessing applications

When all the applications have been received by the due date, the next task is to select those applicants who, on the evidence available, appear to be the most suitable as future employees of the organization, and, therefore, worth the time and cost of further examination in the selection procedures. This task will be based on the published requirements for the job and involves a painstaking and scrupulous study of the information provided by applicants, a comparison of this information with those job requirements and, finally, a decision whether to accept or reject at this stage.

To systematize the process, it is normally useful to carry out a preliminary sift to produce three categories of applicants: suitable, not suitable, marginal. With this method the main effort can then be concentrated on deciding which of the doubtful applicants should be accepted and which rejected. When there are constraints on acceptable numbers – this is the usual circumstance – and a choice has to be made between applicants of apparently equal merits in terms of the essential requirements, a careful consideration of the list of desirable requirements may provide the weighting needed to assist the final decision. A simple description of the sifting task such as this could make it seem a disarmingly mechanical process. It is, in fact, anything but this, and a number of important points need to be made about the general approach to the task and methods used.

To start with the general approach, those responsible for processing applications need to be very aware throughout, first, that they have a responsibility to their employers to be as careful and thorough as possible in selecting the most suitable of the applicants and, second, that they have a responsibility to the applicants themselves to examine their applications conscientiously and fairly. In this situation, applicants are entirely in the hands of those who carry out this task and seldom, if ever, have any chance of query or redress. It is also very important to realize that this is the link stage between the recruitment and selection procedures. It is the first hurdle that the applicant has to overcome in obtaining employment with an organization and is, in effect, the first stage in the selection procedure. The assessment of suitable employees is difficult enough in the face-to-face situations of the selection interview and other selection methods. In deciding, therefore, that an applicant is unsuitable entirely on documentary evidence, the employing organization needs to be as certain as it can be about its reasons for rejection at this stage. In short, the task must never be approached as a routine post-office exercise in which junior clerks are told to weed out all applicants who, say, do not have five General Certificate of Secondary Education (GCSE) passes, or are over thirty-nine years of age. Since the task is virtually part of the selection procedure, it has very important implications for the choice of staff to perform the task. Biodata, which can be automated, and provides a good prediction of the likely success of applicants, is a useful way of handling large numbers of applicants, but requires a regular recruitment requirement to be cost-effective – as in the case of the Inland Revenue. Biodata is described more fully in Chapter 9.

A further important point that has to be made concerns the need for flexibility in making the final decisions about acceptance or rejection. This relates to the previous comment on the problems of making decisions solely on the basis of documentary information. To illustrate by example – if a job demands a heavy goods vehicle (HGV) licence as an essential requirement, then all applicants who do not have this qualification could be rejected immediately, no matter what their other qualifications may be, but if, say, at least five years' experience in the type of job in question were included as an essential requirement, it might be very short-sighted to rule out an apparently otherwise excellent candidate whose experience happened to be only four years. There is no way of confirming from paper evidence whether the four years' experience of this applicant is not, in truth, superior in quality and value to the longer experience of other applicants. It is best not to be stubbornly inflexible or over-precise about matters such as length of experience, age, etc. in the first place. When job requirements are being established, room must always be left to decide individual cases on their merits, as we balance and weight various attributes.

Finally, a word needs to be said about the use of testimonials and referees' reports. Reports of this kind will regularly be used as evidence to assist in the final decisions of the selection procedures, but they also play some part in this phase of the recruitment procedure. Testimonials, despite some obvious limitations, are not always quite as useless as they are sometimes thought to be. For example, in the assessment of the merits and suitability of an application an attached brief report from a present or previous employer may at least confirm the applicant's experience and ability effectively to perform a job. Referees' reports, which are invariably confidential, will not normally be sought until a short list of applicants has been produced. There is no point in incurring the time, trouble and expense in calling for referees' reports for all candidates, when a proportion of these will be rejected during the processing of applications. Referees' reports are, therefore, usually required as supplementary evidence for use in the assessment of candidates during the selection procedure. Employers are often more frank in telephone conversations so we should not overemphasize the importance of written references.

Notifying applicants

The final step is to notify the chosen applicants of the arrangements for the selection procedure, and the rejected applicants that they have not been chosen. The letter to the successful applicants will need to give full details about the arrangements for the selection procedures, i.e. time and place together with other administrative information such as travel, expenses, etc. At the same time it is often very helpful to include any available literature about the organization and its work. In this way a number of questions that candidates might otherwise wish to ask, for example, about locations, opportunities to travel, career opportunities in general, educational, training, social, sporting, welfare facilities, etc. can be anticipated. There is not much that can usefully be said about letters to rejected applicants that is not already obvious. These should be brief and sympathetic, but not curt. We must bear in mind the need for maintaining the corporate image. All letters informing applicants of the results of applications should be sent as soon as possible. Apart from the natural tensions and anxieties that most people experience when waiting for the post to bring them news of any decisions that affect them personally, they have a special need for speedy information that concerns the planning of their working lives.

Administration of the recruitment process

The responsibility for administering and supervising the task of recruitment belongs to the HR staff. They act as the representatives or agents of their employers and are a link between the managers of the organization who require staff, the external sources for finding employees and the people who respond to the advertisements and apply for employment. The main elements of the task are:

1 *Acting as the focal point for co-ordinating the organization's needs for staff*: in this function they use the data of the human resource plan and job analysis.
2 *Providing specialist knowledge about factors affecting the availability of required staff, and of current legislation affecting recruitment for employment*: in this context they may also make recommendations about recruitment policies that the organization should adopt.
3 *Using specialist knowledge to decide what sources are likely to be most fruitful in the search for suitable staff*: here it is particularly important that the HR staff establish and maintain harmonious and profitable relationships with those agencies and consultants who are most likely to satisfy the recruitment needs of the organization.
4 *Formulating and administering the details of the recruitment procedures, related to the publication of information, processing of applications and notifying applicants*: HR staff need to liaise closely with line managers in the various stages of the recruitment process. The phases of the recruitment procedure when consultation between personnel staff and line management is most likely to occur are the publication of the advertisement of the job vacancy and the processing of applications. Line managers should be asked to verify that advertisements accurately reflect requirements before they are finally released for publication. They should be consulted when a shortlist of candidates is being produced.

5 *Maintaining records and data on what happened*: to satisfy any research or audits on equal opportunities, and to check the most cost-effective selection source.

Increasingly, organizations consider employing people with contracts that depart from full-time, normal working hours. These include short term, part time, job-sharing, working from home, term-time working, annualized hours, compressed work hours, twilight shifts and call-out contracts amongst the variety of working time available. At the same time franchise operations and subcontracting arrangements provide opportunities for work to be carried out without the employer bearing the costs and risks of traditional recruitment and employment methods. At a time of labour shortage, these types of flexible arrangements attract applicants from outside traditional sources.

See Figure 8.3 for a summary of the recruitment process.

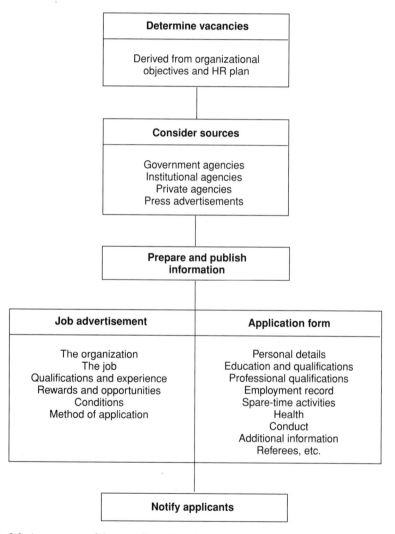

Figure 8.3 A summary of the recruitment process

Questions

1 What should be the aim of an effective system of recruitment?
2 What are the five stages of a systematic process of recruitment?
3 What are the main sources of recruitment available to an organization? Briefly describe and assess each of these sources in terms of the kind of vacancies for which they would be most suitable.
4 Prepare a job advertisement using the main headings as a guide and the example of the Training Administrator, for your own job (or the last one you held).
5 What actions need to be taken to ensure that the processing of applications is as systematic, effective and fair as possible?
6 What are the main responsibilities of the HR department in the recruitment process?

Chapter 9

Selecting employees

In this chapter attention is focused primarily on the selection of employees from outside the employing organization. However, it should be emphasized that the systematic approach to the selection of employees may and should apply to people who are already employed by the appointing organization. Whilst there will always be inevitable problems in predicting future behaviour in a new job, employers obviously have considerable advantages when dealing with people already in their employ. The employers already know what knowledge and skills existing employees have. Perhaps more importantly, they know what attitudes and personal attributes these people display in performing their jobs.

Two basic questions provide the foundation for an effective system:

1 What are the criteria for effective performance against which selectors must judge the suitability of candidates for appointment?
2 What methods are most likely to reveal the evidence they need to make judgements and decisions about the suitability of candidates?

The crucial importance of selecting people who can meet the requirements prescribed in the job description and person specification hardly needs to be stressed. It is equally evident that mistakes in selection can have very serious consequences for corporate effectiveness. Such mistakes may very adversely affect colleagues, subordinates and clients. Employee incompetence may lead to costly mistakes, loss and waste of valuable resources, accidents, avoidable expenditure on training, etc.

Employee selectors face an inevitable dilemma. They have to carry out a vitally important task, but one that is at the same time fraught with problems to which there are either no answers or no easy answers. The abiding problem is the dependence on subjective human judgement. Let us not forget that so-called objective lists are devised by fallible human beings. The essential problem can easily be seen by reference to the example person specification in Chapter 7. Considering the attitudes and personal attributes identified as necessary for effective performance, how can the selectors identify these requirements in a person whom they do not know during the short acquaintance of the selection process?

In view of the importance and difficulties of the task, employers need to take it most seriously. Appropriate investment at this stage can and will be cost-effective if it avoids the possibly enormous and incalculable costs that faulty employee selection may produce.

In general terms, effectiveness in employee selection requires:

1 Awareness of the essential nature of the task and its inherent problems.
2 Clear and comprehensive definitions of the criteria for effective performance by job analysis.
3 Understanding the implications of the concept of reliability and validity for employee selection.
4 Awareness of the range of possible selection methods, their potential value and predictive capabilities.
5 Thorough training for selectors to make them aware of the inherent problems and to develop the necessary skills for effective practice, for example training in interviewing skills.
6 A follow-up system to check how well the predictions made in the selection process have turned out in practice.

The selection task, as we have already seen, is difficult enough with all its inherent and unavoidable limitations. In the absence of the systematic approach described above, selection becomes little more than a lottery.

There is one final important point that needs to be made in discussing the selectors' task. The definitions of effective performance, contained in the job description and person specification, are prescriptions for total effectiveness of performance. There can be few jobs, if any, where the job applicant would be capable of meeting these standards initially. They would normally only be achievable after work experience and training. The selector's task, therefore, is to assess candidates' potential to meet the prescribed performance criteria.

The first of the main questions described above, concerned with the definition of criteria, has already been thoroughly explored in the chapter on job analysis. The remaining part of this chapter will, therefore, deal with the second main question, which concerns the methods available to produce the necessary evidence of potential.

Methods of employee selection

Reliability and validity

In choosing methods of employee selection the selectors need to find methods which are practicable enough, to be used in the short duration and restricted environment of the selection process and which provide the closest possible correlation between the predictor and the criteria for effective performance of the job. Before we look at the range of possible methods in any detail there are fundamental requirements by which the effectiveness of all selection methods have to be judged. In the literature of psychological testing, these requirements are known as reliability and validity.

Reliability

Reliability here means that the selection methods, tests and ensuing results are consistent and do not vary with time, place or different subjects – that is, test and retest reliability. Thus, a ruler is reliable as an instrument for measuring dimensions whether the subject is wood or cheese, and whether the measurement is done in summer or winter, in Russia or Africa. By this criterion, human selectors of employees are inherently not reliable because standards may vary between selectors and within one selector over a period of time. The issue is the degree of unreliability. This may be reduced by using a variety of measuring devices (tests, interviews), and by training assessors, and using more than one assessor.

Validity

A valid method or test is one which truly measures what it purports to measure. For example, to ask a candidate at interview to define the requirements for effective management might be a valid measure of knowledge. It is certainly not a valid measure of the candidate's performance potential. The answer could in no way be of any use in predicting how successful the candidate might be in practice as a manager.

Criterion-related validity is the extent to which the test measures what it is intended to measure, for example, whether the results of the test do predict job performance or the attribute in question. This requires validation of the performance by some independent means, and a statistically significant relationship between performance and the test results for the population involved.

Content-related validity and *construct-related validity* are issues about the technical construction of the test. Content-related validity is the extent to which the content domain is tested by the method chosen. Construct-related validity explores the independence and presence of the psychological construct or trait, and the validity of the test in finding this.

There are three aspects of validity that selectors need to understand:

1 What are the criteria for successful performance, and are they being assessed in the selection process? (The criterion problem.)
2 Are the criteria being used valid and reliable (i.e. consistent) measures of behaviour, experience, personality or whatever, which predict the performance of candidates?
3 Do the tests actually used predict what they are purported to predict?

The answers to these questions therefore are:

1 Agree in advance what constitutes a desirable range of attributes, or competencies, which are required for successful job performance.
2 Operationalize these so they can be tested.
3 Select, after research, the test or methods that will accurately predict the possession of these attributes or competencies.

The search for methods that may provide the evidence needed for decisions has produced a wide variety of tests. These tests could be categorized in various ways, but in broad terms they may be conveniently divided into two main types according to their purpose. They are designed to assess candidates' potential to fulfil the requirements of the job in terms of:

- knowledge, skills and attitudes which already exist
- knowledge, skills and attitudes which might be developed after training and experience in the job.

In other words, in a comparison between the test situations and those actually occurring in the job, prediction may be based on evidence derived from actual past behaviour, or from a calculation of potential future behaviour.

To illustrate the difference with a simple example, let us suppose we are told that a particular job requires the ability to speak Japanese fluently. Having first determined what we mean by speaking fluent Japanese and the criteria by which it is to be assessed, we could make a direct test of all the candidates who claim to speak the language fluently and then assess their abilities against our predetermined standards.

But if there were a shortage of easily recruitable Japanese speakers, we might decide to invest in training suitable candidates to the standards required. In this situation, we should need to devise some test designed to show whether candidates with no knowledge of Japanese have the latent ability to learn to speak the language fluently in a given period of time. This alternative test clearly could not be a test in Japanese itself, but it would have to be some kind of aptitude-revealing test. We might decide, for example, that proven ability in other languages would be a sufficient indicator of the skills required, but to assume a correlation between, say, the ability to speak French fluently and a potential ability to speak Japanese fluently would be unwarranted. This is also an illustration of the need for specialist guidance, because any aptitude test devised would have to be based on a very careful analysis of the factors that seem to be important in speaking Japanese fluently. Furthermore, the reliability and validity of the test would need to be proved by confirming that an acceptable number of people chosen by this method have, in fact, become fluent speakers of Japanese. This kind of proof takes time, and the original test may well need regular modifications before the employing organization is finally satisfied with its predictive qualities.

To give some idea of the variety of methods used in Europe Table 9.1 reports on the percentage of use in the countries shown.

Table 9.1 European comparison of selection methods (percentage of organizations using these methods)

Country	West Germany	Spain	France	Netherlands	Sweden	Turkey	UK
Application forms	96	87	95	94	15	95	97
Interview panels	86	85	92	69	69	64	71
Biodata	20	12	26	20	69	39	8
Psychometric testing	6	60	22	31	24	8	46
Graphology	8	8	57	2	0	0	1
References	66	54	73	47	96	69	92
Aptitude tests	8	72	28	53	14	33	45
Assessment centres	13	18	9	27	5	4	18
Group selection methods	4	22	10	2	3	23	13

Source: Brewster and Hegewisch (1994: app. III, table 3.6).

It is interesting to note the popularity of handwriting analysis (graphology) in France. There is no evidence to confirm the validity of this method.

In the practice of personnel selection, there are many different methods that may be used, as listed below:

1 *Ability tests of achievement*: these are designed to test what the candidate already knows or can do, relative to the requirements of the job (e.g. skills in driving, keyboard skills, foreign languages; knowledge of the law, antique furniture, etc.).

2 *Ability tests of aptitude*: these are designed to predict latent potential to meet job requirements which can be developed to required standards by training and experience. Aptitude tests may include intelligence tests, designed to measure a broad range of generally applicable abilities, or more specialized tests, designed to indicate particular aptitudes, e.g. mechanical skills. The ability tests included under this heading are too numerous and varied in purpose to enumerate. Nevertheless, a well-known example of the use of these kinds of tests is worth quoting to illustrate their practical applicability and potential efficacy. Because the training of pilots to fly aircraft is enormously expensive, it is particularly important that selectors should make as few mistakes as possible in selecting potential pilots. However, because selectors are faced with the central problem of predicting future success they need predictors which are as reliable and valid as possible, i.e. where the test data have the highest possible correlation with the performance criteria for flying. Over a number of years a number of aptitude tests have been developed which have been validated in practice and can be shown to be very sound predictors in terms of the success rates in flying training. When tests of this kind are used in combination, as they are in selecting aircrew, they are known as a 'test battery'.

3 *Tests of personality*: traits of personality undoubtedly have a very important effect on performance of work, and especially any kind of managerial work, where judgement, and influence on and relationships with others, are crucial. A number of tests have been developed and used by psychologists over the years in an attempt to determine personality characteristics as a basis for predicting likely future behaviour at work. Various methods have been designed, for example:

(a) *Projective tests*: a method in which the subject is required to react freely and spontaneously, usually to visual stimuli. Reactions are then interpreted by the tester as indicators of personality traits, interests, etc. The best known examples of this kind of test are probably the Rorschach Ink-Blot Test (interpreting responses to ink-blot shapes) and the Thematic Apperception Test (interpreting responses to a series of pictures). The interpretation of the results of these tests is a task for specialists.

(b) *Inventories*: with this method subjects are required to respond to questionnaires normally concerned with how they feel about certain subjects and situations. Well-known examples of these kinds of tests have been produced by Cattell (16 PF), Eysenck and Saville and Holdsworth (the Occupational Personality Questionnaire – OPQ – for example. Some inventories are designed to be administered and scored by anyone using the instructions and key provided. With others the tests have to be administered by people trained in their application and interpretation.

4 *Group situational tests*: in these tests, candidates are observed by the selectors over

a period of time as they perform a variety of tasks as a team, sometimes with and sometimes without an appointed leader. Tests of this kind first became well known during the Second World War. They began in the UK with the War Office Selection Boards (WOSBs) and are now widely used by the armed forces, governmental and private sector organizations for the selection of potential leaders. The tests are designed to reveal data about the personality traits and interpersonal skills required in managing or co-operating with others in the performance of actual tasks. They undoubtedly provide useful insights into candidates' behaviour as members of groups in a way that no other individual selection method can do. Nevertheless, in essence they represent behaviour measured by the personal, subjective interpretations of human observers in artificial circumstances and are, therefore, open to question in terms of their reliability and validity.

5 *Interviews*: whatever other tests could be used, the selection process invariably includes an interview. Quite often it is the only method used, and in various ways. There may be several interviews covering general and specialist aspects of the job, and interviews may be conducted by individual interviewers or by a board of interviewers. Apart from the information obtained at the interview, interviewers also make use of accounts provided by candidates themselves in the form of completed application forms, CVs, letters, etc., and by others competent to comment on the candidates in the form of open testimonials or confidential reference reports. The interview is by far the commonest method used in personnel selection. At the same time it is an entirely subjective method and, thus, of dubious efficacy. Moreover, any value that it can have may be still further reduced because of lack of skills on the part of the interviewers. Since it plays such a significant part in the selection process, it needs a separate and detailed examination by itself.

It is vitally important to the effectiveness of the system that results should be followed up. This means that the selectors need to have a regular flow of feedback from line managers reporting how effectively selected employees are actually performing. These data can then be used to trace and remedy weaknesses in the selection process. Formal validation studies are rare, but some organizations do analyse labour turnover, and sometimes appraisal assessments, to check the effectiveness of selection decisions.

Assessment centres

During the 1980s organizations increasingly used assessment-centre type approaches, especially to the selection of young graduates and for those organizations where there was likely to be a group or cohort entry.

Assessment centres are not necessarily physical places – the term is used to describe the collection of assessment methods, including group situational tests, applied to a cohort entry where there are specifically designed tests and exercises applied to all applicants (sometimes based on the competencies researched within the organization which are associated with effective entry level or higher level performance). The activities may span several days and include assessment by senior line managers and informal discussions as well as psychometric and other tests conducted by psychologists and other experts.

At the end of the exercises judgements are recorded on each candidate and, of necessity, there must be a final discussion between the assessors, after the exercises are over, to determine an overall rating. The following principles apply to the establishment of assessment centres:

1 They are costly, and need expert assistance to design. Therefore, they are only really cost-effective if there is a large repeat demand for the job in question (e.g. graduate management trainee).
2 The assessment-centre exercises must be researched to establish validity and reliability in that particular organization.
3 The observers/assessors must be properly trained and must have practised observation.
4 The administration of the centre must be professional, with suitable accommodation available, and documentation well prepared in advance.
5 Candidates must be advised in advance that this is to be an assessment-centre approach.
6 Candidates, whether successful or not, should be given expert feedback on their performance, and reasons for selection or non-selection.
7 Confidentiality must be maintained with data, apart from in 6 above. However, training plans for successful candidates should address any needs revealed.

The selection interview

The selection interview has already been briefly discussed above in the general survey of selection methods. However, because it is the one method that is always used, and is of proven and demonstrably limited value as a predictor, it merits a separate, detailed examination. This examination will cover why its value is limited and, since it has to be used, what steps can be taken to give maximum possible effectiveness. How can a limited instrument be used to best advantage?

For many years the selection interview has been the subject of research in order to determine its value as a method. In general, the research has produced a pessimistic evaluation of the selection interview, but has also indicated that its value may be significantly enhanced when interviewers have been trained. If the interview is analysed in the light of the general problem of human communication and of the particular requirements for reliability and validity, it is not difficult to see why it has inherent barriers to success as a selection method. The selection interview is not reliable for the following reasons:

1 The instrument of measure is human.
2 No two interviewers will interpret and assess information in the same way.
3 The same interviewer will reveal fluctuations in interpretations of data and assessments over a period of time.

The interview cannot be a valid test of candidates' suitability for employment for the following reasons:

1 It is a contrived, interrogative conversation, involving a meeting invariably between

strangers and seldom lasting for more than about an hour. It is, therefore, an artificially distorted and entirely stressful situation, no matter what efforts the interviewers may make to reduce the tension. The larger the number of interviewers the greater the tension is likely to be.

2 It cannot possibly test the important areas that add up to suitability for employment, i.e.: competence effectively to perform the professional requirements of a job over a period of time; the personal disposition to relate co-operatively with future work colleagues in smaller groups and within the organization as a whole; the capacity for self-development and the potential to assume wider responsibilities.

3 The interview may indicate that a candidate is presentable, fluent or quick-thinking under the conditions of the interview, but to suppose that the pattern of interview behaviour would be repeated in the very different circumstances of work over a long period of time would be a quite unwarranted assumption.

The only kind of validity that the interview can confidently be said to have is to test whether people can cope with the special and unusual conditions of the interview. Nevertheless, it is often very difficult to persuade selection interviewers that much of the evidence that they require about a candidate's potential for effective performance of work cannot be properly tested by the interview.

It is pertinent to ask why the interview is so widely and prominently used if it is a method of such demonstrable limitations. The reasons are these:

1 It has a high face-validity, i.e. both selectors and candidates have long been accustomed to its use and appear to have much greater faith in its efficacy than the research evidence warrants.

2 Sooner or later there has to be a meeting between the employer and prospective employee, if only so that a number of routine checks may be made on both sides and to give the employer an opportunity to amplify and clarify information provided by application forms and any other documents. It is also an opportunity for the employer to inquire into any inconsistencies, and to explore the evidence.

3 Despite continuous research and the introduction of possibly promising advances in new directions (e.g. assessment centres), a method that will solve the basic dilemma of accurately forecasting future behaviour in employment has yet to be found.

Since the interview is likely to continue to play a major role in the selection process, it seems sensible to adopt a realistic approach, which means making the best possible use of the interview. This is the really important question to which attention needs to be given. As the research data have shown, anyone who is likely to have responsibilities for personnel selection needs to be trained. At the same time the following caveats have to be made about interview training:

1 Because of its innate limitations the total attainable efficiency of the interview as a selection method can never be any more than moderate. Therefore, any improvement produced by training can only be relative.

2 Trainees need to be made fully aware of these limitations. Otherwise they may be led to believe that if only they can learn to apply in practice conventional maxims about sound interviewing (essential though this is) then all will be well.

3 There is sometimes a particular problem in training senior managers. Having interviewed without any formal training perhaps for many years, they inevitably develop confidence in their own styles and methods, and often come to believe that seniority and experience are the main requirements for making decisions on suitability for employment. They may find it very hard to accept that the selection method that they have been using for so long is a very fallible instrument, or that they lack system and skills. Training courses can have a particular value in helping to overcome problems of insight and sensitivity in unskilled interviewers. Trainees can participate in selection interviews that are very close to reality. Discussion with observers and tutors, supported by video tape replays of the interview, can demonstrate the inherent problems of the interview itself and the methods that are likely to be effective in practice, in ways which no amount of lecturing or reading could ever achieve.

A well-planned course should include the following main areas of study:

1 The general nature and problems of personnel selection.
2 The particular limitations of the interview as a selection method.
3 The application of systematic interviewing through practice interviews as a means of making the best use of the interview.

The emphasis of the course needs to be laid almost entirely in interview practice in small groups as a basis for a structural analysis of the interview itself. In this connection it is worth noting that the views and feelings of the interviewees should be used to provide a very valuable and powerful feedback to the interviewers – a learning experience which they can never have in real life.

Variations in patterns of interviews

The following variations are possible in the patterns of interviews:

1 A single one-to-one interview.
2 A series of one-to-one interviews at the end of which interviewers compare views and discuss final conclusions.
3 A board or panel interview with a group of interviewers.
4 A combination of one-to-one and board interviews.

As always, there are arguments for and against each variation. The main criteria to be considered in assessing the merits and demerits of a particular interview pattern are:

1 Acquiring the best possible evidence on which to base judgements and decisions.
2 Giving candidates the fairest possible opportunities to provide the most accurate account of themselves in the difficult circumstances of the interview.

If we assess the possible variations in the light of these criteria, we could draw the following conclusions:

1 A single one-to-one interview is likely to be the least stressful, but has the disadvan-

tage that the acquiring of evidence, judgements and decisions rely on one person only.

2 A series of one-to-one interviews overcomes the problem of the single interview and has the advantage of providing a range of views and judgements.

3 Board interviews are potentially more stressful than one-to-one interviews because the candidate is faced with several interviewers at the same time. The board interview has the advantage that all interviewers are provided with the same evidence, but are able to make independent interpretations and judgements. There is research evidence to show that boards are more likely to make successful selection decisions than single one to ones.

Because of the perceived stress inherent in board interviews, it is very important to keep the number to the absolute necessary minimum, for example, three or four members at the most. Interview boards of large numbers of interviewers are not only likely to intimidate many candidates, they are also much more difficult for the chairperson to control.

Using the interview effectively

A systematic interview is based on three interdependent chronological phases:

1 The pre-interview preparatory phase.
2 The interview itself.
3 The post-interview assessment and decision phase.

Each of these elements contributes vitally to the effectiveness of the total operation, and weakness in any one element will adversely affect the other parts. For example, if the essential pre-interview preparatory work is unsound, then, no matter how well the interview itself may be conducted, the quality of the final decision will inevitably suffer.

The main requirements for a sound interview can now be considered under these headings.

Pre-interview preparatory phase

1 Use the data of job analysis to determine the requirements for effective performance of the job and the criteria by which these may be identified and assessed. These data provide the foundation for the whole selection process.

2 Determine acceptable entry levels for new staff *vis-à-vis* the job requirements for fully effective performance.

3 Consider and, whenever practicable use, other tests and information to supplement the evidence provided by the interview. Any other selection methods used need to be validated, i.e. shown to improve the predictive quality of the process.

4 Decide on the number of interviewers. When an interview board is used, the membership should be the smallest number necessary to fulfil the task.

5 Pay particular attention to all important environmental details such as time, place and setting to enable candidates to feel as comfortable as possible.

6 Produce a coverage plan designed to provide the maximum possible significant information. The plan that is the simplest and likely to be most effective is a systematic,

chronological survey of the important areas of the life history. The coverage plan is not the same as the seven- or five-point plans, the applicability of which to selection interviews is described below.

7 When interview boards are held, discuss and agree the objectives, criteria, the coverage plan and the areas that each board member will cover. The leadership of this discussion is a major responsibility of the chairperson.

Interview-coverage plan

The criteria for assessing applicants' suitability for employment are contained in the person specification, which is a definition of the knowledge, skills and personal attributes needed for effective performance. Applicants may already possess some of the required qualifications or have the latent ability to develop others with training and work experience.

Within its known limitations the interview is used to ascertain what qualifications candidates already have in terms of the person specification, and what potential they may have for further development. As we have already seen, specific tests may be used to ascertain existing and latent abilities. When the interview is used for these purposes, information on which to base judgements about either existing or latent abilities can only come from the evidence of past achievements and behaviour. It follows that the broad plan for the interview that is most likely to provide the required information is a systematic, chronological investigation of the main areas of a life history. A comprehensive interview-coverage plan should, therefore, take the following form:

1 Introductions and brief explanation of purpose and scope of the interview.
2 General and domestic background.
3 Education (full and part time).
4 Work (full and part time) and training.
5 Spare-time interests and activities.
6 Knowledge of and interest in the job.
7 Opportunity for applicant to:
    (a) add any further information.
    (b) ask any questions.

The investigation of these areas should aim to reveal the maximum possible relevant information, that is, it should be directed towards the requirements of the person specification. For example, the discussion of spare-time pursuits may reveal valuable information about ability to organize, sociability, initiative, etc. It should aim to reveal not only factual information about actions, decisions and achievements, but also as much as possible about reasons for decisions, motives, values, attitudes and personal attributes.

The interview

1 Concentrate initially on establishing a sympathetic, productive atmosphere to encourage candidates to talk freely.
2 Begin with introductions and a brief explanation of the purpose and scope of the interview.

3 Follow the broad chronological, systematic coverage plan throughout in order to ensure a comprehensive coverage. Deviations are likely to create gaps in the information obtained.

4 In board interviews arrange for each interviewer to interview in turn. If the situation is allowed to become a free-for-all, then control is lost, the coverage plan cannot be methodically followed and candidates are likely to become unsettled and confused.

5 Pay the utmost attention to the form of question, i.e.:

   (a) concentrate on acquiring as much evidence as possible of potential ability to do the required job, based on the facts of past behaviour and achievements

   (b) in general, avoid hypothetical questions, especially those which have no bearing on the job. They can only produce hypothetical answers

   (c) use a simple, open question form which does not imply answers, make unwarranted assumptions or influence candidates in any way (e.g. why? what? where? when? who?, etc.).

6 Be constantly alert to the possible effects of the interviewers' non-verbal behaviour and manner, and the possibility of the misinterpretation of intentions by candidates. In general, a demeanour that is sympathetic and avoids extremes of *bonhomie* or coldness is the most appropriate.

7 Place information in perspective. The fact, for example, that a candidate was in charge of a section would be of little value unless the important circumstantial details were also ascertained, such as: the work objectives; whether they were achieved or not; if not achieved, what the reasons were; what remedial actions were taken; other problems and how they were handled; responsibilities for staff in numbers and types; other responsibilities.

Post-interview assessment and decision

1 Systematically assess the evidence obtained in the light of the job requirements. For this purpose, the discipline implied in the seven- and five-point plans is invaluable (Table 9.2).

2 In assessing evidence, concentrate on solid facts of past behaviour as indicators of motivation, attitudes, values, personal qualities and abilities and, in sum, of potential to do the required job. Behaviour in the highly artificial situation of the interview itself should be treated with extreme caution. There is little correlation between this behaviour and likely behaviour in the actual environment and conditions of work.

3 In the assessment process, take account of all available evidence. When the interview is the only method used, the other main sources of information are usually referees' reports and testimonials. These documents can be very useful when written by authorities competent to confirm the facts of past performance. They are of much more doubtful value when they purport to assess suitability for employment, because of the likelihood of bias and the writers' probable lack of direct knowledge of the job requirements.

More often than not there are more candidates than vacancies. Whilst the selection process is in progress selectors should not become involved in any comparison of the merits of candidates. Their task is to concentrate single-mindedly on assessing the suitability of each individual candidate in terms of the defined criteria for effective per-

Table 9.2 The seven-point plan as a model for a selection procedure for potential aircraft pilots

	Essential	*Desirable*	*How identified*
Physical	100% fitness	–	Comprehensive range of medical tests
Attainments	Specified subjects and grades in A levels and GCSEs	Degree or equivalent qualifications	Documentary evidence amplified by interview
General intelligence	Levels specified in terms of psychometric tests	–	Ability tests of education/intelligence supplemented by interview data
Special aptitudes	Co-ordination, mechanical comprehension, speed of reaction, handling rapidly changing information	–	Special ability tests of aptitude related to success in flying training
Interests	Aviation and related subjects	World affairs	Documentary evidence amplified by interview
Disposition	Equable temperament, sociable and co-operative	–	Documentary evidence amplified by interview
Circumstances	Mobility	Initially free from heavy domestic/family commitments	Documentary evidence amplified by interview

formance. It could well be that all candidates are assessed as suitable. In situations where there are more suitable candidates than there are vacancies, the selectors then become judges in a competition. They need to review the credentials of each suitable candidate very carefully and conscientiously, comparing their merits and demerits and assessing the stronger and the weaker. Eventually they have to produce an order of merit. In this situation the availability of several judges is obviously preferable to reliance on a single judge.

Employment law and personnel selection

Employment law is discussed in detail in Chapter 21. However, we need to stress here the importance of legislation about discrimination on grounds of race or sex in personnel selection. Current legislation and codes of practice require employers to take all possible measures to ensure that there is no direct or indirect discrimination in their job descriptions, person specifications, advertisements and selection procedures. Direct discrimination (for example, white males only) is blatant. Indirect discrimination (for example, asking women but not men questions about the effects of domestic commitments on employability) is more difficult to combat. It is usually the result of long-established attitudes, and selectors are often not alert to their own unfair discriminatory practices.

To reduce and eliminate discriminatory behaviour that is particularly likely to be unfair to candidates who are female, from ethnic minorities or disabled, positive action is needed by work organizations. They need to publish and distribute the relevant sections of employment law and to produce their own codes of practice, and to train their personnel selectors with particular emphasis on the requirements of employment law in this context and on the need to guard against unfair discriminatory practices.

A summary of the main elements of a system for the selection of new employees is shown in Figure 9.1.

Questions

1 What is the first essential stage in an effective system of employee selection?
2 Describe the various methods by which selectors might identify suitable employees.
3 What is the significance of reliability and validity in the use of selection methods? Give examples to illustrate these terms.
4 What are the limitations of the interview as a selection method?
5 Describe the main areas that need to be included in an effective interview-coverage plan.
6 What significance does employment law have in the process of personnel selection?

Reference

Brewster, C. and Hegewisch, A. (1994). *Policy and Practice in European Human Resource Management*. International Thomson Publishing.

Further reading for Part Three

Bennison, M. and Casson, J. (1984). *The Manpower Planning Handbook*. McGraw-Hill.
Bethell-Fox, C. (1992). *Identifying and Assessing Managerial Competencies*. Open University.
Boydell, T. (1970). *A Guide to Job Analysis*. BACIE.
Fordham, K. G. (1983). *Job Advertising in Recruitment Handbook*. Gower.
Herriott, P. (ed.) (1989). *Assessment and Selection in Organizations*. John Wiley.
Her Majesty's Stationery Office (1974) *Company Manpower Planning*. HMSO.
Institute of Personnel Management (1975). *Manpower Planning in Action*. IPM.
Institute of Personnel and Development (1999). *Recruitment*. Survey Report No. 5, May. IPD.
Jackson, C. (1996). *Understanding Psychological Testing*. British Psychological Society.
Jessup, G. and Jessup, H. (1975). *Selection and Assessment at Work*. Methuen.
Lewis C. (1992). *Employee Selection*. 2nd edn Stanley Thornes.

Munro Fraser, J. (1966). *Employment Interviewing*. Macdonald and Evans.
Pearn, M. and Kandola, R. (1986). *Job Analysis*. IPM.
Rodger, A. (1973). *The Seven-Point Plan*. Paper No. 5. National Institute of Industrial Psychology.
Sidney, E. and Brown, M. (1961). *The Skills of Interviewing*. Tavistock.

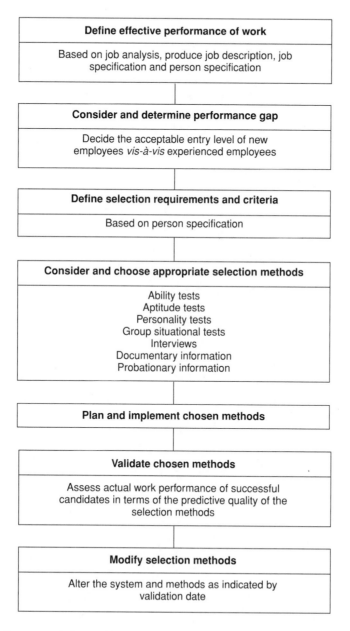

Figure 9.1 Summary of the main elements of a system for the selection of new employees

The effective employment and development of human resources

The effective employment and development of human resources

Having expended a considerable outlay in its efforts to obtain suitable employees, a work organization has a very strong vested interest in ensuring that these human resources are employed as effectively as possible. The weight of research data points to the significance of people management for organizational performance. To do this, an organization has to start by recognizing that people are its most valuable asset, that they are not simply another factor of production for the achievement of short-term objectives, and that they are a reservoir of knowledge and skills, which must be nurtured and developed for the survival and growth of the organization in a constantly changing and increasingly complex environment. An enlightened, long-term view such as this needs to be based on a psychological insight and awareness of the complexities of individual needs and motivation, and hence the potential, inherent conflict between the needs and objectives of the organization and those of its employees. Here, the main problem that the organization has to face is how to create a working environment that enables its objectives to be achieved and at the same time is able to motivate people by providing meaningful and satisfactory work.

This part of the book describes the necessity for a systematic approach to the employment and development of staff in general and, in particular, to the induction period of employment, to the assessment of work performance and potential as a basis for determining needs for work experience and training.

Chapter 10

Induction

The induction crisis

The induction of new employees into an organization is such an important part of the management of people at work that it merits separate and special consideration. There is good evidence that the subject seldom receives the very careful attention that it truly needs by employing organizations. Regular analyses of labour turnover statistics show that a higher turnover during the first years of employment occurs. The wastage (Figure 10.1) in financial and human terms needs no elaboration. Undoubtedly, a portion of the blame can be attributed to faulty recruitment and selection procedures. Equally certainly, the reasons why so many people leave organizations shortly after joining them are connected with the treatment they receive from their employers during this initial

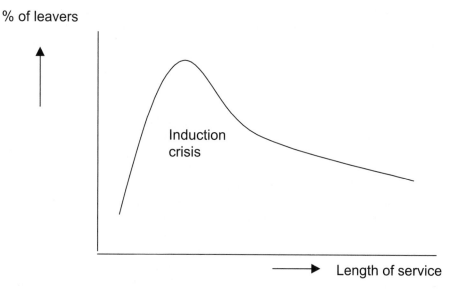

Figure 10.1 Wastage curve

phase of employment. The problems of social adjustment that newcomers have to face are simply not always appreciated or sympathetically handled. This may seem surprising, since all human beings at some time in their lives experience loneliness and a sense of disorientation when finding themselves in a new and unfamiliar environment.

Because of the rigours of contemporary living, stress has become a subject that is receiving increasing attention. It is interesting to note that, where research has produced data on the various factors that cause stress, a change of job receives a high weighting. Thus, the early phase in a new job is well known to be a stressful period both from personal experience and from the evidence of research data, and yet organizations continue to tolerate high rates of labour turnover and often do not seem to be able to deal effectively with a problem that has been described as 'the induction crisis'. Apart from the effect of a high labour turnover on the performance of the new employee's team or group of fellow workers, the effect on those who work throughout the organization could be demotivating. If employers wish to develop well-motivated staff, it is most important that they should demonstrate their values by their actions from the very outset of their employees' engagements.

Causes of the induction crisis

It could be said that the assistance of the behavioural sciences is not necessary to understand why people have problems when they join new work organizations. The cause can be partly ascribed to the strangeness of a new environment, which is an inevitable discomfort that everybody has to face and accept, and which will pass with time. Other causes include a failure to appreciate the variety of work, the supervision, the travel to work, payment system and so on, due to overselling of the job or poor supervision by the employer. It is probably this kind of reasoning that lies behind the failure of many organizations to pursue the causes of the problem more deeply and to find effective remedies. People taking up new employment are clearly in a position of particular insecurity. The continuity of their lives has been broken for the moment and they are making a fresh start in a situation in which they have no previous history. In general, their past achievements tend to count for little in the new work environment, and they have to prove themselves anew, both professionally and socially. Most of these difficulties stem from well-established phenomena of group and organizational behaviour, and especially from factors of the following kind:

1 Organizations and groups develop norms of acceptable and expected behaviour of their members. Newcomers have to learn what these are and to accept and internalize them before they become accepted members of groups. These norms may be very different from those of the previous groups that the newcomers have recently left, and may make the process of adaptation more difficult.
2 Group cohesiveness does not always operate in productive directions. It may also be employed antagonistically towards other groups or individuals who are perceived as non-conformist or deviant. Newcomers may be perceived as threats to groups for various reasons, and they may experience difficulties in gaining acceptance. For example, the work group may perceive that the newcomer will be making too small a contribution, thus increasing the workload of others, or even that they will outperform incumbents and show them up.

3 The psychological contract may often be a source of difficulty in the induction phase. As we have seen earlier, apart from the formal contract agreed between employing organizations and individual employees about the hire and rewarding of labour, both have expectations about each other's behaviour that are not formally prescribed. For example, new employees may regard a sympathetic, democratic style of management as their basic right. If, however, new employees encounter unexpectedly authoritarian styles, they may believe that they have been somehow deceived by their new employers, although there is nothing in the formal contract about the styles of management that may be adopted.

The organization's responsibilities for induction

To mitigate the induction crisis, to help new employees to adjust to their new surroundings, to gain their confidence and commitment and to avoid costly levels of labour turnover all require positive attitudes and actions on the part of employing organizations, based on an awareness that:

1 The induction phase is much more critical and stressful to the new employee than it is often recognized to be.
2 The length of the critical phase will naturally vary and depend on the adaptability of each individual, but it may well last for many months.
3 The causes contributing to the general problem may be found in the psychological and sociological factors affecting organizational and group behaviour, as described above.
4 The induction phase needs to be very carefully planned and supervised, as the first stage in staff development.

The induction programme

The induction of new employees has to be regarded as a comprehensive and systematic programme continuously monitored and evaluated. Too often it has come to mean little more than a day or two set aside, during which time new employees may have interviews, attend short courses, listen to talks about the organization, receive a quantity of literature, be taken on quick guided tours to glimpse the various sections of the organization and meet a variety of people. This is the kind of programme that might be prepared for visitors with limited time available, rather than for people who presumably are expected to stay with the organization for several years. Induction arrangements of this kind could well do as much if not more harm than good. When a mass of information – much of which may be unnecessary – is crammed into a very short space of time, and many of the questions on which newcomers need reassurance are left unanswered, it is likely that initial feelings of confusion, inadequacy and insecurity will be increased rather than allayed.

For the induction programme to be comprehensive and effective the employing organization has to begin with a clear view of what it intends to achieve as a basis for designing the programme. This means that an aim and set of objectives have to be produced similar to that described in Example 10.1.

Example 10.1
Aim

That new employees become integrated as soon as possible functionally and socially into the organization and its environment.

Objectives

1 That they should understand the function, aims and objectives of the organization as a whole.
2 That they should understand the specific objectives to be achieved by their sections, and their personal responsibilities and expected contributions to the achievement of these objectives.
3 That the necessary initial training and work experience should be planned to enable them to fulfil these responsibilities.
4 That comprehensive information should be provided on the following subjects:
   (a) conditions of employment, salary, pension arrangements, holidays, sickness rules
   (b) working arrangements in particular, software packages used, reporting relationships and any key facts about the job not yet covered
   (c) the system of HR management and especially the arrangements and opportunities for staff development
   (d) the whole range of facilities provided for the benefit, welfare and recreation of employees.
   Basic information about catering arrangements, health and safety rules, and what to do if there are any problems are most important.
5 That positive measures should be taken to facilitate the social adaptation of new employees (e.g. welcoming parties, notifications in house journals, introducing newcomers to significant others).
6 That the induction programme should be continuously monitored and its total effectiveness assessed.

The main responsibility for implementing, supervising and evaluating induction lies with the responsible line and HR managers. In fact, the induction phase should be regarded as the first stage in the process of staff development in which line and HR managers have complementary parts to play. The contents and methods of induction programmes will necessarily vary considerably in their details, but will need to include the following main elements in order to meet the prescribed objectives. In additional to a formal programme (off the job) there should be an induction check list, with a system for all the people involved to tick that they have completed their part – line manager, supervisor (if different from line manager), HR staff, security staff, IT staff, etc.

Interviews

Induction interviews need to be given to all employees taking up jobs for the first time, whether from inside or outside the organization. These interviews are carried out by the HR manager responsible for supervising the career of the newly appointed job holder, and, obviously, by the line manager. Coming as they do at a time when employees may well be feeling insecure and anxious about an unknown future, induction interviews are extremely important. They need to be carried out with particular care and skill because of the obvious importance to newcomers of making a good start in their new jobs. The three main purposes of the interviews are:

1 To provide all the necessary information that new job holders need about the job and its attendant circumstances.
2 To allow them to ask questions about any matters on which they are uncertain.
3 To give reassurance and to develop positive attitudes, confidence and motivation. Induction interviews should cover the following points:
  (a) The job description and person specification so that job holders fully understand what is required of them. A description of any software packages should be given and an opportunity to try out any office equipment with a friendly colleague (e.g. fax, e-mail, telephone, computer keyboard, printer) arranged.
  (b) How the job relates to the work and purposes of the group and the organization as a whole.
  (c) All the attendant circumstances of the job (e.g. pay, conditions, welfare, etc.).
  (d) The performance appraisal system and what part the job holder will be required to play.
  (e) An assessment of any training and developmental needs that require immediate action.
  (f) General plans for training and development.
  (g) The 'norms' or unwritten rules, if any, in the organization (e.g. 'Friday is always dress-down day', or 'we can only take private phone calls during the lunch break, unless it is an emergency').

In some organizations, the specific jobs to which new employees will be assigned are covered in the recruitment selection process. In others, this is left for individual departments, branches or sections to decide. In those situations, a placement interview will be needed in which the line or HR manager will discuss in detail with new employees the question of the jobs to which they should be allocated.

The next formal interview that is required in the induction programme will probably take place after about six months' employment, when managers assess progress to date, prospects for the future and any changes needed in existing arrangements. Apart from the formal interviews, informal discussions may take place between management representatives and new employees at any time, as required, to check progress or to deal with difficulties that may arise. It is especially important that the employees themselves should not feel inhibited in discussing any problems that they may encounter with their senior managers or responsible line or personnel managers.

The induction phase broadly comprises three elements – training, work experience and social adaptation, as described below.

Training

Induction training is mainly vocational and designed in order to give new employees the skills and knowledge required for productive employment. It may take the form of short full-time courses or very much longer programmes where a high level of performance is essential, such as, for example, during engineering apprenticeships, flying training, etc. Sometimes induction training is given on the job itself. More often than not the programme is a combination of both forms of training.

Work experience

This covers a very wide range of possibilities and is a matter for each organization to decide. Whether new employees remain with one occupation, or are rotated to meet particular requirements of experience, an imaginative approach is necessary to widen new employees' knowledge of their organizational environment as much as possible. This could include, for example, a schedule of visits or short attachments to other units. Increased knowledge of the organization will help to develop confidence and is a significant means of stimulating interest and motivation.

Social adaptation

As we have already seen, this is a particular source of difficulty in the induction phase. Managers cannot expect to control the subtle interplay of intragroup relationships, but they need to develop a psychological awareness of group and individual behaviour in order to assist their new staff to settle down. This requires a close knowledge of the individual members of their groups, the ability to anticipate where interpersonal difficulties could arise and how the social forces within the group could be used to advantage. In this way, the varied experience and strengths of the different members of the group may be used skilfully to help newcomers to adapt. The more members of the group that can be usefully involved in this process the better.

Finally, because of the complexity and variability of the initial phase of employment from the individual's point of view, employers cannot naïvely assume that a formally planned induction programme coincides with each individual employee's induction phase, as though the programme covers a fixed period at the end of which new employees cross, as it were, a boundary that separates the novitiate from full membership. The process of socialization is infinitely subtle and varies with each individual. Although new employees may often undertake parts of an induction programme together, such as, for example, formal courses, their induction into the organization still has to be regarded as an essentially individual process. Programmes, therefore, need to be very flexible and to take full account of individual differences and needs.

Figure 10.2 summarizes the main elements in an induction system.

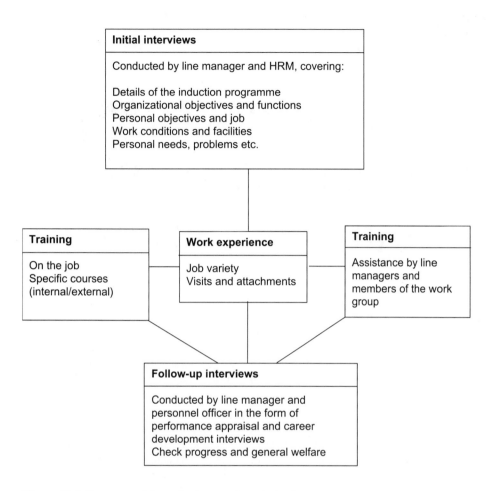

Figure 10.2 Summary of the main elements in an induction system

Questions

1 What is meant by the induction crisis?
2 What are its causes?
3 What steps can an organization take to mitigate the induction crisis?
4 What should be the aim and objectives of an induction programme?
5 What are the main elements that should be included in an induction programme? Give a brief description of all the items you would expect to find on an induction check list. Who should be responsible for each item?
6 What should an effective induction interview aim to achieve and cover?

Chapter 11

Assessing performance and managing careers

The fundamental importance of defining the criteria for the effective performance of work has already been stressed in Chapter 7. The assessment of performance, potential and rewards involves eliciting evidence of past and recent achievements and shortfalls to be related to the criteria as evidence and a basis for judgements and decisions. In this way, managers and HR staff are in a position to provide reasonably confident answers to important questions arising from assessments, for example:

- Are employees meeting the criteria for effective performance?
- If not, what action needs to be taken (e.g. training, further work experience, counselling, change of job, inefficiency or disciplinary procedures)?
- What does the evidence of assessment show in terms of potential for promotion and advancement?
- What does it show in terms of rewards that are merited?

The 'psychological contract' is the term used to describe the 'deal' between employer and employee, not the legal contract, but the bargain implicitly struck about what each party can expect from each other, and about the obligations each has to the other. The central features are the notions of 'exchange' and the reciprocity of a personal relationship. When we assess performance we enter into the debate about the bargain at an individual level – topics such as the promotion opportunities available and the challenges and developmental aspects of the work. Increasingly employers cannot offer careers, but can offer learning opportunities, which improve the employee's chances of employability, and they can sometimes offer flexibility in working arrangements. In return they may expect flexibility and commitment on the part of the employee.

The main requirements for effectiveness in systems of staff assessment are:

1 Purposes should be very carefully thought out, defined and published. They indicate organizational philosophy and determine the nature and details of the schemes used in practice, and of the way the psychological contract is acted out.

2 The purposes and details of appraisal schemes should be carefully explained to all newly appointed employees during induction interviews, following the discussion of their job descriptions and person specifications.

3 Formal arrangements, which are simple and not excessively bureaucratic, should be established for the effective implementation of appraisal schemes and to ensure uniformity in practice.

4 All staff involved in appraisal schemes should be given training in the requisite knowledge, skills and attitudes. Training should include purposes, details and requirements of schemes in use in the organization, the problems of assessment and means of mitigating these problems, the skills required for effective practice and practical exercises to illustrate what is required.

The assessment of work involves three types of review: performance appraisal, potential and reward reviews. These reviews are closely interrelated and linked by the main theme of assessment but they serve different purposes, require different methods and cannot all be undertaken by a sole manager. All three reviews have a major impact on the psychological contract. Assessing work performance of an employee in a particular job is clearly the responsibility of the line manager concerned. Reviewing potential has long-term implications. It needs to take into account all available information about performance over a period of time in a variety of jobs, and may require the use of specialist techniques and methods for the assessment of potential. Potential assessment has to be seen in an organizational context, related to organizational needs, objectives and opportunities. For these reasons it is a task for the HR staff, who, by definition, have an overall view of the organizational HR function. Reward reviews would normally be carried out by line management, but could well involve HR staff.

We can now discuss in detail these three aspects of the assessments of staff.

Performance appraisal

The development of performance appraisal in practice

Historically, performance appraisal in this country originated mainly in the public sector of employment – the armed forces and the Civil Service. Now, formal schemes of performance appraisal are widely used in the majority of work organizations in both public and private sectors. The details of these formal schemes vary considerably depending on the purposes and preferences of individual work organizations. These differences are reflected in terms of the format of reports, degrees of confidentiality and openness, who conducts the appraisal, the level of participation by those being appraised, and the nature of appraisal discussions between those appraising and those being appraised.

In the development of performance appraisal schemes, two broad approaches are discernible. For convenience of description and comparison we may label them as Theory X and Theory Y, after McGregor's thesis on managerial attitudes. The essential difference between the two is that in a Theory X scheme managers produce assessment reports on their subordinates but in a Theory Y scheme assessment reports are the product of joint discussion between managers and their subordinates. A Theory X performance appraisal scheme has the following typical features:

1 Managers are the sole judges of work performance.
2 There is an apparent confidence in the manager's ability and authority to judge and, therefore, no training is given to appraisers for this task.
3 Assessments are based on numerical ratings of abstract qualities, e.g. initiative, drive, energy, reliability, intelligence, loyalty, integrity, etc.
4 The appraisal includes a narrative report made by the manager, which is not divulged to the appraised subordinate and is open to personal bias, to misunderstandings of meanings and sometimes even to sarcasm.
5 There are no formal provisions for feedback to, or discussions with, those being appraised.
6 The main purpose of the appraisal is to identify those seen by management as good or bad performers.
7 There is little or no attention paid to the developmental needs of employees.

A Theory Y form of performance appraisal has objectives which are quite different from the Theory X approach, these being:

1 To identify and remedy problems in the job itself.
2 To identify strengths and weaknesses in performance as a basis for future action.
3 To identify needs for training, development, further work experience and suitability for advancement.
4 To develop constructive manager/subordinate relationships.
5 To develop individuals' capacity for self-assessment and self-awareness, for seeking ways to solve their own problems and to find ways for self-improvement.

The Theory X approach to performance appraisal in its extreme form, as described above, was prevalent in earlier times when styles of management were generally more authoritarian than they are now. In recent years there has been a visible move towards the Theory Y end of the continuum. Nevertheless, vestiges of a Theory X approach to performance appraisal still survive. In some organizations it remains very much in its traditional form. In others, whilst their schemes may reveal noticeable changes in the direction of a Theory Y approach, for example, more openness in discussion between managers and their subordinates, they still retain some of the essential features of Theory X attitudes. For example, in spite of the demonstrable and proven problems of defining and measuring abstract qualities, and the obvious advantages of concentrating on the objectives and tasks of the job, some managers are still required in some schemes to give marks for abstract traits (initiative, reliability, etc.). Again, although open discussions may be held between managers and their subordinates, these may in practice amount to little more than attempts by managers to justify their own views and marks, which have already been written into reports and are not likely to be affected by anything that appraised subordinates may say during discussions.

The main difference between these extremes is the limitations of the one and the opportunities afforded by the other. All the evidence of academic research and practical experience strongly emphasizes the advantages and potential effectiveness of performance appraisal schemes based on a Theory Y approach. We can now examine in more detail the general requirements for an effective scheme that applies this philosophy in practice.

The requirements of an effective system

The requirements described below are based on the premise that a Theory Y philosophy applied to performance appraisal is likely to produce the most effective system, because it emphasizes in particular the importance of helping individuals to improve their performance, to develop their abilities and to encourage their commitment.

1 The first step is to define the requirements for effective performance to provide the criteria without which sound and systematic judgements cannot be made.
2 Next, the purposes of the scheme should be defined and published as a basis for effective practice, e.g.:
    (a) To assess whether defined requirements and objectives of work are being met.
    (b) To identify strengths and weaknesses and to take any appropriate subsequent action.
    (c) To help employees to develop themselves by self-analysis, self-reliance and by finding solutions to their own problems.
    (d) To identify employees who are performing well or badly for purposes of retention, advancement, rewards, inefficiency or disciplinary procedures.
    (e) To develop and improve communication and relationships between managers and their staff.
3 The purposes and details of the appraisal scheme should form an important part of the induction interview between managers and new employees. Managers should adopt and explain the following measures to be taken in practice:
    (a) Performance appraisal is a continuous process involving a joint assessment by managers and individual members of staff. It should not be an annual ritual in which managers make confidential judgements about their employees.
    (b) Managers and their members of staff need to make regular notes about performance, e.g. successes, failures, reasons, suggestions for remedies, etc.
    (c) Managers and their members of staff should meet regularly for appraisals of performance so that any action needed is taken there and then. There is no point in delaying such necessary action until a formal annual performance takes place. For example, an identified training need requires immediate attention.
    (d) A periodic review should be held to conform to organizational policy and practice, to summarize the appraisal discussions that have regularly taken place and to plan for the future.
    (e) Before the periodic review takes place, managers, and members of staff who are being appraised, need to confirm the time, place and agenda for the review.
    (f) The details of the agenda will naturally vary with different situations, but the broad outlines for appraising performance by means of joint discussion between managers and their staff should cover the following headings and questions:
        (i) *The job*: the job description, objectives, component tasks, methods and resources. Are these satisfactory? If not, why not? What changes are indicated? What precise action is recommended by whom, and how and why?

(ii)   *Job performance*: what are the objectives that have to be met and the tasks to be fulfilled? Have these been achieved? What is the actual evidence from work performance, indicating success or failure? What are the reasons for success or failure? How far have any failures been within or outside the job holder's control? What does the evidence of past perform-ance show about strengths and weaknesses in the knowledge, skills and attitudes of the job holder? What precise action is recommended by whom, and how and when to build on strengths, to remedy weaknesses and to develop the individual by means of training and further work expe-rience?

(iii)   *Summary of action proposed*: what action has been agreed to be taken by whom, how and when?

4 Before the appraisal discussion takes place, the manager and individual member of staff separately work through these headings to answer the main questions, using any notes that they have made throughout the period under review. This exercise is the crux of the process and of the philosophy underlying this approach, because it emphasizes and concentrates on:

(a)   joint assessment, involving both managers and their staff

(b)   the key issues – the job, performance and future needs

(c)   observable, measurable evidence from actual work rather than abstract qualities.

5 Having made their separate notes and assessments, the manager and the individual meet to compare their views, to find out how far they agree or disagree, to explore reasons for any disagreement, to try to find constructive solutions and to decide what action is needed for the future to resolve problems in the job and to meet the indi-vidual's development needs.

6 The manager leads the discussion and is, therefore, responsible for seeing that it sys-tematically follows the agenda in order to achieve its purpose. At the same time, it is very important that it should be conducted in an atmosphere that is as informal and relaxed as possible. The manner in which the discussion is conducted is extremely important. The manager is 'in the chair', but if performance appraisal is intended to help to improve performance, to develop individuals and to improve communication, then the discussion needs to be an open two-way exchange of perceptions and not a managerial monologue. Thus, managers should try to find out how far perceptions coincide, where and how they differ and what any differences of views might imply. They need to stimulate people to think, to encourage them to analyse, to become more self-aware and to put forward constructive proposals. In practice, this requires managers to start by asking questions and listening. Having noted what those being appraised have to say, they are then better placed to make helpful comments, to give their own views and any advice or instructions that they think appropriate.

7 At the end of the discussion, the main points covered and the action agreed need to be summarized, recorded and, above all, followed up. These decisions will be the first items on the agenda of any subsequent appraisal discussions.

Behaviourally anchored rating scales

This method represents yet another example of the move away in recent decades from unprofitable attempts to assess abstract qualities and to focus attention on actual performance and behaviour, for example, considering not whether an employee shows initiative, but what he or she actually does that indicates 'initiative' or lack of it.

Scales and ratings are produced through discussion, observation and analysis (for example, critical incident technique) by managerial and HR staff. The first task in this process is to identify key categories of performance, that is, core competencies, as described in Chapter 7. Scales of behaviour, derived from actual experience of the job, are then produced for each category, ranging from definition of the most efficient to the least efficient behaviour and performance.

For example, a key category for a manager might be training and development of staff. The highest rating on the scale might be 'is totally committed to the training and development of staff and makes effective use of on-job and off-job methods'. The lowest rating might be 'does not understand the importance of training and development of staff and takes no action in this direction'.

According to those with experience of the production and use of behaviourally anchored rating scales (BARS) in practice, it is as yet a matter for debate whether the method represents a particularly significant advance in performance appraisal. The identification of comprehensive and detailed criteria, based on actual job requirements, is undoubtedly an important contribution to sound judgement. On the other hand, experience of the scheme indicates that the production of the categories and scales tends to be a time-consuming and expensive process, needing to be regularly reviewed as job descriptions change. As we have already emphasized, criteria are vitally important as the first stage in any judgemental process. But so is the task of producing valid evidence, and in any open joint system of appraisal this could sometimes result in unresolvable differences between the manager and the employee being appraised.

Forms of performance appraisal

If the recommendations for effective practice based on a Theory Y approach described above are put into practice, this will logically be reflected in the details of formats used for performance appraisal. Ideally, therefore, the format should:

1 Be based on the definition of criteria for effective performance, as described in the job description and person specification.
2 Require the need to produce evidence related to the criteria.
3 Require the need to produce judgements, based on a comparison of evidence and criteria, followed by recommendations for future action.
4 Require completion by managers and employees being appraised as a joint exercise.
5 Be simple, easy to understand and accompanied by explanatory notes based on organizational policy, purpose and required practice.
6 Be uniformly applied throughout the organization.

Problems of performance appraisal

Whatever scheme of performance appraisal is used, there will always be fundamental, inevitable problems. In essence, performance is a human judgement which, as we have already seen when considering personnel selection, suffers from problems of reliability and validity. Human judgement depends on the unique genetic and environmental influences that form each individual's values, attitudes, expectations and perceptions. Inevitably, therefore, there may be differences of view on each of the basic questions of performance appraisal, and this complicates the whole process from start to finish. Fundamental questions are:

- What does the job require?
- What does the job holder have to do to perform effectively?
- What evidence from work performance would indicate effective performance?
- What does the assessment of evidence of performance indicate about future actions required?

These questions are systematically interdependent. Each requires a judgement that affects the next question in the sequence. An approach that seeks to make use of a wider range of relevant opinions is 360-degree feedback.

360-degree feedback

There has been an increase in the use of 360-degree feedback processes in the assessment of people. The notion of 360-degree feedback is that employees benefit from feedback from those who are colleagues, customers, their manager and their subordinates from all 'directions': below, above and at the same level.

Feedback is designed to build confidence, to reinforce desired behaviours, clarify problems, improve self-awareness, give recognition and, ultimately, to improve performance.

The process usually follows a procedure whereby competencies having been established and defined, individuals are asked to nominate up to, say, six significant others whom they know within the categories (subordinate, colleagues, etc.) to whom feedback forms are sent asking for the respondent's opinion of the subject on the competency dimensions. The respondents may well use a rating scale.

For example, one large organization introduced eight main competencies, which were broken down into their component definitions, and rated by respondents in terms of the importance of the competencies to the job, and the individual's performance (effectiveness). Thus, for example, the competence 'making things happen', included 'establishing and maintaining contacts in all areas of the organization', 'balances day-to-day operations with important projects', 'encourages collaborative working' and seven more parts of the competence.

Each part is rated on the Performance scale and the Importance scale (see Figure 11.1), for example: 'Balances day-to-day operations with important projects.'

Averages of the data can be taken, and improvements over time can be plotted. The reports of all the respondents are usually grouped together for each individual, showing how respondents in general rated each competence. Taking these ratings, individuals are encouraged to share the data with their manager (but this is not mandatory) and to discuss what the feedback means. From the discussion, a personal development plan can be drawn up.

The HR Department usually runs the scheme, but the data is 'owned' by the individual in most 360-degree systems. This means confidentiality is preserved, although

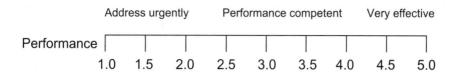

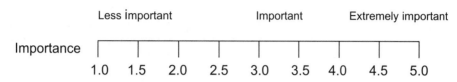

Figure 11.1 Example of performance scales

clearly there are sensitivities involved. Respondents are anonymous as far as the subject is concerned, and if the subject chooses to share the data with their manager or colleagues, it is usually their own decision.

The need for training

Because a system is only as good as the people who operate it, managerial staff at all levels need training in performance appraisal to make it effective in practice.

The objectives of training should be:

1 To standardize practice.
2 To explain the organization's system and give opportunities for staff to discuss and question.
3 To identify general requirements for effective practice.
4 To provide practice in the important skills, such as giving and receiving feedback, assessing and discussing performance.

Details of potentially effective training exercises are outside the scope of this chapter. However, they should simulate reality as closely as possible in the following ways by requiring trainee managers:

1 To make assessments of real, but unidentified, job holders, so that the discipline of the appraiser's approach may be analysed, i.e. defining criteria for effective performance, making sound and fair conclusions.
2 To carry out role-play discussions, based on credible scripts, in order to practise the general performance appraisal agenda described earlier and the necessary skills.

The learning opportunities provided by simulated role-play exercises will be significantly enhanced by the use of video recordings for purposes of analysis and discussion.

The assessment of potential

In practice, the review of potential serves two main purposes: the identification of those who appear to be suitable for promotion, and the assessment of the general potential of individuals in order to decide how their abilities may best be employed in the interests of the organization and of the individuals themselves.

One way in which organizations can bring together the parties interested in potential and career management, is through career development panels. In such a system, the data on high potentials is gathered (usually via the appraisal process) and is fed into the HR department, who prepare the papers for a panel of senior managers with accountability for staffing key roles in the organization. The panel then makes decisions based upon the development needs of individuals, the opportunities available and the needs of the business.

Such systems often operate internationally, with country managers submitting data to the head office HR function. In this way the 'cream rises to the top' and the high potentials from around the world can become known to senior management. In 3M this was known as the 'Consensus Review Process', in AT&T, 'HR planning and development'. Such schemes may be operated in conjunction with career workshops, personal development guides and succession planning. Organizations such as Kodak, 3M, BP Exploration, Amoco and many others conduct such schemes, often with innovative approaches and tools to help individuals take responsibility for their own careers. The degree of centralization or devolvement to business units and to individuals for career planning varies. Sometimes, as with Kodak career services, there was a support service to individuals with personal career plans and workshop software to help people make decisions, to understand what they can do and what is available.

Identifying staff for promotion

The selection of staff for promotion is, in essence, the same process as the selection of new employees. Everything that has already been said about the problems of selecting new employees, the limitations of predictive methods and especially the interview, apply equally here and need not be repeated in detail. A job vacancy has to be filled and there is usually a field of several candidates. The requirements and criteria for effective performance at the higher level need to be defined in exactly the same way as for recruitment selection: the task and problem of the selectors is to predict likely behaviour in a new job situation.

However, there are some significant differences between recruitment and promotion situations. In the former situation the employing organization is dealing with unknown people. When selecting staff for promotion, it already has a store of information both formal and informal about candidates. Furthermore, there are important areas in which prediction is not necessary, namely, compatibility with the organizational culture and relationships with colleagues. Nevertheless, examples regularly occur of employees who are very effective at one level, but prove to be far less successful at a higher level, as if to confirm the well-known Peter principle that people eventually find their own level of competence/incompetence. Such promotional failures seem to be rather more frequent in situations where a capable specialist transfers to what is essentially a managerial job. For example, medical staff or scientists who take over managerial roles or scientific projects, or sales representatives who are promoted into management, or in educational and academic posts, where appointing authorities seem to be prone to converting able teachers into incompetent heads of departments, because apparently they fail to understand that managerial skills are just as important in these posts as professional knowledge and ability.

The methods adopted by organizations for the promotion of staff vary considerably. In some cases, promotions may be made virtually by the unilateral decision of heads of companies or departments on the basis of demonstrated work competence. This method is more likely to occur in a business enterprise. In the public sector of employment and in a number of large industrial and commercial concerns there are formal procedures for selecting candidates for promotion. Since most of these also have a system of formal periodic staff reports, these are used as the basis for decisions about promotion. They provide a total picture derived from a series of reports on performance in a variety of jobs and situations by a range of managers. Since staff reports also suffer from the same difficulties of subjectivity as the selection procedures themselves, the problem is in fact compounded, hence the importance of ensuring that the system of staff reporting is as sound as it can possibly be.

Assessing general potential

The essence of this task is to assess the types and levels of work that employees have the potential to perform. This assessment has to be based on the evidence available from personnel records, staff reports, performance reviews, training and education records, which are centrally maintained and co-ordinated by the HR staff. These records cover a period of several years and extend beyond the confines of the present job. Since the assessment of the general potential of employees is set in the wider organizational context, it is a task that is especially appropriate to the HR managers responsible for supervising the career paths of individual employees. In some organizations, the review is carried out jointly by the responsible HR and line managers. This method is not only feasible, but could also be seen as a logical and sensible method. However, much depends upon the nature and culture of the organization.

Attention has already been drawn to the responsibilities of individuals for self-development, but people cannot take a detached view of their own potential. They may easily overestimate or underestimate their own capabilities. Personal interests, past conditioning or narrowness of experience may also play a part in restricting individuals' capacities to assess their own potential. Nevertheless, it is very important that individual employees be fully consulted in any review of their potential in order to help them see themselves as the organization sees them, to enable them to put forward their own views and wishes, and to develop their commitment to any plans for their future employment. This can be achieved by means of a schedule of career-development interviews, in which personnel staff use the history of past assessments and the career record to date as a basis for joint consultation with employees about their potential and the opportunities for employment and development that are or may become available.

One popular idea comes from Ed Schein of the Massachusetts Institute of Technology. He developed the notion of career anchors. A career anchor is 'a combination of perceived area of competence, motives, and values that you would not give up, to represent your real self' (Schein, 1993: 1). He identified eight different career anchors: 'Technical/Functional Competence', 'General Management Competence', 'Autonomy/Independence', 'Security/Stability', 'Pure Challenge' and 'Lifestyle'. The 'Pure Challenge' career anchor is one when the intellectual challenge is the motivating force, such as for some engineers and consultants. The 'Lifestyle' career anchor is concerned with balancing family needs, work needs and personal needs, in an integrated way. Career anchors are one way of describing the values people have about work, and provide a starting point for a career discussion.

The potential review/career-development interview

This interview is very similar to the performance-appraisal interview in terms of the basic framework and general approach that are appropriate to the situation. The three phases of the interview should be planned and conducted in the following way.

Pre-interview preparation

1 As with the performance appraisal, members of staff to be interviewed need to prepare themselves by considering their personal career objectives and by analysing their own strengths and weaknesses, training and educational needs and employment preferences.
2 HR managers conducting the interviews need to study the relevant personnel records, i.e. career histories, staff reports, performance-appraisal summaries and training records. They will usually need to consult responsible line managers to ascertain whether any changes have occurred since the last report and generally to amplify information about current performance and potential.
3 Finally, they will need to determine the specific objectives to be achieved in each particular situation.

The interview

1 The interview should be based on the following broad plan:
   (a) Explanation of the general purpose and scope of the interview.
   (b) Discussion of the individual's career to date in terms of perceived strengths and weaknesses, likes and dislikes, employment preferences (e.g. 'career anchors'). Data from 'life line' or other such exercises may be helpful.
   (c) Discussion of the future in terms of the potential revealed by past performance, the opportunities that the organization is able to provide and the individual's needs for training and education.
   (d) Summary of agreements about action required.
2 Like the performance appraisal, this is essentially a problem-solving, counselling situation, and the prerequisites for its successful conduct are basically the same. However, there are some special aspects of this interview which are worth stressing:
   (a) Because of the fundamental problems associated with the egocentricity of human perception and individuals' natural pursuit of personal objectives, the essential task of the career or HR staff in this review is not only to assess

potential, but also to help to reconcile organizational and individual perspectives.

(b)   Therefore, because a joint commitment and agreement between employer and employee is necessary for success, the general purpose to be pursued by HR staff in this kind of review is to help individuals in the following ways: to make as realistic an assessment as possible of themselves and their own potential; to adopt realistic expectations of what is achievable and available; to understand that, whilst the organization has a duty and a vested interest to provide all possible opportunities for growth, individuals must accept responsibility for personal development.

Post-interview action

Immediately after the interview, managers should produce a brief summarized report of the interview, the main points of discussion and agreements reached, for retention in the personnel records, and liaise with line managers.

Assessment centres

We discussed assessment centres in Chapter 8. However, assessment centres are also used for promotion and development purposes.

In recent times, increasing use has been made of assessment centres for assessing the potential of candidates for employment and that of existing employees. The earliest example of the assessment centre was the WOSB, which provided the basic model for the assessment centres in current use for the assessment of potential. They are used mainly for identifying staff, especially managers, who show potential for advancement to senior positions. These centres may be established internally by the organization, or they may be external, offering an assessment service to all organizations that wish to send staff for testing. Internal organizational centres will normally be staffed by senior managers of the organization, trained in the methods of the centre, and by occupational psychologists. External organizations will often be staffed by occupational psychologists.

The problems of predicting future behaviour at work have already been discussed in the chapter dealing with selection procedures. The main advantage of assessment centres lies in the opportunity to give candidates a chance of demonstrating skills that they may not yet have had a chance to exhibit in their work. Because they are run by trained specialists, the predictions produced are likely to be considerably more reliable and valid than those of untrained managers and a further benefit comes from training managers to make valid assessments. A possible disadvantage is cost. The costs of establishing a 'centre' include the research and development necessary into the behaviours of successful applicants, and devising and validating tests that will predict those behaviours. Only very large companies could afford the expense of setting up their own centres. In any case, organizations have to make a cost-benefit analysis. They have to ask whether the results justify the outlay. In view of the costs of promoting staff to senior posts, who later prove to be incompetent, it may well be worth while investing in predictions, which could avoid serious managerial problems in future years.

On the basis of the model already described for making systematic judgements, the first task of the assessment centre is to define the required competencies. For example, a process for assessing managerial potential might be based on the following criteria:

1 *Personal attributes*: self-confidence; emotional stability; tolerance of stress; breadth of vision; flexibility and adaptability; sociability and co-operativeness; sense of humour; tolerance and patience; balanced views; impact of personality; moral courage; ability and readiness to learn.
2 *Competence in practice*: analytical and reasoning powers; problem-solving and decision-making skills; identification of priorities; planning and organizing abilities; team membership skills; leadership and communication skills.

The methods commonly used to test and reveal these attributes and competencies are:

- psychometric tests of intelligence, aptitude and personality
- group situational tests involving problem-solving and decision-making exercises
- leadership and team membership role-play exercises
- presentations to group members
- individual written and oral problem exercises
- outdoor exercises to test mental, emotional and physical characteristics.

Assessing rewards

As the term suggests, the reward review is the process whereby managers have to decide who deserves increments, bonuses and other tangible incentives based on individual performance. It is a potentially uncomfortable and contentious situation because inevitably there will be winners and losers and the potential exists for charges of unfair treatment. These problems are always likely to occur, however sound the scheme may be, but it is obviously vitally important to give thought in preparation and practice to ensure that any scheme for reward review is as fair and efficient as it can be. Although in the main the same basic information is used as for the appraisal of performance, all informed opinion on the subject says that appraisal of performance and reward reviews should be separate processes and not combined into one review. If they were combined, the purposes of the appraisal of performance for development purposes could well become confused by considerations of assessing performance in financial terms.

A summary of the main elements of a staff assessment system are shown in Figure 11.2.

Questions

1 What are the main purposes of assessing staff?
2 (a) What is performance appraisal? (b) What fundamental problems does it involve? (c) How may they be mitigated? (d) What are the characteristics of 'Theory X' and 'Theory Y' approaches to performance appraisal?
3 What is 360-degree feedback? What are the potential benefits and difficulties of this approach?

4 How may potential be assessed?

5 What is an assessment centre? What does it do?

6 How can effective performance management be introduced as a system into an organization?

7 Comment on the approach to appraisal and performance management revealed by the Standard Life 'contribution management' system in the following case study.

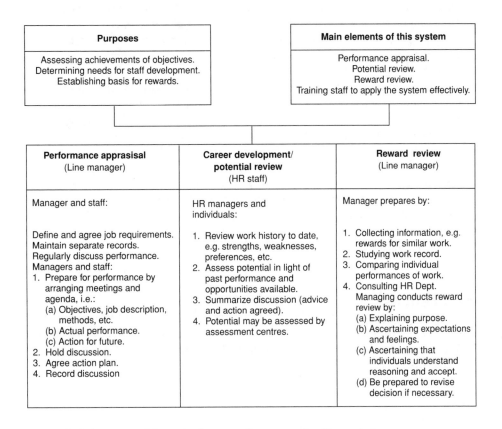

Figure 11.2 Summary of the main elements of a system of staff appraisal

Case study: Standard Life

The concept of 'contribution management' has been introduced as a method for ensuring continuous improvement. The contribution system is linked into job competencies for each person's job through the contribution plan.

The contribution plan is a mechanism for identifying how each individual can contribute to the organization's objectives. The Contribution Management Project was initiated by the Personnel Division in order to create a more flexible work force, focused to produce results and to encourage staff to learn new skills/behaviours, which were needed to implement the total customer satisfaction approach. The contribution system focuses on feedback and development, and on the key competencies – customer focus, preference for action, teamwork, and business knowledge, leadership, people development, openness to ideas, contribution to results, and strategic thinking, against which to assess performance at quarter yearly reviews.

The system operates through a combination of results (or outputs) and the extent to which the employee has learned and demonstrated key competencies. A contribution plan is produced from a 'planning partnership' between the manager and employee around what is expected on the one hand, and what the employee thinks he or she can deliver – the plan results in a record of the team purpose, planning of forecast outputs and performance indicators, and a plan of development activities based on competencies and career aspirations. Outputs are defined and must be specific.

Support from management can be expected in the process by taking an active role in producing the plan, tracking progress, preparing for review meetings, providing coaching and support, and giving and receiving feedback. The employee is expected to take an active part in the process, to show commitment to learning, preparedness to change and receptiveness to new ideas. There are support instruments (for example, Horizon, a PC disk-based self-assessment tool), open access development centres, a company learning directory, secondments both inside and outside the company, and internal vacancy bulletins. Training is given in the process for the staff and management.

Source: Adamson, Doherty and Tyson (1997).

References

Adamson, S., Doherty, N., and Tyson, S. (1997). *Standards of Excellence in the Management of Human Resources*. Human Resource Research Centre. Cranfield University.

Schein, E. H. (1993). *Career Anchors*. Pfeiffer.

Chapter 12

Training and development

Definition: the foundation for effective practice

Helping employees to become effective in their jobs is one of the most fundamentally important tasks in people management that any work organization has to undertake. Employers depend on the quality of their employees' performance to achieve organizational aims and objectives; employees have motivational needs for development, recognition, status and achievement that can and should be met through job satisfaction.

The initiative for providing this help must come mainly from the employers. The vocabulary to describe this kind of help in the context of work includes terms such as training, development, education and, more recently, human resource development. Attempts are made by some authors to separate these terms by differential definitions. For example, 'training aims to achieve short-term specific organization objectives', 'education is directed towards the long-term development of individuals'. Definitions of this kind oversimplify a very complicated process. What, for example, is to be said about the universally accepted term 'teacher training'? This process is certainly not concerned with short-term objectives and certainly includes educational and developmental purposes. As the common denominator of all of these terms is learning, it is better to see training as a learning process, as defined below, rather than to engage in debates about semantic differences.

There is no adequate, all-embracing term to describe this process, although 'work-directed learning' comes close to our view. In the meantime, the word 'training' will be used throughout in discussing the process in the widest possible context, starting with the following comprehensive definition as a foundation for effective practice.

> Training in a work organization is essentially a learning process, in which learning opportunities are purposefully structured by the managerial, HR and training staffs, working in collaboration, or by external agents acting on their behalf. The aim of the process is to develop in the organization's employees the knowledge, skills and attitudes that have been defined as necessary for the effective performance of their work and hence for the achievement of the organizational aims and objectives by the most cost-effective means available.

The importance of using a comprehensive definition as a basis for practice is that it focuses attention on the main aim of training, that is, effective performance, and leads logically to certain important conclusions and questions arising from the definition that determine the degree of effectiveness in practice:

1 Training is always a means to an end and not an end in itself. Unless it leads to the effective performance of work it inevitably incurs a waste of valuable resources.
2 Precise definition of the requirements for effective performance in terms of knowledge, skills and attitudes by means of job analysis is of fundamental importance.
3 Because it is directed towards effective performance of work, it must be seen as an integral and vital part of the whole work system. Training is not, for example, an extraneous activity for which training staffs are largely responsible.
4 Since managers are responsible for the effective performance of work to achieve the organizational aims and objectives, they logically must have the responsibility for ensuring that employees are effectively trained for this purpose. Management must take the initiative in setting up, resourcing and monitoring the effectiveness of the training system and its provision in practice.
5 Whilst management bears the main responsibility, all staff in the organization are involved in the training task. Effective practice requires the collaboration of managerial, HR and training staffs.
6 The purpose of training may be achieved by a variety of means, e.g. by planned work experience in a series of different jobs, by planned experience within one job, by formal training at the workplace or at training centres. The sole criterion for choice of method is whatever is most likely to achieve the training aim.
7 The development of an organization's human resources applies to all its employees from the most senior to the most junior. When training is defined in traditional narrow terms, it tends to be directed towards junior and middle grades of employees. But all employees are likely to need training of some kind throughout their working lives. It surely could not be assumed that senior staff, on whom so much depends, have no need for further learning – especially in view of the demands of economic, social and technological changes in the present times.
8 Because of the vital contribution that training makes to the development of human resources and the achievement of organizations' aims and objectives, all those responsible for training in any shape or form must themselves be trained for the task, e.g. full- and part-time trainers, managers and instructors, as well as first-line supervisors.

Cost-effective training: a systems approach

In a nutshell, cost-effective training means training that actually achieves the purpose of helping people to perform their work to the required standards and is at the same time affordable, that is, not unnecessarily lavish, when simpler, less expensive forms would equally well achieve the aim.

How is cost-effective training to be achieved? It is achieved by applying basic principles for cost-effective management to the specific situation of training, assuming that effective systems of job analysis and performance appraisal have been established so that performance criteria are defined and assessable. The steps are as follows:

1 Identify training needs – who needs training and what do they need to learn?
2 Taking account of learning theory (how people learn); design and provide training to meet identified needs.
3 Assess whether training has achieved its aim in terms of subsequent work performance.
4 Make any necessary amendments to any of the previous stages in order to remedy or improve future practice.

This process is commonly known as the systems approach to training (SAT). It has been successfully applied for many years by many organizations in the public and private sectors as one main way of achieving cost-effective training.

A more educational approach to long-term development is another model, which stresses the development of basic skills, techniques and self-development as a basis for developing adaptability in employees. An 'action learning' approach is also possible. But all these have some notion of systematically determining what development is needed.

The SAT is so called because it is a series of interdependent systems, functionally linked together and integrated into the whole work system. The interdependence of the stages is crucial, since the malfunction or neglect of any one of them inevitably affects the others and the total system. Thus, if job analysis has not defined the criteria for effective performance, training needs cannot be identified by performance appraisal. If needs have not been properly identified, it is not possible to design and provide needs-related training, or to assess ultimate effectiveness in terms of subsequent work performance.

We shall examine the various stages of the SAT in detail later in the chapter.

Identifying training needs

An analysis of training needs is an essential prerequisite to the design and provision of effective training. This is the first main stage in the problem-solving process that characterizes the SAT, that is, the diagnosis that systematically precedes prescription. In simple terms, the purpose of this diagnosis is to determine whether there is a gap between what is required for effective performance and present levels of performance. If any deficiencies are revealed, the causes and remedies may be various, and training is only one of a number of possible solutions.

Training needs arise at three levels – organizational, group and individual levels. They are interdependent because the corporate performance of an organization ultimately depends on the performance of its individual employees and its subgroups.

The corporate needs of the organization and its groups may be identified in the following ways:

1 *The evidence of human resource planning*: this provides information about the demand and supply of human resources and the possible implications for training

needs. Thus, a forecast of a possible difficulty in recruiting people with required entry levels in knowledge and skills could affect recruitment and training policy, compelling the organization to recruit at lower levels and then to provide compensatory training to fill the performance gap.

2   *The introduction of new methods*: whenever new methods of work, e.g. computers, are introduced, this changes the requirements for effective performance, creates a performance gap in knowledge and skills (and with new technology, in attitudes also, perhaps), and hence a training need.

3   *Collective evidence from performance appraisal and formal methods for needs assessment*: information emerging from the performance appraisal of individual employees or from formal methods such as meetings, interviews or questionnaires, in which line managers, HR and training staffs and individual employees are involved, may reveal needs for training that are common throughout the organization or to groups of employees.

This systematically acquired information is an essential basis for seeing what centrally provided training is really needed. Without this information it is very easy for central trainers to provide training on the basis of unsubstantiated views and personal preferences.

Accurately diagnosing the specific training needs for individuals requires the following system:

1   Job analysis to determine:
   (a)   the objectives and component tasks of the job
   (b)   the knowledge, skills and attitudes required for the effective performance of these tasks.
2   Assessment of the performance gap by line managers and individuals, based on a comparison of the required levels with present levels.
3   Specification of training needs indicated by this comparison.
4   Specification of the forms of training needed to satisfy the identified needs.

The joint participation of line managers and their individual members of staff to assess training needs is very important. It is more likely to produce a comprehensive and systematic analysis, and commitment on the part of the individual. It is also an opportunity to encourage individuals to assess their own needs and possible solutions as a part of their development.

It requires time and conscientious effort to make a thorough analysis of jobs and their specific requirements and then to set up formal arrangements for assessing needs, but there is no other basis for designing and providing the training that is really needed. Specific training needs for individuals may arise at any time during their working careers. However, there are particular occasions when a formal assessment is needed, based on the system described above, that is:

1   *Starting employment*: new employees will invariably need some kind of training to fill the gap between their present levels of knowledge and skills and those needed for effective performance of work.
2   *Appraising performance*: in performance appraisal recent performance is compared

with required levels. The comparison regularly reveals deficiencies and needs, which have to be remedied by training.

3 *Changing jobs*: people changing jobs are in a similar situation to those starting employment. The requirements for the new job may well create a performance gap that needs to be filled by training.

Apart from the specific needs described above, individuals have continuing general needs for training in the broad developmental sense. They need to develop their experience within particular appointments. This is the responsibility of line managers, who must determine these needs by careful observation of performance and regular discussions with their staff, and provide the necessary opportunities by informal methods such as delegation, job rotation, etc. People also need the wider experience that comes with a variety of jobs. It is the responsibility of these HR managers, in their career development role, to ascertain these developmental needs and to meet them by career planning as far as operational demands will permit.

The learning organization

In recent years the degree of change in organizations has encouraged the view that organizational change through continuous learning is necessary for organizations to survive. This is well expressed in Peter Senge's (1990) book, *The Fifth Discipline*, in which he suggests that learning organizations are those that know how to make use of five 'component technologies', these being:

1 *Systems thinking*: the notion developed in this book of a systemic approach to learning, seeing the whole as well as the relationships between the parts of the system.
2 *Personal mastery*: 'continuously clarifying and deepening our personal vision' using our energy to develop ourselves.
3 *Mental models*: challenging the stereotypes and mental maps that managers carry around with them.
4 *Building shared vision*: leadership through communicating vision and values.
5 *Team learning*: encouraging team members to think together, through dialogue, using teams as the main learning unit.

Management development is frequently one plank in the change platform, and the notion of continuous development, aimed especially at improving employees through personal development, has gained ground. The two classic management development strategies for dealing with discontinuous, unpredictable change are personal development and action learning. Management development strategies are therefore now integral to change strategies, the argument being that the pace of change is so rapid that employees need to be highly adaptive, intelligent and educated so that they will know how to learn and will be prepared to go through retraining or re-educational programmes many times in their working lives. This is also consistent, when applied as a principle throughout the organization, with the notion of empowerment – devolving responsibility to work teams and to individuals.

Learning theory

There is an argument that instead of emphasizing training, in HR, we should emphasize learning. The move towards action learning approaches is one sign of this.

Since training is essentially a learning process, all those who are in any way involved in training need to have an understanding of learning. Because learning is a continuous human activity, it has always occupied an important position in psychological studies. The main questions to be discussed are what learning is and how people learn. There is a general consensus about the first question, but much more debate about the second.

Learning may be defined as a more or less permanent change in behaviour, which occurs as a result of the influence of external, environmental stimuli on the inherent, genetic disposition of the individual. In the context of training it is useful to consider learning and behavioural change in terms of knowledge, skills and attitudes needed for effective performance. In formal learning situations this change is demonstrated and assessed by examinations or tests. In everyday life it is ascertained by observable changes in behaviour patterns, for example, an employee without commitment demonstrating through behaviour that he or she is now hard-working and conscientious. Since training is directed towards the effective performance of work, ultimately this is the point where learning or behavioural change really matters and needs to be demonstrated. There is no point in such changes being shown at the end of a training course if they are not transferred into observable changes in practice in real work.

How people learn has been the subject of continuing discussion and some controversy for many decades. Much of the evidence leads to the conclusion that mostly we learn from experience. Kolb's (1974) learning cycle (Figure 12.1) suggests a cyclical process of continuous learning.

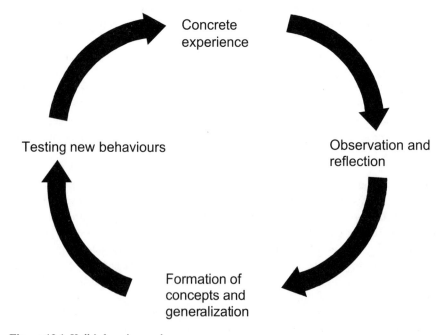

Figure 12.1 Kolb's learning cycle

Figure 12.1 demonstrates the role of experience in learning where we generalize from our experience, and experiment with new ideas, as a consequence of what we have learned, taking into account the feedback we have received from significant others. The challenge for development processes is to find ways of creating learning environments where new behaviours can be tested, and where there is assistance with observation and reflection, to facilitate the learning process.

From the theories, it is possible to distil some basic, simple, general truths about learning which are fundamentally important to those responsible for the design and provision of training, which we can summarize as follows:

1 People must be motivated to learn. They must see a beneficial outcome for themselves. They must see how training could help them to perform their work effectively. They must see a personal need for this to happen and to accept the methods chosen to achieve the training objectives.
2 Feedback is important to motivational and learning progress. People need to have feedback on their learning achievement.
3 Because learning depends on motivation, it is essentially an individual process. People will learn, if they want to, in their own preferred ways and at their own pace, depending on a variety of genetic and environmental factors and on age.
4 People learn from experience, therefore from example and by imitation. As a consequence, they may demonstrate behaviour that could be regarded as socially unacceptable or not conducive to the effective performance of work. In other words, people may easily acquire bad habits and practices and regard these as good.
5 Learning can only take place through the human senses. All senses may contribute to the learning process, but the visual is the most powerful and, to a lesser degree, the auditory.

What implications does the individual orientation of the learning process have for trainers?

1 Training is a learner- and not a trainer-orientated process.
2 The trainer is essentially a catalyst in the learning process. As Galileo is reputed to have said, 'You cannot teach people anything. You can only help them to learn'.
3 In the practice of training, trainers need, therefore, to:
   (a) Show why people need to learn certain things, how it will help them, how their learning fits into a total picture and the relationship of parts to a whole (e.g. the rationale of a whole training programme and of a single subject in a course).
   (b) Make training as experiential and active as possible, i.e. using real work as the learning medium, or methods that relate to real work as closely as possible.
   (c) See that people learn from good examples and practice as far as possible.
   (d) Use an imaginative approach, involving interesting, varied and stimulating methods for learning, supported by helpful audio-visual and similar aids.
   (e) Be interesting and stimulating themselves through their own presentational skills.
   (f) Structure learning so that people have regular assessments of their performance and achievement. Although tests are an obvious means of providing feedback, it can be given informally by the skilful choice of participative, active methods,

video recordings, of the exercise, with feedback for the participants, for example.

The design and provision of needs-related training

This question is the second stage of the problem-solving process. The first stage was diagnostic, that is, to determine what the needs are. The second stage is prescriptive, that is, to decide what action is most likely to meet the identified needs. This requires generating and analysing a range of options in the light of objectives to be achieved and the economic use of available resources. As we have already seen, options available to meet the requirements of work, that is, to fill the performance gap, could well cover a wide range, and training is only one of these possibilities. When training is, in fact, the selected option, the same problem-solving principle applies – the next step is to determine in detail what form of training is most likely to meet identified requirements cost-effectively. In the light of a broad interpretation of training, the range of possible options is wide. Making these choices raises questions such as who should provide training, of what kind, where and by what methods. The answers to all of these questions will be determined by training objectives.

Training objectives

Producing clear objectives is crucially important to the design and provision of cost-effective training. In general, sound objectives should specify what learning trainees should be able to demonstrate by the end of training. If objectives do not provide this criterion, how can trainers and the trainees themselves assess whether the required learning has been achieved or not?

Training objectives should meet the following criteria. Objectives should be:

1 Expressed in learner-oriented terms, e.g. 'By the end of the programme trainees should be able to demonstrate specified knowledge and skills'.
2 As specific as possible about terminal performance, standards required and attendant conditions, e.g. 'By the end of training, the manager will be able to use the computer to prepare spread sheets to create a project plan showing all the main stages in the plan accurately.
3 As measurable as possible and capable of achievement in the time allowed for training.
4 Expressed in language that clearly states what the trainees have to do.

Training objectives that fail to meet these criteria are still regularly seen in published training programmes. For example, an objective for a management training course might be expressed in something like these terms: 'To familiarize students with the principles of effective management.' In no way could any objective such as this be used as a criterion for measuring learning achievement. If the objective had said 'By the end of the programme students should be able to define the principles of effective management and support their answers with real examples drawn from practice and personal experience', the refined assessment of learning is then possible.

In fairness, it has to be said that it is much easier to produce objectives that enable learning achievement to be confidently assessed for some training subjects than it is for others. It is a relatively straightforward task to define objectives in measurable terms for specific activities such as computing skills, driving, flying, playing instruments, carpentry, plumbing, cooking, etc. It is much more difficult with a subject such as management. The task is simpler for specific managerial activities such as chairing meetings, interviewing, etc. Here the criteria for effective performance can be reflected in the training objectives and used to measure learning achievement. The solution to more abstruse topics is therefore to break the topic down into subordinates objectives, parts of the topic, and to measure these.

Once training objectives have been defined, it is possible to address the next stage in the process and to consider questions such as: who will provide the training? What form will it take? What will be the contents? Where will it be held? What methods will be used?

Training designers and providers

The theory that training should be viewed as an integral part of work, requiring the involvement and collaboration of all employees, leads to the logical conclusion that training concerns all the staff of an organization. Organizational staff may be involved in providing training in a variety of ways, for example, managers or their deputies, who provide or supervise on-job training, coaching or open and distance methods at the workplace, or management development advisers, who give formal training at training centres or assist line managers in the design, provision and supervision of training at the workplace.

It is generally claimed that full-time training or teaching requires particular qualifications, especially in communication skills. This is undoubtedly true, but it also needs to be said that essentially there is no significant difference between the requirements for effectiveness in managers and in trainers. Both require the ability to identify, pursue and achieve work-related objectives, to manage human and material resources and time, to show qualities of leadership, interpersonal, communicational skills and presentational skills. The fundamental requirements are the same. The particular techniques can be learned by trainer-training and experience.

Very considerable benefits may be gained from a policy of exchanging staff between operational and training duties. A few years spent by managers during their careers in full-time training duties could provide invaluable experience and opportunities and develop their skills. In this way, they may return to managerial work the better for the experience and committed to the importance of training for the effective performance of work.

Traditionally, the training of trainers has been directed almost exclusively to permanent training staff. But if the need for employing managers, HR managers and other staff in training roles is accepted and practised, then clearly they too should be trained for these tasks and given some basic training in the principles and practice of the SAT, in the use of various learning methods and in instructional and presentational skills.

How can the integrated work and training systems be effective, unless all concerned share the same philosophy, speak the same language and apply the same principles in practice?

Training methods and locations

Training methods and locations can be discussed under three broad headings, i.e. training at the workplace, training at organizational or external centres (off-job training) and a combination of training at the workplace and training centres. The choice will be determined by whatever is assessed as most likely to achieve the objectives of training and work by the most cost-effective means.

Training at the workplace

Training at the workplace may take a variety of forms. In its very broadest sense it may be identified with career development and the acquisition of required knowledge, skills and attitudes from the continuous experience and opportunities provided by work itself. Here, the HR department has the key role in the supervision and direction of career paths to enable employees to widen their horizons and to develop their capabilities to assume wider responsibilities for the future. Line managers also obviously have the main responsibility for training their own staff at the workplace. They may do this in the course of normal work by delegation, job rotation, attachments and visits to related work units, placing individuals under the tutelage of selected, experienced employees or by the use of formal workplace methods such as coaching, open and distance learning. In recent times, as a result of the ever-increasing emphasis on cost-effectiveness, there has been a noticeable tendency for much of the training that was formerly given at training centres to be now carried out at the workplace. This shift applies particularly to training related to individual proficiency, i.e. what is sometimes described as trade or vocational training. It has been stimulated by developments in open and distance methods, often based on computer and video technology It has also led to a change of emphasis in the central trainers' role. Nowadays they are tending to be increasingly employed as consultants to local managers in the design and provision of training at the workplace and less in their traditional presentational and instructional roles. The cost-effectiveness of this approach has already been demonstrated by a number of organizations in terms of saving the very high costs of central training and in improved performance.

Off-job training

Most people are familiar with formal methods of training centres and many organizations use centres or hire hotel and conference accommodation for central events. Here the training is conducted by full-time staff, assisted as necessary by occasional lecturers and tutors. Trainers usually work in groups, and the methods commonly employed are lectures, discussion groups, case studies, simulation, computer based training, role-play and exercises of various kinds, supported by video, closed-circuit television (CCTV), PowerPoint projections and other audio-visual aids. Training usually covers subjects where needs are identified that are common to groups of employees of similar grades or jobs. The choice of methods and locations must be determined by the criterion of cost-effectiveness.

Whilst centrally based training is costly and requires people to leave their places of work, it is necessary and essential for some forms of training, especially in managerial and related subjects. Here people need to work in groups and to learn from each other in a residential setting. Just as line managers need the assistance of central trainers to plan local programmes, so the central trainers must design central training in collaboration with line managers to ensure that it provides what they and their staffs need for effective performance of work.

Combining workplace and central methods

The drive for cost-effectiveness, the widespread use of the systems approach and technological developments in computers, television and video films have added a new dimension to the design and provision of training. The combination of workplace and central methods of training, broadly speaking, takes two forms: a series of modules; and open and distance learning methods.

The use of a series of modules has proved to be a very effective means of providing training for complete subjects such as management, training of trainers, etc. Instead of cramming training into a few weeks, the subject is broken down into component subjects. Thus, a course on management might comprise the following modules: basic principles of effective management; problem-solving and decision-making; time management; human aspects of management; interpersonal skills of management; financial management; summary. Assignments at the workplace would be supervised by the managers of the trainees or by a suitable experienced deputy.

Open and distance methods of learning are familiar to most people through correspondence courses and the Open University. Learning material consisting of textbooks, video films, computer programs and interactive video programmes are centrally produced by trainers, and trainees study at the workplace, at home or at the training centre itself. Here again, progress is supervised by central training staff and line managers. In recent times, these methods have been used with conspicuous success in cost-effective terms in both the public and private sectors.

This combination approach to training has a number of potentially significant advantages:

1　It uses the advantages of the individually oriented workplace and the group-oriented central training methods.
2　It is very flexible.
3　There is no pressure to cram training into a short period of time because of the demands of work or the costs of central training. Training can be extended as long as is necessary, e.g. over several months, to cover subjects in the required depth and breadth.
4　There is a continuing achievement-oriented partnership between line managers, trainees and central trainers.
5　The crucial importance of line management and the integration of work and training is very apparent.

6 When training is extended over longer periods and is directly work oriented, the assessment of learning achievement is more valid.

7 It is especially useful for management training, which can never be satisfactorily encompassed by short central courses.

8 It is likely to be more cost-effective than other methods.

Assessing the cost-effectiveness of training

Assessing how far the investment in training has been worth while is the 'bottom line' of the SAT. The main question is, has training had the effects on individual and corporate performances that it was intended to have?

Evaluating training is notoriously difficult. This is especially true of management development, where outcomes are less easy to determine. There are a number of principles we should follow in evaluating any training or development activity. Following the ideas of Hesseling (1966), we need to be aware of the different stakeholders in the organization and to evaluate the effects of training and development in terms of the outcomes for participants, managers, staff, customers and any other groups who are involved. Similarly, we should not just evaluate the development or training process (so often evaluated by the 'happy sheets', responses from trainees at the end of the programme) but also we should evaluate the content and the objectives of the development, or training.

Data sources include:

- questionnaires to participants and their managers
- 360-degree feedback before and after the events (i.e. over a one-year period at least) showing any improvements
- surveys of morale, climate, attitudes with appropriate questionnaires (again before and after over a one-year period)
- data on improvements, changes to output, service quality or similar performance data before and after tests, examinations of trainees at the end of programmes and later to evaluate learning retention
- interviews with trainees, their managers, and their staff and customers, to judge what improvements have been achieved.

A form of triangulation of the data is to be recommended, with several independent data sources used to confirm any changes.

When trainees return to their work on the completion of a central training course, there also needs to be a constructive, systematic discussion with their line managers. The main purpose of this discussion is to ascertain the trainees' views of training, but especially to plan how line managers may help their staff to develop through their jobs the knowledge and skills that they have learned in training. It is a very demotivating experience for trainees to return to work from a central or external training course with an awareness of their needs for improvement, and stimulated to put their new learning into practice, only to be ignored and sometimes even discouraged by the attitudes of their line managers.

The second stage in the assessment of training effectiveness for individuals after a lapse of time is the ultimate verdict. It is very easy after a lapse of time, when people are caught up once more in the toils of work, to forget about recent training. A formal system is essential, therefore, to impose the necessary discipline for action and to standardize organization practice. This assessment is of particular concern to line managers and ex-trainees, and should be automatically included in a formal scheme for performance appraisal. When the training is provided centrally or externally it is also very important for the training staff to receive feedback. The questions to which answers are needed are:

1 How far has training met the specific needs of work for which it was designed?
2 What changes need to be made, if any, in future training, i.e.:
   (a) Was any material included that has subsequently proved to be of limited or no value?
   (b) Was any material omitted that has subsequently proved necessary?
   (c) How appropriate were the training methods for learning purposes?

There is a very important postscript that has to be made to the discussion of the final stage of assessment. Judgements can only be made after a lapse of time, when line managers and former trainees have gained some perspective about work performance after training. However, the fact that a lapse of time is necessary at once eliminates the possibility of a pure assessment. In the interval between the end of training and the point of assessment other influences will inevitably affect work performance for better or worse, for example, personal problems, managerial styles, working methods and conditions, etc. There are many factors both inside and outside work, some hidden from view and not measurable, which may affect behaviour. The influence of training over a period of time cannot, therefore, be isolated as a single measurable factor.

Finally, it is necessary to estimate the cost-effectiveness of training from an organizational point of view and whether the investment of human and material resources made a justifiable contribution to the achievement of organizational aims and objectives.

The problems of assessing the effectiveness of training become even more complicated at organizational level. A whole range of factors may contribute to an organization's success or failure. The admitted difficulties of organizational assessment cannot be an excuse for neglecting or avoiding making the best possible attempt. As always, since sound judgements can only be made if criteria have first been defined, each organization must decide for itself what the appropriate criteria for assessing the cost-effectiveness should be and what evidence should be acquired. The kinds of criteria that might be used, for example, are productivity, profits, customer satisfaction, levels of complaints, labour turnover, accident rates, mistakes at work, wastage of materials, etc. The ultimate responsibility for providing and assessing cost-effective training rests with management, and especially with senior management responsible for central direction of policy and practice.

The central direction of training

Because training permeates the whole organization and is related directly to all its main functions, the central direction of training must involve the collaboration of senior representatives of the organization's central staff, that is, operations, finance, HR, training, etc. The details are a matter for each organization to decide for itself. The daily supervision of training should be the responsibility of either the director of HR or the director of training, depending on whether these are separate but interrelated departments, or whether the training function is located as a subunit of the HR department, in which the director of training reports to the director of HR. Whatever form central direction may take, the general responsibilities for the staff concerned may be defined as follows:

1 To formulate and publish policy and plans for training (see Example 12.1).
2 To provide the people and material resources needed.
3 To set up all the formal apparatus needed to make the SAT work effectively, i.e. formal systems for:
   (a) identifying work-related training needs
   (b) designing work-related training to meet identified needs
   (c) assessing the effectiveness of training in terms of training objectives and actual work performance.
4 To define the responsibilities of all staff responsible for implementing these systems, i.e. line managers, HR and training staff and individual employees.
5 To prescribe all the formal communication methods needed for the effective functioning of these systems in practice, i.e. scheduled meetings, interviews, forms, questionnaires, etc.
6 To co-ordinate the training work of the various subunits of the organization.
7 To act as a focal point for the exchange and dissemination of ideas about training design and provision throughout the organization.
8 To act as a link with the external world of training and to bring new ideas into the organization to improve cost-effectiveness.
9 To monitor the effective functioning of the SAT and the cost-effectiveness of training in the organization.

Training policy

The statement of training policy is a key document. It describes how cost-effective training is to be achieved by means of central control and the application of the SAT in practice. Example 12.1 indicates broad outlines. The statement would need to be adapted to suit the specific requirements of various organizations. Training makes a vital contribution to the development of the organization's human resources and hence to the achievement of its aims and objectives. To achieve its purpose, training needs to be effectively managed so that the right training is given to the right people in the right form at the right time and at the right costs.

Example 12.1: Statement of training policy

The effective management of training requires central control, the collaboration of all the component divisions of the organization who share the available resources, a specific structure and the detailed provisions necessary for an effective system.

The necessary central control will be achieved by:

1 A central training committee (CTC), comprising the heads of all component divisions.
2 A director of training.

The CTC should meet regularly (for example, every six months) and at any other time as necessary. The purpose of its meetings will be to:

1 Issue and revise training policy and practices.
2 Plan, approve and control a training budget for the allocation of available resources.
3 Set up and monitor the various functions essential to the effectiveness of the system, e.g. human resource planning to determine quantity and quality of staff needed to fulfil the organization's functions and purposes, job analysis to define requirements for individual effective performance and performance appraisal to identify training needs and assess effectiveness of training recently provided.
4 Ensure close collaboration between all component divisions in the design and provision of training so that useful views and ideas are regularly exchanged and wasteful duplication is avoided.
5 Take reports from the director of training on the effectiveness of the system and to consider any proposals for change.
6 Monitor the total cost-effectiveness of the training system.

The director of training has a delegated responsibility from the CTC for:

1 Implementing its policy and supervising the effectiveness of the system and reporting to the CTC.
2 Establishing the means for organizing training on the basis of the systems approach, i.e. identifying work-related needs; designing and providing needs-related training; assessing the ultimate cost-effectiveness of training; initiating any necessary changes.
3 Monitoring the cost-effectiveness of the training system.
4 Liaising with external training organizations and activities to keep abreast of current developments and practices in order to introduce any beneficial innovations into the organization's training practices.
5 Providing all central training courses (e.g. management, training of trainers) identified as necessary for groups of employees.

Line managers at all levels are responsible for the effective training of their staffs, that is, for identifying their needs and for ensuring that they are given the training they need by the most cost-effective means (at the workplace, by attendance at courses internal and external or by other means such as open and distance methods).

Line managers and training staff are to collaborate continually to ensure that the aim of the training policy is achieved:

1 In the design and provision of needs-related training.
2 In the assessment of the effectiveness of training provided.

To achieve this purpose, the director of training will set up and supervise the necessary

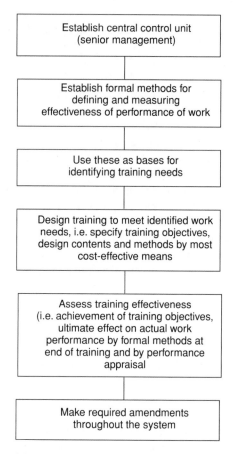

Figure 12.2 Summary of the main elements of a training system

apparatus so that the required collaboration between line managers and training staff may be effective in practice (for example, consultations, meetings, conferences, questionnaires).

Figure 12.2 summarizes the main elements of a training system.

All staff involved in any way in training activities (training staff, line managers, occasional speakers and tutors, training support staff) are to be trained in the knowledge and skills required for the effective design and provision of training. This training will be provided and supervised by the director of training.

Questions

1 Define training and the main consequences that arise from the definition.
2 What is meant by the systems approach to training?
3 What are the responsibilities of central senior staff?
4 What does the identification of training needs entail?
5 How does learning theory affect the design and provision of training?

6 What should training objectives attempt to achieve?
7 Who may be responsible for training?
8 Describe the various forms that training may take in terms of methods and locations.
9 How may the effectiveness of training be assessed?
10 Comment on the British Aerospace BEST OD and management development programme objectives (see the following case study).
   (a) How would you seek to incorporate a systems approach to development to meet the needs expressed here?
   (b) What kinds of development activities would in your opinion be most suitable to meet these needs?
   (c) How can you integrate HR policies such as 360-degree feedback and the identification of potential into such a programme?

Case study: British Aerospace's BEST programme

BEST is the name given to the programme aimed at developing the 1500 executive group members of British Aerospace (BAe). A modular programme, it combines skills development with problem solving techniques, using the competency framework, in such areas as leadership, transnational analysis, role modelling, case studies, etc.

The objectives, expressed through the BAe values are as follows.

Innovation and training
BEST delegates will:

- encourage a flow of new ideas
- create opportunities and environments for creativity
- challenge accepted ways of doing things
- implement ideas which benefit the business
- champion new applications of technology which meet customer needs.

People
BEST delegates actively develop the BAe leadership competencies, including:

- providing clear direction
- focusing on customers
- knowing BAe and its products
- promoting teamwork and encouraging two-way communication
- developing and coaching, motivating and supporting
- demonstrating drive and commitment
- innovating and solving problems.

Customers
BEST delegates will lead their teams in:

- providing the best quality service to both internal and external customers
- responding quickly to changing customer requirements
- building strong relationships
- measuring customer satisfaction
- responding constructively to complaints.

Partnerships
To help BEST delegates:

- create long-term relationships with partners based on trust
- share information within BAe, and with customers, suppliers, distributors and industrial partners
- overcome barriers to sharing information between business units
- co-operate with others to develop products and services, eliminating the 'not invented here' syndrome.

In addition to the variety of learning methods suited to developing these attitudes and behaviour changes, there were also 360-degree feedback techniques and personal development plans to reinforce defined desirable behaviours, and a team-based value planning system. The teams use a value planning workbook, and a network of coaches to help them interpret and understand the values, in their everyday work.

References

Hesseling, P. (1966). *Strategy for Evaluation Research*. Van Gorcum. Assoc.
Kolb, D. A., Rubin, I. M. and McIntyre, J. M. (1974). *Organizational Psychology: An Experiential Approach*. Prentice-Hall.
Senge, P. M. (1990). *The Fifth Discipline*. Century Business.

Further reading for Part Four

Burgoyne, J., Boydell, T. and Pedler, M. (1978). *A Manager's Guide to Self-Development*. McGraw-Hill.
Connock, S. (1991). *HR Vision: Managing a Quality Work Force*. IPM.
Fletcher, C. and Williams, R. (1985). *Performance Appraisal and Career Development*. Hutchinson.
Gutteridge, T. G., Leibowitz, Z. B. and Shore, J. E. 91993). *Organisational Career Development*. Jossey-Bass.
Herriot, P. (1992). *The Career Management Challenge*. Sage.
Hesseling, P. (1966). *Strategy for Evaluation Research*. Van Gorcum. Assoc.
Kenney, J. and Reid, M. (1988). *Training Interventions*. IPM.
Kolb, D. A., Rubin, I. M. and McIntyre, J. M. (1974). *Organizational Psychology: An Experiential Approach*. Prentice-Hall.
Long, P. (1987). *Performance Appraisal Revisited*. IPM.

Pepper, A. (1984). *Managing the Training and Development Function*. Gower.

Randell, G. et al. (1974). *Staff Appraisal*. IPM.

Schein E. H. (1993). *Career Anchors*. Pfeiffer.

Senge, P. M. (1990). *The Fifth Discipline*. Century Business.

Sparrow, P. and Marchington, M. (1998). *Human Resource Management: The New Agenda*. Financial Times/Pitman.

Woodruffe, C. (1990). *Assessment Centres*. IPM.

York, A. E. C. (1990). *The Systems Approach to Training*. Institute of Supervisory Management.

Part Five

The reward and conservation of employees

The theories of motivation we outlined in Chapter 1 exhibited the complexity of reasons for working. The theory we considered by Porter and Lawler gives full weight to the different values that individuals place on rewards. Their model suggests that employees calculate the amount of effort required and the probabilities that the accomplishment of the task will result in the achievement of rewards and satisfactions. Since the calculation of these probabilities is influenced by the individual's expectations about his or her role in the organization, he or she is likely to have preconceived notions of the relative worth of different jobs and will also match his or her own values against the norms of the organization he or she joins.

The reward and treatment of employees is bound up with the overall conditions under which the person works. Holidays, sick pay, pension and company car schemes, for example, provide a framework of benefits associated with salary and job level. Although Herzberg argues that 'hygiene factors' such as these are not positive motivators, he acknowledges that failures in these areas result in what might be termed 'demotivation' to work. The interdependence of 'hygiene factors' and 'motivators' makes the distinction between the two factors hard to see in the actions of people that relate to their working intentions. Apart from the obvious physical conditions of the work (such as the geographical location, surroundings, the danger, etc.), there are influences such as the style of supervision, the stress of some jobs and different decision-making habits which go to create the 'feel' of a job, and which are part of the culture of the organization. This 'feel' is as much a consequence of HR policies as of the ways in which the job is regarded by the incumbent and colleagues. The policies managers pursue towards employees carry implications for the types of relationships they create.

It is of prime importance, therefore, that managers understand how to evaluate jobs and how to construct systems for rewarding people as part of their employee relations strategy. The treatment of employees is underwritten in the UK by rights, the sources of which are in the various collective agreements between employers and unions and in the employment contract around which there is a framework of employment law. We will look at these in the chapters that follow.

The starting point for the manager is to design reward systems that take into account relativities and that represent the philosophy of management and the organization strategy that the organization has decided to adopt. There is then a need to control the wage and salary policies by systems that are flexible and that grant a place to the interest groups – managers and unions – who want to be represented. The HR policies that form the general conditions of service are also related issues, since they contribute so much to the organization's culture and the individual's sense of well-being. In the following chapters we will look at job evaluation in its many forms, how to design pay systems and at salary administration. Finally, we will make an assessment of the policies that are, in the most general sense, for employees' welfare.

Chapter 13

Job evaluation

In this chapter we are concerned with the question: how can the different forms of pay be developed for the organization's economic efficiency? This leads us to look at job evaluation as a prerequisite of any reward structure.

Definition

The purpose of job evaluation techniques is to measure the relative worth of jobs so that the relationship between the jobs can be expressed in salary and wage scales, based on a logical, ordered system. 'Job evaluation' is a term used in a general way for a number of techniques that are in different forms. These techniques entail analysing and assessing the content of jobs so that they may be classified in an order relating to one another and to the marketplace.

Common features of job evaluation techniques

1 Job evaluation is concerned with differences in the work itself, not in differences that are found between people.
2 Reference is made to the 'content' of the job, i.e. what the work consists of, what is being done, what skills are deployed and the actions that are performed. This is normally discovered by job analysis.
3 There are predetermined criteria, or factors, against which each job is measured. These may be descriptions of the whole job, or of its component parts.
4 The practice of involving those who are to be subject to the job evaluation at an early stage helps to ensure both accuracy in job analysis and a commitment to the job evaluation scheme.
5 The outcome of a job evaluation should be wage and salary scales covering the range of evaluated jobs.
6 All systems need regular review and updating, and have to be flexible enough to be of use for different kinds of work, so that new jobs can be accommodated.

What do we mean by the word 'job'?

This may seem to be a silly question to ask, but we must remember that 'jobs' have no physical bounded existence. There is no way of 'seeing' or using any of our senses to comprehend the 'whole' of a job. The idea of 'job' is an analytical one – it enables us to describe a set of actions that are associated with the execution of a range of tasks. 'Tasks' consist of a number of elements that are actions (that is, intended behaviours) that are both observable and measurable. In thinking of tasks we have to think of people performing them, and therefore the major difficulty experienced by the job analyst who wishes to describe a 'job' is to be able to divorce the essential nature of the job from the people performing the job.

Jobs are now often regarded as less important than the skills and competencies employees possess, which can be used competitively in a number of ways. In this flexible world, the apparent bureaucracy of job evaluation sits uneasily with its emphasis on job descriptions and procedure. People often now work in teams, in matrix structures where accountability is spread between posts. Organizations change quickly, putting demands for flexibility on all roles. Job evaluation, however, is a process, not a single technique, and can be applied in any work situation where it is necessary to have a rational basis for rewards.

Problems of measurement

As people are at the centre of all 'jobs', either in the perceptions of others or in the written descriptions of jobs deriving from observations of how they are done, the evaluation is of human activity, not of some kind of impersonal act. This is our first problem of measurement. It is the problem of the inherent subjectivity contained in the discriminatory judgements of the work of others. Our second problem of measurement emerges here also – because the criteria or benchmarks on which evaluation will be made are based on aspects of human action. We may illustrate this last point by thinking about the amount of discretion involved in any job. People seem to want to make choices about their work, and typically seek to extend the areas of discretion they already possess. Even the most routine job contains choices; sometimes about rest pauses, the amount of work or its quality. Even if, according to the operator's manual, the sequence and timing of actions are preset, there are always other aspects of the total job (such as collecting materials, reading drawings, talking to the supervisor) when the worker can exercise some freedom of action.

Job evaluation requires the acceptance of the assumption that there is sufficient typicality in the way the work is performed to make comparisons between groups of jobs worth while. The differences between people and the consequences for the way the work is done may not be significant. It is not until job evaluation has been undertaken that we can see what the differences are. The changing activities of an organization have to be put into an ordered context for pay purposes. Change emphasizes the need to conduct evaluation on a continuous programme, to update rewards and keep the balance in our rewards in the direction which best suits the organization's objectives. The problems and advantages of job evaluation can be summarized as follows.

The problems of job evaluation

1 Schemes take time to establish and involve some formalization of rules regarding job hierarchies.
2 The measures that are selected determine the outcome. The decision of what to measure, therefore, partly preconditions where the job is to be placed in the hierarchy of jobs which is being constructed.
3 Job evaluation committees, where they exist to reconcile interest groups, have to reach compromises over what is 'politically' acceptable within the organization. Trade-offs occur between the interest groups.
4 Job evaluation introduces some rigidities into pay systems, and reduces the opportunity for managers to exercise complete discretion.

The advantages of job evaluation

1 Some form of evaluation is necessary to introduce rationality into pay scales – enabling comparison to be made on an explicit basis. This reveals where the differences in rates are a consequence of tradition or custom rather than for economic reasons (see Chapter 21 on 'equal value' legislation).
2 Any inherent bias in the process can be recognized, and partly dealt with, by using committees to help in the evaluation, and perhaps outside analysts to describe the jobs.
3 Job evaluation can be applied to different situations – it is a process which can be adjusted to the requirements of the organization (its size, the kind of work, etc.).
4 By involving employees at an early stage in establishing the system, it is possible to draw on their own feelings of fairness, their concepts of what should be rewarded, and to gain their commitment to the reward system.
5 Job evaluation helps organizations to create salary structures that can be compared with market rates.
6 Given the considerable sums of money in pay budgets, the control of costs implied by job evaluation rules may be essential for business success.
7 Sexual discrimination should be reduced, since the basis for pay scales is made explicit and can be challenged under the equal value legislation.

The argument that organizations want total flexibility is rather spurious. In reality, whilst there may be flexibility within some job families (jobs which share common basic skills, purpose and activity), there is little movement across job family boundaries, and specialization is still regarded as very important where there are individual skills and competencies (for example, the different hospital consultancy specialisms, camera crew in television production, airline pilots, chefs, etc.). Job evaluation can, therefore, be used to establish the benchmarks for job families, which can then act as control points for other job family members, for example, for production jobs, clerical jobs, warehouse jobs, to cite three kinds of job families.

Computer-aided job evaluation (CAJE) can also remove much of the bureaucracy and the time-consuming processes of comparison. There are two ways in which CAJE can be used:

1 As a software system, giving a data management service (e.g. in whole job ranking schemes).

2 As a rapid evaluation process, by computing the output from completed question-naires using predetermined criteria (e.g. in a points rating scheme).

A job description and a person specification are essential first stages to job evaluation. The procedure is the same as we described in Chapter 7, the person specification being an outline of the qualifications, experience and other attributes needed to do a job. The person specification should show the job factors. Both the description and the specifi-cation should be summarized into a 'job profile', recording the responsibilities, skills, competencies – in other words, the factors on which the job is to be evaluated.

Different kinds of job evaluation schemes

Broadly speaking, there are two main dimensions on which job evaluation can be delin-eated: whether they are quantitative or qualitative in the schemes' treatment of job factors; and the extent to which they are analytical of a job's content.

A brief description of each of the most well-known schemes is given below.

Whole job ranking

This is a non-quantitative and non-analytical method. It is a technique in which jobs are placed in order of importance or value relative to each other. The main guide is usually the amount of responsibility in each job or the importance of the job to the organiza-tion. This method looks at the whole job, not its component parts, and is concerned with the rank order of jobs, not differences in any absolute sense.

The procedure to be followed is:

1 Benchmark jobs are identified. These are jobs that are 'yardsticks' or standards against which others can be compared. They should be chosen because they are rep-resentative of job requirements, and there should be no controversy about their content, value or importance.

2 The benchmark jobs should be drawn from various levels in the organization.

3 Each job to be evaluated is compared with the benchmark job and a judgement is made to determine its relationship with the benchmark job.

4 As the number of ranked jobs increases, we can compare new jobs with those that have already been ranked.

5 In large organizations, we can use 'job families', where there are similarities, as finite populations – for example, accounts department staff.

6 It may be easier from an administrative point of view to use a computer program to make the comparisons.

7 A further refinement is the paired comparison method, where each job is compared with all the others in turn until a consensus is reached among the assessors on the ranking. This should improve the reliability of the ranking, but the number of com-parisons increases exponentially (from 1225 comparisons for fifty jobs to 4950 paired comparisons for 100 jobs).

Generally, the whole job-ranking method is thought to be appropriate for small organizations. There are problems in handling the number of comparisons if the number of jobs is larger. It is also difficult to choose benchmark jobs that do not have some flaw as yardsticks if a number of different departments and specialisms are involved.

Classification or grading scheme

This is also a qualitative and non-analytical method. It is a centralized approach that may best be seen as part of the design of the organization to which it is applied.

This approach requires the examination of jobs in the light of predetermined definitions of the grades, as part of a planned organization structure, where the level of work in each grade is founded on what is thought to be appropriate functionally. New jobs are then compared with the predefined grade descriptions to indicate the placing of the job in a relationship with other graded jobs.

Assuming that the grading scheme is to be integrated with the design of the organization, the following steps should take place:

1 The shape and size of the organization's hierarchy has to be determined. This becomes a question of how many levels there should be in the hierarchy, and the span of control (the numbers reporting to each supervisor) at each level.
2 The job hierarchy is divided into a number of grades, with written definitions for each.
3 The definitive grade descriptions are associated by outside analogues with appropriate pay rates, and effectively become the benchmarks against which other jobs are graded.
4 The broad differences that management wish to apply are written into the grade descriptions, often being in terms of the level of skill or responsibility.
5 Jobs are fitted into the structure by evaluation committees, who arrive at a consensus by comparing the ungraded jobs with the grade descriptions.

There are similarities between whole job ranking and grading schemes, in that jobs are taken as wholes. The hope with a classification system is that it will produce a planned organization. There are benefits in the approach for staffing budgeting and career planning. However, there are problems in making comparisons where an in-house scheme is used. If the categories or grades contain a wide range of skills or job requirements, this reduces the usefulness in discriminating between jobs.

Points rating

The points rating technique entails the analysis and comparison of jobs according to common factors, which are represented by a number of points, the amount depending on the degree of each factor present. Jobs are then placed in order of their total points rating. Pay is usually determined by reference to benchmark jobs. Points rating is therefore both a quantitative and an analytical technique.

The technique requires a number of steps that must be undertaken with care:

1 'Job factors' are discovered by an examination of the most essential elements in the job. Job factors need to be present in all the jobs to be evaluated. This is accomplished by taking a significant sample of jobs for which complete job descriptions and person specifications should be prepared. The factors selected from the descriptions and specifications should be those that are critical for differentiation between jobs.

2 The factors – categories such as 'engineering knowledge' required to do the job, or 'physical effort' – are sometimes taken to be at a broad level and can be termed 'generic factors'. There are then a number of specific subfactors that comprise the 'generic' factor – for example, 'engineering knowledge' could be broken down to different aspects of mechanical engineering, or in the case of 'physical effort' the physical demands can be qualified more precisely.

3 The subfactors should then be weighted according to the degree of importance they have in each job. This is done by dividing each subfactor into a number of 'degrees'.

4 In order to resolve the problem of how to award points to each factor, and degree, it is useful to begin by assuming that the value of all factors present in any job will add up to 100 per cent. The evaluation committee can then give relative values of each factor in each benchmark job so that the generic factors are given a percentage which totals 100 per cent, and each subfactor a percentage which adds up to 100 per cent of the generic factor. The evaluation is of each subfactor, so that each subfactor should be broken down into degrees. At this stage we have an indication of the relative importance of each generic factor and each subfactor. The number of degrees used should not go beyond what is likely to be recognizable, up to five degrees of a subfactor being the maximum for most purposes. Definitions of each degree used for each subfactor are required. The total number of points can be any number, but the maximum number for all factors must add up to this total, and therefore the number of points is dependent on the number of factors, and evaluators should allow room for the maximum combination of points. A popular number is 500 points.

Table 13.1 illustrates this part of the process.

Since acquired 'skill and knowledge' is rated relatively high in the example in Table 13.1, and training and previous experience is rated high on this, we may grant the highest degree of this subfactor, 100 points, of the 500 points total possible (that is, 40 per cent of 500 = 200, 50 per cent of 200 = 100). The number of points in each degree can be an arithmetical or a geometric progression, and the subfactor's degrees need definitions. For example, 'Experience':

1st degree (up to one month)	20 points
2nd degree (over one and up to four months)	40 points
3rd degree (over four months but less than twelve)	60 points
4th degree (twelve months to eighteen months)	80 points
5th degree (over eighteen months)	100 points

using an arithmetic progression.

5 A chart should then be drawn up, which shows the values for each subfactor, broken down into degrees present, with clear, agreed definitions of the subfactors and degrees.

6 Each job is then evaluated, preferably by a committee which will arrive at a consensus on the total number of points for the individual jobs being evaluated. Out of this the jobs may be placed on a range or scale.

Table 13.1 Points rating scheme (the factors are drawn from the BIM 'Job Evaluation' Scheme)

Generic factor	Importance %	Specific subfactors	Importance %	Maximum points
Acquired skill and knowledge	40	Training and previous experience	50	100
		General reasoning ability	20	40
		Complexity of process	20	40
		Dexterity and motor accuracy	10	20
Responsibilities and mental requirements	30	For material equipment	5	7.5
		Effect on other operations	40	60
		Attention needed to orders	40	60
		Alertness to details	10	15
		Monotony	5	7.5
Physical requirements	20	Abnormal position	60	60
		Abnormal effort	40	40
Conditions of work	10	Disagreeableness	90	45
		Danger	10	5
Total				500

Although the points scheme may seem complicated, this technique has been widely used in Britain and the USA since its invention in the 1920s.

There are a number of variations on the method outlined here, which indicates the flexibility of the points scheme. The use of points should not be seen as a sign of scientific objectivity, as the points system relies on judgements by evaluation committees. Nevertheless, the technique is useful in comparing many different jobs that contain the same job factors, and has been developed into tailor-made schemes to fit the specific requirements of companies.

Guide chart profile of Hay MSL Limited (now Hay/McBer)

The guide chart profile method was developed by management consultants Hay MSL Limited as a variant of the points rating technique. The scheme provides a total wage/salary package, and the widespread use of the scheme globally permits direct comparisons with other organizations to establish the market rate for particular jobs. A summary of some of its main aspects shows the *modus operandi.*

Following the scheme's extensive use, the consultants have identified three generic factors, and further subdivisions into subfactors. No doubt there may be further adaptations to the scheme as it evolves. The generic factors and subfactors are defined in Table 13.2.

Table 13.2 Guide chart profile factors

Accountability (a) Freedom to act (b) Magnitude of accountability	Dependent on the job's purpose, which should be related to the organization's goals
Know-how (a) Skill, education, training (b) Breadth of knowledge, including planning, organizing, etc.	
Problem-solving (a) The 'thinking environment' (constraints) (b) The 'thinking challenge' (how creative, routine, etc.)	Dependent on frequency and importance of problems

Accountability and know-how are evaluated on a points scale with varying degrees and problem-solving is shown as a percentage of the know-how required for each job, the final results being converted into a geometric scale of scores under the three generic factors.

Job profiles are produced to show the different aspects of each job, under each of the factors, and help to reveal the relationship between the required performance and the organization's objectives, and show where the main job demands are, whether in acting or advising.

There is a points value in a pattern of numbers for each factor, depending upon a definition given in the guide chart, with 15 per cent intervals in progression, this being the step change which indicates a significant difference in job content. A judgement is made about the balance between each of the three factors in the job under consideration.

One of the benefits of this scheme is its recognition of the variable nature of managerial jobs that cannot be classified without taking the person specification into account in an individual way. However, although the concept of accountability has a wide application, in practice the method seems to be favoured in tackling the problems of white-collar and executive rewards.

The HayXpert software can be used to conduct a benchmark evaluation which is then a basis for the remaining jobs in the organization.

Factor comparison

Factor comparison is another analytical technique that uses some of the ideas of both the points rating and the ranking methods. One version of factor comparison, illustrated here, is a 'direct to money' approach. This system entails evaluating jobs in terms of each other, on a basis of a certain limited number of factors, and reconciling these rankings with money values for each factor derived from benchmark jobs. Out of the first stages of the exercise comes a table of factor rates for the benchmark jobs against which all the other jobs can be evaluated. There are two parts to the early stages, therefore: factor ranking, and factor evaluation.

The method is more involved than the others described, as there are difficult judgements to be made at each juncture.

1 The first step is to agree on the factors which are found in each of the jobs to be evaluated, so that these can be defined. The number of factors chosen is usually limited to a few broad factors, not less than four or more than seven.
2 Early studies suggested: mental requirements, skill requirements, physical requirements, responsibility and working conditions, but the factors chosen will need to be those that are appropriate for the jobs.
3 The next stage is to choose benchmark jobs, which must contain all these broad generic factors. These benchmark jobs must clearly be representative of the factors, and, there should be an unambiguous wage or salary for the job in question.
4 The payment for the benchmark jobs can be either the current rate (if this is thought correct) or the intended rate for the job, based on evidence from salary surveys or negotiated agreements.
5 The evaluation committee then ranks the factors contained in each benchmark job. Taking the four generic factors we used in our previous example (Table 13.1), we can follow the factor comparison procedure for two jobs, say, a secretary and a data entry clerk concerned with computer input (see Table 13.3). It must be appreciated that full job descriptions and person specifications would be needed for these two jobs before evaluation, and we will assume for the sake of simplicity that these have been prepared.

Table 13.3 Factor comparison

Generic factor	Rank order for secretary (£260 total)		Rank order for data entry clerk (£195 total)	
Acquired skill and knowledge	1	£100	2	£60
Responsibility and mental requirements	2	£70	1	£70
Physical requirements	3	£60	4	£25
Conditions of work	4	£30	3	£40

6 The committee must approach the benchmark jobs also from the perspective of factor evaluation, when money values are given to each factor. Given that the total job is worth 100 per cent of the composite wage, a percentage of the wage can be attributed to each factor on a basis of its importance in the job. In Table 13.3 we have shown money values against each factor.
7 The reconciliation between the factor rankings and the factor evaluation is a crucial stage for resolving any differences. Because two different scales are being applied and there are not necessarily equal intervals, it is possible that there could be wide variations. Thus, 'acquired knowledge or skill' is worth much less for the data entry clerk than for the secretary, although there is only one difference in rank. Problems such as these would need some compromise solution by the committee.
8 A pilot study would help to resolve any serious difficulties in reconciling the factor

rankings with the money evaluation and, should the factors or benchmark jobs prove unsuitable, then the whole process must be restarted.

9 The remainder of the jobs to be evaluated can be dealt with more speedily once this early work has been done and, as each job factor is ranked and then evaluated, the network of values and rankings should reveal a pattern on which decisions can be reached more easily. Full descriptions of all the other jobs to be evaluated need to be prepared, of course, and the pay for each factor after the job has been analysed can be settled by reference to this table of rates for the key jobs which has been constructed.

Factor comparison schemes are often treated with suspicion by employees, and are not as popular in the UK as the other three methods we have outlined so far.

The benefits of the scheme are that in the early stages, when benchmark jobs are being evaluated, two different approaches to the same job are reconciled to produce a practical compromise on the relative value of the job. This is likely to result in greater accuracy than the ranking method as far as management or the evaluation committee is concerned.

Time span of discretion

This is a somewhat theoretical approach to job evaluation, developed by Elliott Jaques (1964). It borders on being a social philosophy. The assumption is made that individuals have a subconscious awareness when their work, payment and capacity are all approximately at an acceptable level of demands and rewards. When a person's work and capacity are equally matched, there is, according to the theory, an amount of payment (including salary and benefits) of which the individual is aware that matches the work and capacity level. Thus, people can feel underpaid or overpaid, worked or utilized.

A second aspect of Jaques's theory is the view that the discretionary work activities that an individual performs can be measured in terms of the time that elapses before a manager is aware that his or her subordinate has performed this discretionary element satisfactorily, in balancing the pace and quality of his or her work.

These two aspects of the theory are related, in that what people feel is 'fair' pay is understood by individuals in conformity with the time span of discretion that their work demanded. The pay norms which are felt to be fair are intuitive understandings by people of the rates that others receive for similar work, their own standard of living, and conceptions of equity, all conditioned by their feeling of the extent to which their capacity is being used or developed.

Research in the UK and the USA has indicated that there is a high correlation between felt fair pay and time span measures. The implications are that at each level in the organization there are time span measures that should, therefore, correspond to pay levels. Jaques also claims that individuals have 'capacity growth curves', these being the rates at which an individual expects his or her capacity to grow in the future and, therefore, the salary progressions that he or she would anticipate. Salary scales could be constructed, therefore, using this information.

The theory has aroused a lot of interest, and has informed discussions on rates of pay and questions of social justice. However, its practicality as a proposal for the evaluation of jobs remains in doubt. There is disagreement over the validity of the research where such vague concepts as subconsciously held pay norms are used and where there are different interpretations of what is discretionary. Because of the tendency for people to draw on their own experience, there must be a bias towards maintaining the status quo in any organization, that is, the time span approach does not make clear which is the dependent variable. Do people believe that they have a certain time span of discretion because they are paid at a certain level in relation to others? If so, the theory becomes a self-fulfilling prophecy. Finally, there are difficulties in obtaining acceptance of these ideas by those in industry and commerce.

Decision banding

This method starts with the premise that all organizations tend to reward their members in terms of the decisions they make. This is similar to the time span of discretion, where the quality of the decision varies at each level of the organization. Paterson, who invented the decision-banding method, postulates six basic kinds of decision:

Band E – Policy-making decisions   (Top management)
Band D – Programming decisions   (Senior management)
Band C – Interpretative decisions   (Middle management)
Band B – Routine decisions   (Skilled workers)
Band A – Automatic decisions   (Semi-skilled workers)
Band O – Vegetative decisions   (defined by others – unskilled workers)

All bands except O can be divided into two grades, upper and lower, thus giving eleven grades.

The stages recommended by Paterson are:

1 The establishment of job bands according to the kinds of decisions.
2 An analysis of the content of the jobs, from which jobs can be put into the appropriate subgrade for Band B, using points rating, and by ranking for Bands C and D into the agreed band.
3 Monetary values are assigned to each level. The increase between grades for pay rates is exponential, requiring equal distances between the midpoints.

Paterson claims that his method can be used for all jobs in the company, and that given proper consultation it is possible to achieve a consensus on the difficult question of differentials. Among the possible problems one can envisage with the decision-banding approach are the rigidity of the bands, the reliance on the job analyst's descriptions, and the difficulty of convincing employees that this rather perplexing scheme has initiated an accurate rate of pay.

Direct consensus method

The direct consensus method is another derivative of the time span of discretion theory. Again, there is an assumption that a consensus of opinion will be found in any working group concerning the relationship between jobs. It is argued that a wages structure will be acceptable to employees if it embodies their conventional wisdom.

The method is simple, but for most practical purposes requires the use of a computer, both to produce the ranking of jobs and to calculate the variations of assessors' opinions.

1 Job descriptions are prepared from a representative sample of jobs. The number of jobs should be a 'prime number' between eleven and seventy-nine.
2 A representative committee is established with a sufficient number of assessors to make it possible for each one to rank an equal number of jobs, using a standard form for the computer input.
3 The jobs are ranked as 'wholes' using the question of how important is the job (presumably to the organization) in relation to each other job.
4 Jobs are ranked using the paired comparison method. All possible pairs of jobs are compared; the total number of comparisons is

$$\frac{N(N-1)}{2} \qquad\qquad (13.1)$$

where N = the number of jobs.
5 Reconciliation between job rankings is usually left to a computer, which will also calculate the variation between the assessors' ratings.

Ranking jobs as wholes can lead to rather difficult ranking decisions, and it is possible that, given computer facilities, jobs could be ranked under the broad factor headings that is one variation of this approach. The direct consensus method is expensive as regards assessors' time. Since job content is likely to change, a comparison of factors would probably help to make the method flexible. Multiple regression can be used to weight factors relative to what is thought appropriate.

The introduction of job evaluation schemes

We have devoted a proportionately large amount of space to the description of various forms of job evaluation because it is an essential first step towards the creation of a salary/wage structure that has a rational basis in the eyes of both management and workers. However, the way job evaluation is applied will be of fundamental importance in the acceptance of a scheme as a rational instrument.

Job evaluation committees have already been mentioned. Employee involvement is a part of the overall sharing of power. How management ensures the representation of the different interest groups is dependent on organization structure, size, the current state of union/management relationships and existing relationships among the groups of employees affected by the evaluation. Job evaluation committees are less used at present, reflecting the stronger sense of managerial prerogatives.

Where they are formed, as a general rule small rather than large committees are recommended and they should reach decisions by consensus. 'Consensus' here means that each member of the committee should be allowed to express an opinion, and where there are genuine differences the reasons for the differences of view should be argued out until a broad measure of agreement is found, even though there may be minor objections. The chairperson's role is obviously important in directing these discussions. Whoever fulfils the role should be capable of balancing judgements and drawing together disparate outlooks, and should command respect from both employees and management. Whatever approach is adopted, senior line managers must be represented.

Payment systems arising from job evaluation

The outcome of a job evaluation scheme is an ordered and accepted pay structure, where there is a logical relationship between the amounts paid and the job factors and where the differentials between jobs fit into the structure and are approved. In practice, this is difficult to achieve. If there are committee meetings, interest groups will achieve the redefinition of certain factors and will manage to push up or down the relative worth of some of the jobs, on the grounds of what is acceptable, comprehensible and traditional. The fitting of the results of the evaluation to the market rate prevailing may, therefore, be a result of negotiation.

The same job evaluation schemes are rarely used for both blue-collar and white-collar employees. Jobs that are highly technical in content, or scientific and professional, do not fit easily with administration, sales or managerial jobs. This imposes further constraints on each group, as the salary and wage structures that emerge are related in the minds of employees, but not through job evaluation, so the final structures will have to be convincing.

The provisions of the Equal Value Amendment, described in Chapter 21, mean that employers should ensure that the factors used do not discriminate in favour of one sex. There is potential for an equal value claim if there is a special scheme for lower-level employees if they are mostly female, while more senior employees covered by a different scheme are mostly male, for example.

We have already mentioned some of the techniques of putting a money value on a job. In the factor comparison example, this is intrinsic to the technique. From the points system, a salary band can be defined by plotting the values on a scattergraph. From such a scatter, a line of best fit can be drawn through the midpoints to help create the grades. The cut-off for each grade will always be a matter of judgement. To fit market rates to jobs requires a survey of the comparative data, including employee benefits. Job evaluation provides the database on which judgements can be made, but we must turn to the problem of devising salary/wage scales for the important stage of setting up and administering scales.

Questions

1　What are the advantages of job evaluation in establishing a reward structure?
2　Describe the methods adopted in an *analytical* job evaluation scheme.
3　What have the ideas of Elliott Jaques contributed to the principles of job evaluation?
4　Discuss the proposition that job evaluation schemes should reflect organizational needs for flexibility and diversity.

Reference

Jaques, E. (1964). *Time Span Hand Book*. Heinemann.

Chapter 14

Pay and benefits

Reward policy

A prerequisite for the strategic management of pay and benefits is a reward policy.

The objectives of a policy towards payment could be best described as 'to remain competitive for labour whilst rewarding good performance and adopting a position on pay which controls costs and is felt to be fair by all employees'.

Single status issues such as whether or not to make distinctions between groups of employees in the benefits and conditions they receive are matters of company policy. They reflect the company's personnel philosophy. Some of the other issues which are also questions of policy, and which should be decided by the company's executive board, with the advice of the HR manager, are:

1 Where the company wishes and can afford to be in the labour markets (e.g. whether or not to follow a 'high wage' policy, demanding sustained effort of a high standard for large rewards, by positioning the company in the top quartile relative to competitors).

2 What kind of total remuneration package it wishes to offer (e.g. whether or not to give a range of 'perks', such as cars, inflation-proof pensions, etc., or whether to let the employee make the choice through a flexible benefits policy).

3 A further question is whether or not to trade off benefits against wages. Consideration will have to be given to the consequences, for the retention of employees, for the kinds of people who work for the company and for their motivation to work.

4 Profit share bonus schemes also have to be thought through, to see whether they reflect an incentive element in the employee's wage, and whether there will be any real feeling of participation as a consequence of the profit share.

5 The policy on variation of pay has to be resolved. The questions here are: whether or not pay is to be regarded as the main incentive to good performance; what job families are to be identified; how new jobs are included; and what kind of job evaluation scheme to adopt and how to run it.

6 To what extent will company policy on pay be delegated to local managers, and how

does the degree of autonomy fit in with policies on profit centres and management accounting?

7 The frequency of pay reviews, who is to be consulted, what kinds of evidence will be sought and the negotiation posture of the company have to be decided.

These are some of the policy options available, the choice of what is suitable being dependent on individual company circumstances and the philosophy of management espoused.

Wage structures

Wage rates for hourly rated personnel sometimes include a proportion that is calculated on the individual's output. The various terms used are described below.

The basic or flat rate

This is the amount of money paid for an hour's work. It is also sometimes called the 'hourly rate'. Time rates are predetermined rates per hour paid at the end of the week or month. The flat rate is often used where the work does not lend itself to any kind of measurement. Sometimes in addition to, or instead of, the basic rate an individual bonus payment may be made.

Payment by results systems

Payment by results systems are either of the following:

1 *Straight piecework*: this is the system whereby the employee is paid according to output. The method is either to agree a fixed amount of money for the production of each item, or a period of time is allowed for making the item. In the latter scheme, sometimes called the 'time allowed' system, if the employee completes the work in less time than planned, he or she is still paid for the original time and thus is able to increase earnings by completing more of the pieces, the calculation of the bonus being based on the difference between the time allowed and the actual time expressed as a percentage of his or her wage.

2 *Differential piecework*: this is similar to the 'time allowed' system of piecework, except that the amount of the bonus earned (which stems from the time saved) is shared between the company and the individual, the wage cost being adjusted with output, so that the company takes a proportion of the bonus as production increases. Schemes of this sort may be known under various names, such as 'premium bonus schemes'.

The employee has a choice with piecework on the level of output he or she wishes to achieve.

Measured daywork

The pay of the employee is fixed on the understanding that he or she will maintain a specified level of performance. This level of performance, known as the 'incentive level', is calculated in advance, and the employee is put under an obligation to try to achieve the level specified, as his or her pay does not vary in the short term.

There are individual rates and bonus systems. In addition, there are bonus schemes that aim at providing a group incentive, either to a work group or factory-wide.

Small group incentive schemes

Typically, a bonus is given to group members when their output targets are achieved or exceeded. There are numerous schemes, which vary according to the timescale adopted for measuring output, the size of the group, and the intergroup competitiveness that they encourage. Payment of the bonus may be equal among the group's members, or proportionate to an individual's earnings or status.

Advantages of group schemes

1 They draw on the natural tendencies of working people to develop norms based on what the group believes is an acceptable and 'comfortable' level of production, thereby harnessing the team spirit.
2 They are administratively simpler than individual schemes; the cost savings come from less clerical and inspection work, and savings on time study.
3 'Indirect' production workers, such as cleaners, stores assistants, etc., who also contribute to the production process can be included.
4 Flexibility within the group is encouraged, and one might anticipate that workers would be anxious to help remove production bottlenecks and to encourage training.

Disadvantages of group schemes

1 The impact of group pressures on the less efficient individual may not be beneficial where he or she needs advice and help in order to work up to the target.
2 Holidays and sickness may upset the working of the scheme. Special arrangements may have to be made to stagger holidays carefully, and a shutdown may result in lower pay for the holiday weeks.
3 Variations in production targets due to problems of supply, or a sudden fall in demand can be a cause of complaint, and disillusionment with the scheme could set in.
4 Members of large or scattered groups may not respond to the implicit appeal to group cohesiveness that is at the heart of these schemes.
5 Group norms of production may not be adequate, and if translated into official 'targets' will then not create any real increase in production. If a level is set which is too high, the group scheme will be a non-starter. It is, therefore, very dependent for its success on the targets being achievable but also very worth while for the company.

Bonus schemes stand in different ratios to the base rate, and a guaranteed or fall back rate is frequently part of the wage for pieceworkers. There are agreements and legal requirements concerning lay-offs and short-time working in the UK (see Chapter 21).

Long-term, large group schemes (gainsharing schemes)

The main difference between these schemes and those outlined above is that they apply on a long timescale, usually across the whole unit, and are often seen as an attempt to involve the staff in the organization of operations. They are sometimes called gainsharing schemes. The bonus calculation would typically be made monthly, and would be based on changes in the value of goods produced, or improvements in the actual output per person-hour against the standard.

There are many variants of these schemes. For example, the Scanlon plan (originated in 1947) was both a suggestion plan and a collective incentive scheme. The suggestion scheme was part of a system for drawing on ideas from the workforce about improvements that could be achieved jointly by management and union. It operated a bonus depending on reductions achieved by the workforce in labour costs compared with the sales revenue. Reductions in sales revenue could result in no bonus, however, although employees worked as hard.

The Rucker plan (in 1955) used 'production value' (or added value) as a basis for a collective bonus scheme. This value is defined as the difference between the sales revenue and the cost of the raw materials and supplies (that is, the inputs to the production process).

'Added value' bonus schemes make use of the idea that if the ratio of total employment costs to sales revenue falls below the level it has been, then the improvements in productivity this represents should be shared by granting a bonus to the people who have produced the change. A scale of bonus payments (as a percentage of basic pay) may be calculated. This approach is less susceptible to market forces. ICI is among a number of companies who pioneered a similar scheme.

Advantages of long-term, large group schemes

1 The long-term aspect should provide steady earnings.
2 Employee participation through production committees helps to overcome the 'them and us' attitudes that can be destructive, and it helps to build trust.
3 There is a wide range of applications to different businesses.
4 Value added schemes can be adjusted more readily to the company's trading position than those that use simple numbers of items produced.

Disadvantages of long-term, large group schemes

1 If applied across a whole factory or unit, there may not be a sufficient sense of identity from the scheme to help create teamwork.
2 For the schemes to have any incentive value, a bonus of at least 10 per cent would be expected by employees to make it worth while. The larger the numbers covered, the less the percentage to each employee, hence reducing its usefulness.
3 It is questionable whether individuals see how their own particular effort will

contribute to the achievement of the target over a long timescale. Here it is worth remembering the many variables that can intervene (changes in personnel, supervision, customer requirements, machinery, etc. – a list that increases as time passes).

Gainsharing schemes can be designed with a variety of objectives, measured by indices besides output or revenue growth. Cost reduction and performance measures may be a significant part of the gainshare, but to these objectives can be added customer retention, safety, environmental impact, customer satisfaction and profitability, amongst many others. For example, in addition to the normal business measures BP Exploration had safety and environmental goals. Each of their oil and gas rigs in the North Sea (managed separately as 'assets') were on separate gainsharing schemes. Whilst this brought benefits, there was also the effect of discouraging staff transfers between the rigs, deriving from this approach.

Design features of gainsharing schemes include the following:

1 The basis for the calculation – company-wide, team, or individual measures.
2 If a team approach (often favoured), then team goals are needed.
3 What will trigger the pay-out – does the team have to pass a profitability gate before any pay-out is made? Are there variable shares according to participation in the scheme, the amount of profitability achieved, length of service, grade, occupation or other variables? Will the amount be a percentage of pay, or an equal amount for all team members?
4 Gainshare bonus may also vary according to the issue (e.g. 2 per cent for safety targets, 5 per cent for productivity targets). Very often the scheme produces a pool of money over time from which employees share according to a predetermined policy.

Choices over these design features can only be made according to the context.

Salary structures

Salary structures range in flexibility, from the most rigid rate for age or service scales to those which are entirely based on management discretion. The salary administrator's objective is to retain consistency in approach, to keep the rationality of scales whilst keeping sufficient scope to be able to reward outstanding performance.

Most scales relate salary to the grade of the job. Following a job evaluation, a series of job grades may be constructed, using any of the methods we discussed in the previous chapters (not only as an outcome of the classification method of job evaluation). If the scales are drawn on a diagram, with grades lettered A–E (A being the lowest), a salary scale could be as shown in Figure 14.1.

Clearly, one of the questions to be decided is, should the scales for each grade overlap (as in Figure 14.1) and, if so, by how much? Related to this is the question of what should be the range for the scales.

The overlap needs careful thought because of the implications for transfers between grades and promotions. To determine the range of the salary, as a rough guide, an

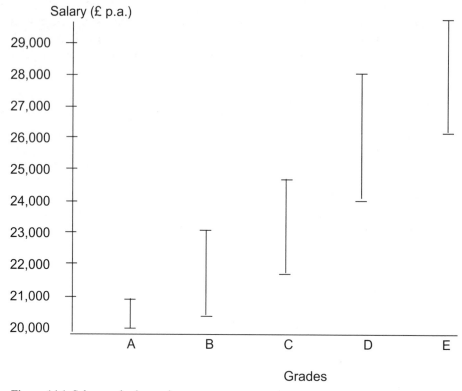

Figure 14.1 Salary scales by grade

overlap of 10–20 per cent is usual between associated grades, the salary level at the top of the range being 20 per cent to 50 per cent higher than at the bottom of the range. Higher percentage spreads for higher-grade jobs are normal, so that in Figure 14.1 the range for A is £1000, whereas for E it is about £3000.

Broadbanding

The need for flexibility at work, the flatter organization structures and the pace of change have resulted in a move away from the large number of individual grades. Careers increasingly are lateral rather than vertical, and employees work in many different teams, often within matrix structures.

Broadbanding is one suggested response to these new pressures. Broadbanding means collapsing numerous grades or salary ranges into a few wide bands. These bands cover a number of job families that formerly would each have had their own pay ranges. Companies using broadbanding usually reduce the number of salary ranges or bands by a half or two-thirds of their previous number in the traditional structure. These new broadbands may not use the same salary points as the old bands, so in the case cited in Figure 14.1 there might be three bands or ranges instead of five, say, from £20 000 to £23 000, from £22 000 to £27 000 and from £25 500 to £29 000, for example.

Creating scales from job evaluation results

In our discussion of job evaluation, the various techniques are all seen to have as their outcome an ordered positioning of jobs relative to each other. The result will be a list of job titles placed in order, but they will still need to be placed into specific grades (unless a classification scheme has been used).

Creating a scale

1 The list of jobs is placed in order, together with the associated salary and, if a points scale has been used, the points value. We will then have to decide the number of grades required. This will be dictated by the size of the organization and, in a traditional structure, the percentage salary difference between the midpoints of the grade. If we take the average salary for those ranked lowest, and the average for the highest, we can get some idea of the spread of salaries, and the step intervals will then have to be decided taking the job evaluation results into account, using the principles on overlap between rates outlined above. It would be as well to aim for only as many levels as is consistent with the evaluation results.

2 As a matter of policy, it may be that more than one set of grades is thought necessary. In this case, the top group of grades will have different criteria applied from those at lower levels.

3 When there is a points scheme we can allocate an equal span of points to each grade. The 'classification' techniques of job evaluation will provide a predetermined list of grades, but in the ranking methods some kind of arbitrary cut-off point for each grade will be needed. Jobs which fall on the boundary of two grades will have to be looked at carefully, to ensure that a correct decision on the grading has been made, looking, for example, at the salary progression implications of the grading decision.

4 Finally, we need to show the relationship between the jobs on the new scale, by plotting the relative position of jobs which can be listed along the horizontal axis with their grades, whilst salary per annum is shown on the vertical axis, as in Figure 14.2. From this, the midpoints of the new scales can be calculated and the range of the scale then decided, in a traditional salary structure.

In a broadbanded system, the midpoint will not be a significant control point. The salary ranges are usually too great, and the job families are related in a different way to the marketplace. The options are to maintain the job-evaluated results and the marketplace relationships based on these (for example, to keep the points rating as in the Hay system) and to introduce the broadbanded scales at a second stage, or to use two or three control points in the band which are related to market rates.

Assuming that a salary survey has been undertaken, or that information is available to deal with the question of what is the new market rate for jobs of each category, existing scales will need to be updated. The design and interpretation of salary survey information is rather a specialized task, and details of how to tackle that problem are given later in this chapter ('Wage/salary survey' section). A new line will have to be drawn on a graph similar to Figure 14.2 which will be the new midpoint for the updated scale (see Figure 14.3). Such an important policy step has enormous policy implications for costs, recruitment and existing relationships, since it will form the basis for the new scales.

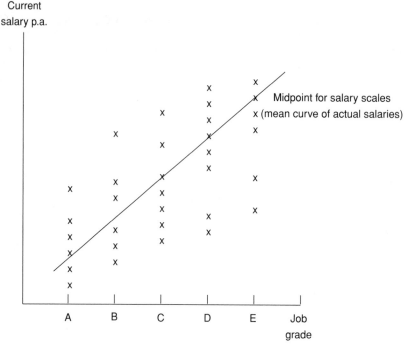

Figure 14.2 Midpoint for salary scales

Scales may have to be adjusted and any anomalies identified. There will almost invariably be a few people who do not fit easily into the salary bands and, once identified, plans for the individual's increments to bring him or her into the scale will be required.

Value/cost analysis

Outsourcing, market testing and 'best value' principles have now become common ways to reduce costs and to check the value of internal service provision. This approach can also be used to establish benchmark jobs or service values. For example, cleaning and catering services that are labour-intensive can easily be priced by reference to outside contractors. The analysis may be conducted by, first, calculating the impact on profit of the costs of replacing employment with an outsourced service and, second, comparing with this figure the costs of employment as a percentage of salary for the same service. These latter costs would need to include total compensation costs and all the 'oncosts' (National Insurance, recruitment, training, support staff, sickness/holiday cover costs, etc.).

Salary administration

How the policy is operated within the agreed structures is a matter of salary administration. Large companies will usually have a specialist salary administrator, and in the

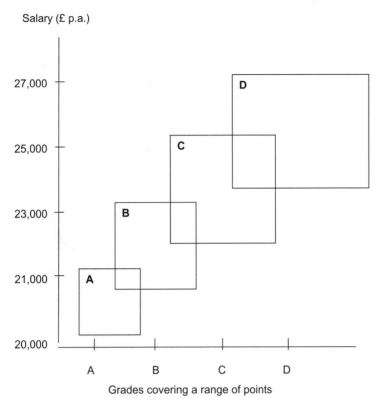

Figure 14.3 Overlap between grades

small- to medium-sized organization the task will probably fall on the HR manager, or could be performed by the chief executive, company secretary or chief accountant.

There are two types of scale to administer. There are those which have scope within each range for rewarding varying levels of performance differently, and there are those which grant automatic increments based on age and/or length of service. There are sometimes scales that give a mixture of the two.

The type of scale which provides for varying levels of performance over time can be shown as a 'box' on the graph, with overlaps between the grades (Figure 14.3).

The issues for administration are how to move individuals through these scales, and how to shift the scales themselves.

Wage/salary reviews

The impact of inflation and the annual cycle of wage negotiation have made an annual review of salaries and wages normal practice in many organizations. The distinction between the hourly rated and monthly paid is often made with different review dates. This can lead to serious problems when trying to maintain a rational basis for salary/wage differentials – evidenced when hourly rated employees transfer on to the monthly payroll, and when increases for monthly paid supervisors or indirect workers such as stores staff are considered in isolation from their hourly rated fellow workers. It is strongly recommended, therefore, that the same review dates for both groups are used.

Preparatory work on the reviews should be started well in advance. We would suggest three to six months beforehand, depending on the size and complexity of the organization. Wage and salary increases can be for one or more of the following reasons:

- cost of living
- merit
- service
- age
- market shortages (in skills, for certain groups)
- the correction of anomalies
- consolidating bonus or overtime, or other restructuring.

Managers ought to be involved at various stages in the reviews. If the increases are to be negotiated, the preparatory work will include the development of a negotiating strategy, and much supporting evidence will be required, together with the financial consequences of various prospective agreements (see Chapters 17 and 18).

Assuming either that negotiations agree the new scales and the criteria for merit increases, or that there are no union negotiations for the salary review, the following procedure is consistent with good practice:

1 HR department initiates and pilots through a job evaluation (may take some months to complete).
2 HR department undertakes salary surveys of local companies, or obtains national survey data.
3 Estimates of costs are prepared for new scales which are constructed using the data of the survey. These are submitted to the board for approval.
4 Once approved, senior line managers are given guidelines for recommending increases for merit, and an indication of the cost of living increase which has been incorporated in the new scales.
5 Line manager recommendations, confidential at this stage, are vetted by the HR manager.
6 HR manager refers back any problem cases, taking particular note of the costs and trends, notably the effect on relativities, progression policies and recruitment.
7 HR manager summarizes costs and presents consolidated list to the board (this may not include details of individual cases, but should be a breakdown of the costs into different groups). The report should include an outline of any trends and the likely effects of the increases.
8 Once approved by the board, notifications are sent to individuals through their managers, and to payroll. The information is entered on personnel records. The new scales are then published.

The same procedures can be followed for hourly rated or monthly paid staff.

Cost-of-living increases

Inflation ran at double figures in the UK for most of the 1970s, although it fell in the 1980s. Other Western European countries were similarly afflicted, as were the USA, Canada and many Third World countries. Real wages (the amount of goods and services that money wages will buy) would therefore fall unless maintained by cost-of-living increases. It is argued that this in turn fuels inflation, producing a cost push for prices to rise, rather than a demand pull. The pressure from groups of employees to gain cost-of-living increases, and the practice of incomes policy norms in the UK that set out expected percentage rises, resulted during the 1980s in all wages being under upward pressure on an annual cycle. Although inflation has subsided, there is still a residual effect as employees often anticipate cost-of-living increases in their demands.

When a scale is revised upwards, employees will expect to rise to at least the same position relatively on the new scale. However, it is possible, with the employee's agreement, to use the increase as a means of lowering the relative position in the grade, where an employee is being downgraded, for example, or where job evaluation and comparison with market rates has shown the employee to be overpaid in relation to the job. In these circumstances, rather than lower the pay the employee is best kept on a 'standstill' rate until the increases in the new grade affect the salary (so-called 'red circling'). This reflects a convention that wages are rigid downwards (see also the section on constructive dismissal in Chapter 21).

Performance-based pay/competence-based pay

One of the tests of a salary scale's adequacy is its efficiency in matching ability, potential and current performance with satisfactory rewards. To retain employees, the recognition of their performance must occur on time and equate with their own sense of what is fair. Following Elliott Jaques we might expect individuals to have a preconceived notion of what is a 'correct' salary for the work they perform.

Merit increases are therefore given to show recognition and to imply the kinds of actions and attitudes that the company wishes to reward. This has a bearing on how other employees define success in that organizational context, and thus merit increases are an essential element in the drive towards the company's objectives. There is increasing interest in performance-related pay, through merit increases tied closely to objectives. This places greater emphasis on appraisal schemes.

Competence-based reward programmes use improvements in competence or job-related skills as criteria for increases. Other performance-based systems relate salary increments to performance against objectives.

The main criticism of competence-based pay is that it is centred on the inputs to the organization, rather than the outputs. Skill acquisition is only valuable if it can be converted to outputs that generate profits/sales or reduce costs. The combination of competence and objectives as criteria for increments are, therefore, to be recommended. Skill-based increments can fit readily into a broadband salary structure, where the intention is to encourage flexibility and the deployment of a range of skills. In total compensation schemes, where there is a total value placed on the job including benefits and other costs, a core standard value is the proportion of total job value that relates to competence, which usually includes the core salary (that which it is felt should not vary with performance), as well as pensions and social security benefits. (See below for a discussion on total compensation.) Pay increases using skill or competence criteria are designed to improve an employer's skill base, to improve flexibility and to assist in the implementation of technical change. When this has been achieved, new priorities may emerge, with a consequential change to reward policy objectives.

The debate on performance-based pay has intensified recently, as schemes have spread up the managerial hierarchy and from private to public sector. There is no evidence that performance improves in the long run purely due to performance-based pay. The issues raised by Herzberg are still valid today. People are less likely to be motivated by money than they are by challenge, personal development, good supervision, feedback and a sense of achievement deriving from the work itself.

The arguments for and against performance-based pay can be summarized as follows.

Against

1 Does not motivate (the Herzberg theory).
2 After initial improvements, there is diminishing marginal utility to the organization as job holders have less and less that can be done to improve their work.
3 It is inappropriate for some jobs, for example, where quality and personal service are important.
4 Objectives change too quickly to be used annually in performance reviews.
5 The variable element would have to be considerable to have an effect, but if the rewards are highly volatile individuals are unable to plan financially (e.g. their mortgage payments).

In favour

1 In a period of low inflation, when zero increases are the norm, the only possibility for increases in pay is through productivity improvement.
2 Compensation has a high symbolic value. It symbolizes achievement and attracts peer group approval, and has a wider meaning in society.
3 If rewards can be linked to objectives, it will help to drive the objectives.
4 By basing reward on competence acquisition, there can be a coherent recruitment, appraisal and development policy.
5 There is clarity about rewards, and since all staff can have objectives all can participate.

To summarize, performance-based pay can be useful, provided objectives can be easily set and there is good communication about the scheme. In addition, the amounts of the increases must be significant and be related to organizational objectives.

Table 14.1 is an example of a performance-based pay scheme in a large financial services company. All employees are appraised and an overall performance level is agreed for each employee:

Table 14.1 Relating performance to percentage increase

Performance level	Multiple of increase (decided each year)	% amount of increase company can afford (decided each year)
1	2.0 ×	
2	1.5 ×	e.g. 5%
3	1.0 ×	
4	0 ×	

Note:

Performance levels

1 Excellent – Has exceeded all objectives and made an outstanding contribution.

2 Good – Has achieved all objectives.

3 Average – Has achieved most objectives.

4 Not rated/unsatisfactory – Has not been in job long enough to be assessed, or has not met most objectives.

A multiple of the increase is then awarded and applied to the general company increase, this being the amount the company can afford, given the distribution of performance amongst employees. Sometimes a forced distribution is created with a consequential raising of performance standards, or changes to the multiple. The reward decision is made after the appraisal review.

Fixed incremental scales

Some organizations have fixed scales. A regular increment is given on completion of each year's service. This is similar to rate for age increases (see Figure 14.4), but continues to the maximum for the scale. To retain some elements of discretion, double or triple increments can be provided for within a scheme or, indeed, no increment.

Discretional increments

A further method is to make judgements at the stage of starting (or being promoted) as to how long it will take for an individual to perform the full range of duties satisfactorily. If this is, for example, four years, then the difference between his or her starting rate and the top of the grade is divided by four years to give an even rate of increases. Should performance change during the four years, then the remaining difference between his or her current salary and the top of the scale can be made divisible by a smaller or larger number.

The divided box

The salary box (that is, the range over time) can be broken down into subranges that show appropriate rates for performance predictions on a basis of previous experience

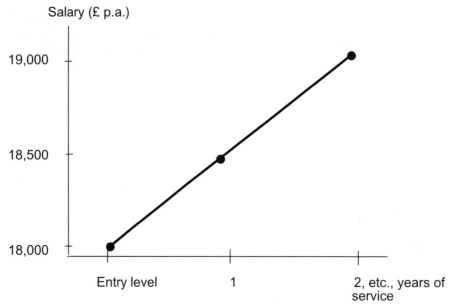

Figure 14.4 Rate for age scales

and evidence of track records. Again, an individual can be switched from one salary progression line to another if his or her performance warrants it. An example of the divided box is shown in Figure 14.5. This shows three performance levels, outstanding, good and adequate, with three different progression curves through the range.

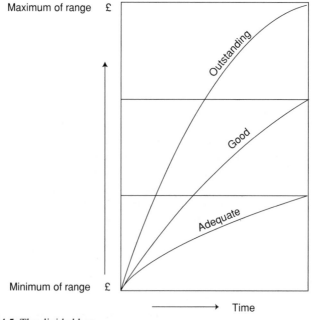

Figure 14.5 The divided box

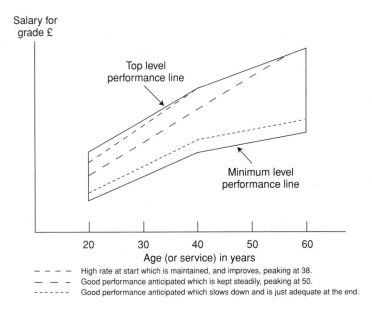

Figure 14.6 Grade funnel (three rates of progression)

Grade funnels

This is a way of describing minimums and maximums of a range, which can change with the length of service or with the age of those in the grade. The placing of the individual's salary between these parameters would, therefore, give room for high levels of performance at any age, reduce the uncertainty on where to place the new starter or those who were promoted, whilst giving room for changing the line of the salary progression if performance changes. An example of the grade funnel is shown in Figure 14.6.

Market pressures

The reaction of managers to market rates and pressures is partly a problem of how to cope with short-term changes in market rates due, for example, to a temporary skills shortage, without upsetting an agreed grading scheme that has arisen from job evaluation. If the change is not temporary (for example, a shortage of various kinds of computer specialists) the benchmark jobs will reflect the importance and rarity of the skills when the next job evaluation takes place, and a negotiation for a new pecking order will occur when the job evaluation committee meets. In practice, in the example cited, it means the organization has to place a higher value on computing or system skills because of their scarcity.

Short-term (say, up to two years) fluctuations may be met by considering a market rate supplement, which gives the shortage jobs a temporarily higher rate, which is recorded separately on their documents and records. It should be explained to the people concerned that such high percentage increases will not always be given. When market pressures abate, the salary will be brought back to the place on the salary curve that has been projected. Special bonus payments and other premiums are sometimes used to retain staff, but the use of special payments outside the scales is to be avoided, as these anomalies create precedents for other groups, distort existing relativities and, if allowed to persist, make a total nonsense of the scales.

Overtime payments

Overtime is most frequently paid to hourly rated employees; the premium may be full time and a quarter, time and a half or double time. Overtime is yet another 'plussing-up' tendency that needs careful control. The concept of overtime is usually seen as a means of overcoming a short-term requirement for longer hours. Where companies have started to rely on overtime, either because of labour shortages, or because it is a way of increasing earnings without revising scales officially, there is every likelihood of serious problems in the offing. A time will surely come when an employee does not wish to work 'compulsory overtime', or there will be a lull in orders, or a new manager will be appointed who does not agree to the 'blind eye' overtime, which is not really overtime at all but just an excuse to increase earnings. There are now legal restrictions on the number of hours an employee can be expected to work in a week. As expectations are not met, there is the making in all those situations of an industrial dispute.

A few simple rules for the control of overtime may help:

1 Overtime should always be authorized in advance by a senior manager (not the immediate supervisor).
2 A return showing the number of hours worked, and the reasons, should be made, and statistics of overtime by department kept.
3 Some allowance should be made in the wage/salary budget for overtime when it can be projected (e.g. during holidays or at peak periods).

Salary planning

We have already pointed out the importance of a policy on salaries and wages. To carry through a policy necessitates planning for both the individual's salary and for the groups of people under review. Piecemeal salary decisions are likely to result in distortion to the overall policy unless careful planning takes place. For example, there is a steady attrition of salaries when a high labour turnover brings in new employees at lower rates than existing staff to the extent that the salary mean for the grade is reduced. Although this does afford opportunities within the overall salary budget for adjustments to other salaries, the global effect is to distort differentials and to make reviews more crucial. Salary administrators can turn to a number of devices for planning salaries.

Total compensation

The high costs of employment, and the variety of additional benefits, perks and incentives are such that companies which wish to manage their human resources efficiently seek to control their total employment costs and to ensure that these expenditures are put to best use. At executive level there have always been a variety of costs associated with employment. However, benefits such as private medical insurance and pensions are spreading down organizations. There is an argument for using total compensation management for all jobs. This means that employers can communicate the total value of their compensation and negotiate on total costs with trade unions. The total compensation approach is a necessary first step towards flexible rewards and flexible benefit packages – so-called 'cafeteria' schemes. Most importantly, comparisons between different company reward systems can be made, making it possible to agree a market rate.

The elements in the package include: *perquisites* (perks), which are such elements as company cars, free use of facilities, club memberships, cheap loans, housing. *Long-term incentives* are stock options, stock appreciation rights and the like. The value taken for these is the value at the time of the award. *Benefits* are pension, medical insurance, holidays, accident, disability and death insurance. These are valued using actuarial advice for the population in question. *Short-term incentives* include commission, monthly bonus and similar schemes. The final element is the *base salary*. It would not be unusual for the base salary to be less than 50 per cent of the total compensation package in, for example, sales jobs or senior executive positions. The percentage of each component is worth recording so that changes in the balance of the total compensation package can be monitored and kept in line with the market. The monitoring of all the component parts of the total compensation package is also necessary to ensure that the most tax-effective reward policies are adopted.

Maturity curves

Projections of salary curves for groups of staff can be plotted to establish future trends. This is simply achieved by recording the salaries of people within the group on a graph, showing salary against time or age. The median salary of the group is usually taken to be a good enough measure for planning purposes. Future trends can be plotted using regression techniques. The benefits of planning a group of salaries, as distinct from individual salaries, are in the build-up of data concerning performance by the group – how long do they typically take to reach maximum for their grade and at what stage in their careers would you expect the increases in salary to level off, are two of the questions this approach helps to answer. The more stable and career-minded the group is, the greater the benefit from this kind of planning. As far as actual salaries are concerned, one can either make allowances for inflation, or predict salaries at present levels, assuming constant price/wage levels, and adjust later.

Compa ratio

The compa ratio is a measure of the general level of salaries in a grade compared with the midpoint. It is calculated by applying the following formula:

$$\frac{\text{Average of all salaries in the grade}}{\text{Midpoint of the salary range}} \times 100 \qquad (14.1)$$

This can reveal that the salaries in the grade are unusually high if the ratio is over 100, for example, or that attrition in the salaries for the grade has taken place when it is low. It is sometimes useful to calculate the compa ratio for each of the grades in a department at the time of the salary/wage review so that in discussions between the department manager and the HR manager an overall view of the salaries for the department can be taken into account. The HR manager, or salary administrator, may also wish to use the compa ratio in comparing the recommendations for merit increases between department/line managers by calculating compa ratios for the different departments. Further useful comparisons can be made across the whole company to see how the salaries for each grade stand in the structure and thus what actions are needed to correct anomalies.

Wage/salary surveys

Where the company stands in relation to the wage/salary rates being paid in the labour markets is a question that exercises all those concerned with recruitment and with pay negotiations.

There are many published sources that one can draw on. In the UK, the *Department of Employment Gazette* contains regular tables of current earnings and comments generally on the prices index as well as on wage rates, overtime and hours worked. The major reward consultancies all publish data to their clients on reward package trends in the UK and internationally. Another useful source is the information supplied by Incomes Data Services, which disseminates details of wage settlements, surveys, trends and also comments on a wide range of matters related to employment.

In spite of all these secondary sources, up-to-date information is often needed quickly, and the HR manager frequently has occasion to conduct his or her own survey. Details of local rates and salaries for specialist groups may not be available from anywhere else.

If the company is well known in the locality, or if there are good personal contacts with colleagues at other companies, a quick telephone survey will give a general indication on salaries. However, to establish accurate comparisons, something of a more formal nature has to be done.

A postal survey will require careful preparation, and will also require much effort in the analysis of results. A quick guide on conducting a survey is given below, but it should be emphasized that experience is necessary to carry out this rather difficult exercise without problems, and that time spent in piloting questionnaires and reading about survey design will pay dividends.

1 The scope of the survey must first be decided – who is covered, and the amount of information which is to be sought.
2 In order to make accurate comparisons, detailed descriptions of the jobs to be covered must be included. (You should avoid using company jargon.)
3 Make clear what you are looking for: basic wages, total earnings, the hours these represent, overtime rates and bonus earnings need to be separately recorded.
4 If the salary information given is in the form of scales, responding companies should be asked to indicate where new starters enter and where most of their current staff are

in the scales. A total compensation approach allows you to gain the most accurate data, assuming your respondents can reciprocate.

5 Information on other benefits, for example, company cars, pension schemes and holidays, is also a useful guide to the total package. Some of this may be quite sensitive – e.g. where senior staff are concerned or where sales commission earnings are involved. A guarantee of confidentiality, by avoiding naming individual companies when publishing results and ensuring that there is no way that a particular company could be identified, should be a part of your arrangements with the responding companies.

6 It is only to be expected that participating companies will require some feedback, and a copy of your analysis of results should be sent to them.

7 The results should be collated in graph form, with each graph clearly labelled and each axis marked. A short narrative report summarizing the findings will be helpful. To facilitate the analysis of the results it is often useful to consider the kinds of graphs you will find beneficial when designing the questionnaire so that the questions can be phrased to produce results in a convenient form.

8 A high non-response rate to a postal survey would not be unusual, but can be minimized by including a personal letter with the questionnaire and a prepaid reply envelope, by keeping the format of the questionnaire short and simple, giving adequate time for completion, and by telephoning those people whose reply is still outstanding after the due date.

International comparisons of salaries

An HR director once illustrated his problems in trying to harmonize pay and benefits throughout his European companies by referring to the occasion when the manager of the Greek company pointed out that the annual bonus was given in kind to his employees in the islands and that they expected to receive one or more goats each year, depending on the level of profits achieved.

Although there is now freedom of movement for labour among the European Union (EU) countries in Europe, in practice there are wide variations in conditions, hours, holidays and state regulations, so that comparison is difficult. One of the biggest problems in comparing pay internationally is the variability of exchange rates, where, for example, a rate change of only 0.5 DM to the £ sterling would lead to a large increase or decrease in pay per annum at the higher salary levels. The introduction of the Euro across most of the European community will bring its own special problems, arising from the direct comparisons of pay packages and benefits across Europe, where differences between countries will remain because of tax and social security differences.

Since the value of money is dependent on the goods and services it can buy, comparisons of earnings must also include some kind of weighting according to the level of prices in each country. However, this in itself is not enough, since there will be different patterns of purchasing between countries. Assuming that a representative range of goods and services can be found in each country, the ratios of the costs of these between countries can be determined. These ratios are referred to as 'purchasing power parities'. Although, if exchange rates and purchasing power parities are taken into account, the results of a comparison of salaries between countries will be more accurate, there is bound to be a margin of error because of the non-salary elements in the total remuneration, because exchange rates are volatile, and because patterns of consumption in such matters as transport and housing may not be comparable at all.

Pay-related benefits

Profit share

We have already described some of the schemes operated for hourly rated employees. These are typically related to output. There are other types of schemes that are more often applied to monthly paid staff where the level of net profit determines the bonus. The intention behind profit share schemes is to make the employee feel involved and to give him or her a sense of participating in the company's future growth.

A number of schemes exist. To give one example, the employees may receive a number of ordinary shares each year after the annual dividend has been calculated. The number of shares can be determined by translating the money set aside for the bonus into shares purchased at the current rate, and then issuing these to employees. The number of shares, and the cut-off point of the scheme, may include qualifications of service, grade level, etc., and a clause stipulating that the shares should not be sold for a fixed period after the bonus. Some companies retain the shares for a term after the bonus, only issuing them to employees after a year or, if the employee leaves, the bonus may be paid out in cash.

One of the difficulties of giving shares to employees is that there is a risk that the share value will fall and the employee then receives less than if they had taken cash. If the option to take cash is part of the scheme, since the number of shares granted is likely to be small, and the dividends of only a token amount, there may be less inclination for the employee to build up a sufficiently large portfolio of shares to make it worth while. There are various tax incentives given by the Inland Revenue from time to time.

The motivational force of a profit share scheme is open to doubt. Long-serving, stable groups of employees are most likely to benefit, and these are more likely to be loyal and interested in the company than the short-serving employee. The amount of money represented by the profit share is unlikely to be sufficient by itself to make employees wish to stay. It is as part of a total remuneration package that profit shares may have most importance.

Sales commissions

There are some groups of employees for whom commission payments represent their main earnings, such as sales staff, sales managers and various kinds of representatives. Questions about the usefulness of self-employed agents are beyond the scope of this book. However, it is worth considering the impact on relationships of a high percentage of commission earnings. If a small basic salary is supplemented by high commission, or bonus earnings, the sales staff become almost self-employed agents. Commission earnings not only provide an incentive, but also give employees a choice on the work they do, where they concentrate their efforts and how they plan their time. Whilst this is necessary for the typical sales job, it does entail a loss of control and a lack of stability in earnings. Some kind of balance is necessary. To provide an incentive, at least 10 per cent of earnings should be in commission, but more than 30 per cent of earnings as commission provokes a heavy reliance on immediate performance, which is inimical to training and development and gives an instability to earnings. This might encourage the employee to supplement their income by working for other companies at the same time, or to regard themselves as self-employed.

Among the items on any check list for commission schemes are a number of items worth considering in advance; the check list produced by Keith Cameron gives a good guide:

Commission schemes	
Type of target:	Number of products; sales revenue, etc.
Targeting:	Who is responsible, what target?
Eligibility:	Sales staff, internal, external, management.
Assessment intervals:	How often assessed (monthly, weekly, etc.)?
Payment intervals:	How often paid?
Threshold:	Minimum sales before commission is triggered.
Ceiling:	Maximum amount of commission (per week, month, etc.).
Accelerator/decelerator:	According to profitability of different products, percentage increase or decrease in commission.
Returns:	What happens if product is returned (defective) or if deal falls through?
Controls:	Who checks, what is checked? Paperwork?
Communication:	Telling people *what* the scheme is for and why. Communicating changes.
Time span:	Life of scheme.

Company cars

Policy on company cars will need to be laid down at the same time as the salary scales. Here the choice is whether or not company cars should be provided for use by employees privately as well as on company business, and at what level this extra benefit is to be granted. For some companies, a car goes automatically with the level of the job, and in some cases two cars are now provided, one for the manager, the other for the manager's spouse.

The main consideration here is to ensure that there are rules that govern the award of a company car and that these rules should refer to the job content. If the use of a car is essential for the job, then it is easy to justify, both to the rest of the employees and to the Inland Revenue.

Alternatives to this approach include company car purchase schemes, which allow the employee to own the car by granting a loan that is repaid over a period. Maintenance, petrol and running costs are borne by the company.

Total benefit packages/flexible benefits

When planning salaries, an approach that takes account of all the benefits and their interrelations is to be preferred. Salaries and wages should, therefore, not be examined without considering the other HR policies on holidays, sickness, pensions, hours, etc., and also the differential effect of taxation on the take-home pay of employees.

The tax-effectiveness of benefits such as company cars, and the increasing range of benefits such as private health insurance and stock option schemes, has led some companies to offer a flexible benefits package from which employees may select the mix appropriate to their needs. Originating in the USA, where the prevalence of private health insurance started the trend towards flexing benefits according to individual needs, there are around three-quarters of all companies offering flexible benefits in the USA, whilst in the UK the take-up is slower. The numbers in the UK are increasing, with companies such as Royal Bank of Scotland, Allied Domecq, W. H. Smith, Nationwide, and Cable and Wireless offering schemes.

Flexible benefit packages normally operate under the following conditions:

1 There are certain core elements in the package that cannot be traded or changed, e.g. a significant proportion of base pay, pension, life insurance and medical insurance.
2 There are rules concerning how much of the perks and benefits can be changed, e.g. the extent to which the model of company car can be traded up or down, the maximum amount of additional contributions to the pension scheme, etc.
3 There is a finite list of benefits/perks in the scheme.
4 Employees are only allowed to make changes, to exercise their flexible options, at set times (e.g. on appointment, promotion, when the car is due for change, etc.).
5 Employees receive a detailed statement showing the value of the benefits and sometimes free financial counselling periodically.

There are a number of different variations in flexible benefits, with different degrees of choice for the employee. These range from core benefits only (no choice, but basic benefits including car, pension, etc.), to 'core plus' schemes where the standard benefits given to all employees are augmented with a few limited optional extras (e.g. private health insurance), to modular schemes where as in a cafeteria, employees are able to choose a selection of benefits from a choice of set menus. The final version is either total choice of all benefits or ultimately all benefits paid in cash for the employee to use on benefits or not, according to choice.

An example of a flexible reward structure (closest to a 'core plus' scheme) from a large retailer shows a summary of benefits (see Table 14.2).

Top executives pay and remuneration committee

There is a long-standing debate about the rewards achieved by chief executive officers (CEOs) and top corporate executives. A great deal of this debate arose because of concerns that shareholders were not able, or willing, to control high pay rises well above inflation and unconnected to firm performance, granted to senior executives; the belief being that senior executives were paying themselves more because there were few

Table 14.2 Summary of benefits and their value/cash alternative

Benefits	Value	Cash alternative	Trade-up/value to buy	Comments
Company car	Maximum leasing allowance according to grade	1. 'Trade out' – the amount of your annual leasing allowance 2. 'Trade down' – the difference between your annual leasing allowance and the actual cost of the chosen vehicle (with extras)	As required within limits	
Fuel card (private petrol)	*	*	Not available to buy	
Medisure	*	*		You will be able to rejoin at any level, but obviously foregoing the cash alternative
London traveller	*	*	*	
Dental plan	*	*	As required	Additional cover can be bought for your partner and/or children
Optical plan	Depending on cover chosen	n/a	Depending on chosen cover	
Financial services	Depending on option(s) taken	n/a	Depending on option(s) taken	
Overseas holiday travel insurance	Depending on cover chosen	n/a	Depending on cover chosen	

Note: * Values in £ to be shown, according to the amounts/rates prevailing, dependent upon premiums or contract.

checks on their power to do so. There was scepticism from all political parties about the capacity of senior executives to police themselves. As Kenneth Clark (then Chancellor of the Exchequer) stated in March 1994, 'I do not think any government has the power to stop people being paid by their companies. But . . . with the rate of taxation having been reduced, people should think twice before allowing their boards to award them excessively high salaries' (quoted in *The Times*, 3 March 1994).

For some years, attempts at reforming corporate governance arrangements have been made, through reports from Cadbury, Greenbury and Hempel. These reports recommended numerous changes for companies to adopt voluntarily, and there have also been attempts by reforms to the Company Acts, persuasion by investors organizations such as the Association of British Insurers to give more power to shareholders, to separate the role of chairman from CEO, to involve non-executives in annual reports, and to regulate board and senior executive pay through remuneration committees. These committees are constituted to review the remuneration of the board, and other executives at senior level. They consist of non-executive directors, and are usually serviced by specialist compensation advice either from in-house specialists or by consultants.

The debate on whether directors' pay is excessive continues however. A report by the reward consultants, William Mercer, in 1998 who surveyed twenty of the larger UK companies showed that executive pay has overtaken inflation: salary increases were at around 23 per cent for the period 1995–8, for senior executives, whereas price inflation averaged around 6 per cent during that time, and wage inflation at around 14 per cent. The current base salary for CEOs in 1998 was £549 000. In addition there were bonus payments and share option gains. The CEO average package therefore looked as follows:

	UK
Base salary	£ 549 000
Share options	£1 389 000
Bonus	£311 000
Total	£2 249 000

The average total package was over £2 million per annum therefore. Whilst executive salary increases of 23 per cent may seem excessive, total shareholder return has increased by 98 per cent in the last three years. However, shareholder return is calculated by measuring the increase in share price, plus the dividend receipts. The massive increases in stock prices in the UK and the USA are arguably not entirely the consequence of senior management actions. The US salaries for CEOs are much higher than in the UK – 38 per cent higher base pay, and 212 per cent higher bonus. For example, over 50 per cent of US CEOs in the largest 350 companies there earned a base salary in excess of $1 million in 1997, with share option gains to match.

In 1999, the Department of Trade and Industry issued a consultation document on directors' remuneration. This recommended that all quoted companies should have remuneration committees with access to expert advice, that there be a general framework linking performance to pay, which should be disclosed, as should any gains made by directors on exercising these share options.

The linkage disclosed should set out the long-term objectives in relation to board performance, the criteria for performance measurement and the comparator companies, and the relationships between firm performance and director rewards. Disclosures should include details of contracts and compensation arrangements. The government would also like shareholders to vote annually on director remuneration.

Behind these recommendations is the concern that in a number of high profile cases, director remuneration has increased whilst firm performance has declined. There are also concerns about social justice, the widening gap between the rich and the poor, and the difficulty of maintaining pay restraint by the mass of working people, to avoid cost push inflation, if the top executives in companies are seen to be receiving massive pay increases.

Questions

1 What should be the main objectives of a modern salary/wage policy? How can we ensure that it is being applied equally?
2 What are the advantages of long-term group bonus schemes? Illustrate your answer by reference to an added value scheme.
3 How can we introduce flexibility into salary structures without losing control of costs?
4 How can we overcome the problems which are associated with performance-based pay schemes?
5 What are the steps to take in conducting a salary survey?
6 What place should profit share schemes have in a total reward package?

Chapter 15

Conditions of service

We outlined earlier the significance of those HR policies that provide a framework of conditions influential in creating the quality of work life. Conditions of service governing such issues as hours of work, holidays and pensions are fundamental to the contract of employment that exists between the employer and the employee.

Companies face a number of options when constructing their HR policies. The decisions made will reflect their philosophy of HR work. A number of factors will have to be taken into account by managers who confront the range of options available:

1 *Financial considerations*: the direct and indirect returns on investment have to be investigated, which entails a cost/benefit analysis of each policy.
2 *The stability of the labour force*: here, the impact of the proposed policy on those groups who seek organizational careers should be examined.
3 *The age and sex distribution of the labour force*: this raises the question of what influence these measures have on the operation of the policy.
4 *The administrative costs involved in servicing the policy*: for example, the costs of running a pensions scheme.
5 *State welfare benefits*: how do these affect the policy?
6 *Industrial relations implications* which may derive from the policy – such as the sort of groupings which are created, and the interests which are reinforced or weakened by the policy chosen. What are the consequences for the company's industrial relations strategy?

In this chapter we will look at hours of work, holidays, sick pay, pensions and welfare policies.

Hours of work

The hours of work for any job are a result of tradition, collective bargaining, technical necessity, convenience for management control and for communication needs. There are some people, such as sales representatives, for whom there may be no normal hours of work.

The distinction should be drawn between 'basic hours' and the normal hours worked, which may include overtime. For some of the major industries, the basic hours are subject to negotiation between employees and trade unions at a national level. When thinking of basic hours, we have to be sure of what is included: for example, does the time include tea breaks, lunch breaks, time for starting machinery, for cleaning up, etc.? Overtime is more common in the UK, where until recently around 16 per cent of employees work more than forty-eight hours per week, which is more than in other European countries. As a way of bolstering earnings in low-paid jobs it is clearly an unsatisfactory approach by which whole occupational groups and management come to rely on longer hours. The tendency to use overtime as a common way to flex labour in response to changes in demand is diminishing, in preference for changed working time arrangements.

There is legislation in the UK covering the permitted hours of work for women and young people, and for occupational groups such as drivers, for health and safety reasons. There is also European-wide legislation on hours of work, as described in Chapter 21.

The Working Time Directive came into force in the UK on 1 October 1998. This stipulates a forty-eight hour week, four weeks paid holiday per year, weekly rest period of at least twenty-four consecutive hours every seven days, a daily rest break of at least twenty minutes during a working day of six hours or more and a daily rest period of eleven consecutive hours in every twenty-four hour period.

The rules about working times are complex. Air, road, and seafaring workers are excluded from the rules. All those on a contract of employment are included, but a minimum of thirteen weeks service is required and the genuinely self-employed are excluded. Exemptions are few. For example, partners are exempt (but not solicitors), as are very senior autonomous workers. Under Regulation 21 certain provisions are excluded in specific circumstances, for example, where there is a need for continuity of service or production, such as hospitals, prisons or the media.

The calculation of the average weekly hours is over a seventeen-week reference period. If an employee or employer opts out of the forty-eight hour week, for special reasons, the employer or the employee must keep a daily record of the hours worked. Night workers cannot opt out, and their average normal hours should not exceed eight hours for each twenty-four hour period. Night workers are entitled to a free medical assessment.

Holiday pay may be accrued and paid at the termination of employment. The regulations only deal with minimum leave entitlement. Regulations are enforced through employment tribunals.

There are many variations in hours, according to industry, occupation and, of course, where there is shift working or where flexible hours are used. These two aspects of hours are worthy of special attention.

Shift working

Shift working is introduced to make more efficient use of machinery, to increase production, or because the market or the technology requires continuous staffing. There are five main types of shift working, as shown in Table 15.1.

In addition to these shift patterns, there are different forms of part-time working used,

Table 15.1 Example of shift-work patterns

Shift type	Hours per shift	Typical start times and finish times	Cycle
Double day	8 hours per day	06.00–14.00; 14.00–22.00	2 groups of workers rotate each week, early/late shift
Day and night alternating	10 in 24 hours	08.00–18.00; 22.00–08.00	2 groups of workers alternating weekly or fortnightly, with rest days in between
Permanent nights	11 in 24 hours	18.30–05.30	2 groups of workers, 2-week cycle, with rest days: 3 rest days after 1st week, 2 rest days after 2nd week
3-shift discontinuous	8 in 24 hours	06.00–14.00; 14.00–22.00; 22.00–06.00 Monday to Friday inclusive	Weekly or fortnightly for the 3 groups of employees
3-shift continuous	8 in 24 hours	As above, but 7 days Monday to Sunday inclusive	4 groups of employees' cycle for 3–24 weeks. 1. Traditional pattern one week of each type for each person, with rest days; 2. 'Continental' pattern: 2 or 3 shifts of the same kind, with rest days in between

and mixtures of the systems outlined in Table 15.1, for example, one part of a factory may be working, say, permanent nights, whilst another part operates a 'twilight shift' from 16.00 to 22.00.

Shift working leads to problems with domestic and social life for many employees, and may give rise to health worries. Most of our lives seem to be structured to a working existence where 8.00 to 17.30 is the norm. In the provision of children's schooling, travel and services, the assumption of daytime working is made. There are trends towards twenty-four hour shopping, and telephone banking, which are gearing people's lives to a different style. Although there may be compensation in being at home when others are at work, partners and children can be upset by the irregularity of hours and absences in the evening. The change of the shift cycle from days to nights, and then back, disturbs the bodily functions – the circadian rhythms of heart, respiration, body temperature, blood pressure and digestion. 'Stress' manifested in sleeplessness, digestive disorders and even depression, may therefore be felt by some shift workers.

The research on the effects of shift work on health is inconclusive so far, but it is possible that some people are better able to accept the disturbance of different shift cycles than are others. The extent to which the shift worker's family accepts the pattern of the hours, and whether or not the worker is psychologically prepared to accept the changes, may be the key factors.

There are also managerial problems with shift work. Communications between the members of each shift are often inaccurate, the night-shift personnel may feel left out or come to regard themselves as a separate unit. Friction between the shifts can arise from apparently trivial incidents, such as the cleaning up of machinery or failure to report a new technical problem. It follows, therefore, that management must make a special effort in:

- training managers in the special problems of shift work
- attending to shift workers' communication problems, for example, by working along with shift supervisors and using written communications
- the provision of welfare, occupational health and catering facilities, such as canteens, social clubs, etc., which cater for the needs of the shift worker.

Clock time and task time

Hours of work are not important to those whose activities are directed towards the accomplishment of tasks irrespective of when they occur. To use Berne's terms, we can distinguish between 'clock time' and 'task time'. Attendance at work at particular times may be essential for jobs that give a service to others, but for other posts where there is an amount of work that has to be completed, quite apart from the time, attendance can be more flexible. It may also be possible to only pay people when 'called out' to work – that is, to employ them on zero hours contracts. The development of a more flexible approach to working hours stems from the desire of employees to avoid rigid time-keeping and from the difficulties that employers have in recruiting and retaining staff in some areas.

New technology in the form of laptops, fax machines and on-line facilities has revolutionized the way work is done and, just as significant, where work is done. Homeworking and flexible contracts fit together well for some people, where work may be completed in the evening or at weekends at home without any loss of efficiency. There are potential gains – by working at home and avoiding wasteful journeys to and from work more productive hours are available, able staff whose contribution would otherwise be restricted through childcare, care of the elderly or through disability are able to work, and creativity is encouraged. However, homeworking does potentially reduce the socializing benefits of congregating with fellow workers and, in spite of tele-conferencing, makes meetings less easy to attend and to run. Homeworking for managers who also go to the office may create a situation where work becomes intrusive in the home.

Flexible working hours

The basic principles of flexible working hours have been described by Baum and Young (1973: 19) as: 'The essential aim of the flexible working day is to replace the traditional fixed times at which an employee starts and finishes work by allowing him/her a limited choice in deciding his/her starting and finishing time each day.'

A 'core time' (see Figure 15.1) is established by the employer when attendance is required – usually the middle period of the day, excluding the meal break. The start and finish times are variables on either side of this. The contract between the employer and

Core times 10.00–12.00 and 14.00–16.00. Lunch: a minimum mandatory lunch break of half an hour to be taken between 12.00 and 14.00. Contracted hours: seven per day, thirty-five per five-day week, four-weekly accounting period.

Figure 15.1 An example of a flexible working hours scheme

the employee fixes the number of daily contracted hours, which are assessed over periods of from one week to one month. The employee thus starts and leaves work at times that are convenient for him or her, times which can vary day by day to suit his or her own circumstances. When an employee works longer than the contracted daily hours a credit is carried forward or, if he or she works less, a debit. The period over which the employee is expected to balance debits and credits is known as the 'accounting period', and can be a week, two weeks, four weeks or a calendar month. The idea was pioneered in Germany, but has now spread to the UK where there are a number of different types of flexible working hours schemes (FWH) in operation. Electronic recording equipment is used because of the necessity for large numbers of accurate records to be processed.

As an illustration of the variety of schemes, we can note that there are those that have flexibility over the lunch break, and there are different approaches to the amount of core time, the total debits and credits allowed to accumulate, the length of the accounting period and the methods of calculating holidays and overtime.

In the case of Figure 15.1, the employee may start any time between 7.00 and 10.00, and the time of leaving is flexible from 16.00 to 18.00. He or she must take at least half an hour for lunch between 12.00 and 14.00.

A further refinement is used where the employee can carry credits over to the following accounting period, and these can be put towards holiday entitlement. The company would need to have agreed a formula for credit leave units, which could be half or whole days based on the number of contracted hours per day.

The introduction of an FWH scheme requires care and preparation. Care is needed in the early stages of the negotiations with employee representatives to make clear the opportunities for personal choice and the attendant responsibilities that such a scheme offers. Consultation with employees over a number of months before the scheme is to come into operation may help to surface hidden doubts and misconceptions, and give time to explain what the scheme is about. A company policy on the 'core time', the accounting period and how credits and debits will be dealt with should be thought out well in advance. Questions about how overtime is to be calculated, what to do about domestic crises, the problem of part-time staff and explanations about the equipment on which records will be kept must be dealt with early on in the planning. Communication about the scheme needs expert handling, and the role of the first-line supervisor is crucial in this process.

The overriding constraint on FWH schemes is the needs of the business, and there will be many occupations where it is not practical. Flexible working hours schemes seem to be most used where there are large numbers of administrative staff, such as in national and local government departments and large insurance companies, and the benefits of the scheme for recruitment in tight labour markets are clear.

Flexible working hours should be distinguished from agreements made between employers and trade unions to work a total number of hours per year, the precise start and finish times to be decided by management. Such annualized hours contracts allow organizations to match closely the amount of labour to market demands. This is helpful, for example, so that there is sufficient labour to meet the peaks in a seasonal demand. Annual hours agreements give control to management over working time, the flexibility is at their discretion, whereas flexible working hours are (within limits) under the control of the employee.

Holiday entitlement

Employees now have a right to four weeks paid holiday per year. The main difference is between rules under which the employee has to build up his or her entitlement first, by working for the full 'holiday' year, and schemes where the employee can anticipate his or her completion of a year's service.

The holiday entitlement year is the year during which entitlement is built up. This may be the same as the calendar year, or based on 'financial', 'accounting' or other 'years'.

Shutdowns for the whole holiday period

Factory shutdowns are common in some industries, for example, the 'Wakes Week' in northern England, and there are localized traditional days such as the 'Glasgow Fair'. There are often good technical reasons for a total shutdown, which provides time for essential overhauls and maintenance on the factory buildings. Shutdowns also avoid difficulties where the work is so interlinked that staggered holiday arrangements would not be practical. Where families are working in different companies in the same locality, local shutdown helps cases where husband and wife want to go on holiday together. If the couple work for different employers, however, and they have different shutdowns, this can result in an employee leaving, or wanting holiday without pay.

Joint careers

With the advent of both members of the household pursuing careers, domestic problems can arise where there is insufficient flexibility by either partner's employers to make joint holidays possible.

Other than a general commitment to be sympathetic to this problem, a policy response is not really required, difficulties being better dealt with on an individual basis. Department managers can help to relieve the problems of joint careers and clashes in holiday dates by initiating a holiday roster early in the year, giving priorities where there are severe family problems and ensuring that people with firm dates record them on the roster as quickly a possible.

Sick pay

The fear of losing earnings through sickness absence haunted workers until social security and sickness schemes were introduced.

The main rules regarding statutory sick pay (SSP) are that employers pay SSP where there is an entitlement for up to twenty-eight weeks to employees who are sick for at least four days consecutively (including weekends and bank holidays). Entitlement is determined by the following:

1   SSP is paid for whole days (not parts of days).
2   Employees must comply with the employer's rules regarding notification of absence.
3   Payment is only made for the fourth and any subsequent qualifying days.
4   A period of entitlement begins with the first day of incapacity to work and ends when the first of any of the following events occurs: SSP is exhausted, the incapacity period ends, the employee is in prison, the contract of employment ends, or the maximum period of entitlement (three years) is reached.
5   There are special rules regarding pregnancy, invalidity pensions and trade disputes.

The overall effect of these arrangements is to put pressure on employers to curb sickness absence.

Personnel records and statistics

Personnel records and statistics provide the information that is an essential part of a system for effective HR management. They are continuously necessary as a basis for decisions affecting major functions such as human resource planning, recruitment and selection, employment of staff, performance appraisal, training, career development, management development, succession planning, transfers, promotion, rewards, health and safety, etc. They are also needed to supply information to a variety of external authorities and agencies, for example, Department of Employment, Health and Safety Executive, employers' association, trade unions, etc.

It may seem too obvious for comment, but the importance of up-to-date, accurate data cannot be overemphasized. A sound information system needs to satisfy the following criteria: the information recorded and available for use should be actually necessary, up to date, regularly revised, accurate, comprehensive, as simple as possible, accessible and instantly retrievable. It is needed in two forms, organizational and individual.

Organizational information

Organizational statistics serve two very important functions: they provide essential information about main areas affecting the general state of the organization at a particular time; they also indicate trends that need to be made apparent, so that timely measures may be taken to improve conditions of work and performance. The main statistics that normally need to be kept are briefly described below.

1 *The state of the labour force*, that is, the number actually employed as against the budget, or establishment, figure. This needs to be for a specific period, and we will assume that this is *one year* in the ratios below. We discussed labour turnover in the chapter on HR planning. In addition, statistics on labour stability and on a variety of other indicators should be routinely examined.
2 *Timekeeping/attendance*: ratio

$$\frac{\text{Number of person hours lost}}{\text{Total possible person hours worked}} \times 100 \qquad (15.1)$$

3 *Accidents* (including types): ratio for frequency

$$\frac{\text{Number of lost time accidents}}{\text{Number of person hours worked}} \times 100\ 000 \qquad (15.2)$$

(100 000 total of hours in an average working life)
4 *Health* (including types of illness): sickness statistics, showing average length of absence.

These statistics need to be broken down into departments, locations, occupations, grades, sex, age groups and, where applicable, causes.

The information organizations need for purposes of effectively employing individuals and for looking after their interests are these:

1 The original application for employment and the contract of employment.
2 Notes and results recorded during selection procedures.
3 Up-to-date personal details, e.g., address, sex, date of birth, family, National Insurance number, tax references, etc.
4 Career history (education and training, qualifications, jobs and experience, responsibilities, promotions, noteworthy events, covering previous and present employers).
5 Assessments of performance, appraisal, rewards.
6 Records of health.
7 Records of absence, accidents, conduct and any consequential action (e.g. formal warnings, inefficiency, grievance procedures).
8 Records of any career interviews with HR staff.
9 Details of salary, bonuses, merit pay, pension contributions, etc.
10 Membership of unions, staff associations and societies, including any offices held.
11 Notes on termination of employment, e.g. reasons, dates and consequences if known (new employer, retirement, etc.).

The main elements of a personnel records and statistics system are shown in Figure 15.2.

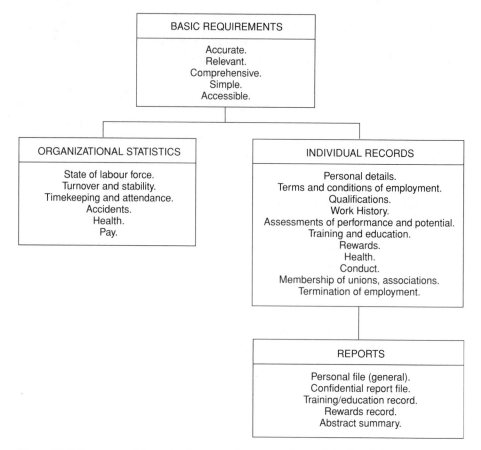

Figure 15.2 Summary of the main elements of a personnel records and statistics system

How this considerable quantity of varied information is organized will depend upon the requirements and practices of each organization. Nowadays, computer-based systems are usual, although some paper-based files may be kept with original documents, such as contracts of employment.

Except for small, private organizations it will usually be necessary to use several records or databases, some of which are kept centrally, that is, in the HR department, and what is to be kept by each department. The main, comprehensive records will certainly need to be kept centrally in the HR department, but departments and branches will probably need some basic items for regular daily use. One would expect line managers to have access to the computer system from their personal computers (PCs) to HR records.

The requirements of the Data Protection Act should be kept in mind (see Chapter 21). The rapid development in recent times of data processing and information technology based on computers has revolutionized the maintenance of personnel records. As a result, a considerable quantity of detailed information can now be stored and instantly retrieved.

The great benefit of receiving regular reports from the desk-based PC in the HR department is obvious. Only in this way can reports on sickness absence, the availability of particular skills, or wage/salary information necessary for planning and controlling be rapidly made available. There are many different software packages available, which will help to collate and analyse information for succession planning, development and competence recording. Systems which bring up prompts for example to ensure appraisals are completed on time, and the direct entry on to the system by line managers are all routine matters now.

Absenteeism

Unscheduled absences from work give rise to serious management problems. Planning is brought to nothing by the absence of a significant number of the workforce.

Sick-pay schemes are sometimes blamed for influencing those who are not genuinely ill to stay at home, because the threat of loss of earnings has been removed. However, the subject is more complicated than it may appear. There may be more illness among certain groups of workers because of the nature of their work. Hourly rated personnel may have to take days off for spurious illnesses, since, unlike their monthly paid counterparts, they are more stringently supervised and can only attend to personal problems in this way. Although it is easy to accuse someone of malingering if he or she takes a number of single days off for rather unconvincing reasons, the person concerned may be under some form of stress or just have a general feeling of unease, tiredness and fatigue. Absenteeism may also be a safety valve preventing serious industrial unrest, as it allows individuals a way of expressing a token protest.

There are more clearly identified trends in absenteeism. Alcohol is a significant cause of absences on Mondays. There are occupational reasons for illnesses – drivers often suffer from ulcers and digestive complaints, and 'jet lag' has come to be accepted as a reason for absence for globe-trotting executives, for example. The stress of each job is not obvious to outside observers.

Stress

'Stress' is a generic term for a whole area of problems arising from physical and psychological reactions to perceived challenges or threats to well-being which are beyond the subject's normal capacity to meet. There are physical symptoms of stress, such as high blood pressure, eating disorders, sleeplessness, irritability and so on. The extent to which the person affected is feeling adverse reactions to a stressor will be mediated by the perception of the stressor, the individual's personality type, the degree of control over the situation felt by the subject and the coping style adopted.

Many people will experience some mental difficulties in a lifetime. It is estimated that around 20 per cent of people will suffer a major depressive episode in their lifetime (that is, lasting two weeks or more), 15 per cent will suffer from some kind of anxiety disorder, 33 per cent have had at least one panic attack and 11 per cent have suffered from some kind of phobia. There is growing evidence that illnesses such as immune system problems (for example, opportunistic infections, allergies), some cardiovascular disease, memory loss and even sexual dysfunction have a stress-related element. 'Burn out' symptoms, such as irritability, persistent sense of failure, blame or guilt, feelings of discouragement, lack of concentration, rigid thinking, suspicion of others and social isolation can be traced often to a long exposure to stressful situations.

Those with mental ill health problems are often frightened to reveal their difficulties to others, so great is the stigma, and where it is obvious research has shown 38 per cent of people with mental health problems reported being teased, harassed or intimidated at work (Read and Baker, 1996). The amount of work intensification has recently been seen as one cause of increasing reports of stress. The most highly rated causes named recently were time pressures, deadlines (60 per cent), 54 per cent work overload, 52 per cent threat of job losses, 51 per cent lack of consultation and 46 per cent understaffing (Cooper, 1997).

There is now a legal requirement to deal effectively with work-related stress (the *Walker* v. *Northumberland County Council* case) and the Department of Health estimated in 1995 that 9.1 million working days are lost each year due to stress-related illness, costing £3.7 billion.

Corporate reactions include Employee Assistance Programmes, where employees can talk to counsellors independent of the company, better occupational health policies and health education relating to eating, exercise habits and stress reduction workshops. If managers are fretting about malingering, they must separate out the genuinely sick from those who are not genuinely ill. Illness has no precise definition; it is, therefore, best left for managers and supervisors to deal with individual cases with the help of occupational health specialists and HR managers if necessary. Perhaps the most useful approach is to try to create conditions under which employees want to go to work and look forward to the experience rather than fear or dislike it.

Pension schemes

The decision by the European Court in *Barber* v. *Guardian Royal Exchange Assurance* (in 1990) that pension schemes are a part of 'pay' has resulted in a number of rulings that have brought pensions within the equal pay provisions, to remove discrimination against women on pension matters. Pension ages for state pensions will be equalized gradually from the year 2010 onwards.

Part-time employees must now also have the right to enter pension schemes. It is the duty of pension fund trustees to comply with European law, and employers can be told to make up contributions to the pension fund to enable the trustees to meet their European law obligations. The Pensions Act 1994 introduced a general principle of equal treatment between men and women in respect of pensions, and rights to trustees for paid time off for training and further duties. All occupational pension schemes must treat maternity and parental leave as pensionable service. Pensionable service must accrue at the normal rates of pensionable salary and cannot be reduced by lower pay during the leave. In money purchase pension schemes the employer has to pay any shortfall in normal employee contributions based on normal salary. For final salary pension schemes, the employer is not required to pay the extra contributions, but is liable for the solvency of the fund as a whole.

The wave of redundancies in the late 1990s has resulted in an expansion of early retirement. That is certainly one option, albeit an expensive one for any employee below sixty years of age.

The government has introduced a measure that allows employees to opt out of an occupational scheme, provided they enter a private scheme of their own choosing. 'Portable pensions' should encourage labour mobility.

Redundancy/early retirement

The general trade recession, and the structural changes in the older industries of Western Europe, such as steel, mining and transport, have led managers to look at how they can reduce their labour force in a 'painless' way. Early retirement is one approach used to overcome the trauma of dismissal.

The benefits can be summarized as follows:

1 The support given by a retirement pension takes away some of the financial anxiety, giving time for the employee to look for other employment.
2 Older employees may have fewer financial responsibilities (children have left home, mortgage has been repaid, etc.), whereas redundancy for a younger person may have a more harmful effect on the family.
3 Early retirements can 'unblock' promotion opportunities in the future, and create a more dynamic organization.
4 It may be less psychologically damaging to be 'retired early', given that a person who is going to retire in a year or two will already be preparing for his or her retirement. The term 'redundancy' is also rather unpleasant to some, implying uselessness and reflecting on the job holder rather than the job.
5 Early retirement gives some financial advantage to the person who can find other employment, as he or she may still draw his or her pension.

The disadvantages of using 'early retirement' to slim down a labour force are:

1 Early retirement is costly to the company. The costs of paying both the employee's and the employer's contribution to the pension scheme will obviously be higher the longer the employee would have served. Ten years is the maximum most employers would expect to buy for all practical purposes. A straight redundancy payment (even including a 'golden handshake') is likely to be cheaper.
2 The option of early retirement is only open when there is a pension scheme of which the employee has been a member for some years. The loss of increments up to the normal retirement date, although mitigated by extra allowance by the company in its pension calculations, will be felt as a serious blow if settlements in wage rates are higher than the allowance made to compensate for inflation.
3 The early retirements that are voluntary may be from groups from which losses are not required, whilst others hang on to their jobs when they ought to leave for the sake of economic efficiency.
4 The company loses its most experienced workers. The loss of skills is potentially damaging to the training of younger employees.

Outplacement

There is now extensive use of outplacement for those made redundant. This consists of the provision of special counselling and help through the transition, as well as the creation of a job search strategy for the individual affected. Approximately 75 per cent of companies in the UK use either external (consultancy-based) outplacement or internally provided outplacement services. These are in various forms, from one-to-one counselling and help (often for executives) down to group schemes for shop-floor workers. There is a burgeoning outplacement industry in the USA, as well as in other parts of Europe and the UK. The objective, from the employer's point of view, is to ease the pain of redundancy by including outplacement in the package, and also to demonstrate to the 'survivors' (those who remain after their colleagues have been made redundant) an acceptable level of care in order to maintain the motivation and morale of the survivors – who are a key group in any restructuring.

Welfare policies

Personnel management originated in part from the early welfare workers of the 1890s to 1918. With the growth of employment management from the 1930s, specialist welfare departments have become only adjuncts to the main HR department. The welfare role has moved into specialist services, and has also become more diffuse in its general applicability to all managerial jobs.

The management of people now brings managers into contact with a huge variety of personnel problems and organizational issues, ranging from drug abuse, alcoholism and Aids, to overwork, stress and problems arising from single parenthood, care of the elderly and interpersonal disputes about smoking or other habits.

We will consider policy responses to some of these problems in our chapters on health and safety and employment law, but we should note here the scale of the problem and the need for line managers and their HR colleagues to be alert to the difficulties these problems can cause. Smoking (even passive smoking) causes around 100 000 deaths each year in the UK. The number of people reported HIV-positive rises each year, along with the smaller number with full-blown Aids. Smoking and Aids can cause disruption not just from absence due to illness, but also from the reactions of others around them. However irrational, these need to be taken into account.

Drug abuse is becoming a major problem. In 1991, in Manhattan, New York, a subway accident caused the deaths of five people, with 170 injuries. A vial of crack cocaine was found in the driver's cab, and later the driver was found, drunk. In the USA 66 per cent of drug users are employed, and the dangers are obvious. There is a growing trend towards testing employees, and prospective employees, for any evidence of substance abuse.

Specialist assistance and care is needed to help these people, but before that can be provided line managers and HR staff have to manage the referral of employees to the appropriate agencies, as well as manage the communications issues.

The welfare role of the manager

All managers have a welfare role to perform for their staff. The immediate line manager or supervisor will be first to notice the signs that an individual has a problem – poor performance, absence, sickness and difficulties in relationships will be seen by the perceptive manager, who should be conscious of the importance of a sense of well-being for the achievement of results.

Such an approach by managers does mean that they see themselves as helpers to their staff. Helping in this sense is being supportive, problem-solving with subordinates and constantly seeking ways to make the employee successful. Given such a manager–subordinate relationship, personal problems and sickness, for example, will be problems the subordinate will want to share and, if it is feasible, to seek help in solving.

There will be occasions when expert assistance is required. The skill for the manager in his or her welfare role therefore, has two aspects. He or she must be able to diagnose with the employee what the problem is and, if possible, help to solve it, and he or she must be able to persuade the employee that expert help is required where necessary.

Occupational health

There have been occupational health initiatives since Dr Thomas Legge's appointment as the first Medical Inspector of Factories and Workshops in 1898. The World Health Authority defines health as 'not merely an absence of disease or infirmity but also a state of physical, mental and social well-being'. The Health and Safety Executive lists the modern environment for occupational health as:

1 Comprehensive Health and Safety legislation – actively promoted by the European Union.
2 Concept of risk assessment firmly established in practice.
3 Increased professional standing and organization of occupational health disciplines, including medical (organized through the faculty of occupational medicine, as a part of the Royal College of Physicians) nursing, ergonomics, etc.
4 Greater expansion of the general biomedical science base.
5 Widespread public and media interest.
6 Greater access to sources of information, including via the Internet.

The Health and Safety Commission is constantly pushing forward the frontiers; witness the proposed new code of practice on stress at work. Nevertheless, organizations do not often invest in their own medical officer, so there is a danger that HR staff may not always have access to medical opinion trained in employment matters if they rely on reports from the general practitioner rather than use specialist occupational health advice.

Counselling at work

The first stage in seeking help is the 'counselling interview'. This kind of interview requires a problem-solving approach. To apply this technique, experience and training are needed, but the following outline gives an impression:

1 *The identification of the problem*: this requires a non-directive approach, using open-ended questions which allow the problem holder to explain his or her problem, listening and *not* offering advice or evaluative comments. The manager or welfare officer must remain neutral at this stage. To allow the employee to talk about topics that are highly sensitive, it is important that he or she be given time to think and express him or herself – thus silences should be allowed, and techniques for opening up the problem should be used, for example, 'reflecting back' key phrases to elicit some further expansion of the issues raised.

2 *The conditions under which the problem occurs*: by exploring the conditions under which the person experiences the problem, the 'boundaries' of the problem can be found. If the conditions changed, would the problem change? The 'conditions' include the feelings of the person whose problem it is. These feelings are facts. By allowing problem holders to reveal what their own feelings are, they will come to accept their own part in the problem. Active help that a supervisor might contemplate to alleviate problems could include changes within the job, relieving pressures for a temporary period, getting the subordinate to use his or her workmates in helping to resolve a problem.

3 *Solutions to problems will only be real solutions if the person who believes there is a problem also believes in the solution*: it is most likely that people will believe in the solution if they put it forward. They should therefore be encouraged by the manager to do so, and a useful role for the manager is to get the subordinate to evaluate his or her own solutions rationally.

4 *Where a problem is identified which requires expert help*: this switches the focus to the problem of how to achieve a fruitful conjunction between the problem holder and the expert agency (e.g. drug addiction centres, marriage guidance, etc.). Various types of supportive behaviour will assist – for example, giving time off, respecting confidentiality, accompanying a nervous person on the first visit, etc.

It is clear from the above rather brief account of counselling that there is a difference between 'counselling' and 'discipline'. The distinction is in the concept of discipline that the manager possesses. If he or she believes that the employee can change him or herself then the counselling role is appropriate. Only when this has been tried and failed should he or she move into the discipline procedure (see Chapter 21).

Specialist welfare roles

Specialist welfare officers can offer a unique role. Where they are neither part of senior management, nor within the employee groups, they can portray a kind of neutrality which makes them valuable as helpers in the wider social problems that society faces. The personal problems experienced are sometimes so serious that they need to be discussed with someone outside the chain of command. For the person with problems of alcoholism, or whose children are in trouble, for example, the neutral welfare officer may also have useful contacts with outside help. Their specialized experience will also enable them to recognize problems more readily. The most productive arrangement is where there are both a well-trained, sympathetic line supervisor and an experienced welfare officer. Given a mutual desire to help employees, much can be accomplished by these two working together.

Typical welfare problems

Young employees

Line managers and welfare officers should take a particular interest in young people. Line managers are giving a lead to youngsters by their example, and are building up the new entrants' supervisory skills when they inculcate a helping, caring attitude. Welfare officers should make themselves known to new employees and should be active in bringing sports and social activities to their attention. It is particularly valuable for the welfare officer to bring together young people who can then share common problems in a mutually supportive relationship. Accommodation is often a problem for new employees in large cities, and one might expect a register of accommodation to be kept within the HR or welfare department that should be vetted for standards and the list kept up to date.

Sickness

Long-term sickness produces problems of coping with a lower income and extra costs for hospitalization, as well as a variety of other difficulties, such as emotional upsets and finding help to look after children. Here, expert help from a welfare officer, plus assistance from the HR department with sick pay, time off problems, etc., is necessary. Sick visiting has long been a function of welfare and line management, and shows that a real interest is being kept up in the employee's welfare.

Retirement

Retirement comes as a shock to many people. The whole of a family's domestic and social existence is predicated on the assumption of a regular income and the security provided by employment. Patterns of behaviour that have come to be regarded as normal for forty years are suddenly changed on the sixtieth or sixty-fifth birthday. There is a need to prepare people for retirement, therefore, by attending pre-retirement courses and discussion groups. The preparation will cover the practical questions about pension and social security benefits, taxation problems, how to keep fit, how to develop new interests, and will give employees a chance to become acquainted with the idea of retirement. Welfare officers and senior line managers should continue meeting ex-employees after retirement and be on the lookout for hardship.

Canteen facilities

Welfare policies are not only concerned with individuals. Canteen facilities, sports and social clubs, company outings, long-service awards and preferential purchase schemes are just some of the areas that welfare policies cover. Of these, canteen facilities tend to be most contentious. Among these general welfare policies, the quality of the canteen facility and the amount of subsidy are most likely to affect relationships. This is quite disproportionate to the costs, but it reflects the concern of people who will take even minor failures in catering very personally. Matters such as cleanliness, the quality of the cooking and the prices are among the most crucial. To help diminish the contention, many companies have put the control of the canteen in the hands of a committee representing employee interests, or have outsourced the restaurant or canteen to high-quality specialist providers.

Conclusion

In the broadest sense, employee well-being is what HR management is about. To grant employees a sense of well-being requires more than just a felt fair pay and benefits policy; it needs a positive approach to the welfare of people at work, by managers and specialist welfare staff alike.

Questions

1 What are the problems of shift working?
2 What are the benefits of FWH schemes? How do FWH schemes differ from annualized hour schemes?
3 What factors would you have to weigh up when considering an early retirement option in order to reduce the organization's labour force?
4 Read the case study below and consider what went wrong here, and what are the actions which should have been taken.

Case study: The marketing director who wasn't

SB was part of a chemicals, consumer products and engineering group. SB made a range of window products, venetian blinds, roller blinds, vertical blinds etc. and also co-ordinated soft furnishing products, kitchen utensils and small items of furniture for the kitchen and bathroom. SB employed around 1000 people spread over five sites.

The products were sold via retail outlets, including all the large stores, for example, John Lewis, House of Fraser, etc. The marketing role was performed by the Managing Director (MD), this being one of his main interests. However, the growth of the company and the demands on the MD's time resulted in the decision to appoint Larry Grant who had been the General Sales Manager (GSM) to a new marketing role. The promotion was generally welcomed. Larry was aged forty-five and had been a very successful GSM, for the ten years since he started with SB. He was regarded as a good people manager, a good organizer and someone who could build good customer relationships.

The old structure was as shown in Figure 15.3.

Under the new structure he kept the product managers and product publicity department, but also had a marketing assistant, and was expected to grow the role. He had a seat on the company's executive board now. He was given broader responsibilities for analysing markets, strategic marketing planning and for generating the creative ideas of the future. An assistant sales manager was promoted to take on the GSM role.

Around three months after Larry was promoted, the MD expressed concerns about him. Larry seemed to be slow in producing reports, he became more irritable when challenged and was unable to keep up at meetings. This was attributed to his new role and the MD had a number of friendly discussions with him.

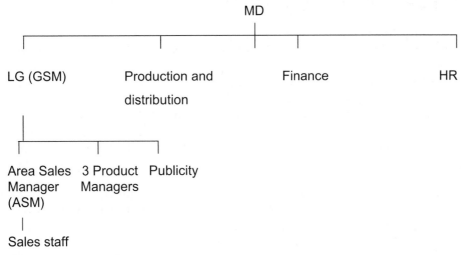

Figure 15.3 The marketing director who wasn't: organization structure

Larry became increasingly vague and indecisive after six months. Eventually, he was unable to decide on even the most simple issues, for example, whether to have a lunch meeting etc. His secretary became worried about his behaviour. Before she could report to anyone on this she arrived one day to find Larry in rather a casual style of dress and with his office walls covered in hessian (a kind of sack-cloth). He told her he was trying out a new product, then left the office shortly afterwards, saying he had a headache.

His wife called the next day to say he had seen his doctor, who had recommended a complete rest. The phrase 'mental breakdown' or mental ill health was never used. The company made generous provision for him after several visits to his home when it became clear that he would never return to work for them.

Over the ensuing months the MD discovered that during his period of appointment as Marketing Director, Larry had agreed a number of large discounts with customers, and had made various costly promises to the company's major suppliers.

References

Baum, S. J. and Young, W. E. (1973). *A Practical Guide to Flexible Working Hours*. Kogan Page.

Cooper (1997). In Arnold, H. (ed) Crisis Talks. *Personnel Today*, October, 29–32.

Read, J. and Baker, S. (1996). Not just sticks and stones. *Mind*. November.

World Health Organisation (1986). Constitution of the World Health Organisation. In *Basic Documents*, 36th edn. WHO Geneva. P1.

Further reading for Part Five

Armstrong, M. (1996). *Employee Reward*. IPD.

Baum, S. J. and Young, W. E. (1973). *A Practical Guide to Flexible Working Hours*. Kogan Page.

Brewster, C. and Hegewisch, A. (1994). *Policy and Practice in European Human Resource Management*. Routledge.

Conoley, M., Nugent, M. and How, M. (1997). *Flexible Benefits*. 2nd edn. Croner Publications.

Doherty, N. and Tyson, S. (1993). *Executive Redundancy and Outplacement*. Kogan Page.

Egan, G. (1976). *The Skilled Helper*. Cole.

Hewitt Associates (1991). *Total Compensation Management*. Blackwell.

Incomes Data Service (1999). *Benefits: Costs and Values*. IDS Focus, No. 89. IDS.

Jaques, E. (1964). *Time Span Hand Book*. Heinemann.

Livy, B. (1975). *Job Evaluation: A Critical Review*. Allen and Unwin.

Pritchard, D. and Murlis, H. (1992). *Jobs, Roles and People: The New World of Job Evaluation*. Nicholas Brearley.

Part Six

Industrial relations

The term 'industrial relations' is used in a general sense to describe the formal relationships between employers and trade unions or other collective groupings of employees, together with the institutional arrangements that arise from these relationships.

In granting only one part of our book to this subject, we are aware that it is impossible to cover the whole range of topics that could be included, but it is our intention to provide a general introduction to the subject of industrial relations in the UK. We hope that in doing so we will give managers with HR responsibilities some practical insight into industrial relations issues, and that our discussion of techniques and approaches to understanding these issues will prove helpful.

Unitary and pluralistic 'frames of reference'

The approach managers take to formal relationships at work is crucial because their success in this field depends upon their own values, their deep-set beliefs about the legitimacy of managerial authority, and the distribution of power in organizations. Fox has suggested that the 'frame of reference' which managers adopt conditions their response to the problems they face. The 'frame of reference' is a term coined to describe the typifications and tacit understandings people use to make sense of their everyday world.

We argued in Part One that each individual is socialized by experiences which result in possessing values and attitudes that come to be regarded as conventional wisdom. The possession of these values is reinforced by the groups within which the individual moves (management colleagues or workmates). Thus, 'frames of reference' become touchstones for making judgements and the filter through which evidence is passed.

The 'unitary' frame of reference is common among managers. According to this unitary perspective, all people in the organization are working towards one goal, where there is one sense of authority and where conflict is anathema. Managers often see themselves and other managers in the company as part of a 'managerial team', and they expect their subordinates to subscribe to the same point of view.

An alternative way of looking at organizations is to see them as pluralities of interest groups, each with differing and sometimes competing interests, which may come together in alliances, although these alliances shift and change as circumstances dictate. Whatever the long-term interdependence of interest groups, in their day-to-day struggle for resources and in their operational activities, they assert sectional interests. The manager's role from a pluralist frame of reference is to balance the various interests in order to achieve objectives, including those of shareholders, customers, the government and employees, allowing as much freedom of expression and action as possible. Each group, in addition to having markedly different interests, is also subject to schisms and will become part of various cross-cutting alliances. The management process thus becomes one of creating an open climate of relationships in which these varying competing interests can be expressed, and agreements can be made with an acknowledgement in an open manner of the real differences that exist.

The British system of industrial relations

The idea of a 'system' is used in this context in an abstract manner. The notion is helpful when analysing and describing an interrelated set of activities. The most famous formulation of industrial relations as a 'system' is given by Dunlop:

> Every industrial relations system involves three groups of actors: (1) Workers and their organizations, (2) Managers and their organizations, and (3) Government agencies concerned with the workplace and the work community. Every industrial relations system creates a complex of rules to govern the workplace and work community. These rules may take a variety of forms in different systems – agreements, statutes, orders, decrees, policies, practices, customs. The form of the rule does not alter its essential character: to define the status of the actors and to govern the conduct of all the actors at the workplace and work community.
>
> (Dunlop, 1970: viii)

Given the significance of income and status deriving from the occupational position taken in society, it is inevitable that broad political questions arise when we consider the institutionalization of the relative power positions of management and unions. This 'institutionalization' has taken the form of the large-scale organization of working people into trade unions to protect their economic interests, and the development of employers' associations which seek to protect and further the interests of employers. The internal structure of the unions, and their relationships with each other, derive from their history, the industries where they operate and the work situation of their members. Employers' associations are groups of employers who combine to form a 'club' that negotiates wages and other conditions of service, and for mutual support and advice in such areas as training, and to operate with the unions a common disputes procedure.

The main tradition of the British system of industrial relations has been the tradition of voluntarism, where employers and trade unions have negotiated and agreed terms at the national level, without recourse to legal backing for the agreements.

The growth of committees of shop stewards at the local level and trends towards productivity bargaining have led to more local negotiations in the private sector of the economy. A counter-trend has been the increasing involvement of the state and increasing militancy in the public sector where some bargaining is at national level. During both world wars, and from 1945 at times of crises, the state has become concerned with the regulation of labour. The need to manage a mixed economy, and the control of inflation specifically, brought the government directly into the industrial relations arena during the postwar period.

Political ideologies are, of course, linked to management ideologies, since both are concerned with the use of power. The Labour Party gains its main financial support from the trade unions, a movement in which the party had its early roots. The Conservative Party has long been associated with the City of London, and with professional and upper middle-class beliefs.

A simplistic view would see the two main political parties as representatives of polar differences in society between the interests of labour and capital. However, another interpretation of recent events would see the state interventions through employment law, incomes policy and trade union law by governments of both political persuasions as a sign of a new trend. In this, the state may be seen as acting on behalf of a third party interest, separate from capital and labour. This could be construed as a stance where the state takes to itself the pluralist role of maintaining the balance between different interest groups, so that essential freedoms in our society are maintained and the individual's rights (as consumer or worker) are protected. The role of the state in industrial relations over the 1960–80 period could be said to have intensified. The state's adoption of a pluralist mantle (a role which it has traditionally fulfilled in other areas of social life) was a sign of management's failure to create and sustain trust with workers, and of the unions' failure to reform their procedures. More recently, the UK government proposed the notion of 'partnership', and the 'third way'. Whether or not that means a way of recognizing the pluralities of interests in organizations or is really a return to a unitarist frame of reference is a question at the heart of the debates about what HRM should mean in practice.

It is the function of Part Six to go into the practical problems that are encountered in the management of industrial relations. The history of trade unionism helps us to understand the traditions and conventions of industrial relations that are influences on current actions. The arrangements that exist for collective bargaining and the industrial relations policies available will be considered, together with techniques for negotiation and procedures for the resolution of disputes. Finally, we will examine the law relating both to individuals and to collectivities in employment.

Reference

Dunlop, J. T. (1970). *Industrial Relations Systems*. Southern Illinois University Press.

Chapter 16

The history and development of trade unions

This chapter is a very short summary of the development of trade unions in Britain. Our intention here is to set out the history of trade unions only in relation to three main areas: trade unions and the law; the political consciousness of trade unions in the UK; and the main changes that have occurred in unionization. Although this is a limited account of union development, knowledge of these areas will inform our discussions in succeeding chapters.

The early history of trade unionism up to 1914

In the early history of trade unionism we should distinguish between unskilled unions and the craft societies. The craft societies were unions of workers who had served an apprenticeship, which was seen by the craftsman to give him a right to a customary wage, control of entry, the maintenance of standards and the general regulation of the craft. Craft societies set down rates and offered their members friendly society benefits, notably benefits in cases of sickness, accidents and retirement.

Local control of rates was soon augmented by national organization in the mid-nineteenth century, so that the engineers, iron-founders, boilermakers, carpenters and joiners each formed amalgamated societies out of local or regional societies, which gave sufficient local autonomy in custom and practice while providing standard minimum rates, hours and benefits to members. Trades councils also developed in the towns from the mid-1850s, representing all trades in one district, and were a forum for ideas on unionism to spread.

The political ideology of the craft societies was based on an individualistic doctrine represented by the Liberal cause. The artisans believed that self-help and the freedom to associate with their colleagues to further the aims of the craft were not incompatible objectives, since it was through hard work and sacrifice that the tradesman learned his craft, and the benefits granted by the union were based on the insurance principle through contributions.

The industrial revolution fundamentally changed employment conditions. Some of the newer industries adopted apprenticeship schemes; others relied on training through experience.

One of the features of early trade unions was the discontinuity of their organization. They rose and fell in strength and influence with the trade cycle, growing in booms and falling in slumps. Cuts in wages were not unusual, since employers regarded labour as a variable cost that should be subject to the same principle of price determination as other 'commodities'. The casual nature of the employment contract, together with the large pool of unskilled, poor people anxious for work, made the organization of unions difficult. Unions possessed little in the way of financial reserves. Until the 1880s, there were many small unions with localized membership.

There are few statistics, but by about 1890 union membership is thought to have covered approximately 5 per cent of the working population, that is, 10 per cent of adult male workers. Half the membership was in the north of England, and the density of membership (the proportion of actual to potential members) varied across industries, the largest numbers being in metals, engineering, shipbuilding, mining, quarrying, the building trades, printing, textiles and woodworking.

The mid-Victorian period of unionism was characterized by a rather pragmatic non-militant approach, deriving from the policy of a 'Junta' of union secretaries based in the London Trades Council. The opposition to the Junta's domination of policy, and emerging working-class radicalism, led to a counter-movement. A Trade Union Congress was organized in Manchester in 1868, and in Birmingham in 1869, by the provincial trades councils. After 1871, there were annual TUCs that conferred on questions of importance to unions and working people. The TUC has never sought either to control individual unions or to be a federation of unions. One of the main information-gathering arms of the TUC was its Parliamentary Committee, which also sought to influence Ministers and Members of Parliament.

In the late 1880s a new unionism emerged. This was the start of large-scale organization of unskilled and semi-skilled workers on a national basis, pursuing claims for better wages by hard-fought strikes as exemplified by the famous London Dock Strike of 1889, the seamen's strike in the same year and the improvements gained by the gas workers. These 'general' unions owed their stability and growth to their success in a few large industries and the larger works where the strength of the leadership could exert an influence. These general unions had a more militant outlook on collective bargaining, and put forward a broad socialist doctrine on the redistribution of ownership and the removal of the worst abuses of capitalism.

The legal status of trade unions has always been uncertain. The law has frequently been used to repress groups of workers. In the early nineteenth century there were the Combination Acts, and it was not until 1871 that the position of the unions was clarified by an Act, which established that members were not liable to prosecution as criminal conspiracies because they were in 'restraint of trade'. The Act also sought to make unions responsible for their own internal organization, whilst granting them protection for their funds and allowed them to register as friendly societies. Unfortunately, the contemporaneous Criminal Law Amendment Act made most of the actions of a union in dispute subject to severe penalties, and it was not until 1875 that a new law, the

Conspiracy and Protection of Property Act, permitted peaceful picketing and strike action. Similarly, the 1875 Employers' and Workman's Act made breach of contract a purely civil matter.

The union cause received a further setback from the Taff Vale Judgement in 1901, when the House of Lords held, on appeal, that employers have a right in law to sue trade unions in the courts and to obtain damages from their funds for the actions of their officials during disputes. The judges found that, although trade unions were not corporations, the rights granted to them in the earlier legislation gave them a corporate character so that they could be sued for damages. In 1906, the new Liberal government reversed the effects of this judgement by passing the Trade Disputes Act, which again made peaceful picketing legal and gave trade unions and their officials immunity from any claim for damages caused by actions in furtherance of a trade dispute.

The rising cost of living and declining real wages in the period 1896–1914 resulted in a strengthening of the newly emerged Labour Party, and more people joined the trade unions. There was a further legal tussle in 1909 about the political levy which trade unions paid to the Labour Party. The House of Lords decided, on appeal, that payments of money from union funds to the Labour Party were *ultra vires*. The 1913 Trade Union Act again reversed the decision, although the Act required union members to ballot for a political contribution. It is not difficult to see the origins of trade unionists' suspicion of the law in these cases.

1914–18

We have already commented on the development of welfare work during the First World War. The war had a significant effect on industrial relations for a number of reasons:

1 The involvement of government in directing employment, and the regulation of wages, moved thinking to the position where the cost of living was seen as a basis for wage determination.
2 For the first time, a government had to develop a dialogue with the unions over such issues as 'dilution', and the planning of staffing encouraged bargaining at a national level.
3 With the advent of large-scale production, employers sought the help of local union representatives in exercising control over labour.
4 The war was important in the political experience of the Labour Party and trade union members. They saw what the state could do to organize production on a large scale.

At the end of the war society had changed from prewar times. There was a feeling expressed in the slogan that 'homes fit for heroes' should be built, that life should be better and that we should not return to the old class conflicts. The revolution in Russia gave encouragement to the belief that some form of worldwide social change was possible.

1919–39

Unions were more militant and sought long-term benefits in negotiation immediately after the war, when labour was scarce. This was a period of amalgamations between unions, which resulted in the formation, for example, of the Amalgamated Engineering Union, the Transport and General Workers Union and the Amalgamated Union of Building Trade Workers. Financial problems were one reason for amalgamations. The small local unions could not compete, and were soon to disappear. The combinations of employers who faced the unions were another major reason for seeking to present a united front.

Towards the end of the 1920s, unemployment rose and trade unions went on the defensive, aiming to protect jobs rather than to increase wages. Employers sought to restore wages to a supply and demand basis. This was the time of the famous 'triple alliance' between the miners, transport workers and the railway workers – an alliance in areas of policy and for mutual support at a time of difficulty and confrontation. The attempts by the unions to maintain their socialist gains from the wartime economy were opposed by the employers and the government, which sought to decontrol the mines and the railways.

The General Strike of 1926 lasted nine days and was a result of a breakdown in the negotiations between the Miners' Federation, the coal-owners and the government over the employers' demand that the miners should work longer hours for less pay. The TUC was not a 'revolutionary body'. It would appear that all the TUC wished to do was to put pressure on the government by the threat of a general strike, and it was quick to call off the strike when it was pronounced illegal.

Up to 1926 the unions had retained their political objectives. They sought a different kind of society, although not outside the concept of parliamentary democracy. After 1926, until the war in 1939, the unions were more concerned with local industrial matters.

The result of the General Strike was the Trade Union Act of 1927. This made all sympathetic strikes illegal, state employees were prohibited from joining any union whose membership was open to workers in other occupations and 'contracting in' to the political levy was made necessary.

Large-scale unemployment, together with the draconian approach of the 1927 Act, resulted in less militancy by the unions by the end of this period.

The General Council of the TUC was concerned to reduce the problems of inter-union clashes over recruitment of members, and in 1924 the Congress approved an inter-union code of conduct. More precise and binding rules were laid down by the TUC in 1939, when meeting at Bridlington. The 'Bridlington Agreement' stipulated that where a union already represented and negotiated on behalf of a group of workers at an establishment, no other union should attempt to recruit members there. Although restricting choice, this agreement helped to introduce order into collective bargaining.

1939–51

The Second World War was again the occasion for co-operation between unions and government. This 'total' war involved everybody, and from the perspective of trade union development was significant for two reasons. First was the need for local control, and co-operation in production assisted the growth of the shop steward movement. Managements needed stewards as much as did the union as a vital communication channel with working people. The large-scale and increased pace of work made communications even more important. Second, with the changed role of the state and with a Labour government, initially as part of a coalition during the war and, at the end, elected with a large majority to carry through reforms, union leaders felt that the tide of history was with them. The welfare state and the nationalization of basic industries brought socialist aims nearer. Indeed, one of the first steps of the new Labour government was the repeal of the 1927 Act, making sympathetic strikes legal and returning the position on the political levy to 'contracting out'.

However, even during the Second World War, in spite of compulsory arbitration, a number of strikes did occur, and after the war there was an 'outbreak' of unofficial strikes. It could be argued that as unions become more associated with the centre of power so their role as advocates of the non-managerial cause is weakened. The large-scale organization of unions made members remote, and their involvement in union affairs sporadic and problem-centred. Rifts between rank and file and the leadership are a feature of the large-scale organization of people. Since unions are supposed to be operated democratically, this can result in the leadership having to take a less moderate view than they would wish.

1951–70s

The membership of trade unions grew mostly in the white-collar area (see Table 16.1), although the density of white-collar membership did not increase dramatically until the 1970s.

Table 16.1 Increase in trade unionism from 1948 to 1974

	Membership %	*Density %*
White-collar	+ 117.1	+ 9.2
Manual	+ 0.1	+ 7.2

The reasons for the growth in white-collar union membership were as follows:

1 There were more white-collar jobs due to changes in the occupational structure. The growth areas in the British economy were the service areas and process industries. More women joined unions as a result.
2 White-collar unions achieved a higher density, possibly due to incomes policies and a need felt by their members for professional negotiation on their behalf.
3 White-collar jobs emerged in large concentrations – the 'clerical' factories, especially in the public sector. The standardization of functions helped to create a common identity.

4 The duty imposed by governments that nationalized industry should bargain with the unions also encouraged white-collar union growth.
5 Most of the growth was in the public sector, and it was in this area that employment expanded sharply; so that local and central government became largely unionized.
6 Associated with the previous point, the impersonal relations and standardization of conditions of service stimulated the representation of interests through union officials.

Having achieved a good penetration of most sectors (including junior and middle managers) and increased the density, white-collar unions were more militant in pursuit of wage claims, as was seen during the winter of 1978/9.

One of the major areas for confrontation between unions and government was over the issue of pay controls. Since 1945 there have been numerous attempts to control inflation by some form of prices and incomes policy. There have been two main effects of incomes policy and price rises:

1 A 'threat effect' caused employees to join unions to protect themselves against falling living standards.
2 There was also conflict over pressure for local-level bargaining against incomes policies which are more readily applied at national level.

The 1960s were years of low unemployment and union militancy. There were large numbers of unofficial strikes, and it became common for Britain's economic problems to be blamed on the union movement. A Royal Commission under Lord Donovan investigated some of these issues, and its report was published in 1968. It concluded that management should assume a more direct responsibility for industrial relations and that, among other improvements, bargaining should be at a local level.

This, in fact, has been the trend. We will discuss the emerging role of the shop steward more fully in Chapter 17. Here, it may be noted that shop stewards, encouraged by the size of companies and their independence from employers' associations, had come to fill a vital place, both for management and workers.

The advent of incomes policies and the 'social contract' slowed down the movement towards local autonomy in bargaining. It was clear, however, that the greatest difficulty with incomes policy was for the union leaders to obtain the agreement of the members. The growth of employment legislation since the 1960s will be commented on in the chapters that follow. Both Labour and Conservative governments have sought to introduce some kind of legal framework within which trade unions should operate. The Labour government's White Paper, *In Place of Strife*, was never translated into legislation, but the Industrial Relations Act of 1971 under the Conservative government provoked an enormous wave of protest over its attempt to make collective agreements legally binding on the parties, and the extension of controls over union affairs. With the defeat of the government following its confrontation with the miners over pay, the new Labour government repealed the 1971 Act.

Industrial relations in the 1980s

The industrial relations scene changed in the 1980s. Some previous trends, such as the move to company-level bargaining, continued and the individualistic ideology of the

1970s grew in the 1980s, finding political expression through government policies. A new climate for relationships at work emerged. What caused these changes?

1 High levels of unemployment reduced trade union militancy.
2 The move from 'smoke-stack' industries to a service-based economy meant that unions lost support in their traditional areas, especially in the nationalized industries.
3 The changes to the occupational structure, blue-collar to white-collar jobs, affected the number of trade union members.
4 New technology has changed job and working practices. There was now more competition between unions for members (as, for example, in the printing industry and in the active recruitment by the Electrical, Electronic, Telecommunications and Plumbing Union – EETPU).
5 There were more women in the workforce. Approximately 5 million people (mostly women) now worked part-time. It is always difficult for trade unions to organize part-time employees.
6 The Conservative government legislation removed the possibility of secondary action, and forced unions to ballot before strikes. The whole aim of the Thatcher government policy was to reduce trade union power. Managements showed themselves ready to obtain court injunctions against unions.
7 New approaches to industrial relations were brought to the UK from Japan. There were now over seventy Japanese companies operating here, their preferred approach being one union, single-status employees with emphasis on employee involvement.
8 The recession caused managers to act more strategically in the way they handled industrial relations. This entailed managers opening up parallel communication channels to the unions, seeking longer-term agreements, bargaining for gains in productivity and looking for quality improvements.

These trends therefore had an effect. Trade union membership fell by over 3 million people, and the number of days lost through strikes also fell. Some trade unions, notably the Amalgamated Union of Engineering Workers and the EETPU, sought ways to modernize the movement with new approaches. Trade unions were merging in an attempt to pool their financial strength and to obtain economies of scale. 'No strike' deals with employers, single-union agreements and strong local involvement of employees in the company were some of the threads which emerged as a basis for the new approach.

However, during the 1980s recession, productivity improved. Output increased by 12 per cent between 1983 and 1986. Inflation at that time was running at around 3.9 per cent per annum, whereas wage settlements were on average 7 per cent per annum, showing that some of the productivity gains were shared by the workforce. In spite of the loss in membership, the number of trade union members held up as a proportion of full-time employees represented, given that almost half the working population in the UK was either employed part-time, self-employed, unemployed or on various training schemes.

From industrial relations to employee relations

During the 1980s the trade unions were put on the defensive. Union membership fell, and a range of laws were passed to make unions more accountable to their members, to outlaw closed shops and sympathetic strikes, and to institute the ballot box as a key control on union leaders.

The increased incidence of derecognition by employers, and the lower recognition rate among newer workplaces in the 1980s, were attributed by Millward (1994) to the removal of statutory support for recognition in the 1980s and the higher rate of turnover among establishments in the 1980s. New offices, factories and warehouse units were being rapidly set up, just as others were closing. Other reasons included changing occupation and employment structures, the use of the secondary labour market of part-time, subcontract, temporary and casual workers, and the increased trend towards outsourcing. In the period 1984–90 the number of workplaces with recognized unions fell from 66 per cent to 53 per cent, and from 1990 to 1998 to 45 per cent, and the number of employees who were trade union members in those workplaces had fallen to 36 per cent in 1998, many of these changes being caused by derecognition.

At the same time, employers have been increasing direct communication with the workforce and have put the work group, with the supervisor as a central figure, as a focal point for human resource policies. Supervisors now undertake most communication with the workforce, but there has also been an increase in the use of multimedia techniques, corporate videos, business television, with live interaction between workers and chief executives, and attitude surveys.

The broader term 'employee relations' is coming to be used more frequently to describe the relationships at work, intended to encompass both union and non-union members, and to include all those policies adopted by employers towards managing the relationships with the workforce. The second recession in the 1990s to hit the UK reinforced the changes occurring in 'industrial relations'. Large-scale European unemployment kept wages down and maintained pressure on prices. Big companies as well as small were hit by this second recession, which affected the service industries as well as manufacturing, and the south and south-east of England as well as the Midlands, the north of England, Scotland, Wales and Northern Ireland. This recession has resulted in greater attention to organization restructuring and to the delayering of organizations. 'Empowerment' became a term in common usage. Given flatter structures, there were wider spans of control, and it was now necessary to give the work group a high degree of autonomy. Semi-autonomous work groups have been used since the 1950s – what was different in the 1990s was a raft of HR policies in development and rewards and business process redesign policies aimed to move organizations towards a process rather than a functional base. Total quality management policies have been introduced to support this new approach.

The early 1990s was a period when trade unions began to see the need to change and to address the problems of the new industries, new occupations, new contractual arrangements and the diversity of the workforce. Much of the history of trade unions had pushed them towards a strategy of dependence on the return of a Labour government. When that happened, in 1997, it became apparent that times had changed, and that they were more likely to be successful in following what has been described as a 'British version of social partnership' (Lloyd, 1997).

The ebb and flow of power in industrial relations over the centuries has pushed the frontiers of control back and forth between management and workers. From this abbreviated history of trade unions in the UK, we can see how they play a part in the political processes of the nation. Conflicts with the law have been a feature of their relationship with the state. Unions are democratic movements, and their power is dependent upon the support of ordinary working people. The emergence of shop stewards, and the move to local-level bargaining, leads to the conclusion that it is at the company level where industrial relations policies and strategies can forge productive relationships.

Questions

1 What differences in their history and development exist between craft and skilled unions and unions of unskilled people?
2 To what extent have state policy and the law influenced the development of trade unions?
3 What reasons are there for recent changes in trade union growth?
4 Do trade unions play a part in the political life of the nation? Give examples from the history of trade unionism to support your argument.

Reference

Lloyd, J. (1997). Industrial Relations in Britain. In Tyson, S. (ed) *The Practice of Human Resource Strategy*. Pitman, p. 51–72.
Millward, N. (1994). *The New Industrial Relations*. Policy Studies Institute.

Chapter 17

Collective bargaining

The conduct of British industrial relations must primarily be the concern of those working at the plant or office level. We have seen from our discussion of the history of industrial relations, however, that there are a number of national institutions that impinge on relationships, and therefore actions and reactions at the local level have industry-wide and national dimensions. The relative power positions of the participants are crucial determinants of the outcomes in collective bargaining.

In this chapter we will describe the roles of shop stewards, union officials, employers' associations and managers so that we can identify the parts they play in collective bargaining. We will go on to set out the different forms of bargaining, and to suggest a model industrial relations policy which could be applied at the local or 'plant' level.

Trade unions and employers

The trade unions

A rough classification of trade unions into the categories of 'craft', 'general', 'industrial' and 'occupational' is sometimes made. In practice, trade unions are not organized on these principles as there are so many exceptions, often derived from historical precedents, that such generalizations are inaccurate. There were approximately 224 trade unions, listed as at 31 December 1997. The total membership was around 7.8 million members (1997 figures). Listing by the Certification Officer is voluntary, and it is likely that there are other, non-listed trade unions and employers' associations. The largest single union is UNISON, formed from the amalgamation between the National and Local Government Officers Association, the National Union of Public Employees and the Confederation of Health Service Employees, with around 1.3 million members. Following closely behind is the Transport and General Workers Union, with just over 880 000 members, and then the Amalgamated Engineering and Electrical Union, with 720 000 members and the General and Municipal Boilermakers Union with around 709 000 members.

Shop stewards

Shop stewards were simply described as 'trade union lay representatives at the place of work' by Lord McCarthy in his research for the Donovan Commission. The title of worker representatives varies according to the industry and trade: for example, from the quaint 'father' or 'mother' of a 'chapel' in printing, to 'works representatives', or 'staff representatives' in small factories and offices. There are also many variations in the size and nature of the constituency the steward represents. The duties a steward would be expected to perform are:

1 Recruitment of new membership, seeing new starters and explaining the union's activities to them.
2 Maintaining membership, through the inspection of union membership cards, and by keeping the interest in the union alive.
3 Collecting subscriptions. This is now often arranged through the company, who collect for the union (a 'check-off' system), but stewards do still collect in some establishments.
4 Operating at the heart of the communication network between management, union and members, collecting views, passing on information, and sometimes determining the position which the membership should take up. The steward represents this to management, union officials, and passes back to members the management response.

There is a difference between the *de jure* and the *de facto* rights and duties of shop stewards. Although few union rule books contain specific references to shop stewards, their performance of the duties summarized under (4) above has granted them a vital place at the centre of British industrial relations. Their functions have extended to the negotiation of terms and conditions, pay, piecework rates, overtime and hours of work, the regulation of work rules and staffing levels, and together with stewards from other unions they influence inter-union relationships.

The practice has emerged, therefore, for shop stewards to occupy positions of power at the focal point of collective action in the daily interface with first-line supervisors.

Shop stewards are usually elected by a show of hands, and their representative functions are conducted in informal meetings with members, and in meetings with management, arranged through local procedures. In multi-union environments, their meetings will probably be between the management and a joint shop steward committee. This latter body may be elected or appointed by the shop stewards, and where there is a large number of stewards there is likely to be some form of seniority granted to facilitate organization. Shop stewards may represent workers from other unions where it is impractical for a separate steward to be appointed. The extent of management recognition of stewards varies according to whether or not the company or an employers' association negotiates pay and all the terms with the unions at national level, and also on the extent to which there are local negotiating procedures even where national agreements exist.

The official organization of trade unions

There are many variations in the structure of trade union organization. This is because of the origins of their constitutions, which have often emerged from amalgamations, and because of the structure of the industry in which they bargain. The organization of people into unions follows the distribution of the labour force – geographically and in accordance with the type of work and the size of the employer's unit. Generalizations about union organization are therefore, hardly possible, but for the sake of simplicity we will outline the usual union organization.

Many unions have local branches that are organized into districts and/or regions. The members of the union elect the executive committee or council, which is responsible for administering the union's activities and for conducting agreed policy. All unions have general secretaries, who are full-time officers and who are responsible to the executive committee. The larger unions also have presidents. The general secretary and, where applicable, the president, share responsibility for the day-to-day business and are responsible for the work of the other full-time officers. The policy of the union is decided by a representative conference, the delegates to which are elected by the membership, voting in their branches. In many of the white-collar unions, this conference elects the executive.

There are a number of checks on the power of the leadership, which prevents an autocracy developing: for example, the local autonomy of district committees, the trade group structure of some unions and the balances within the unions' constitutions. In addition to checking power, such constraints also make for less decisive leadership and restrict the freedom of the union leaders to act quickly in the settlement of disputes. Moreover, the requirement for secret ballots for elections, and for industrial action, forces a degree of democracy on all unions.

Shop stewards are not only representatives of the working groups, but also are frequently active in the local union administration, as one might expect. In some cases, the branch and district committee representatives are shop stewards, strengthening the steward's role in grass roots administration. McCarthy's research found that there was a marked variation in the degree of assistance that union officials gave to their stewards. Since then, a good deal of effort has gone into the training of stewards by their unions. The use of workplace branches seemed to McCarthy to be the most efficient form of organization, although the solution to problems arising at multi-union sites still seems dependent on informal *ad hoc* arrangements made among the shop stewards.

Trade union membership

From our survey of the history of trade unions we can say that union members possess different characteristics according to whether they are skilled or unskilled, blue- or white-collar union members, and that there are regional, occupational and industrial variations. Different types of behaviour might therefore be anticipated from these different groupings.

Briefly, members of the skilled sections of the unions tend to be more conservative than the unskilled. Skilled tradespeople very often have more at stake in the organizations where they work and probably have more stable working careers. Unskilled workers are more likely to be laid off or to be made redundant. Skilled blue-collar members are concerned to protect their skill through maintaining the craft training systems. Occupational differences in outlook are exemplified by electricians, whose job opportunities, rewards and conditions of working are different according to whether they are on construction contracts or maintenance work. As there are wide variations in levels of unemployment regionally, union members' reactions will depend on their local context.

This was shown by union members in the steel industry, where the reactions to closures in South Wales reflected the despair of men faced with no job prospects elsewhere. The growth of white-collar unionism, and the increasing density, reflect a changed status and work situation for white-collar workers. We mentioned in the previous chapter that white-collar employees were becoming more 'unionate'. Perhaps as significant as this attitude is the unionization in the public and service sectors, attracting more women into union membership.

There are a number of general trends that have an influence on members' actions:

1 Improved education has made members more demanding and less easy to lead. They have high expectations, but are interested in their union 'delivering the goods', in the form of shorter hours, more pay and greater job security. Paradoxically, they are not active in union affairs.
2 Stronger emphasis on change within industrial relations policies resulted in demands for professional bargainers.
3 The activities of successive governments through public policies and employment legislation have made trade union members more aware of the law and industrial relations.
4 The evidence suggests that for most union members attachment to work is instrumental. They work in order to obtain for their family and home the consumer goods, holidays, etc. and opportunities for satisfaction outside work which better living standards offer. This gives a centrality to the home and family so that work fulfils a secondary role.
5 We can no longer make the assumption that union members automatically support the Labour Party. The spread of unionism into white-collar areas and the absence of any real political objectives mean that union members have more volatile political affiliations. For example, it is estimated that around half the membership of unions voted Conservative in the 1979 general election. The agenda of 'New Labour' no longer corresponds to the 'cloth cap' socialism of the earlier periods, adding further complexity to the analysis.
6 Trade union members want to be involved in the decisions that are taken at a local level. They do not accept managerial beliefs in authority or unwieldy union bureaucracies, and are much more inclined to seek their own local remedies to problems rather than go through a lengthy disputes procedure.

The working group

In Chapter 2 we outlined the features of working groups. In any understanding of the institutions and procedures that are involved in collective bargaining we should not forget the influences of work groups on the process of collective action. We have already described how groups develop norms that are maintained by sanctions on group members. These norms govern output as well as behaviour.

The famous Hawthorne experiments documented the sanctions imposed on those in the 'bank wiring room' of Western Electric's works in Chicago in the 1930s, and the restrictions on output that resulted. Then, the group being studied said there should be 'no rate busters' (no one should produce more than the norm), 'no chisellers' (no one should produce less than the norm), and 'no squealers' (no one should pass information about the group to management). Studies by Roy, Lupton and others show that work groups are interest groups, which seek to promote and maintain their interests through the manipulation of incentive schemes and the control of work rules. Face-to-face relationships between members of the group are more important to workers than relationships with management.

Group loyalties may bring working people into conflict with shop stewards or union officers as much as with management. Sayles points to the importance of technology when he suggests that it is possible to distinguish four types of work group, according to their level of skill and the amount of interaction between group members. Thus, where there is a high degree of interaction between unskilled group members the group will be 'erratic', and where there is less interaction the group will be 'apathetic'. On the other hand, skilled workers with high interaction form 'strategic groups'. If skilled workers do not normally interact much at work, they will form 'conservative groups'.

These conclusions about working groups are of importance to managers in the assessment of the bargaining strength of the groups with whom they negotiate. For example, erratic groups without good formal representation produce difficulties in the negotiation of change, as exemplified in the docks. Groups that occupy strategic positions, such as maintenance workers, are often able to use these positions in wage bargaining, as in the electricity supply industry. The strategic use of power by work groups is also found in the continuous bargaining process which occurs over piecework and bonus rates, sometimes with informal work-sharing to ensure job security.

Managements must accept a degree of independence by work groups as a fact of life, and the controls they seek to exercise over the work need to take account of the workforce's orientation. One approach by management is to encourage participation at the local level or through the supervisor's leadership qualities to create interesting, rewarding work. The empowerment movement seeks to push power down to semi-autonomous work groups. Another approach is to establish honest relationships with worker representatives, and to be prepared to exercise patience and sensitivity in bargaining around an increasing range of issues whilst maintaining management's decision-making function. We will explore these questions in Chapter 19.

Employers' associations and management

Employers' associations

Employers' associations consist of large and small organizations ranging from self-employed members, master craftsmen and the like to public companies and large conglomerates, which may be members of several associations covering different industries. They seek to further the interests of a group of employers within an industry or section of the associations' economy.

According to the Certification Officer's report, there were 107 associations listed at 31 December 1997, and twenty-one associations with an income of more than £2 million per year. They covered organizations in 1997 that varied in size from the Engineering Employers' Federations, which had around 5 065 members, to the Test and County Cricket Board, with thirty-nine members. The largest number of individual members is in the National Farmers Union, which had 127 024 members in 1997.

The structure of employers' associations is extremely variable. The national federations are made up of a number of local associations who elect a committee or council. This national committee usually appoints other committees (for example, executive, finance and negotiating committees), the members of which would normally be drawn from senior executives of the constituent companies. These committees are supported by full-time officers, who service the committees with policy documents, give advice and help with research rather in the mode of a civil servant's relationship to a government minister.

The major functions of employers' associations have changed in emphasis from the days before the Second World War. Nowadays, they are less concerned with the control of members' activities and are much more interested in providing advice and support. The present functions of the larger associations are to:

- act as trade associations, offering commercial advice to members
- act as pressure groups on government, public authorities, etc.
- provide uniformity of collective action with trade unions
- negotiate at a national level with trade unions
- operate a disputes procedure with trade unions
- disseminate information and advice about industrial relations to members.

The advent of productivity bargaining and the refusal by large employers to adhere to a uniform line with smaller companies or their competitors on wages issues have resulted in pay structures being determined at the local-plant level. According to Clegg, industry-wide negotiations add to the amount rather than alter the pay structure. Local agreements usually take industry settlements into account, but add or vary them according to local conditions. Some conditions of service and minimum hours are determined at national level, and this does enable some order and rationality to be achieved, since the unions have usually had to come together in order that negotiations could take place – for example, between the Confederation of Shipbuilding and Engineering Unions and the Engineering and Allied Employers' National Federation.

Another useful function of employers' associations is in dealing with disputes. The aim of these procedures is to prevent the occurrence of stoppages that could be resolved by meetings between employers and unions, taken through a series of stages to national level if necessary. The disputes procedures offer a means of conciliation on domestic disputes, and if the procedure is exhausted the employer can expect moral support from the remainder of the employers in the event of a strike. There seems much less possibility of employers taking concerted action themselves, however, and the uniformity of action which can be anticipated is more a means of preventing trade unions from succeeding with leapfrog claims, or establishing precedents which they can use to the employer's disadvantage.

Management

Industrial relations is an integral part of the management of any business. Throughout this book we have stressed the importance that managers must place on relationships if they are to be successful, and of the need for consultation and good communication. Increasingly, larger companies are appointing HR directors to company boards, and the spate of employment legislation as well as the need for organizational change have given an impetus to this move. In smaller companies, the managing director or chairperson may take responsibility, but in all companies these senior managers should be involved in the establishment of a sound industrial relations policy.

Management's role in industrial relations begins, therefore, with recognition of the implications for relationships of the decisions that are taken. For example, when deciding corporate strategy on the acquisition or disposal of assets, when planning new products, investment in new machinery or increases in the size of the workforce, there are implications which must be picked up at an early stage so that they can be weighed in the decision-making process.

The responsibilities for the implementation of policies should be spelt out at an early stage also. The board, having determined policy, will no doubt look to its functional heads – in production, sales, finance and HR – to put the policy into practice. Responsibility for industrial relations is thus made diffuse, and because the most probable areas for conflict are in production it is the production and works managers who have been in the forefront of negotiations with the unions in the past.

The trend towards 'professional' HR management has provided a counterweight to professional union negotiators. So much seems to depend on personality and negotiating skills that it is not possible to generalize about who should take the lead in negotiations. The model of a senior HR manager as the responsible person with perhaps a line manager supporting has certain advantages if the personnel HR manager reports to the board:

1 The 'distance' between the board and the negotiator can be used during the negotiations and subsequently, as the negotiator is not expected to be privy to all management's future plans, and if negotiations break down there is room for further action in compromises from the board.
2 A senior and well-briefed HR manager should have a wide knowledge of the existing agreements, and may be familiar with the union officials through other negotiations. A line manager may tend to act in a sectional interest, or look for a short-term expedient that may have unfortunate long-term consequences.
3 HR managers should be able to offer continuity since it is their specialism, whereas line managers may anticipate promotion or movement to another job.
4 Given an HR manager as lead in the negotiating team, a knowledgeable line manager is invaluable as a member of the team because of awareness of the technical processes and the job content of the unit.
5 If a senior line manager is accountable for the whole group on whose behalf negotiations are being conducted, he or she should be a member of the team also. Alternatively, he or she could be involved in briefing sessions before, during and after (debriefing) the negotiations. He or she is more likely to accept that the best deal was gained, however, if he or she has been concerned in the negotiations themselves.

If the policy on industrial relations has been carefully thought out beforehand, the implementation is less difficult. Where companies are proposing the rather dangerous step of leaving their industrial relations strategy to the negotiations themselves, clearly the parameters will need to be set beforehand.

The internal bargaining process

Too little attention has been paid to the internal bargaining process within companies, and the assumption of two power groups, employers and unions, facing each other across the bargaining table to set the seal on the company's future industrial relations is an overstatement. Just as in trade unions, there are different groups – stewards, officials and militant or non-militant members forming a loose coalition – so on management's side there are interest groups. Local-level management, for example, may not agree with a group policy, or supervisors may see an identity of interests with shop stewards and seek to frustrate any deals that produce extra work.

Management organization is, therefore, not a monolith, and the informal processes that occur include attempts by boards to control their negotiators and the organization of workshop pressure against the unions. The real control of what happens is on the shop floor or in the office. This is where the internal bargaining process is utilized to maintain order and to control the rules of work, the participants in this process being the supervisors, the shop stewards, the department managers and the workers themselves. No doubt this is a source of inertia in British industrial relations, but it is also a force preventing the more radical or zealous among senior management and union officers and stewards from forcing changes on to a traditionally minded, conservative workforce.

Different approaches to bargaining

Collective bargaining comprises the settlement of wages, conditions and procedures by bargains expressed in the form of an agreement made between employers' associations or single employers and trade unions. The objective of all bargaining is to find an agreement. Agreements may be conveniently divided into procedural and substantive agreements.

Procedural agreements set out the rules by which the formal relationships between the company and the union will be regulated. These could include disputes procedures and procedures by which substantive agreements are to be interpreted.

Substantive agreements are agreements about the terms, conditions and pay of a group of workers. These would include hours of work, holidays and the rules governing how the work is to be done. A further subdivision is into bargaining at industry and at domestic level. At the industry level, bargaining between employers' associations and a confederation of trade unions settles both broad procedural and substantive areas. In the domestic bargaining of particular companies with the unions representing their workforce, the rates paid for specific jobs, and the regulation of the work, as well as local procedures for dealing with discipline and grievances, are negotiated. Examples of this fourfold classification are given in Table 17.1.

Industry-wide bargaining usually has to take into consideration sectional or occupational interest. For example, craftspeople in the steel industry and on the railways negotiate separately.

Table 17.1 Substantive and procedural agreements

Agreement	Domestic	Industrial
Substantive	Wage agreements, productivity agreements	Hours of work, apprenticeship schemes, holidays
Procedural	Local disputes, discipline and grievance procedures	Industrial procedures (applied through various joint councils, for example)

Productivity bargaining

A productivity agreement is arranged where an employer agrees to higher pay and/or to improvements in benefits in return for an agreement from the union to changes in working practices or numbers employed that will result in an improvement in productivity, measured by unit costs, total output or by some other sign.

A new era in productivity bargaining was started at the ESSO refinery at Fawley in 1960 where, for the first time, workshop representatives of all the unions were brought into an agreement with the management in which the company agreed to increases in pay in return for changes in working practices.

Productivity bargaining has since proved to be an approach that other companies have adopted as a means of removing demarcation lines between jobs and problems caused by different union membership. These changes in bargaining have helped to move the main arena for negotiating down to the 'domestic' or plant level. Some employers' associations have left the settlement of pay rates to individual plants so that local productivity agreements could be concluded. Domestic bargaining has also been encouraged by the spread of measured daywork and by the need to rationalize payment schemes.

Productivity schemes focus attention on the role of the supervisor, and by making him or her responsible for the achievement of improved performance there is the opportunity to build up his or her role. But for the agreement to be effective, supervisors have to have powers of control which make their already difficult intermediary position even more stressful. For schemes to be implemented satisfactorily, therefore, the supervisors down to the shop floor workers must be given training and support in what is probably a new role for them. The introduction of quality circles, where employees work with their supervisor on ideas to improve the quality of their work, has also given greater emphasis to the supervisor. Productivity agreements result in management looking for more information on output, and may put the spotlight on performance standards. Clearly, in negotiating new schemes companies should be aware of the likely effect these schemes will have on worker/supervisor relationships, formal control systems and on the pay relativities with other groups in the organization not covered by the scheme.

Industrial relations policy

The management's industrial relations policy will increasingly be based on local circumstances. Most industry-wide agreements are largely used for guidance, with the emphasis on day-to-day affairs at the domestic level, so that a policy on industrial relations is essential.

From the perspective of the company, there are a number of areas of major concern when framing an industrial relations policy:

1 The preservation of harmony in relationships, or the creation of harmony where none exists. This does not imply that management should avoid disruption of the business at all costs, but it does mean that a main objective of an industrial relations policy will be to keep the respective groups of workers contributing to the organization's success.
2 The orderly introduction of change. No industry can avoid technological change, and there are implications for the customs and practices that have grown up over decades with management's tacit agreement. To gain the advantage of improvements in productivity, the changes need to be introduced in a way that is acceptable to the workforce.
3 The costs of employment must be controlled and have to be compatible with the company's pricing policy. The pricing policy will have been set with the marketplace in mind. Labour costs are an important element in total costs, so any change in the proportion of costs attributable to labour results in a reduction in the company's profit margins and there are implications, therefore, for the corporate plan.
4 Industrial relations policies should influence the productivity of the organization. In many recent instances, this has been achieved by introducing greater flexibility in contracts, in working time and in jobs, and by pushing through a greater concern for quality.

The company should express in writing its industrial relations policy as part of its human resources strategy, which may then be communicated to all levels of staff and to the unions. Ideally, union officials should be involved in consultation before the policy is finalized.

The statement should cover the following:

1 The company's attitude/philosophy towards trade unions. The circumstances under which the company will recognize unions for bargaining purposes, and any agreement on membership.
2 The negotiating procedure and the people with whom negotiations will take place (junior shop stewards, district officials, etc.), the frequency of negotiations and procedures for resolving disagreements and for interpreting provisions of agreements.
3 The scope of the negotiating bodies, and the numbers and positions of the members. For example, if the company has a number of subunits (a group or divisional structure) the arrangements for collective bargaining should be set out. Sometimes joint negotiating committees are formed, or a senior committee may be established with responsibility for several bargaining 'units'. The scope of each committee's negotiations should also be stipulated, together with the mechanism for referring problems to the appropriate committees.
4 The facilities and information to be given to the union representatives. These topics are covered broadly by the legislation (see Chapter 22) and by codes of practice, but particular headings of information and the practical facilities will have to be decided.

Procedures for determining the number of union representatives granted facilities will be one of the procedural issues that must be negotiated. The relationship of the consultative processes in the UK to any European works council, and the respective roles of the works councils will also have to be covered.

5 The relationship of any plant or company agreement to the industry agreement must be established. This is a statement of what will be followed automatically from the industry-level agreements (for example, on hours, overtime rates, etc.) and what will be the subject of further negotiation at domestic level. The policy should state how the arbitration and conciliation arrangements will be put into force at the local level.

To be successful, a statement that covers the areas listed above should involve everyone (from senior management to worker representatives) in consultation.

The next stage is the negotiation of the substantive and procedural issues that are in the scope of the policy through the bodies which have been established:

1 The substantive areas for negotiation include the wage and salary systems, incentive schemes, grading and job evaluation schemes, recruitment, training, promotion and redundancy policies.
2 The procedural and consultative arrangements on discipline, grievance procedures and the procedures for redundancy and dismissal.

In most cases, management does not have the chance to set up a policy from scratch. Only in a greenfield situation will that be possible, but the model above is still valid as a framework that can be adapted to circumstances. Typically, the area over which negotiations can take place has extended, and recognition of this fact within the policy is within management's control. The objective is to keep bargaining orderly, and in many companies it is now necessary to recognize that there is joint regulation of the rules governing work.

Where it is possible to negotiate a plant/company agreement, it is advisable to start from those matters over which there is already agreement. First, a tentative agreement on each area in turn should be sought, before moving on to the next. Nothing is finally settled, however, until both parties have agreed the whole range of issues, so alterations are still possible (see Chapter 18 for negotiation techniques).

A further complication can arise when there is no obvious single union or group of unions with whom to bargain. Inter-union rivalry is still a fact of life. Joint committees of all the unions involved may be one way around the difficulty.

Where management is faced with competing claims by different unions, it must make a judgement as to which union has the power to do the most damage and then should settle with that union first. Management should then seek to promote a more rational basis for future dealings.

Given that a principal objective for any industrial relations policy is to obtain harmony, management should not seek to play off one union against another. A better approach is to work with the unions concerned to try to bring some order into the bargaining arrangements.

Bargaining with a single union brings many benefits. It has been possible for some companies to achieve recognition with a single union in return for no-strike deals, pendulum arbitration (where the arbitrator decides on the merits of either the claim or the offer, not on an average between the two), and agreement lasting two years or more over pay.

These agreements are not easy to secure. This is illustrated by the case of the Ford Motor Company. After a two-week strike, Ford was able to obtain a two-year pay agreement in 1988 for its factories in the UK, but without all the productivity gains desired. The US parent later refused to invest in a new plant in Scotland because the unions could not agree which trade union would represent the workforce (the investment being contingent upon a single union at the proposed new plant).

The growth of inward investment to the UK from Japan and other countries has also stimulated new approaches to collective bargaining. Greenfield sites offer the advantage of no previous history of bargaining and no disharmonious episodes to forget. Such new investment has offered opportunities for single-union deals, or at least 'single-table' bargaining (bringing all the unions into a joint bargaining arrangement). In some cases, for example at Honda, the company has opted not to recognize any trade union for bargaining purposes. Where trade unions are involved, and where managers have a choice, a form of mutuality has emerged. This does not imply that the union is taken as an equal partner with management; rather, trade unions have come to play a significant role only in so far as they have served management's purposes in maintaining a disciplined workforce and as a channel for communication.

Conclusion

In this chapter we have outlined the part played by the protagonists in collective bargaining: trade unions, their officials, shop stewards and members, employers' associations and management at different levels. The plurality of interests these actors represent is reconciled at industry and at domestic level through bargaining processes. To bring order to the process of joint regulation of work, industrial relations policies that cover both substantive and procedural issues need to be devised at the company or plant level. These agreements should provide the opportunity for maintaining harmony in relationships, rewarding effort and promoting high levels of productivity.

Questions

1 What part do shop stewards play in the process of collective bargaining?
2 Why do the attitudes of trade union members differ, between those shown by white-collar and blue-collar members?
3 Why has there been a continuous trend towards local, plant-level bargaining?
4 What is productivity bargaining? What are the difficulties in making a success of agreements on productivity?

Chapter 18

Negotiation techniques

In the previous chapter we outlined the institutional arrangements for collective bargaining between workers and employers. Although the power bases of these groupings will help to determine the outcome of the bargaining, their power is expressed through negotiations.

When the two groups meet, whether in national, company or local bodies, the negotiating strategy that each side has prepared, and the way the strategy is acted out, will affect the result. Negotiations are not usually about winning or losing everything, but rather are concerned with small shifts and marginal gain or losses in pay, changes in rules, working methods, terms of employment and so on. Matters of principle may often be felt to be involved, notably where redundancy schemes, managerial prerogatives or disputes over disciplinary measures are concerned, but agreements are achieved through compromises that avoid a total capitulation by either party.

There are two different approaches to negotiation:

1 *Distributive bargaining*: where the negotiation is about the distribution of resources, which are always finite, where a gain for one party is a loss for another. Distributive bargaining is sometimes called zero sum bargaining. For example, if an increase in pay of 15 per cent is gained against a management budget of 10 per cent, the 5 per cent extra achieved by the union has to be funded either from profits or investment, or from other groups in the company, or by increasing productivity (producing more for the same cost) or by increasing prices (increasing the proportion of wage costs : total costs). If productivity can be improved, then the bargaining need not be distributive.
2 *Integrative bargaining*: this is where the negotiations are about how to resolve a problem to the mutual satisfaction of all parties. The approach entails 'problem-solving' by management and unions looking for the best solution to grievances about management actions, discipline problems and matters that lend themselves to joint management/union co-operation. This is especially appropriate in real productivity deals.

In this chapter we will concentrate on distributive bargaining, leaving the integrative approach to Chapter 20.

Negotiation is not always a formal affair. Managers and shop stewards may find themselves taking a continuous negotiating stance. Pressure from management or pressure from the unions for changes are part of the everyday interaction in which either side may be engaged in persuasion. Our description of negotiation techniques will assume that the negotiation is sufficiently formal for a number of stages to be followed. However formal the arrangements the principles remain the same, and it is the responsibility of management to ensure that they are not rushed into agreements, or give way to pressures, but that they have prepared a strategy that they can follow. The chapter is divided into two sections: preparing the case and conducting the case.

Preparing the case

The aim

The first task is for an overall aim to be set. This should be consistent with the industrial relations policy and should be achievable. For example, one aim could be to change the production system in order to improve productivity, or another to achieve an agreement with the unions in line with the corporate plan on wages/salaries. From the aim, objectives that are not so rigid that they are unalterable in negotiation should be thought through. In the first instance, these may be to do with the types of machines, numbers employed, etc., or in the second example, amounts to be paid to the various groups.

Research

The issues over which the negotiation is to take place should be researched. A good understanding of the history and background to date is invaluable. The researcher will be looking for trends: signs of the way the union is going on particular issues. It is as well to use more than one source for the accounts you gather or to check minutes of previous meetings. Where the negotiation is over pay, recruitment or similar substantive matters, management should be armed with a survey of pay rates or of labour market information.

Bargaining power

The strategy to be followed will be dependent on the bargaining strength of the union. This will be a variable, according to the issues on which it represents the workforce.

One way of analysing power is to list the issues over which the negotiation will take place and then to note the costs and benefits to each party of the different outcomes. Where the negotiation is over substantive issues, most of the costs are likely to be to the company, although as inflation rises a pay increase of less than the inflation rate is a reduction in real wages which is a cost to union membership. Similarly, in productivity bargaining, overtime or bonus earnings may be traded for other benefits, which can be costed.

Chamberlain used the following model to define the relative costs of agreement or disagreement between two parties A and B:

$$\text{Bargaining power of } A = \frac{\text{The costs to } B \text{ of disagreement with } A\text{'s terms}}{\text{The costs to } B \text{ of agreement with } A\text{'s terms}} \qquad (18.1)$$

$$\text{Bargaining power of } B = \frac{\text{The costs to } A \text{ of disagreement with } B\text{'s terms}}{\text{The costs to } A \text{ of agreement with } B\text{'s terms}} \qquad (18.2)$$

Thus if A is the union, B management, the greater the cost of disagreeing in relation to the cost of agreeing to a union's demands, the more power the union possesses. If, for either party, the ratio is less than 1, there will be disagreement. Concessions or strikes can lower the cost of disagreement to the point where a settlement is possible.

The strategy

Given an understanding of what the union is likely to raise, and an assessment of their power on these issues, management should be in a position to predict the demand the union will make, or what kind of offer they should attempt. There is an opportunity now to work out the argument for and against each proposal, notably the benefits/disbenefits to each party of agreeing/disagreeing. In particular, managers should look for the weakness in their own case and try to find counter-arguments.

The position of each side on the issues can be determined under the three possible situations that may emerge, which Atkinson has labelled as follows:

1 If management achieves its objectives entirely, what would be the ideal settlement?
2 If management makes some progress, but with power from the union realistically assessed, what would be a realistic settlement?
3 If management is forced to concede or make no progress, what is its fall-back position?

As an example, if the union is demanding an increase of £20 per week, the three positions for the two parties could be as in Table 18.1. There is clearly room for agreement, since the union's fall-back position and the management's idea of a realistic settlement coincide. If the union is able to discover that management's fall-back position is higher than their fall-back demand, they would no doubt revise their fall-back demand upwards, and the final settlement would be nearer the £16 mark.

Table 18.1 Example of union and management positions

Positions	Ideal	Realistic	Fall-back
Management	£8	£14	£16
Union	£20	£17	£14

Management should now be able to work out what its own demand would be or its response to the union's demand. If management intends to make an opening statement containing a first offer, the amount of movement this will allow should be considered.

Any possible concessions should be thought through and, to gain maximum response from the other side, their timing has to be calculated.

Management's strategy is established, therefore, from the range of issues to be covered, the strength of the parties on each issue, management's position on each issue and where the union is anticipated to stand, and the arguments that can be marshalled for and against the management's case. There is the tactical question of whether or not to open with a bid and how high this should be, which has to be resolved in the light of how much movement is possible and how much power each side has. It is also useful if managers can agree in advance what reaction they will have to any threat of sanctions that the union might propose.

The agenda

This raises tactical and practical questions. It is valuable to have items on the agenda which can be linked so that there is the prospect of gaining movement on problems which otherwise might remain unresolved. The agenda should not be cryptic, however, and must be acceptable to both sides, so that both have time to prepare. The ordering of the items on the agenda can be used to put time pressures on the last items, but it must be remembered that the other side may not accept the order.

Preconditioning

The history of the dispute will already have preconditioned the participants. Active attempts are sometimes made to formulate a climate of opinion in which the outcome of the negotiations is made more acceptable. For example, advance publicity of poor trading results, statements in newspapers and company journals which reflect the strength of the competition and the company's problems all influence attitudes. On the union side, large pay settlements in other parts of industry, results of comparability studies, the inflation rate, etc., may be used in a propaganda war before the negotiations commence.

Providing unions with information

There is now a general duty on employers to disclose information at all stages of collective bargaining to representatives of independent trade unions, and a code of practice for this has been produced by the Advisory Conciliation and Arbitration Service (ACAS). The code gives examples of the types of information covered – which includes cost structures, gross and net profit figures, sources of revenue, as well as data related to performance and details of pay, benefits and staffing levels, including the bases on which these matters are decided.

The management team and the setting

Whoever is selected to conduct management's case must be articulate, persuasive and carry sufficient authority to make decisions. He or she should be acceptable to the other side at a personal level, and his or her intellectual abilities should be sufficient to enable him or her to translate the possible the effects of proposals on company policy. It is a useful ploy to retain some distance between the negotiators and the ultimate authority (say, the board of directors), although the negotiators should always remain in their confidence. While the chief negotiator is conducting the case for his or her side, other members of the team should be keeping a record of what is happening and listening to the interplay of the argument, looking for strategic developments and able, therefore, in an adjournment, to give an analysis of the negotiations. There should be sufficient rapport between members of the negotiating team for the members to pick up non-verbal as well as verbal clues that they are needed to intervene. The setting for the negotiations ought to be comfortable, free from interruptions, with the chief negotiators facing each other in central positions.

Conducting the case

The opening statement

This is a broad statement of the position as you see it. It should leave enough room for further negotiation. No details or contentious counter-demands should be attempted at this early stage. It is sometimes quite effective to give parts of the opening statement to other members of the team to present. In listening to the opening statement from the other side, try to find clues to the strategy they are adopting, and be prepared to revise your strategy accordingly. Look also for areas of agreement. Both sides will derive a sense of achievement from early agreement on part of the negotiations.

The argument

A number of techniques are common in the art of persuasion:

1 Gaining commitments from the other side which can then be used to further your own case. For example, an agreement by the union that its members should not suffer any job loss can lead on to a conclusion that increases in pay would result in a reduction in employment, and then be used to reduce the union's demand.
2 The argument should dwell on the benefits to the other side of acceptance. Opportunities for the other side to agree without losing face should be provided.
3 Appeals to emotional issues as well as to reason may be effective. There is sometimes a sense of relief from all sides when the problems are expressed in human terms, instead of concentrating always on financial or business implications.
4 State the case with conviction and, if necessary, forcefully, but without shouting or using abusive language. You must convey your own belief in your arguments.
5 Information should only be released during negotiations for a reason, and this should have been decided in the planning phase. The timing and method of releasing it (verbal or written) may be important, and the negotiators will have to decide during the negotiations when the moment is right.
6 If no progress is being made on one point, having clarified the problem which is holding up agreement, it is probably as well to set it aside and return to it later.

7 Linking issues together may help over a stumbling block. Conversely, if there is a halt on all fronts because of a sticking point on one of the items, the technique of isolating the issue as in (6) above can be used.

There are interpersonal skills in negotiation which help:

1 Listen carefully to what is said.
2 Ask questions rather than make statements all the time.
3 Do not try to score personal points. If the opposition descends to personal vituperation, either ignore it, or make your stance clear that you will not continue if abuse is used.
4 Avoid taking advantage of any division in the opposing team. It will result either in unifying them against you or in the break-up of the negotiations.
5 Do not use long convoluted sentences; use instead simple language and a tone of voice which treats your opposite number as your equal.

Concessions

The timing of concessions can be crucial to the outcome. Concede too early and the opponent may accept the concession as of right and then move on to his main argument. If a concession is to be made, it will probably yield most value if it is granted in response to the opponent's main argument, and if it is attached to a push for a reciprocal action on his or her part it may result in a modification of his or her demand.

In negotiations one sometimes encounters the 'phoney concession', which is a gesture that appears to be a concession but, on reflection, is seen to be an inevitable or worthless concession. It is a trick, rather like selling a pass in rugby football, and as such may not work. Where it does work, and can be carried off convincingly, your opponent will believe that he or she has scored a victory, and may be prepared to make a real concession in return.

If it appears that you are being forced into concessions, the best plan is to try to slow the pace, either by creating a diversion, taking up another point with a suggestion that you will return to the problem later, or by adjourning proceedings for a short time.

Adjournment

There are a number of reasons for wanting to adjourn. The most important occasion is when the negotiating team needs to consider the other side's proposals. The time should be fully utilized by analysing what has happened and going back through the record of what has been said and agreed. This kind of adjournment allows the team to consult with senior management or to seek advice from experts on a topic (for example, if changes in the pension scheme rules are being discussed, actuarial advice may be necessary).

As indicated above, adjournments can also be used judiciously as a break point to prevent yourself from being swamped. The time can still be used to advantage so that the team is able to formulate a reply.

Finally, adjournments at natural breaks are sensible, for lunch, tea or in the evening. Fatigue in negotiations can be as dangerous as time pressures, since there is a temptation to speak without thinking or to give away an important point merely out of tiredness.

Settlements

The objective of negotiation is to obtain agreement. Before the negotiation teams break up, it is as well to agree how the settlement is to be communicated to the workforce. If a new agreement has been negotiated, the length of time the agreement will run will have been part of the negotiations. Stability is achieved by long-term rather than short-term agreement but, if the agreement is for a long time, it ought to contain provisions for interpretation, and the disputes procedure ought to be sufficient to cope with any disagreement that may result from the long period during which the agreement is in operation.

Conclusion

Good negotiating styles only come from practice. Preparation, and care in the negotiating arena, will help, however, and the summary in Figure 18.1 shows the important steps in the negotiation process.

Questions

1 What preparations should you make before any negotiation?
2 How does the 'power' of the contending parties influence negotiations?
3 Describe the key issue you should think through when developing your negotiating strategy.
4 Under what circumstances should you make concessions?

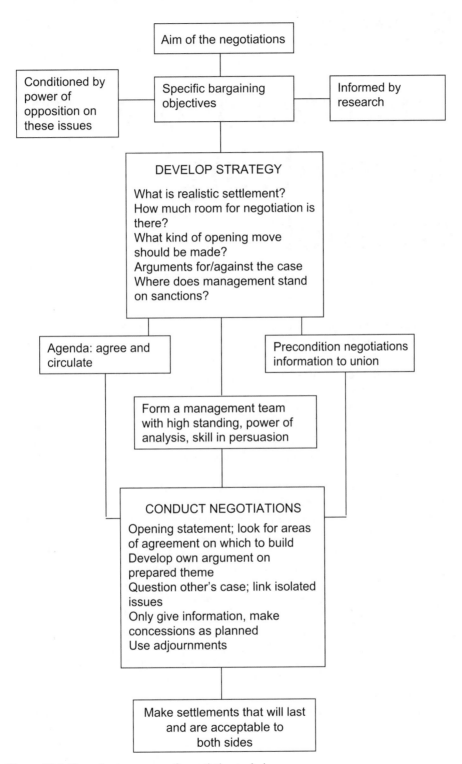

Figure 18.1 Flow chart summary of negotiation techniques

Chapter 19

Disputes and ways of resolving conflict

We suggested at the beginning of Part Six that a pluralist stance towards industrial relations is necessary. What we come to regard as 'conflict' in an organization depends on our interpretation of events.

The reality of most organizations is that people hold a multiplicity of personal objectives. There would seem to be some truth in the claim that employees really work for the material and psychological satisfaction they can achieve, and that their work is therefore an instrument used towards their own ends. In addition to this instrumental attachment to work, interest groups form in organizations, where individual interests coalesce. These groups seek to achieve their ends through alliances and by following group strategies.

A number of sociologists have suggested that our attention should be addressed to the explanation of 'order', or lack of 'conflict', which is perceived by some to be unnatural, the normal pattern being one of disagreement, conflict and often violence. One outcome of such a view is that 'political activity' is necessary to avoid a state of anarchy. This political activity includes the formation of alliances, the representation of interest groups in consensus decision-making, and mechanisms for containing and canalizing opposition.

The values of managers govern their attitudes towards workers taking action in pursuit of claims and condition the manager's response to 'industrial action'. Whether such action is regarded as a legitimate part of the bargaining process will depend on a manager's view of conflict in organizations as a whole. Questions we must face are: can we expect to have the total commitment of people to their tasks? Do groups of workers have the right to express their disagreement and to use their power in confrontation?

In this chapter we will examine the nature of industrial conflict and its resolution.

The conflict cycle

There are a number of distinct phases in a conflict cycle. The cycle begins with substantive or emotional issues being triggered by an event, which seems to focus attention on what are regarded as the underlying issues. Tension escalates to the point where sides are drawn, and the two sides make judgements on the opposition's power and goals. Those involved in the situation experience fear at the confrontation according to the risks they are taking with family, income, job, prestige, etc. There is negotiation or a series of meetings where both sides work through their disagreement. The outcome either will be a resolution by compromise or the conflict cycle will start again.

Conflict takes place at different levels. There may be a 'running fight' between a supervisor and a group of workers over a period of years, with occasional outbreaks of overt conflict in the form of 'wildcat' strikes, or the conflict could be at a national level, as in the famous miners' strikes in the 1970s and 1980, or an event such as the pay offer by British Steel in 1979 that sparked off feelings of insecurity, fear of job loss as well as a prospective loss of income and status (these being some of the problems union members felt were important during the 1980 strike). Even in the recent past, there have been threats of industrial action in ports, airlines and one-day stoppages in schools and universities.

Different types of dispute

There are signs of disaffection with organizations, which are explicit, such as strikes, confrontation leading to lockouts and various forms of withdrawal of co-operation by workers in furtherance of their claims. High labour turnover, absenteeism, high accident rates due to inattention, poor training, and customer complaints could also be regarded as implicit conflict in the sense that they are indicative of at least a lack of interest or motivation to work, and at worst animosity towards the company and what it represents. Strikes are, therefore, not of themselves an indicator of low productivity (except, of course, for the period of the strike itself). A study of coal-mining, for example, revealed that the pits with few strikes were not outstandingly productive. Apathy and a low level of energy at work are probably more damaging than outright confrontation over differences.

Industrial conflict takes a variety of forms. Overtime bans, working to rule, refusal to use new machinery have all been seen in different industries over the past two decades. The draughtsperson's union invented an ingenious form of pressure on management: 'working without enthusiasm'. White-collar workers and managers who are unionized have considerable scope for this type of action since their work frequently requires them to use their initiative and creativity.

Apart from sanctions against management, workers sometimes take action against those of another union, or employer, by 'blacking' the goods they produce, that is, refusing to use or handle them. For example, dock workers have 'blacked' goods manufactured by employees who did not obey a strike call by the union and have refused to unload imported cargoes of coal when the miners were on strike, out of sympathy for their cause. Sanctions against individual workers who do not obey the majority decision also occur. Unofficially, these may include 'sending to Coventry' (that is, not communicating with the offender at work), and physical sanctions have been known, although never officially approved by unions. We may recall here the way in which offenders who broke group norms were struck on the upper arm, as recounted in the Hawthorne research.

Strikes

A strike is not the only type of sanction that workers can apply. It is, however, one of the most effective. Withdrawal of labour puts pressure on an employer immediately, and although there are costs to employees in the form of loss of pay the employer faces an immediate need to negotiate so that a return to work and a resumption of business takes place. Other forms of industrial action can become a 'running sore', and may cause as much difficulty for employees as for management. Overtime bans are only effective when overtime is regularly expected, and working to rule can be inconvenient for the workers. The 'lockout' by an employer is not so frequent nowadays, this being where the employer refuses to allow a group of employees to return to work unless they accept management's terms.

Strike action on a selective basis has been used to minimize the cost to the union and to maximize the effect on the employer. This is exemplified by the withdrawal of a small number of key workers, such as those operating a computer installation. For a strike to be effective, the employer's business has to be stopped, and thus strikers place great emphasis on solidarity and regard picketing as an essential element in their tactics. The use of pickets on the premises of employers not directly related to the dispute, but who can bring pressure to bear on the employer who is engaged in a dispute (secondary picketing), have been banned (see Chapter 21).

Strikes and other forms of industrial action are not always sanctioned by the union. We can, therefore, differentiate between official and unofficial strikes, the former providing the benefit of strike pay to those on strike and the use of the union organization. Matters are not always so clear-cut. Strikes that start as unofficial are often made official as they progress.

The classification of strikes for comparative purposes is, therefore, problematic because each strike is a complex phenomenon in which people with different and changing motives are acting out the various stages in the conflict cycle. As there are many other forms of industrial action, statistics on strikes cannot be taken as a definitive measure of industrial unrest. There are also serious difficulties in collecting strike statistics. It is probable that many small strikes are unrecorded, and the different methods of recording in each country make international comparisons imprecise. Strike statistics are usually kept on the total number of stoppages beginning in a year and the aggregate number of working days lost due to stoppages in progress during a year. The caveats extended above counsel caution when interpreting these statistics. The benefit gained from studying the statistics is to derive a general impression of signs of militancy, and to see which industries are strike-prone.

Until 1926, the pattern was for large numbers of working days to be lost from a relatively small number of strikes. After the General Strike in 1926, until 1956, the number of days lost was not typically so high, but the number of strikes increased. The late 1960s saw an increase in militancy; from 1968 to 1977 the average number of working days lost per 1000 workers was 452, which was nevertheless better than the record of Italy, Australia, Canada and the United States. The number of strikes starting per year was around 2000 from 1957 to the late 1970s, except for 1970 when almost twice that number started. In 1957, the engineering strike pushed up the number of days lost to 8.4 million, and there have been four particularly bad years since then: in 1972, 24 million working days were lost, in 1974, 15 million days, in 1979, 28 million days, and in 1984, 27 million days (due to the miners' strike).

During the 1980s the strike weapon came to be used less: the number of stoppages fell from 1348 in 1980 to 701 in 1989, and down to the 600 level in the early 1990s. By the end of the 1990s, the number of recorded strikes was negligible.

The recent Workplace Employee Relations Survey (WERS) (in 1998) indicated that only 7 per cent of workplaces had seen ballots of union members in the previous year, industrial action was reported in only 2 per cent of workplaces and strikes in only 1 per cent of workplaces in the previous year. In 93 per cent of workplaces, managers reported no industrial action of any kind in the past five years. Strike activity in 1997 was the lowest since records began in 1891, according to the Office for National Statistics.

This reduction in trade union militancy may be due to a number of factors. First, high levels of unemployment are associated with reduced militancy. Second, the Conservative governments during the 1980s and on into the 1990s expressly sought to reduce trade union power by introducing legislation which made the unions liable for damages caused to employers in a dispute in a wider number of situations. The introduction of the need for a ballot of members before any action is taken gives time for management and unions to reach a compromise on issues in dispute. Third, the collapse of Britain's old industrial base – mining, heavy engineering, shipbuilding and some manufacturing sectors – has changed the occupation structure and labour force characteristics. Increasingly, jobs have become part time, often occupied by women, and are in the service sector of the economy. In manufacturing and construction there has been more subcontract and non-union labour. These changed features of the labour force may also have reduced the propensity to strike.

When militancy was higher, economic reasons accounted for 80 per cent of stoppages and 90 per cent of person days lost. Piecework and wage payment systems used to give rise to many disputes, but in recent years there has been a trend towards measured daywork and incentive schemes are less of a factor. However, the threat of inflation and the urge to protect living standards are more important now. The growth of the public sector, where incomes policy and cash limits have been felt most, has resulted in a number of confrontations there, where white-collar unions have grown sharply.

Most strikes are short, sharp affairs, where the employees walk out when an event triggers the examination of a number of underlying problems over which there has been frustration and annoyance, for example, over grading decisions or work rosters. The set piece, long drawn-out battles in steel, transport and the mines, for example, have come at a stage when negotiation has broken down. The trend will probably be towards more official disputes, since in the growth area of unionism, the white-collar area, the members are more prone to strike on union instructions.

From research completed by the Department of Employment, we can see a profile of a strike-prone industry:

- labour-intensive
- high union density
- the average size of the units managed is large
- high-paid, skilled labour force
- majority of labour force is male
- industry is subject to fluctuating market pressures.

Procedures for conflict resolution

Discipline procedures

There are many disputes each year due to management's disciplinary actions. Dismissal and suspensions occur for breaches of rules (such as sleeping on the job, negligence, breach of safety regulations) and for more general problems of conduct, including absenteeism and bad timekeeping.

Discipline procedures are local procedures devised by management, sometimes negotiated and agreed with the unions concerned. Shop stewards and/or local union officials may take part by representing their members at any hearings or appeals against management's decision. The advent of unfair dismissal legislation (see Chapter 21) and the ACAS code of practice on disciplinary practice and procedures in employment have led to more formalization of procedures. Under the 1972 Contracts of Employment Act, employers were obliged to provide written information for their employees about disciplinary rules which are applicable to them, and details of the person to whom they should apply if not satisfied.

The following prescription for a discipline procedure is drawn from the Code; discipline procedures should:

1 Be in writing.
2 Specify to whom they should apply.
3 Be quick in operation.
4 State the disciplinary actions which may be taken.
5 Specify the levels of management with the authority to dismiss (usually those at senior manager or director status).
6 Give the individual details of the complaints.
7 Give individuals a right to be accompanied by a trade union representative, or by a fellow employee of their choice, at any disciplinary hearing or interview.
8 Unless it is a case of gross misconduct, no employee should be dismissed for a first offence.
9 Disciplinary action should not be taken until a case has been carefully investigated.
10 Give individuals an explanation of any penalty imposed.
11 Provide a right of appeal with an established procedure.

This leaves a number of questions to be resolved. How should a manager decide whether or not a subordinate's action is misconduct? What is serious misconduct? How and when should action be taken on cumulative problems such as lateness or inefficiency? How many warnings should be given, and who is to be involved in the discipline process?

Let us start to deal with these questions by saying that the purpose of discipline at work is to change behaviour. If an employee behaves in such a way that he or she shows he or she has no intention of being bound by the contract of employment, then the employer can regard the contract as broken. There should be no moral purpose behind disciplinary action, and it is not the responsibility or the right of the manager to impose his or her own moral code. If it is possible for the employee to change his or her behaviour or performance, then the manager has a responsibility to offer an opportunity for improvement and to help the employee to progress.

We can distinguish between four different kinds of problems that result in disciplinary action of some sort, sometimes resulting in the termination of employment:

- inefficiency (failure to perform up to the required standard)
- sickness and unavoidable personal problems (e.g. serious illness)
- cumulative discipline problems (e.g. absenteeism, bad timekeeping)
- Immediate discipline problems (e.g. theft, fighting).

Inefficiency

The incapacity of a subordinate is initially a problem for the immediate supervisor, and before any disciplinary action is taken the procedures we outlined in our sections on appraisal, induction and training should be followed. Only when these have failed to improve the performance of the individual, and the possibilities of transferring the person to a more suitable job have been exhausted, should a discipline procedure be instituted. Having tried all these possibilities, managers should move to Stage 1 of the discipline procedure outlined below, and give the employee a formal warning.

Sickness/unavoidable personal problems

The first step is to spend time on investigation of the problem through sick-visiting or a counselling interview. It is important to ask the employee whether or not he or she is able to return. The decision on termination of employment will depend on the length of the absence and the needs of the work. It may be necessary to terminate the employment if a long absence is likely and there is urgent work to be done. This decision must be taken only as a last step, of course, and employers should show compassion in dealing with sickness. If the employee would be capable of performing another type of job, a transfer should be examined.

Cumulative discipline problems

The stages in the discipline process are:

1 The immediate supervisor should interview the employee to discover the cause. The union representative should be advised, and asked if he or she would like to be present, or a friend/colleague of the employee may come to the discussion.
2 The supervisor issues a verbal warning, recorded on the file by the HR department, and the employee must be told in what ways he or she can improve, what help is available and over what time period the improvement is expected.

3 If there is no improvement, a further interview is necessary, and a written final warning should be given (either by senior management or by the HR department). The steps that are to take place if he or she fails to improve should be explained, and the employee should be given every assistance to improve and extra efforts should be made to help, with a time limit by which an improvement should be made. The union representative should be informed.

4 If the final warning is not heeded, the employee should be told that he or she will be dismissed, with a provision for an appeal to the HR director or managing director if the employee has reason to believe that there has been any unfairness. While such an appeal is taking place, the employee should be suspended from duty on full pay. The appropriate union official should be informed.

Immediate discipline problems

1 An interview should be held to establish the cause of the problem. By the nature of these problems it may be necessary to institute an inquiry, with other employees called in to give their accounts of the incident. When the 'offender' against the rules is asked for his or her version, he or she must be allowed to call other witnesses and to be accompanied by a trade union representative or a friend.

2 If the investigation is likely to take days to complete, it may be wise to suspend the employee on full pay during this time. Suspension under these circumstances should be distinguished from suspension as a penalty imposed as a consequence of a hearing.

3 When the investigation is complete, the employee should be interviewed again and advised of any action which is taken. If a penalty is proposed, written particulars ought to be handed to the employee concerned and a copy given to the union representative. If a warning is proposed, then the manager should continue from Stage 3 of the procedure for cumulative problems as outlined above. There should be provision for appeals against any penalty in the way already suggested.

Provided management follow an appropriate procedure, and the grounds for dismissal are fair, mistakes which could result in an unfair dismissal, with the attendant tribunal problems, can be avoided. We set out reasons for dismissal that are fair in Chapter 21.

Grievance procedures

Grievance procedures are necessary to ensure that employees have a recognized channel through which they can bring their grievances to the attention of management. The objective of grievance procedures is to grant employees the right to have their grievances heard, investigated and, if proved justified, remedied. No matter how good the procedure is, the maintenance of good communications is only possible where the climate of relationships favours open criticism, honesty and fairness in dealings between people. A grievance procedure that is simple, and is respected by employees and management, should help to continue such a climate.

We can draw a distinction between individual grievances, which should be handled by the grievance procedure, and group grievances, which would normally be the subject

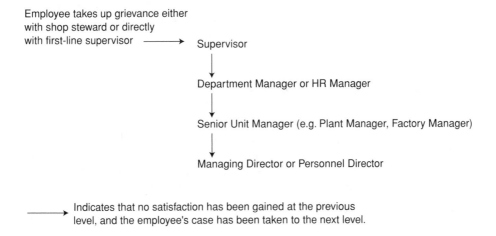

Employee takes up grievance either
with shop steward or directly
with first-line supervisor ⟶ Supervisor

↓

Department Manager or HR Manager

↓

Senior Unit Manager (e.g. Plant Manager, Factory Manager)

↓

Managing Director or Personnel Director

⟶ Indicates that no satisfaction has been gained at the previous
level, and the employee's case has been taken to the next level.

Figure 19.1 Grievance procedure

of negotiation, joint consultation or a formal disputes procedure. The stages of a grievance procedure are represented in Figure 19.1.

There are variations in the role that the HR manager can play in grievance procedures. The HR specialist should not be called in at once, and there are advantages in HR
managers being at the end of the procedure, to avoid clashes over authority among line
and 'staff' functions, and to help preserve the status of HR as the last 'court of appeal'.
The time that must elapse before an employee can move on to the next stage of the procedure should be stated. Grievances should be dealt with quickly. If a delay is unavoidable before a manager can get the answer, he or she should make sure that the employee
knows why and what the timescale is for a resolution of any difficulties.

The clear-cut distinction between individual and group grievances becomes blurred
in some circumstances. Although applying to one person, grievances may be seen as
representative of the actions by management, such as changes in work rules that a group
of people oppose.

Dispute procedures

There are dispute procedures that operate at a local domestic level and procedures at an
industry-wide level. In some industries, the industry-wide procedure will only deal with
disputes about the interpretation of national agreements, whereas in others, any type of
dispute, substantive or interpretative, can be put through the recognized industry procedures. Where industry procedures will only accept interpretative disputes, any other
form of disagreement has to be handled at the local or domestic level.

At the domestic level, procedures work through local committees. Shop stewards
(where there is unionization) take part in the procedures in joint consultative and works
committees, and in combined committees with management. Local disputes are usually
taken up with management by the local employee representatives as part of their normal
bargaining. Long-term questions may overcome the more pressing disputes and the
immediate issue is incorporated into a longer-term strategy, sometimes by the union.

Large organizations have formal procedures at the local level. There are different levels of conflict settlement offered by a series of committees in tiers. A failure to agree at a local level results in the dispute being passed to district or company level, and so on upwards to national or industry level.

Engineering industry procedure

This is a good example of an industry-wide, employers' association procedure. Works committees with a maximum of seven representatives of the management and up to seven shop stewards meet regularly and will consider complaints from individuals or groups of workers. If no settlement is reached, a further meeting of the works committee may be held with the Union District Officer and the employers' federation representative present. If there is still failure to agree, the disagreement may be referred through the procedure's 'provisions for avoiding disputes'. The objective is to avoid either a partial or a full stoppage of work until the procedure has been exhausted. The stages are:

1 Either party may bring a problem before the local conference held between the local employers' association and local union officials.
2 If no settlement is reached at the local conference, either party may refer the disagreement to a central conference (held monthly), with a panel of employers and national officers. The central conference tries to reach an agreement.

If it is not possible to arrive at a mutual recommendation, then the whole matter will go back to the shop floor for settlement by the normal means of collective bargaining.

There are a number of different procedures operated by different joint industrial councils, such as those in gas and electricity and in chemical and allied products. In the building industry, there are four stages:

1 A site meeting with union and association officers.
2 A local joint committee meeting.
3 Regional conciliation panels are held.
4 National conciliation panels are the final stage, with the provision that further disagreement can be referred to arbitration, and there is an emergency procedure that is used for urgent problems when, for example, a stoppage is imminent. Under this emergency procedure, the national officers can refer the dispute directly to a regional joint emergency disputes commission, and finally to a national emergency body.

Arbitration

There is nothing to stop either or both sides in a dispute seeking arbitration. Some procedures for settling disputes have built-in clauses concerning arbitration. These are mostly in the public sector, including the Civil Service and local authorities.

Public inquiries have been used to settle disputes where a long strike is thought to be damaging to the public interest. The Advisory, Conciliation and Arbitration Service is an independent, state-backed body which seeks to conciliate and to offer advice to either or both parties whenever requested to do so. When it is impossible for employers and unions to agree through collective bargaining, ACAS may appoint a mediator from outside, or a board of arbitration if both parties request this. Any attempts by ACAS at arbitration do not have any binding force on the parties.

In addition to ACAS, there is a Central Arbitration Committee, which can hear claims for improvements in terms and conditions of employment if the union is not recognized by the employer.

Within the union movement, arbitration in the settlement of disputes between unions can be provided by the TUC, which has the power to suspend a union and to recommend its expulsion from the congress.

Interpersonal resolution of conflict

Conflict and problems in relationships are sometimes more susceptible to less procedural solutions. There are conflicts that are a consequence of interpersonal relationships, for example, when an individual has problems in integrating into a larger unit. Managers in these circumstances need to adopt a style that keeps communication flowing. This may entail:

1 *Supportive behaviour on the manager's part*: supporting and counselling the individual with the problem. 'Difficult' behaviour by subordinates may be a cry for help rather than a challenge to managerial authority.
2 *Work group problem-solving*: using the resources of the group to resolve the problem. This means opening up a dialogue between members of the group and persuading them to be open about any problems that they experience. This is a strategy which requires a high-trust relationship, and the manager must be prepared to take criticism of his or her own performance.
3 *Job design techniques*: the objective is to design jobs which both give satisfaction for individuals and opportunities for improving performance.

Conclusion

Conflict resolution starts with a careful diagnosis of the causes of the problem. It is then the responsibility of the manager to apply an appropriate procedural, structural or personal solution, or a combination of all three. The manager's greatest assets in resolving conflicts will be his or her own preparedness to adopt a pluralist stance, and the interpersonal skills which he or she can bring to bear – supplemented by perseverance, honesty and pragmatism.

Questions

1 What is the difference between a unitary and a pluralist frame of reference?
2 Describe the main sanctions workers can apply. Why are some sanctions more effective than others in producing an ultimate resolution of the conflict?
3 What are the main reasons for strikes?

4 Set out the main steps in a discipline procedure. What are the different approaches towards cumulative and immediate discipline problems?
5 What are the stages in a grievance procedure?
6 What are the benefits of a formal disputes procedure? At what stage would you expect there to be arbitration?
7 When conflict is a consequence of interpersonal relationships what sorts of solutions are available?
8 What are the main sources of conflict? Summarize each type and note the possible solutions.

Chapter 20

Consultation and participation

The width of interpretation we can give to the idea of participation is reflected in the many levels at which we can see employees participating in a modern democracy. There is participation through national institutions, through industry-wide bodies, and at company and sometimes department or section level. Collective bargaining in its many forms could be said to be employee participation in the distribution of wealth in society.

Descending and ascending participation

One way of distinguishing between different forms of participation was described by Walker in 1977, when he differentiated between 'descending participation' and 'ascending participation'.

Descending participation includes schemes for enlarging and enriching the employee's job, so that some of the functions of the next level of supervision become part of his or her work, and this approach to participation can also be found in forms of supervision where decisions are made by the work group acting with the manager by problem-solving as a group. In this latter case, the manager becomes very much the representative of the group that operates its own control and discipline functions. In the former instance, job enlargement schemes seem to some supervisors to be threatening because they tend to squeeze the middle and junior levels of management. To be successful, therefore, they have to be applied from the top of the organization so that power and responsibility are devolved downwards.

Ascending participation is characterized by joint consultative committees and arrangements that recognize the employee's demand for more information from management and for involvement in decision-making.

There has been a tradition of joint consultation in the UK since the end of the First World War. The advent of both world wars reinforced the need for co-operation between employers and their workforce to achieve the production targets essential for victory. The early experiments in joint industrial councils, which the Whitley Committee advocated in 1919, eventually faltered in most industries, except in the public sector. Nevertheless, the idea has blossomed at a local level in industry, and a number of organizations have maintained joint consultative committees through the years. The principles behind joint consultation have also been influential in the training of HR managers. Other forms of participation, for example, through 'empowerment programmes', quality circles and through financial participation such as Employee Share Ownership Plans, seek to engage the commitment of employees.

Joint consultative committees

Joint consultative committees (JCCs) usually operate at company level. They are committees of managers and workers, with a formal constitution, which meet regularly to discuss problems of mutual interest that are outside the normal area of negotiations. Employee members of such committees are elected and serve for a fixed term. The arrangements can apply to any form of organization structure, irrespective of whether or not the employees are members of a trade union.

The principles on which joint consultation is based are those we have outlined in our comments on problem-solving. The approach to employee relations is integrative rather than distributive, and could be summarized as follows:

1 For employees to be concerned about the achievement of the organization's objectives, they must be made aware of the objectives and understand the reasons for the policies that are followed.
2 Good communications between management and the workforce are vital. Employees should be advised in advance of areas under discussion so that they can express their views and contribute to the thinking that goes into the decision.
3 Problems that stem from the application of rules to local situations, and matters that are of direct concern to the employees in their working lives such as working methods, attendance at work, catering, welfare arrangements and conditions of service, are best dealt with by management and staff representatives meeting regularly to talk and put forward solutions.
4 A reservoir of goodwill and interest should be built up which can be drawn on when unpopular decisions have to be accepted by the workforce. One of the benefits of the JCC meetings is that employee representatives receive training and experience in how to present cases at meetings, to report to their constituents and to research into problems.

The constitution of a JCC should specify:

1 *The scope of the JCC*: the areas which fall within its scope, such as working arrangements, information about products/services, the organization's financial position, security, suggestion schemes, physical working conditions, catering, etc., should be set out in general terms.
2 *The relationship between the JCC and other bodies*: these – notably any committees which are concerned with negotiation, or with the flow of information from management to work people – ought to be agreed and stated. If there is more than one JCC, the areas each is to cover should be set out and the procedure for referring matters to the next level up (e.g. from company to division to group level) specified.

3 *The intervals at which the JCC meets*: monthly or bimonthly would probably be sufficiently frequent to prevent the JCC from being bypassed with urgent problems and its consequent relegation to a 'talking shop'.

4 *A list of the officers of the committee*: such as Chairperson, Secretary and their deputies, together with their functions. At least one of these officers should be representative of the workforce. The method of electing the officers should be set out.

5 *The arrangements for the election of representatives to the committee*: this would normally be achieved by obtaining nominations and then holding a ballot, jointly supervised by management and by the unions or other worker representatives. In some companies the shop stewards may automatically serve on the JCC, or representatives of the stewards may be voted on to the JCC by the stewards voting as a whole.

6 *The length of time members should serve on the committee*: and what to do if members leave in mid-term (e.g. through illness, resignation, etc.). Management members may be co-opted on to the committee.

7 *The agenda should be prepared in advance*: by the JCC Secretary, with the items submitted by any member of the committee. The Secretary should be responsible for the minutes and their circulation to senior management and notice boards. Minutes should be brief and be quickly produced.

Some critics of joint consultation see it as merely a device for preventing militancy by union representatives, as a trick to gain consent. Another criticism is that JCCs become bogged down in trivia. It is sometimes suggested that the meetings are rituals and that no real change occurs as a consequence of them. When JCCs *do* become influential, the argument runs, then they become negotiating bodies.

As a counter to these points, if a JCC is operated as intended, that is, as a forum for a discussion of the matters that are of importance to the workforce, then there is no reason why a JCC should not be an extremely effective way of achieving consensus decisions that resolve problems for the organization as a whole. Much will depend on the qualities of the chairperson and the impartiality and real interest in joint consultation that he or she brings to the role. Trade union criticism of joint consultation is often motivated by the vision of one communication channel between management and workers, which the union controls and which is primarily a channel for negotiation.

The debate on participation

During the 1970s the debate on participation was heightened by the combination of economic circumstances and the mutual dependence of a Labour government and the trade unions. Hyperinflation made an incomes policy essential, while a strong union movement was able to take advantage of a sympathetic Labour government to bring the union leadership into economic policy-making, and to give the unions more say in the operation of statutory bodies. This push for 'industrial democracy' built on attempts by previous governments to bring together the government, the Confederation of British Industry and the TUC in long-term planning, through the National Economic Development Council and its offshoots. 'Tripartism' spread into the control of quasi-governmental organizations such as ACAS, the Manpower Services Commission, the

Health and Safety Commission, etc., while the 'social contract' between the Labour government and the unions in the mid-1970s allowed the unions to trade pay restraint in return for agreement by the government to put some of their political objectives at the top of the policy agenda.

From 1976, the fourth medium-term economic programme of the EEC encouraged participation in management's decision-making, and sought greater capital accumulation by workers. This led to the Bullock Report in January 1977, which contained a number of recommendations on participation in decision-making.

The social dimension of the European Union

The programme to complete the European internal market aims to remove all the remaining barriers to trade between the members of the EU. Among the many proposals, it is those which concern the participation of workers in decision-making which have caused greatest controversy.

The Single European Act, ratified in 1987, added three obligations to the Treaty of Rome. These covered the harmonization of national provisions to improve the functioning of the labour market, improvements in health and safety of workers, and Article 118B, which stipulates: 'the Commission shall endeavour to develop the dialogue between management and labour at European level'. The Social Dialogue was started in 1987 between the Union of Industries of the European Community (UNICE) and the European Trade Union Confederation (ETUC).

The objectives of the ETUC are to influence governments and European institutions in protecting and furthering workers' interests, which are pursued through the twin routes of collective bargaining and legislation. Formed in 1973, the ETUC in April 1995 had approximately 46 million affiliated members, through national bodies such as the British TUC, in 22 countries. The ETUC was an influential body in the discussions that resulted in the Social Protocol at the Maastricht meeting.

The arguments that have been deployed have centred on the need for a 'level playing field' if competition is to be fair. There is a view that poorer member states might avoid improvements to working conditions in order to take advantage of low wage costs, and that a plinth of social rights is necessary to avoid social dumping. A price competition spiral might ensue, when companies in the richer countries might be tempted to try to reduce costs by reducing pay and social benefits. From this destabilizing price war there would be no winners.

The British Conservative government was vociferous in opposing the idea of the Social Charter, largely, it seems, for ideological reasons. Having 'freed up' the UK labour market, there was a desire by the British to keep it free of restrictions imposed by what was seen as the Brussels bureaucracy.

The Community Charter of Fundamental Social Rights, published in September 1989, contained twelve sets of 'fundamental rights'. These included, *inter alia*: rights to social protection, to freedom of association, to vocational education and training, to equality of treatment between men and women, and to information, consultation and participation, as well as to health protection.

However, these proposals were not acceptable to the British at the European Heads of State meeting in Strasbourg in December 1989, and the original ideas were 'watered down' to become more a matter for guidance than a mandate for action. In practice, many of the proposals (such as equality of treatment between men and women) were already enacted in British law.

At Maastricht, Britain negotiated an opt-out from the provisions of the Social Charter on the grounds that flexibility in the labour market was necessary in order to encourage inward investment and thereby to reduce the massive unemployment in the EU (which was standing at around 18 million people in 1998 from a figure of around 20 million at the time of Maastricht).

Some increases to employees' participation in decision-making has been brought about through the health and safety regulations, where the statutory rights for health and safety committees and the free flow of information to employees was accepted as important; more so, than the enforced adoption of German-style 'co-determination', which was once feared by employers. Whatever the objections to formal participation schemes, large modern companies accept the necessity to obtain the agreement of employees to change.

As a result of the opt-out, British employers were originally not required to obey the European Works Council Directive in respect of their UK employees. Following the election of the Labour government in 1997, the new government decided to end the British opt-out from the Social Chapter, and to accept the European Works Council (EWC) Directive. Many companies had, in any case, already negotiated EWC's. At least 430 EWC agreements had been concluded by September 1996. For example, United Biscuits, Coats Viyella, ICI, BP, Marks & Spencer had all concluded agreements, the main reason for which being that they had employees working across Europe and therefore not to create an EWC would have resulted in consultation only with their staff based elsewhere in Europe.

It is worth noting here that statutory works councils were already required prior to the Directive, in Belgium, France, Luxembourg, the Netherlands, Germany, Greece, Portugal and Spain, and some form of employee representative on most company boards of directors in Denmark, Germany, France, Finland, Luxembourg and Sweden. These representational arrangements do not necessarily have an impact on trade union membership, which varies considerably between countries. For example, trade union density in Denmark at around 70 per cent compares to the UK at around 35 per cent and a similar figure for West Germany, with only around 10 per cent for France. The only statutory requirement in the UK (apart from the Transfer of Undertakings (Protection of Employment) Regulations and collective bargaining laws) is for employers to show in their annual reports to shareholders what steps have been taken towards employee communication and representation. The pressure for change on British companies may increase if a European company statute is eventually agreed which would give companies a 'European' identity with tax and legal advantages. Such a 'European company statute' is likely to contain provisions for participation of employees.

We should note that the EWC Directive only applies to undertakings with at least 1000 employees, in the EU, and at least 150 employees in at least two countries, whilst central management is responsible for setting up an EWC or a special negotiating body. To establish such a body would require the support of at least 100 employees or their representatives, in two undertakings or more, or from establishments in at least two or more countries.

Those companies that have established EWCs report a number of benefits, in particular greater awareness of business strategy and priorities, an improved understanding of what is happening in different counties, increased trust, encouragement for higher standards in training, communication and consultation, according to research by the Industrial Participation Association (IPA), which conducted research in companies including Henkel, Zeneca, ICI, Kone and Générale des Eaux.

A variety of selection procedures are used to find delegates to the EWC, including selection by the union, or through election or some combination of selection and election. The EWCs are allowed to invite experts to their meetings (for example, in connection with health and safety matters). There are difficulties reported by companies, for example, in creating a common agenda, and whilst the majority of events start with a pre-meeting of employee representatives to go through the agenda, there seems to be no set format. In most cases, the EWC is timed to take place as soon as possible after the announcement of the annual results.

In the IPA's research into twenty-six companies, the researchers asked what measures for success they use for EWCs:

> on both sides, the most common answer was that the EWC could be considered a success if we feel that there has been a real exchange of views in terms of frank and full disclosure of information, informed discussion and executives listening to and taking on board opinions. Many also hoped that the EWC would break down barriers and improve employee relations.
>
> (IPA, 1998:10)

The increasing pace of change and the importance of gaining commitment are essential. Many large companies have consciously adopted a more participative style, sometimes announced in a statement of the company's philosophy. For example, GEC, ICI, GKN and United Biscuits have developed their own way of dealing with the participation question, through such means as communications exercises, autonomous work groups and committee structures. The public sector Whitley Committees have long been a way of consulting civil servants, although there are signs that the Whitley system is breaking up in the Civil Service because of its unresponsiveness to local problems, and because the individual unions in the public sector are much stronger than before and do not always perceive a commonalty of interests with their other union colleagues.

Movements by workers themselves in response to threats of closure have become more common, as have management buy-outs sometimes with government help as in the case of the Meriden motorcycle co-operative. Direct action by workers, such as sit-ins, and attempts at the formation of producer co-operatives have tended to be unsuccessful, as the circumstances are usually the least favourable for any marketing initiative. In addition, there are a number of problems associated with producer co-operatives:

1 The difficulty of attracting capital for a new venture.
2 A lack of management skills.
3 The apathy of the trade union movement towards this form of participation.

Partnership

In addition to formal participation or consultation systems, managers also encourage direct forms of participation. The former is seen in the JCC or the EWC, the latter in cases where the manager maintains some control of the decision-making process, for example by delegation, empowerment and involvement schemes.

The notion of 'partnership' has come to be used as a way to describe an approach characterized by a unitary frame of reference, and a strong desire to harness the energy and commitment of employees to the flexibility and change orientation necessary for business survival. The IPA defines the partnership approach as consisting of three elements: a commitment to working together to make the business more successful, understanding the need for both flexibility and security, with policies to address these needs, and relationship-building with the workforce. They cite companies such as ICI, Elida Gibbs, Boots, Rover, Blue Circle, John Lewis, Transco, Scottish Power, Thames Water and Welsh Water, as cases where the partnership approach has been developed (IPA, 1998a).

The joint problem-solving aspects central to partnership mean that working groups have been successful at cost reduction involving job cuts and new working practices with more flexibility achieved. Examples here are: the Royal Mail where the understanding of the strategic requirements to be ready for more competition resulted in the reorganization of the sorting offices; a 36 per cent (1000 people) reduction of employee numbers at Blue Circle was achieved; and the case of the Port of Felixstowe where with trade union agreement new technology and more flexible staffing was introduced to make the large container port competitive. We should note that in many of these cases, a relatively militant trade union environment has been turned into a productive relationship where both employer and employee interests can be advanced.

Other cases include Tesco where there is a partnership between management and trade unions to provide a more flexible working arrangement, and many others, where the improvement in communications especially 'employee voice' can be seen to bring business benefits, such as quality improvements with fewer rejects or recalls.

The IPD which sees partnership as being 'about particular processes of management, rather than about structures' (IPD, 1997: 8), argues for a mixture of direct and representational participation. The concept of partnership can be taken further, suppliers and customers could be involved as partners, and the idea of the stakeholder organization implies a long-term agreement to work together for mutual success.

Conclusion

Co-operation between management and workers is essential for success in business, and the way that this is achieved will vary according to the size, structure, market share and financial support of the organization. There are increasing pressures for formal mechanisms to be adopted across Europe, and the need to share information is increasingly accepted.

Questions

1 What is the difference between 'descending' and 'ascending' participation?
2 What does management seek to gain from formal methods of joint consultation? What are the benefits of a JCC for workers?
3 Taking the case of an organization you know well, how would you introduce formal representation of employee interests to the main board of directors or other central decision-making body?

References

IPA (1998a). *Sharing the Challenge: Employee Consultation*. A guide to good practice. IPA.

IPA (1998b). *European Worker Councils*. A guide to good practice. IPA.

IPD (1997). *Employment Relations into the 21ˢᵗ Century*. An IPD Position Paper. IPD.

Chapter 21

Employment law

Changes in the law may be said to represent broader social change. In recent years, the employment contract has increasingly become subject to regulation. General duties towards workers have been laid on employers, and there is now a legal framework encompassing the collective action of workers in strikes, ballots and picketing, and laws to influence the way trade unions conduct their affairs. In addition, the UK is subject to the Treaty of Rome and to the delegated legislation of the European Commission and the Council of Ministers.

The complexities of employment law grow daily, presenting a problem for a general text of this kind. To give a detailed description of each statute would take several volumes, yet in omitting detail we could be accused of misleading readers. The best solution to the problem would seem to be to take the main areas where the law impinges on employment and to describe in outline the current constraints and obligations without going into detail on the specific statutes. This chapter will cover the institutions, contracts of employment, dismissal, redundancy, pay, maternity, discrimination in employment, data protection, collective bargaining, and health and safety.

A number of institutions have come into being to help the interpretation and to administer the law and give advice to management, workers and trade unions.

The Advisory, Conciliation and Arbitration Service

We have already outlined the advisory role of ACAS and its function of promulgating codes of practice. It has a positive role to play in 'promoting the improvement of industrial relations', especially the machinery of collective bargaining, according to the 1975 Employment Protection Act. The possible forms of intervention by ACAS include:

- conciliation (attempts to get both parties together)
- mediation (offers grounds for settlement)
- arbitration (assists in appointment of one or more arbitrators).

The Advisory, Conciliation and Arbitration Service is also involved in individual cases of conciliation, before complaints by individual employees are heard by a tribunal and, where the parties agree to their involvement, settle disputes by adjusting unfair dismissal claims, under the Employment Rights (Dispute Resolution) Act 1998.

The Central Arbitration Committee

The Central Arbitration Committee (CAC) was established under the 1975 Employment Protection Act. It replaced the old Industrial Court, and is a permanent tribunal which deals with referrals on: arbitration, trade union recognition, the disclosure of information to trade unions for collective bargaining purposes, under the Equal Pay Act, and from the disputes procedures of a number of organizations. The CAC can play an important role in arranging trade union recognition agreements under the Employment Relations Act 1999. Central Arbitration Committee awards are published and take effect as part of the contracts of employment of those employees covered by the award.

Employment tribunals and the Employment Appeal Tribunal

The industrial tribunals were renamed 'employment tribunals' in 1998, and exist throughout the UK to deal with most of the cases that are brought under the statutes relating to employment. Tribunals also have jurisdiction in employment-related contractual disputes with awards up to £25 000. These tribunals are informal, consisting of a legally qualified chairperson and two members, one selected from an employers' panel, the other selected from a trade union panel. Evidence is given on oath, witnesses are called and legal representation of the contending parties is permitted. The decision by the tribunal is legally binding. However, their decisions can be challenged either by review (within fourteen days of a decision being entered on the register) or by appeal (within forty-two days of the decision being sent out). The power of review enables an employment tribunal to rehear the whole or part of a case if there has been some administrative error leading to the wrong decision by tribunal staff, or if a party did not receive notice of the proceedings, or a decision has been made in the absence of a person entitled to be heard, or there is important new evidence or, more generally, 'in the interest of justice'.

Appeals against a tribunal's decisions are permissible on points of law to the Employment Appeal Tribunal (EAT), which also has the same review powers as an employment tribunal. Employment Appeal Tribunal appeals are normally heard by a High Court judge and two or four lay persons (although a judge may sit alone if the appeal arises from an employment tribunal decision where only the tribunal chairperson was involved). The EAT may also hear appeals on fact under the Trade Union and Labour Relations (Consolidation) Act 1992 concerning entry on the list of trade unions and issues related to the certificate of independence of trade unions.

Employment Rights (Dispute Resolution) Act 1998

Under the Employment Rights (Dispute Resolution) Act 1998 a case may be dealt with in some circumstances without a full hearing. This latter applies where the parties have given their written consent.

A case may be disposed of by hearing the applicant only where the respondent has done nothing to contest the case, or it appears the applicant is seeking a remedy that the tribunal cannot provide, or with only the applicant and respondent (or their representatives) where the facts are not in dispute, and the tribunal has to reject or allow the claim, because of a ruling by a superior court, or if these are only preliminary hearings.

There are cases that are concerned only with areas where the employee is claiming entitlement to a payment, where the tribunal must consist of the chairperson sitting alone (for example, guarantee payments, redundancy payments).

Compromise agreements are possible under the Trade Union Reform and Employment Rights Act 1993. This procedure makes it possible to settle claims regarding statutory employment rights (including unfair dismissal, discrimination, equal pay) provided there is a written agreement and the complainant has received independent advice on the terms of the agreement on the right to claim in an employment tribunal. In addition to lawyers, trade unions and advice centres may give advice to employees on compromise agreements under the amendments made by the Employment Rights (Dispute Resolution) Act 1998.

Contracts of employment

A contract of employment exists when one person engages another to perform a particular task as part of his or her business, in a manner that he or she dictates in return for payment. The relationship will then imply certain duties on the part of the employer: for example, to pay National Insurance contributions, to deduct income tax and to conform with the requirements laid down in employment legislation.

The contract may be formed by conduct, by a document or orally, or by a combination of these. All that is required to establish that a contract exists is agreement of the essential terms by the parties.

Written particulars of a contract

Employers must provide all employees (full or part time) with certain written particulars of their contracts. These must be supplied within two months of starting work, or after a month if the employment ends in that time or, if the employee is going overseas for more than one month, before the employee leaves to travel. Existing employees who have not received particulars must be provided with them within two months of a request. It is important to check that the particulars are correct. Changes to written particulars must be notified as soon as possible, and in any case within one month.

The following information must be supplied in one document (the 'principal statement'):

1 The names of the parties to the contract.
2 The date the employment started and the date the statutory continuity of employment started (if different).
3 Remuneration scale or rate and method of calculation.
4 Payment intervals.
5 Hours of work.
6 Holiday entitlement, including any roll-over holiday rights from one year to the next.
7 Job title or brief description of the work. (For the sake of flexibility, it is better to use generic job titles.)
8 Place of work, or the employer's address if the work is itinerant.

The employer must also supply up-to-date information in the following areas (which may be in a separate document and may be referred to in the principal statement but which must be accessible) and there must be an opportunity to read these:

1 The rules concerning sickness or injury.
2 Pension arrangements.
3 Notice provisions, referring here to statutory minimum notice periods or whatever has been agreed, or to collective agreements where these are stipulated.
4 Expected duration of the work if employment is not permanent or fixed term.
5 Disciplinary rules.
6 Disciplinary procedures, showing the stages and to whom and how the appeal is to be addressed, for both discipline and grievance procedures.
7 For overseas employees, the duration of overseas employment expected, the currency to be used for pay purposes, any additional benefits and the conditions on return.
8 Any collective agreements into which the employers have entered covering this employment must be explicitly stated.

The employer should state if there are no specific elements to be supplied in the list above (for example, pension scheme).

There is no remedy for failing to provide these – except declaration of terms by employment tribunal, which may be unfavourable to the employer.

Express and implied terms of contract

Express terms are those that the parties specifically agree upon, and these terms of contract will typically include some of the items mentioned above, such as rates of pay. The express terms may also include the nature of the work itself. An agreement between the employer and a trade union may be referred to as containing certain of the terms of the contract.

Implied terms are those which are not stated, but which nevertheless impose obligations and duties on both parties. For examples of implied terms we may quote the employer's duty to give the employee reasonable notice in the event of the parties not having agreed the length of notice, for example, where an employee has not yet served for four weeks.

One of the most practically important implied duties is the duty on both the employer and the employee to maintain the relationship of trust and confidence between them. The other important implied duty is the employee's duty of good faith while in employment, which extends to a duty of confidentiality during employment.

Unlawful contracts and restrictive covenants

Any contract which is unlawful, or which is contrary to public policy, and restrictive cannot be legally enforced.

Under circumstances where an employer is anxious that former employees might set up in opposition, make use of the former employer's trade secrets or in some way damage the employer's interests, recourse is frequently made to some form of restrictive covenant in the contract, forbidding the employee to engage in the same business within a specified period after leaving (sometimes this is coupled with a geographical limitation).

Restrictive covenants are unenforceable if they are considered to be in undue restraint of trade, that is, unreasonable in the interests of the parties and the public. Attempts at removing competition by preventing former employees from exercising their skills may be considered to be against public policy, the test being whether the employer is protecting a legitimate business interest versus the right of the individual to earn a living. However, if the employer merely wishes to protect business secrets he or she might be able to justify a restrictive covenant.

It is difficult to distinguish between the two purposes, but the courts have decided in the past about confidentiality clauses on the basis of whether or not the employer was trying to preserve 'objective knowledge', which is the principal's property, or if it is the employee's skill and expertise or mental/manual ability, which is the property of the individual and should be transferable to other businesses without hindrance. Legal advice is necessary before drawing up a covenant of this kind, in order to ensure its validity. It may be enforced by the employer applying to the court for an injunction to restrain the employee's breach or proposed breach. The employer can also claim damages for losses suffered, and may be able to claim against any new employer if they 'induced' the employee to breach their contract.

An unenforceable covenant does not invalidate the remainder of the contract, although if an employer breaks the contract, a restrictive covenant that would otherwise have been acceptable would not be enforceable.

Part-time workers Directive

The purpose of this Directive adopted by the European Union in December 1997 is to remove discrimination against part-time workers, and to improve the quality of part-time work. The Directive passed into UK law in 2000. The Directive states that part-time workers must not be treated 'in a manner less favourable than comparable full-time workers', in regard to their employment conditions. Wherever possible part-time workers terms should be calculated on a pro rata basis. Moreover, employers must consider requests for part-time work, and movement between full time and part time is to be permitted, unless this is established as not practicable by the employer.

Changes in a contract's terms

If the parties to the contract agree, the terms may be changed. Unilateral attempts to change the terms to the disadvantage of either party would result in the contract being broken. Changes to the terms must be communicated to the employee within one month after the change. This can be done by giving the employee written particulars of the change, or by making the amendment available for inspection. Changes to a contract's terms, if to the disadvantage of the employee or due to the behaviour of the employer, may constitute 'constructive' unfair dismissal if the employee leaves.

Fixed-term contracts

A fixed-term contract is one where there is a fixed end date. It is advisable to give fixed-term contracts in writing for even the shortest periods of time. All fixed-term contracts should be for specific duties, and there should be a good reason for giving one. Fixed-term contracts for twelve weeks or less exclude holders from the rights to minimum periods of notice and to guaranteed pay.

For fixed-term contracts, once the person has been employed for fifty-two weeks unfair dismissal may be claimed. If short-term employment can be justified by the employer, the termination may not be unfair. It may be justified as a redundancy dismissal if the temporary post has to come to an end. For fixed-term contracts, in excess of two years, where an agreement has been signed beforehand waiving the employee's rights to claim redundancy payments when the contract is completed, the waiver is binding, but the expiry of a fixed-term contract is a dismissal under the Employment Rights Act 1996, and a new European Directive on fixed-term contracts seeks to give those on such contracts the same rights as those employees on open-ended contracts.

If the contract is renewed at the end of the fixed term, an agreement is required in writing, stating that the exclusion clause shall apply to the new contract also. It would be wise for an employer who is contemplating offering a fixed-term contract to seek legal advice beforehand.

The termination of a contract

The Employment Rights Act 1996 following the Act of 1978, lays down minimum periods of notice. For the employer this is one week's notice after four weeks' continuous employment, and then increases after two years' continuous employment to two weeks, by one week for each year of continuous employment between two and twelve years, and is at least twelve weeks' notice if the period of continuous employment is twelve years or more. The employee must give at least one week's notice after four weeks' service. The employer's and employee's period of notice may be extended beyond that by agreement expressed in the contract. Payment in lieu of notice may be made by agreement (though this does not deny the employee the right to claim unfair dismissal or redundancy), and, unless stated to the contrary, notice may be given on any day of the week.

An employee with one year's service has a right to a written statement giving particulars of the reasons for dismissal. These reasons must constitute a full explanation, not just be abbreviations such as 'misconduct'. The employee's request, which can be oral or written, must be met by the employer within fourteen days, or a claim to a tribunal may award up to two weeks' pay as compensation. Employees with more than one year's service can claim against their employer if they believe they have been unfairly dismissed, although there are a number of circumstances in which there is no qualifying period to claim, for example, pregnancy or 'whistle-blowing' cases.

Dismissal

Wrongful dismissal

We should distinguish between wrongful dismissal and unfair dismissal. It is still possible for an employee to claim that he or she has been wrongfully dismissed in an ordinary common law action for breach of contract in the civil courts or in an employment tribunal. This applies where the employee claims that the employer did not dismiss him or her in accordance with his or her contract.

This might arise, for example, where the employer had failed to give proper notice as stated in the contract. The amount of the compensation or damages awarded would normally aim at placing the employee financially in the position in which he or she would have been, had the wrongful dismissal not taken place. The employee would not be entitled to reinstatement or re-engagement, however. A wrongful dismissal can have other consequences, however, such as rendering restrictive covenants unenforceable.

Unfair dismissal

Since the Trade Union and Labour Relations Act of 1974, as amended by the Employment Protection (Consolidation) Act 1978 and the Employment Rights Act 1996 and subsequent legislation and case law, employees have had the right not to be unfairly dismissed. There are two aspects to 'unfair' dismissal:

1 The manner of the dismissal must be fair – that is, the tribunal must be satisfied that the employer has acted reasonably and fairly, in all the circumstances, in the manner of the dismissal. The tribunal will decide this 'in accordance with equity and the substantial merits of the case'. In doing so, the tribunal will take into account the size and administrative resources of the employer. The extent to which the employer has followed a discipline procedure that accords with the practice recommended in the ACAS *Codes of Practice on Discipline* is taken by tribunals as evidence that the employer has behaved reasonably.
2 The 1974 Act laid down a number of reasons for dismissal that might be considered sufficient if the manner of the dismissal is fair. These reasons are:
    (a) Redundancy.
    (b) Ill health or lack of capability or lack of qualifications for the job in which the employee was engaged: capability is to be assessed according to skill, aptitude, health or any other physical or mental quality (including the employee's adaptability and flexibility).
    (c) Misconduct: this must be sufficiently serious to warrant dismissal or a culmination of a series of less serious matters.

(d)   Where the employee could not continue to work in the position without break-
      ing the law (for example, driving while his or her licence is suspended for a long
      period).

(e)   Some other substantial reason of a kind such as to justify the dismissal of an
      employee holding the position which that employee held.

With regard to point (e), a number of reasons have been used to justify dismissal under
this heading, including an irreconcilable conflict of personalities, caused by the dismissed employee; and an ultimatum from an important customer which forced the
employer to dismiss the employee. However, the manner of the dismissal must be shown
to be fair, so the employer should make efforts to search for vacancies or try to transfer
the employee to a job where he or she will be successful.

A minimum of one year's service is normally required to qualify for the
unfair dismissal protection, and an employee must be under normal statutory retirement
age.

Unfair dismissal: special cases

Individuals have a right not to be dismissed because of a refusal to join any particular
trade union (Trade Union and Labour Relations (Consolidation) Act 1992
[TULR(C)A]). This also applies where a worker refuses to make a payment to charity
as an alternative to paying union dues. Employees should also not be subject to any
action short of dismissal taken in order to compel them to join a trade union, and
employers should not select people for redundancy because of their union membership
or because they are not members of a trade union. Mass dismissals for industrial action
are unfair (assuming the action has been properly balloted and limited to action within
the authority of the ballot). Commercial contracts which stipulate that contractors
should employ union-only labour, or that require the contractor to consult with trade
unions, are outlawed.

Statements within the written particulars given to employees that they are encouraged
to join a trade union are not of themselves unlawful. However, the legislation is clearly
aimed to establish the absolute right of individuals not to belong to a trade union, and
there is no length of service requirement in this case of unfair dismissal.

Under the Employment Rights Act 1996 there is no length of service requirement in
situations relating to health and safety complaints, where an employer must not act to
the detriment of the employee for reporting an unsafe practice. This is intended to
prevent victimization, and also covers occasions where the employee carries out duties
preventing or reducing risks to health and safety, or leaves the employer's premises in
the event of imminent danger. There is no limit to compensation for unfair dismissals
of those people raising health and safety issues, or for whistle-blowers as per the Public
Interest Disclosure Act 1998. The one-year minimum service requirement also does not
apply in sex and race discrimination cases (see below). However, cases must be brought
within three months of the dismissal taking place.

Dismissals where the reason is pregnancy, or the principal reason is connected with
pregnancy, are automatically regarded as unfair. It is also automatically unfair if the
reason is that the employee took part in industrial action. Similarly dismissal is auto-

matically unfair (with no service qualification) where the dismissal is victimization for exercising rights to representation at disciplinary or grievance hearings or in regard to TU recognition claims, or for asserting other statutory rights such as working time rights etc.

Redundancy

Definition of redundancy

An employee may be redundant if:

1 The company that he or she worked for ceases or intends to cease trading for the purposes of which he or she was employed.
2 The employer ceases to carry on business altogether.
3 There is a diminution of the requirement for employees to carry out work of a particular kind in the place where the person is employed.
4 There is a dismissal for reasons not related to the individual, e.g. reorganization of work.

The employer should terminate the contract with proper notice where there is a change in ownership. If the new owner wishes to take on the contract, he or she may do so with the agreement of the employee, and provided the contract is continuous and the business is transferred to the new owner, so that the nature of the employee's work does not change, there will be continuity of employment and no redundancy will have taken place (but see Transfer of Undertakings [Protection of Employment] Regulations – TUPE – below).

If the selection for redundancy is for some reason other than a diminution in the amount of work, or the circumstances applied equally to one or more other employees in the same undertaking in similar positions but who were not made redundant, or the selection for dismissal contravened a customary arrangement, then the employee may claim that he or she was unfairly dismissed.

Where an employer wishes to offer alternative employment, he or she should do so in writing before a new contract is due to start. The written particulars of the agreement between the employer and the employee should state the terms and conditions of the new employment, rates of pay, location and duties, etc. If the employee does not believe that this is a suitable alternative offer, he or she may apply to a tribunal for redundancy pay.

If there is to be a trial period in the new employment, the trial period will begin with the ending of the previous employment and should not last for more than four weeks unless a longer period is mutually agreed for retraining purposes. Such an agreement must be in writing, and must state the date of the end of the trial period and the terms and conditions of employment during the trial period.

A renewal of contract or a re-engagement should take effect within four weeks of the termination of the old contract. Where the employee accepts the suitable alternative offer, his or her employment is deemed to be continuous.

Rights to a redundancy payment

Employees who are made redundant are entitled to a payment from their employer. The right to receive a payment depends on a number of conditions:

1 Employees must have been dismissed because of redundancy.
2 Some employees may be entitled to a redundancy payment if they are laid off or kept on short time.
3 The employee must have served for at least two years and be over the age of eighteen and under normal retirement age.

Dismissal due to redundancy

Irrespective of whether the employee is given notice, or in cases of redundancy constructive dismissal, leaves, the termination will count as a redundancy if the definition outlined above is met. The date of the dismissal is the date on which the notice expires or the termination takes effect. If the employer, after giving notice, substitutes a shorter or longer period of notice, the date will be the new substituted dismissal date. Employees who refuse to work to the later date may lose the entitlement to the full redundancy payment, depending on the circumstances of the case.

If the employee anticipates the expiry of the employer's notice by indicating his or her intention to leave earlier than was originally agreed, the employee will still be taken to have left due to redundancy, and the effective date will be the new date the employee gives. If the employer objects, he or she can write to the employee, requiring him or her to withdraw notice and to continue in employment until the original notice of the employer has been served, and stating that, unless he or she does so, the liability to a redundancy payment will be contested. The issue might have to be resolved by reference to a tribunal. This is true of dismissals due to misconduct during the notice period, when the employer may withhold redundancy pay, but may equally have to fight out the case at a tribunal hearing.

Tribunals are often asked to decide whether the selection for redundancy is fair. Here the tribunal will take into account the reason for the redundancy, the basis for the selection (for example, last in, first out – LIFO), how this principle was applied in fact and the extent to which reasonable efforts were made to find alternative employment.

Lay-off and short-time working

If an employee is 'laid off' or put on short time, he or she may be entitled to a redundancy payment.

Where there is a diminution of work of the kind the employee is required to perform under his or her contract, and because of this the pay for any week is less than half a week's pay, he or she is legally regarded as on short time. Should he or she be on short time (or laid off altogether) for four or more consecutive weeks, or have been on short time or laid off for a series of six weeks or more in a period of thirteen weeks, then the employee can claim redundancy pay if he or she gives the employer proper notice of his or her intention to do so. If there is a reasonable expectation that, no later than four weeks from the termination date, the employee would enter a period of thirteen weeks without short time or lay-off, then the employer must notify the employee within seven days that he or she contests the redundancy payment, as the employee would not under those circumstances be entitled to it.

Length of service

The two-year minimum service must be continuous, and if any re-engagement has taken place, whether or not the service was broken will depend on the re-engagement, the length of the break being crucial (see above on re-engagement within a four-week period).

The amount of the payment

The amount of the redundancy payment to which the employee has a legal entitlement is as follows. Please note that no redundancy pay is due if the employee has reached normal retirement age for the post, and the amount is reduced pro rata for every month over the age of sixty-four. The following list gives the amount of pay for each year's service in the relevant age bracket:

- age 18–21 = half a week's pay
- age 22–40 = one week's pay
- age 41–65 (60 for women) =one and a half weeks' pay.

This is subject to a maximum of twenty years' service, that is, only the previous twenty years will count. The amount may also be reduced if the employee has a gratuity or pension from the time he or she leaves.

Carrying out redundancies

An employer proposing to make 100 or more employees redundant at one establishment should notify the Department of Trade and Industry (DTI) of that proposal at least ninety days before the first dismissal. If twenty to ninety-nine employees are potentially redundant, the DTI must be informed at least thirty days before the first dismissal.

Advance consultation with appropriate representatives

Advance consultation with the appropriate employee representatives is necessary at the earliest opportunity when twenty or more redundancies are proposed. If there is an appropriate trade union, consultation must be with that union. The appropriate trade union is defined as the independent trade union that is recognized by the employer for bargaining or representation on behalf of that worker or group of workers.

If there is no appropriate trade union, consultation must be with employee representatives. If there are no such representatives, an election should be held to elect representatives. An employer has positive obligations in relation to that election process, including an obligation to ensure that the election is conducted fairly.

Employers must undertake consultations with a view to reaching an agreement with the appropriate representatives. Consultation must begin in good time, and at least thirty days before the first of the dismissals take effect (in the case of twenty to ninety-nine proposed redundancies) or at least ninety days (in the case of the 100 or more proposed redundancies). See Table 21.1.

Table 21.1 Amount of advance notice to DTI for the advance consultation period with appropriate employee representatives

Number of people to be made redundant at one establishment	Within following period of days	Minimum warning before first redundancy (days)
20–99	90 or less	30
100+	90 or less	90

Advance notice

Disclosure of information to representatives in writing when consultation begins

The employer must disclose the following information:

- reasons for redundancy
- numbers and descriptions of those to be made redundant
- total number of that description employed at the establishment in question
- proposed method of selecting who is to be dismissed
- method and timing of dismissals
- details of the method of calculating any redundancy payments other than those required by law.

Where an employer fails to comply with the consultation rules, a tribunal may make a 'protective award' – an order that the employer must pay the affected employees for a protected period, which can be up to ninety days.

Time off to look for another job

An employee who is to be made redundant (provided he or she has at least two years' service) must be allowed up to two days' paid leave of absence to search for other employment. When the normal hours differ week by week, the average weekly hours are taken over a twelve-week period immediately preceding the day on which notice was given.

A code of practice on handling redundancies

A 1972 code of practice set out a procedure that is, although revoked, still relevant as a model policy approach to redundancies, especially where there is no union with whom to consult.

Before contemplating redundancies, the code suggests that management should stop recruitment, reduce overtime, consider retraining or transferring the employees to other work, retire those over normal retirement age and introduce short-time working.

Where the redundancy is inevitable, employers should give as much warning as possible, use voluntary redundancy and early retirement, and offer help in finding other work. Employers must also ensure that individuals are informed before any news leaks out and should try to run down establishments slowly.

Transfer of undertakings

Where a transfer in the ownership of a business is contemplated, then employers (either vendors or purchasers) must follow a similar consultative procedure as specified in the earlier section on carrying out redundancies. Section 10 of the Transfer of Undertakings (Protection of Employment) Regulations 1981 states that appropriate employee representatives (which must be a trade union if one is recognized for collective bargaining purposes) must be informed:

- when the transfer will take place, and the reasons for the transfer
- any legal, economic or social implications for the employees
- whether or not any actions are intended with regard to the employees
- where the employer is making the transfer, the expected actions of the buyer in respect of the affected employees.

Employers are required to consult with any appropriate employee representatives and to consider their representations. Where a reply is required, they must give reasons if they reject the representations.

The representatives can complain to a tribunal about failure to comply with these regulations. If a tribunal upholds the complaint, the maximum compensation is thirteen weeks' pay per employee affected.

The regulations apply to any type of business or undertaking, whether or not it is a commercial or public sector activity. The regulations apply irrespective of whether or not property is transferred (for example, they include franchises) and where there are several stages to the transfer process.

Employees gain a number of rights from these regulations:

1 After a transfer, the new employer must honour the existing contracts of the employees. The regulations do not yet apply to pension schemes.
2 Employees have the right to object to the automatic transfer of their contracts of employment. Such a refusal would not constitute a dismissal, and employees would not need to give notice.
3 Any dismissal because of the transfer will be regarded as unfair, unless it can be shown that the main reason was not the transfer itself but for some other economic, technical or organizational reasons entailing a change in the workforce.
4 Contractual redundancy rights can also transfer with the contractual rights, so that there is no dismissal, and so no right to redundancy pay.
5 Accrued pension rights up to the transfer date must be protected. Amendments to the Acquired Rights Directive will make those who are responsible for the future

employment conditions provide pension rights equal to those in the previous employment.

However, there is still some uncertainty about this complex area, especially concerning what is a relevant transfer owing to the wide variety of circumstances such as outsourcing, insourcing and where some part of the business are transferred whilst others are preserved.

Cases such as the European Court of Justice decision in *Süzen* v. *Zehnacker Gebäudereinigung GMbH* (1997), emphasized that there needs to be an analysis of what transfers, which must be an economic entity, and that sufficient of its assets have been transferred such that its essential identity is preserved in the new organization to which it was transferred.

Pay

Methods of payment

Following the repeal of the Truck Acts, manual workers do not have to be paid in coin of the realm, and payment is increasingly made by electronic funds transfer direct into a bank account, such as the service offered by Bankers Automated Clearing Services Limited.

The National Minimum Wage Act 1998

The Act prescribes minimum rates of pay. For those under eighteen years of age there is no minimum. For employees aged eighteen to twenty-one the minimum is £3.00 per hour, and for employees aged twenty-two and over, during the first six months of working in a job which includes accredited training, £3.20 per hour. For all other employees (with the exception of those listed below) the minimum is £3.60 per hour. Exceptions are listed for whom there is no minimum as follows:

- apprenticeships under age nineteen or in the first year of apprenticeships
- workers on sandwich course secondments, work experience or in certain types of sheltered employment
- prisoners and voluntary workers
- nuns and monks working for religious orders.

Calculation of the wage payments for National Minimum Wage purposes is based on a method which for most practical purposes is the base rate plus any non-premium overtime, that is, gross pay before tax. Allowances such as shift allowances or London allowance are disregarded, as are benefits. The method to be adopted is to include:

1 Total remuneration (gives sum before income tax, National Insurance and compulsory stoppages such as attachment of earnings orders or Child Support Agency payments).

2 But excludes benefits in kind, advances or loans, retirement allowances, redundancy payments, suggestion scheme rewards and vouchers (e.g. luncheon vouchers) or stamps.

3 If free accommodation is provided, a notional rate of 50p per hour worked or £2.85 a day is included.

4 Reduction cumulatively from the figure of pay for absence periods which were not part of the working time.

5 Overtime allowances (e.g. for unsocial hours, or London allowance), tips, and gratuities from customers paid by the customer in cash (i.e. those paid through the payroll would be included), reimbursement of expenses, amount of any payment made by the individual to the employer (except fines for misconduct paid under contract, repayments of advances or loans, payments for goods and services bought from the employer, which are included, unless these are part of a contractual obligation as with compulsory deduction for staff canteens, which would be excluded).

The 'reference period' is the pay period (a maximum of one month). Working hours for the reference period are calculated differently according to the four categories of workers defined. These are:

Category	*Defined*
Time workers	Paid for hours worked; pieceworkers who have a set number of hours.
Salaried hours workers	Paid a stated annual salary for a number of hours in a year, (including annualized hours).
Output workers	Workers paid piece rates or on commission, with no fixed hours.
Unmeasured workers	Any worker who does not fall into any of the other three categories.

The amount paid must be at least the minimum amount required under the National Minimum Wage legislation during the reference period.

Working time includes time spent working, time spent at or near the workplace and when the worker is required to be available (except when the worker is required to sleep on the premises), travel for purposes of work (except between home and work) and time spent on training. Working time excludes rest breaks, industrial action and absence which affects pay.

Employers must keep 'sufficient' records, which must be available for inspection by employees as well as by the Inland Revenue who are the enforcing authority.

Itemized pay statements

Where an employer employs more than twenty people, the employees have a right to receive an itemized statement of pay that shows:

● gross amount of pay
● variable deductions (such as income tax)

- fixed deductions (such as pension contributions); if the employer prefers, a statement can be issued annually showing the aggregate of fixed deductions
- net amount of pay.

Right to time off for study

Under sections 63A–63C of the Employment Rights Act 1996 there is a right to paid time off for study or training. Any employee aged between sixteen and seventeen years of age who has not reached a specified standard is entitled to paid time off to study for qualifications identified in the regulations. These qualifications include five GCSEs, Scottish Qualifications Agency award (SQA) in five subjects, Business and Technology Education Council (BTEC) and vocational qualifications. The courses do not have to be related to the employee's current job.

Guarantee payments

Employees with contracts expected to last for more than three months have a right to a limited amount of pay if laid off or put on short time. The conditions under which this is granted to an employee are:

1 He or she must not unreasonably refuse suitable alternative work.
2 He or she must make him or herself available for work and it must be a day on which he or she would normally be working.
3 The lay-off or short time must not be a consequence of a trade dispute involving his or her own employer. Thus, if there is a strike in the company that is not associated with his or her own employer, then guarantee pay would apply if the employee was laid off.

The amount of guarantee pay is limited to a maximum of five days within any three-month rolling period and there is a statutory limit.
The formula for calculating a day's pay is:

Number of normal working hours $\times$ Guaranteed hourly rate

$$\text{The guaranteed hourly rate} = \frac{\text{One week's pay}}{\text{Normal working hours per week}} \qquad (21.1)$$

If the hours per week vary, the average over the last twelve weeks is taken as representative. Where the employee has less than twelve weeks' service, then the average for similar workers of the same employer is taken.

Collective agreements on guarantee pay

Where a collective agreement exists which would result in the employee receiving more than the minimum guarantee pay under the Employment Rights Act 1996, then the employee receives the larger amount. Whether or not the legal minimum gives more than the collective agreement depends on how many days are involved, and on whether or not the collective agreement guaranteed a proportion of a week's pay instead of a day's pay as a basis for calculation.

The parties to an agreement on guarantee pay may apply to the Secretary of State for exemption from legal obligations, provided their scheme is as beneficial to employees as the state scheme.

Suspension on medical grounds

There are situations where the employee may be suspended on medical grounds because of a health hazard at his or her place of work or because of a recommendation contained in a code of practice. Employees (other than those on fixed term contracts of three months or less) with a minimum period of one month's service, who are not absent for a personal health reason, are entitled to payment for up to twenty-six weeks of suspension. Employees must not unreasonably refuse offers of alternative work during this time.

A number of state payments are now made through the payroll. These are presently statutory sick pay and statutory maternity pay.

Statutory sick pay

This scheme involves employers being responsible for paying the first twenty-eight weeks of sick pay through the payroll. This means that employers must keep detailed records. Details were given in Chapter 15.

Employees should be advised that failure to produce accurate information might be treated as misconduct and lead to disciplinary action.

Family-friendly policies

Parental Leave Directive

This EU Directive (Council Directive 96/34/EC) was implemented in December 1999. In the UK, the Employment Relations Act 1999 implemented the maternity and parental leave regulations entitling a parent to a minimum of thirteen weeks leave (which may be unpaid) in order to care for a child, provided the conditions set out in the regulations are met.

There is a minimum qualifying period of one year's employment, the Directive and the regulations apply to both parents, include adoption as well as birth, and are applicable per child. The time may be taken as a single block, or as an annual allowance (for example, one day per week, for fifteen months). Leave is available up to a child's fifth birthday or eighteenth birthday if the child is getting Disability Living Allowance. In the case of adopted children, the limit is eighteen or the fifth anniversary of adoption, whichever is the earliest. The contract of employment continues throughout the leave, and parents taking leave have a right to return to the same job or, if this is impossible, the employer must offer an equivalent or similar job consistent with the person's employment contract. However, redundancy could occur. There are rules for employers to control the timing of the leave, if it causes difficulty, and there is protection against victimization for employees who seek to assert this right.

There is also a right to absence from work for urgent family reasons, in cases of sickness or accident. This includes relatives (for example, aged parents) as well as children and non-family dependants, and applies where it is essential to have support or assistance from the worker at the time. This absence may also be unpaid. There is no qualifying requirement nor a maximum limit on the amount time off that can be taken. There is no requirement to give advance notice if it is not reasonably practicable to do so.

Maternity provisions

A woman who is dismissed because she is pregnant will be regarded as unfairly dismissed unless by continuing to work she was in contravention of a statute. In this case, the employer has a duty to offer suitable alternative work if there is a vacancy. Women who return have a right to return to the same job, apart from this situation.

Maternity leave

All women are entitled to up to eighteen weeks' ordinary maternity leave, which should start no earlier than eleven weeks before the expected week of confinement. Additional maternity leave, for women with one year's continuous service or more, of up to twenty-nine weeks counted from the actual date of the birth is permitted. All employees have a right to return to the same job that they left, unless reasonably impracticable, in which case any suitable alternative job must be offered. The employee must return in fact, that is, must actually turn up for work.

All the provisions about maternity leave time off, such as start of maternity leave and return to work rules are covered by regulations. The Employment Rights Act 1999 covers the overall statutory framework.

An employer is required to give paid time off for antenatal care as instructed by the doctor. There are special provisions regarding the rights of mothers breast-feeding babies, to avoid risks up to six months after birth, which oblige employers to transfer the mother to suitable alternative work or to suspend her on full pay if necessary.

Discrimination in employment

Equal pay

The Equal Pay Act 1970 was designed to stop discrimination in the contractual area of terms and conditions between men and women. It applies to both sexes, and to employees of any age. There must be no difference in the pay, benefits and conditions of service for women or men in 'like work', or work which is rated as equivalent. The comparisons made are between people working for the same employer, or at the same establishment (where there are differences based on location), or at an establishment observing the same terms and conditions. A 'benefit' has been defined by the European

Court of Justice as pay if there is an entitlement based on the employment relationship. Exceptions are in maternity provisions, and when there is a statutory reason as, for example, where women are forbidden to carry out certain work in factories. An employer must be able to prove that any difference between the contracts of men and women is due to a material difference in the work. Work that is 'broadly similar' is regarded as the same for the purposes of the Act. Job evaluation schemes that use non-discriminatory factors show the value of different jobs in relation to each other, indicating that no discrimination has occurred.

Equal value

Following a case brought by the European Community against the UK government, which succeeded in showing that the Equal Pay Act did not fully conform to the Treaty of Rome and the EC's 1975 Equal Pay Directive, the Equal Pay Act was amended to ensure that the principle of equal pay for work of equal value, compared between men and women, was included in the equal pay legislation.

There are three ways in which a claim (by a man or a woman) may be made in respect of pay, terms and conditions of service:

1 Where she (in the case of a woman making the claim) is employed on 'like work' to that of a man.
2 Where she can show that she is employed on work rated as equivalent to a man under a job evaluation study.
3 Where she can show that the work she does is of equal value to a man's work in terms of the demands made upon her in such areas as effort or skill, etc.

A claim under the Act is made to an employment tribunal. If no conciliation is possible, the tribunal will examine any job evaluation scheme to see if it is valid. Where no job evaluation scheme is operating, the tribunal may still reject the claim if it thinks there are no reasonable grounds for the claim. Where there is a job evaluation scheme and the employer can show that there are no grounds for the scheme to be regarded as sexually discriminatory, the claim will not succeed. However, unless the employer is able to show that there are no reasonable grounds for saying that the work is of equal value (for example, by showing that there is a genuine material factor which proves that the difference in pay or conditions is due to reasons other than sex differences), the tribunal must commission a report from an independent expert. This report will be considered when it is completed (usually within forty-two days) and the tribunal, at its resumed hearing, will make a decision. Tribunals can require information to be given to the independent expert, and there are safeguards if the report is inadequate.

Sex discrimination

The Sex Discrimination Act 1975 aimed at removing discrimination in the non-contractual areas of employment and set up the Equal Opportunities Commission to oversee the working of the Act and the Equal Pay Act.

A distinction is made between direct and indirect discrimination, both of which are illegal. Direct discrimination is where a person is treated less favourably than the opposite sex because of their sex (for example, the recruitment of all males in managerial jobs). Indirect discrimination occurs when, although the conditions are applied equally to men and women, the effect of the condition is to preclude one sex (for example, stipulating that all managers must be over 6 feet 3 inches in height, this being less likely as a female characteristic). Therefore, where the condition is irrelevant, and where the number of women who can comply is fewer than the number of men, then there is indirect discrimination.

Similarly, discrimination against people on the grounds of their marital status is regarded as illegal.

The only exception is where there is a genuine occupational qualification for:

- physiological reasons (e.g. a male actor)
- for decency or privacy (e.g. a lavatory attendant)
- where the employee is required to sleep on the premises
- where special care is provided (e.g. in prison)
- personal services for education or welfare
- legal restrictions
- where there are overseas restrictions and it is necessary for the person to work overseas (e.g. in some Muslim countries women might be restricted)
- where the job is for a married couple.

The main areas where HR personnel managers must watch for discrimination are in:

1 *Advertisements*: these should not have any particular reference to sex. Job titles which have a gender included should be avoided (e.g. 'salesgirl', 'office boy').
2 *Recruitment procedures*: these must avoid discrimination; notably the person specification must not show signs of direct or indirect discrimination.
3 *Promotion, training, transfer policies*: these should be sufficiently well known and obviously non-discriminatory so that accusations of unfairness can be avoided.

Complaints may be made (within three months of the discrimination) to a tribunal, which can award damages. The Equal Opportunities Commission can require an employer to stop discriminating and to advise the Commission of action taken to remove discrimination.

We have already referred to the issue of sexual equality and pension schemes. Following the case of *Barber* v. *Guardian Royal Exchange Assurance* (1990), pension benefits in occupational pension schemes are treated as pay, and therefore men and women must be treated equally with regard to these benefits. The right to join a pension scheme (contributory or non-contributory), contracted in as well as contracted out, public and private sector, is equal for men and women. There was no obligation to equalize benefits for service before 7 May 1990. Effectively, men can now retire at the same age as women (but this is not mandatory). Claims can be brought against the pension fund as well as against the employer.

Race discrimination

The Race Relations Act 1976 follows the same broad principles, in seeking to remove discrimination, as the Sex Discrimination Act and makes the same distinction between direct and indirect discrimination. The Commission for Racial Equality's role in promoting harmony between ethnic groups extends beyond employment.

Racial groups are defined as groups of people of particular origins, of specific race or nationality or colour. Religious affiliations are not part of the definition (although there is legislation in Northern Ireland aimed at preventing religious discrimination).

The segregation of racial groups is illegal. The victimization of anyone who brings a complaint under the Act is also illegal (as is the case with the Sex Discrimination Act). Employers must pay particular attention to their recruitment procedures to ensure that no discriminatory practices enter into their decisions (for example, in advertising, screening applicants, etc.), and should ensure that their employees are treated fairly so that promotion, training and development opportunities are not forgone because of discrimination. Terms and conditions of employment must apply equally to all racial groups, there must be no discrimination during disciplinary action, and unless membership of a particular race is a genuine occupational qualification (for example, for a film or play), then there are no exceptions. The Race Relations Act applies to organizations of all sizes. The complaints procedure is similar to that of the Sex Discrimination Act.

Age discrimination

Although there is no law banning age discrimination, a Department for Education and Employment code of practice on age diversity in employment urges employers to avoid discrimination against people because of their age, for example, when medical reports on older job applicants are sought rather than seeking health checks on young and old alike. The code could be relevant in unfair dismissal cases, and the EU is likely to make age discrimination unlawful in the near future.

Discrimination against disabled people

The Disability Discrimination Act (1995), aims to protect disabled people and those who have been disabled, from discrimination in employment, and places a duty on employers (with fifteen or more employees) to make reasonable adjustments to any physical feature of premises occupied by the employer or any arrangements made by the employer to avoid causing a substantial disadvantage to a disabled person.

This Act covers the recruitment system and process and the terms of employment, and the reasonable provision of suitable physical facilities, such as wheelchair access.

An employer discriminates against a disabled person if the employer, for a reason related to the disability, treats the disabled person less favourably than he or she would treat others, unless one or more of four reasons which may be entered as justification apply. These reasons include:

1 The disabled person is unsuitable for the employment.
2 The disabled person is less suitable than another person.
3 The nature of the disability would significantly impede the performance of the person's duties.
4 The disability would significantly reduce the value of training (either to the disabled person or to the employer).

After the Court of Appeal case of *Clark* v. *Novocold*, it is very easy to show less favourable treatment, for example, any absences related to a disability have to be ignored in deciding whether to dismiss, even if a non-disabled employee absent for a similar period could have been fairly dismissed.

The Act defines 'disabled person' as a person with a 'physical or mental impairment which has a substantial and long-term adverse effect on his or her ability to carry our normal day to day activities' (Section 1). The definition excludes substance addictions, hay fever, and disfigurements such as tattoos and body-piercing. Physical or mental impairments, which are included within the meaning of disabled include sensory impairments (such as those affecting eyesight or hearing) and mental impairments. Long-term effects are those which have lasted at least twelve months, or will be twelve months, or for the rest of the life of the person. Recurring effects such as epilepsy are included.

Typical adjustments that an employer might make include:

- making physical changes to premises
- allocating some of the disabled person's duties to another person
- transferring to fill another job
- altering working hours
- modifying equipment, instructions or reference manuals
- providing a reader
- providing special training.

Employment tribunals hear complaints brought under this legislation, in much the same way as under the Sex and Race Discrimination Acts. There are codes of practice to help employers to eliminate discrimination, and to define disability.

The Rehabilitation of Offenders Act 1974

This Act (which does not apply in Northern Ireland) means that convicted criminals who have completed their sentences, whether imprisonment or fine, have a period of rehabilitation after which the conviction should be regarded as spent. The period of time before the conviction becomes spent is dependent on the sentence. Thus, for example, for sentences of six to thirty months' imprisonment the period is ten years before the conviction is spent, and at the other extreme an absolute discharge is spent after six months. Further convictions during the rehabilitation period extend the time before the earlier conviction is spent so that both convictions are spent at the same time.

As far as HR managers are concerned, when interviewing applicants for employment they may ask about any previous convictions, but must not question the person about any spent convictions. If an applicant does not reveal a spent conviction, no action should be taken against the applicant and he or she must be treated as though the offence had not been committed.

A spent conviction is not grounds for dismissal, or for not recruiting or promoting an employee or in any way treating the employee differently from others. Certain professions, such as barristers, accountants, medical practitioners, etc. are excluded from this generalization, and spent convictions may be taken into account in their case. When giving references, no information should be disclosed about spent convictions. Such a reference would be slander or libel, and would also risk prosecution.

Public Interest Disclosure Act 1998

This Act seeks to protect 'whistle-blowers' whose disclosure is protected if the information shows criminality, any breach of a legal obligation, health and safety dangers, environmental danger or concealment. The employee is not protected if the act of disclosure involved committing a criminal offence. The disclosure is protected if made in good faith or with legal advice. Disclosure should be made to the employer, other responsible persons or to a third party in accordance with a procedure agreed with the employer. Employees in these circumstances are protected from dismissal or action short of dismissal, since such action by the employer would be automatically unfair, with no qualifying period of employment.

Data Protection Act 1998

This Act repeals and replaces the 1984 Data Protection Act, although a number of the provisions are similar, in regard to the need to be careful and to treat data confidentially. The 1998 Act gives the employee rights of access to most personnel data that the employer holds on individuals. It implements the EU Data Protection Directive. The Act covers electronically stored and paper-stored information. It limits the type of information that can be processed and the purposes for which it is processed. Personnel data is defined as any set of information about an individual either processed by a computer or kept manually, which forms part of a file. This covers personnel files and notes by managers.

Processing sensitive personnel data is subject to more stringent controls – including information about a person's racial or ethnic origins, political opinions, religious beliefs, trade union membership, health, sexual life and actual or suspected criminal offences.

The processing of personal data includes all processes used in obtaining, recording and holding data, which covers the processes of organizing, altering, retrieving, consulting, disclosing and using data.

Employers must appoint a data controller who will be responsible for determining the purposes and processes of data collection. The duty of the data controller is not to process the data unless certain conditions are met, such as that the data may only be held for specified, lawful purposes, and not be excessive in regard to purpose. There are further conditions dependent upon whether or not the data is classified as sensitive personal data. The conditions for sensitive personal data revolve around the need for the individual's explicit consent, whether or not processing the data is in his or her interests, or if he or she has already made the data public. For non-sensitive data, many of the same conditions apply – for example, the processing is necessary for the purposes of exercising or performing any right conferred or obligation imposed by law on the data controller in connection with employment. In the case of non-sensitive data, legitimate reasons include if the data controller has to process the information in order to comply with non-contractual obligations such as health and safety requirements, or if the processing is necessary for the performance of a contract to which the individual is a party (for example, payroll).

Employers must ensure that the data protection principles are adhered to, for example, by asking the employee to give consent for different types of data processing. There are also transitional provisions in regard to manual (paper file) data, processing begun before 23 October 1998. From 1999 until October 2001, employees are not entitled to see data that was obtained or processed before October 1998. In the second transitional period from October 2001 to October 2007 there is a right of access to manual data, but the other provisions in regard to manual data do not come into effect until after 2007.

We should note that the Human Rights Act 1998 gives effect to the European Convention for the Protection of Human Rights and Fundamental Freedoms 1950 – under Article 8 of which 'everyone has the right to respect for his private and family life, his home and his correspondence'.

Access to Medical Reports Act 1988

There is a right for employees to access any medical records (whether or not kept on a computer) supplied by a medical practitioner for employment or insurance purposes. This is where the report is prepared by the individual's own doctor (either before or during employment) rather than the company doctor. The employer must obtain the consent of the individual concerned if a medical report is to be requested from that person's own doctor, or a doctor covered by this law, and must advise the person of his or her rights under the Act.

Collective bargaining

Definition of trade unions and role of the Certification Officer

The Trade Union and Labour Relations Act 1974 defined independent trade unions as those that are free from control or interference by the employer. The Certification Officer is responsible for certifying the independence of trade unions and for keeping a list of trade unions and employers' associations. The Certification Officer supervises the scheme for refunding costs incurred by trade unions in holding secret ballots. Under the 1984 Trade Union Act, the Certification Officer hears complaints concerning the ballots for the election of the principal executive committee of a trade union.

European works councils

The European Works Council Directive, September 1994 (94/45/EC) seeks to facilitate consultation and communication with employees in 'community scale undertakings'. It does not cover organizations that operate only in one of the EU countries. A 'community scale undertaking' is defined as any undertaking with at least 1000 employees within member states and at least 150 in at least two member states. Further discussion on European works councils can be found in Chapter 20.

Trade union recognition

Claims for recognition by trade unions are handled by the CAC. There is a tight timetable with short deadlines for each stage, but the intention is not to be too formal. The Employment Relations Act 1999 provides a right (under certain circumstances) whereby a trade union may claim recognition by employers and a procedure for this to take place.

The right to claim recognition is extended to any trade union or two or more trade unions acting jointly, where the employer has at least an average of twenty-one employees (including associated companies in the UK, employee numbers averaged over thirteen weeks), including part-timers, provided another union is not already recognized in the bargaining unit.

In the case of a disagreement, the appropriate bargaining unit is decided by the CAC, which has to take into account the need for the unit to be compatible with effective management, the location of workers, the views of the parties, and the need to avoid small fragmented bargaining units.

Recognition is automatic if the trade union can demonstrate it has a majority of the workforce in the bargaining unit in membership (or joint applicants have a majority). However, the CAC may consider a ballot is necessary if a significant number of members affected tell the CAC they do not want the union to be recognized, or the employer has doubts about membership, such as the circumstances under which people joined the union. In these situations, the CAC will order a ballot to be conducted by an independent party, where there needs to be a majority in the ballot, plus at least 40 per cent of the bargaining unit voting in favour for recognition to be granted. Employers must co-operate in this process.

If the trade union and the employer fail to agree recognition procedures voluntarily, there is a fall-back procedure which will be legally enforceable, based on a model prescribed by the DTI.

Derecognition is dealt with by a similar approach. Applications for derecognition may be made by employers or by a worker or workers within the bargaining unit, and this would only apply if the recognition were awarded by the CAC or under the procedures of the CAC. However, there is a moratorium for three years after a recognition has been agreed, before any application for derecognition claim can be made. The grounds for derecognition are where the number of employees has fallen below twenty-one (where derecognition would be automatic), or if at least 10 per cent of the bargaining unit want derecognition and a majority will support derecognition. The issue would then be decided by a ballot – 40 per cent of the electorate would have to support derecognition, and where the original recognition was based on majority membership, if the union no longer has a majority of members this would also result in derecognition.

Trade union immunities

The 1980, 1982 and 1984 Acts consolidated in the Trade Union Act of 1992 severely limited the immunities previously enjoyed by trade unions from tort liabilities – such as breach of contract, intimidation by threatening a breach of contract, interference with a contract or inducement to break a contract.

Immunity is now restricted to actions which are 'in contemplation or furtherance of a trade dispute'. The disputes to which this applies are limited to disputes between workers and their employers which relate wholly or mainly to one or more of the following:

- terms and conditions of employment, or physical conditions of work
- engagement or non-engagement, termination or suspension of employment or duties of employment of one or more workers
- allocation of work or duties of employment between workers
- discipline
- membership or non-membership of a trade union
- facilities for officials of trade unions
- negotiation machinery, consultation procedures, including recognition issues.

Effectively, this prevents official secondary action and political disputes, stops sympathetic strikes and restricts disputes of an official nature to those involving the workers of the same employer. The TULR(C)A (1992) removed immunities from trade unions which take industrial action without the support of a ballot. This does not prevent unions from threatening action without a ballot, but they cannot carry out the threat without one.

Under the 1992 Act, vicarious liability is defined. A union is only liable for acts 'authorized or endorsed by the trade union'. Examples are members of the union's executive committee and those empowered by the rules to act. Damages are limited according to the size of union membership. For trade unions of over 100 000 members, the maximum is £250 000.

Trade union membership

Every employee has the right not to have action taken against him or her which seeks to prevent him or her from joining an independent trade union or from taking part in its activities (that is, if the union is a party to an agreement with his or her employer).

It is unlawful for an individual's employment to be made conditional upon his or her union membership or non-membership of a trade union. Blacklists of trade union members used for recruiting purposes are banned. Individuals have the right to join the trade union of their choice, which may signal the end of the Bridlington principles because under the 1993 Trade Union Reform and Employment Rights Act it is unlawful for a trade union to expel someone unless for a permitted reason. These permitted reasons are mostly matters of personal conduct, or in cases where the rules restrict membership to those employed in a specific trade, profession, industry, occupation or with particular qualifications. The dismissal of an employee for failing to join, or for proposing to join, a trade union is unfair.

People have a right to join or not join a trade union. Members of trade unions may only be disciplined according to the rules of the unions (according to the 1992 TULR(C)A). Disciplinary action is unlawful in relation to the following conduct (*inter alia*):

- failing to take part in industrial action, or criticizing such action
- encouraging or assisting other people to perform their contracts of employment

- alleging that trade union officials acted unlawfully
- failing to agree or withdrawing their agreement to a check-off arrangement
- working for or proposing to work for an employer who employs or has employed people who are not members of the union or of another union.

Under the same 1992 Act any term of a contract which stipulates that a supplier of goods or services must employ union or non-union labour is rendered void. It is similarly unlawful to refuse to deal with suppliers on grounds of trade union membership.

Rights to time off

Trade union officials (shop stewards, trade union safety representatives, etc.) in recognized trade unions have a right to time off during working hours, with pay, to carry out trade union duties, including training in industrial relations. Members of trade unions have the right to time off to take part in union activities other than strike activities. This includes meetings of the membership, but there is no obligation to pay for this latter time off.

A similar right exists for time off without payment for public duties, such as attendance as a justice of the peace or in local authorities.

Disclosure of information to trade unions

Employers are required to disclose certain information to the representatives of an independent trade union that they recognize for collective union bargaining. This does not apply to employers' associations. The union representative (who could be a shop steward and/or a full-time official) can be required by the employer to put his or her request for information in writing.

The employer has an obligation to produce information only if:

1 It is in his or her possession.
2 It relates to his or her undertaking or that of an associated employer.
3 It is in accordance with good industrial relations practice (as per the ACAS code of practice).
4 The absence of the information would impede the trade union representative to a material extent in conducting collective bargaining.

There is no obligation to produce information relating to particular individuals, information given in confidence, or information which could cause substantial injury to the employer's undertaking, other than its effect on collective bargaining. There are similar exclusions regarding national security, information used in legal proceedings or if giving the information could break the law. The employer does not have to produce any original document or compile data where this would cost more than its value for collective bargaining purposes.

Trade unions may complain to the CAC when an employer fails to comply. In such circumstances, ACAS would normally try to conciliate, but if this fails, the CAC may make an award. To date, most references have been made by white-collar unions and a large proportion of them has been settled without a full hearing.

Election of union officers

Part I of the TULR(C)A (1992) requires a trade union to hold a secret ballot of its members to elect candidates to a union's principal executive committee, a procedure which must be followed at least every five years. All members of the union must have an equal opportunity to vote without any constraint. An independent scrutineer, with a right of access to the union register, will distribute voting papers and will count the votes.

Political objectives of trade unions

Section 71 of the TULR(C)A (1992) requires a union to ballot its trade unions members at least once every ten years if it is to retain the authority to devote union funds to political objectives. This legislation was retrospective as far as the ten-year period was concerned. The rules for the ballot are similar to those for electing union officials, except that a wider constituency, embracing unemployed members, those in arrears, etc., is given. The same rules regarding the independent scrutineer apply.

Check-off arrangements

Employers who deduct trade union subscriptions on behalf of trade unions arrangements are engaged in these arrangements. The written (and dated) consent of each employee is required, and must be renewed every three years. An employee has the right to withdraw consent by writing to the employer at any time. Employers must notify those covered of any increase in subscriptions at least one calendar month in advance, unless the subscription is a percentage of salary.

Strike and industrial action ballots

A union's call for industrial action of any kind against an employer will only be immune from tort proceedings if it is preceded by a full postal ballot. Unions must inform the employer about the ballot in advance and must inform any employers whose employees are affected of the result. If more than fifty people are to be involved in the action, the ballot must be subject to independent scrutiny. Whilst industrial action should take place within four weeks of the ballot, the ballot validity may be extended to eight weeks, by agreement, to allow negotiations.

Picketing

Picketing is only permitted legally where pickets seek, by peaceful means, to communicate with and to persuade workers to work or not to work in support of a trade dispute. Preventing people from crossing the picket lines by physical means and picketing outside a private home are both unlawful. Picketing is permitted only where it is outside or near the employee's own place of work and is conducted by the employees in dispute or with their union representative. The Secretary of State has produced a code of practice on picketing which has to be taken into account by the criminal courts in any litigation. The code suggests that in general the number of pickets should not exceed six at any entrance to a workplace, and recommends liaison between the picket organizer and the police.

Working Time Regulations

The Working Time Regulations, dated 1 October 1998, implemented into UK law the EC Working Time Directive of 1993. These regulations set out maximum working time, minimum rest periods and holidays and rules regarding night work.

Working time is defined as 'any period during which the worker is working, at his [*sic*] employer's disposal and carrying out his activity or duties'.

The regulations state that workers are entitled to:

- daily rest periods of eleven consecutive hours in every twenty-four hour period
- uninterrupted rest break of at least twenty minutes during working days of more than six hours
- weekly rest periods of at least twenty-four consecutive hours in every seven days (this may be forty-eight hours in a fourteen-day period, by agreement)
- paid annual holiday entitlement of four weeks (including bank holidays) per year; after thirteen weeks service
- maximum working week of forty-eight hours average, over a specified period
- limitation on the hours of night workers.

Formal written agreements between employers and trade unions or workers, may be made to restrict or amplify the above provisions, if the workforce comprises more than twenty workers. There are also derogations for 'autonomous' workers and managing executives, these being people who determine their own working hours. Further discussion on working hours can be found in Chapter 15.

Health and Safety at work

The Health and Safety at Work Act 1974 places a general duty on all employers to maintain standards in health, safety and welfare of people at work, to protect the general public and visitors against risks to safety and to prevent pollution of the environment. A Health and Safety Commission exists with a Health and Safety Executive to enforce the law.

Scope

The Act requires the employer to provide for his or her employees, so far as it is reasonably practical, plant, machinery, systems of work, handling, storage and transport that are safe and without risks to health. The employer also has an obligation, so far as is reasonably practical, to provide information, instruction, training and supervision on safety, to maintain any places of work in a safe condition, to ensure a working environment that is without risk to health, with adequate facilities and a written safety policy. It should be noted that mental health as well as physical health is covered. Failure by employers to address the problems of stress at work, for example, can result in successful claims against employers. Employers must now conduct formal risk assessments and appoint competent persons to assist in compliance. The policy must state how it is to be carried out and who is to be responsible. Employers must not charge employees for the cost of safety equipment or for special protective clothing, such as goggles.

Sanctions for breaches of the Act are imposed in the criminal courts. The penalties are a fine of up to £20 000 and up to six months' imprisonment for every person guilty of infringement. Unlimited fines and up to two years' imprisonment may be imposed for some offences.

Employees also have duties – notably to co-operate with management on safety matters.

Risk assessment

Employers must make regular assessments of the risks faced by their employees and non-employees at work 'arising out of or in connection with the conduct of their undertaking'. The purpose of the risk assessment is to identify the measures needed to comply with health and safety rules.

If there are five or more employees, a written record must be kept to show significant findings and any group of people who are particularly at risk. The Health and Safety Executive's *Five Steps to Risk Assessment* explains the process:

1 Look for hazards.
2 Decide who might be harmed and how.
3 Evaluate the risks arising from the hazards and decide whether existing precautions are adequate or if more should be done.
4 Record findings.
5 Review the assessment periodically and revise if necessary.

When evaluating the risks under Step 3 above, employers should assess whether the risk in relation to each hazard is high, medium or low, and then check to see if generally accepted industry standards/controls/measures are in place.

The regular reviews can be prompted by changes to machines, working practices, substances in use, etc. Even if no changes have occurred it is wise to review procedures on a regular basis (for example, annually) and to include non-routine operations in the assessment.

Under 1992 regulations, which were introduced to comply with EC Directives, a range of responsibilities was placed on employers to ensure that all work equipment is suitable and well maintained, that workers are trained and given information on use, and employees are provided with protective equipment and are not obliged to undertake manual handling operations which involve a risk of injury where this can be avoided.

The Factory Acts

The 1961 Factories Act, which has over 200 consequential regulations and orders, details particular duties on employers, such as the fencing of machinery, and rules concerning the employment of women and young persons in factories.

For example, first-aid boxes and, where fifty or more persons work, a trained first aider are required. A minimum temperature of 15 °C (60 °F) after the first hour of work is laid down, and there must be adequate ventilation, etc.

Perhaps the most important provisions are those covering the fencing of machinery, guards being obligatory on all moving parts. The periodic inspection of hoists, cranes, boilers, etc. is expected. Accidents causing absence of more than three days must be reported to the factory inspector, as must any accident which causes an interruption of work for twenty-four hours or more, or causes a death.

It should be noted that, in addition to any penalty for failing to comply with the regulations, there is the possibility of further civil action for compensation for a breach of statutory duty.

The Offices, Shops and Railway Premises Act 1963

This covers the same sort of issues as the Factory Acts but for the premises named in its title. It deals with such matters as sanitary facilities, cleanliness, overcrowding, ventilation, lighting, etc., and lays down minimum standards in these areas.

Questions

1 Describe the main functions of ACAS.
2 Under what circumstances is a contract of employment formed? What written particulars of the contract must be given?
3 What is meant by 'unfair dismissal'?
4 What is constructive dismissal?
5 If you were advised by your chief executive that twelve factory workers (members of the Transport and General Workers Union) would have to be made redundant because of a reduction in sales orders, what actions would you take and why?
6 What groups of employees are exceptions to the minimum wage legislation?
7 How may a trade union obtain recognition from the employer of its members?
8 When is it possible for a trade union to organize a strike without losing immunity from legal action?
9 What is the difference between direct and indirect discrimination?
10 What are the main provisions of the law concerning discrimination against disabled people?
11 When is picketing lawful?
12 What is the main objective of the Health and Safety at Work Act?
13 How does the law protect employees who are involved in 'whistle blowing' cases concerning health and safety?
14 What is involved in a risk assessment?

References

ACAS *Codes of Practice on Discipline, Information to Trade Unions, and on Time off for Trade Union Duties*. Leaflet IND (G) 163 (L). HMSO.
Health and Safety Executive *Five Steps to Risk Assessment*.

Further reading for Part Six

ACAS *Codes of Practice on Discipline, Information to Trade Unions, and on Time off for Trade Union Duties*. HMSO.

Atkinson, G. G. (1977). *The Effective Negotiator*. Quest.

Brewster, C. and Connock, S. (1987). *Industrial Relations: Cost Effective Strategies*. Hutchinson.

Cully, M. et al. (1999). *The 1998 Workplace Employee Relations Survey First Findings*. See DTI website at www.dti.gov.uk/emar

Department of Education and Employment. Various employment and trade union legislation booklets.

Dunlop, J. T. (1970). *Industrial Relations Systems*. Southern Illinois University Press.

Elliott, J. (1978). *Conflict or Co-operation? The Growth of Industrial Democracy*. Kogan Page.

Fox, A. (1966). *Industrial Sociology and Industrial Relations*. Research Paper No. 3. HMSO.

Goldthorpe, J. H., Lockwood, D., Bechhofer, E. and Platt, J. (1968). *The Affluent Worker: Industrial Attitudes and the Worker*. Cambridge University Press.

Gospel, H. E. (1992). *Markets, Firms and the Management of Labour in Modern Britain*. Cambridge University Press.

Guest, D. (1995). Human resource management, trade unions and industrial relations. In *Human Resource Management* (J. Storey, ed.), Routledge.

ILO (1973). *Conciliation in Industrial Disputes*. ILO.

IPA (1998). *European Works Council, A Guide to Good Practice*. IPA.

IPD (1997). *Employment Relations into the 21st Century*. An IPD Position Paper. IPD.

Lewis, D. (1994). *Essentials of Employment Law*. 4th edn. IPM.

Millward, N., Bryson, A. and Forth, J. (2000). *All Change at Work? British Employment Relations 1980–1998*. Routledge.

Chapter 22

Human resource strategy

In this final chapter we will examine human resource strategy as an all-embracing concept, bringing together all the policies and activities that have been described in this book.

The fit between human resource strategy and business or organization strategy is a key determinant of HR effectiveness. The fit between these two aspects of strategy enables HRM to contribute fully to the achievement of organization objectives. The creation of business or organization strategies is dealt with in different ways within different contexts, so here we will present a view based on the most typical approach taken to this process.

Business and human resource strategy

Business or organization strategy may be defined as the attempt by those who control an organization to find ways to position their business or organization objectives so they can exploit the planning environment and maximize the future use of the capital and human assets. Human resource strategy is simply the process of bringing together people plans and programmes of activity within an overall framework, designed to deliver against organizational objectives. As Miller (1987) explains, HR strategy comprises 'those decisions and actions which concern the management of employees at all levels in the business, and which are related to the implementation of strategies directed towards creating and sustaining competitive advantage'. The process of strategy formation is the process by which many different perspectives come to be reconciled. It is the process of taking the influences from the economy and society, and reinterpreting these and organization objectives during a reconciliation of influences from employees, shareholders and other stakeholders. There are external and internal pressures, therefore, which put the fit between HR strategy and business strategy under pressure (Figure 22.1).

There is a need to integrate HR and business strategy at the policy level, that is, to bring together policies into the business processes and programmes, such as those concerned with quality, customer services, cost reduction and productivity improvements. Miles and Snow (1994: 15) have described the process as one of 'fitting organizational

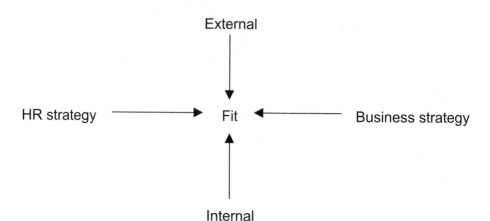

Figure 22.1 The fit between HR and business strategy

structure and management processes to strategy'. This is part of integration, an aspect of the general requirement to fit the strategy to the business starting with fitting the business to the marketplace.

Pressure for change

There are enormous pressures for change upon organizations, which can be found in the business environment: globalization, customer demands for improved quality, technology innovations, demographic and social change. Organizations are changing as part of a dynamic aimed at making both the private sector companies and the public sector more responsive, with a strong capability to change. Acquisitions, joint ventures, mergers and demergers are producing a great variety of organization structures including network and federal structures. This organic approach means organizations are more fragmented, and in the abandonment of stability, rigidity and the rationalistic formal relationships we can see signs of what we describe in Chapter 3 as postmodernism in organization theory.

Amongst the pressures for change which impact as external factors upon the fit, we might expect that general economic and demographic changes will be most important, but also that there are political pressures, for example those related to European integration. One way we can classify these factors is through a PEST analysis.

Political changes are often also seen as economic changes, (for example, the debate about membership of the European currency, the Euro). Consequently we should not be too concerned about precision in the categories, but use PEST analyses as ways of teasing out the factors which are most likely to have an impact upon our business, and the extent of that impact. Demographic and other social changes also have major economic consequences, implying that we should see PEST as represented in Figure 22.2.

It is the economic factors which ultimately influence organization strategy, that is political, social and technological factors provide opportunities or constraints for organizations according to whether they aid growth or not, or produce higher costs or not.

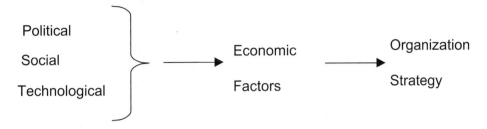

Figure 22.2 PEST analysis: trends

Such factors also may offer new service and product opportunities depending upon whether or not there are appropriate economic infrastructures, such as channels to market, available expertise, and sufficient demand in the economy for the product or service.

If we take demographic changes as an example, we can see how changes forecast may influence the human resource function's ability to deliver desired strategy outcomes and hence these demographic shifts impact upon the degree of fit between the HR and the organization strategy.

The *Sixth Periodic Report* on the social and economic situation published by the EU (European Commission, 1999) examines all the demographic and employment trends in the EU up to 2025. This shows that demographic trends are likely to affect the labour market to a considerable extent in the long term.

'Low birth rates will mean an ageing of the population with consequences for pensions as well as for health care. Over the next 5–10 years this will be particularly pronounced in the Northern regions of Italy, Southern and Eastern Germany, Southern France and mainland Greece' (European Commission, 1999: 8). For example, in Northern Italy and Central France by 2025 the number of people aged sixty-five and over will have doubled, increasing to 40 for every 100 people of working age, and the over eighties will increase everywhere (especially in Greece, Spain and Italy). Dependency rates are often shown as guides to the net demographic impact of changes. The dependency rate is the total number of people above and below working age (fifteen to sixty-four) as a proportion of those of working age. For the outlying parts of the UK (for example, north-west and east Scotland) these dependency rates will be around 0.50, and for much of the rest of the UK 0.55, with some parts (for example, the Southern Counties, eastern England, and the Midlands) being closer to 0.60 by 2025.

The ageing labour force may find adapting to technological change more difficult with a consequence for HR development and training policies and practices, and organizational responsiveness. There are also projected increases in labour supply up to 2005 due to increasing numbers of women in the labour force and due to continued inward migration. The labour force is expected to start to decline from about 2010, but with many different regional effects.

Looking forward to the twenty-first century

The labour force will become increasing diverse, and the policies needed by organizations to assimilate and manage diverse values, cultural backgrounds, religious beliefs and different customs, are likely to require a major effort in policy initiatives to make the workforce cohesive and effective.

This has already become a critical aspect of HRM, for many organizations. For example the city of San Diego created what they described as a diversity commitment:

> The city of San Diego, California, uses the term diversity commitment rather than diversity programme. A programme conveys a short-term effort, one that has a beginning and an end; but commitment is ongoing, organizational and comprehensive. San Diego's Diversity Commitment is designed to create cultural change, where both individuals and the organization adapt.
>
> (American Association of Retired Persons, 1994: 2)

The activities embraced age diversity, as well as being designed to remove ethnic and religious discrimination.

Organizations have a need to be representative of the populations with whom they interact. Local authorities that are elected by that population are especially sensitive to this issue. Similarly, private sector organizations need to have staff who broadly represent their customer base, and engage in diversity programmes to ensure they remain representative as well as for broader social reasons.

Current growth rates in Europe are in the region of 2.5 per cent per annum of gross domestic product (GDP). Growth rates in the UK are around this norm, with slightly higher GDP rates in East Anglia, and greater than 2.7 per cent in central and southern England, and in the north of Ireland. According to the EU, there is no evidence that GDP per head of the population is converging towards the EU average. However, there are 18 million unemployed people in Europe (as at 1997) with the lowest unemployment rates in Denmark, Portugal and the UK at around 5–7 per cent.

New technology is moving so fast that the effects on employment and on organizations, for example, of a move towards business via the Internet are not readily known. For example, Silicon Valley in the USA has around eleven new companies founded per week, has 20 per cent of the largest information technology (IT) companies in the world, and claims that there are sixty-two new dollar millionaires being created every day. Increases in personal spending are growing in financial services, and in home PCs by nearly 20 per cent per annum. We probably do not know what will be the new products or services that will dominate our marketplaces in the next fifty years

These developments are promoting the globalization of economies in the major developed countries, and are producing new occupations. Amongst the technological developments which seem likely to impact on HR is the development of 'spontaneous computing', whereby employees, managers, customers, suppliers for example can access information anytime, anywhere, through portable 'wearables' (computers that will be part of clothing, spectacles etc.). The various stakeholders in the organization are destined to be networked together.

At the same time, office space, which is costly and inefficient is likely to be replaced increasingly by working wherever the employee wishes or needs to be – at home, travelling, on the golf course, in restaurants, whilst shopping and so on. The 'personal assistant'-type of software will research data and prompt its owner with information at appropriate moments, releasing time to be spent on other things. The central hosting of information at either a corporate IT department, or at a software vendor's web site means that PCs will not need to have individually supplied, expensive packages.

At the level of the individual, we are all knowledge workers now. We mostly earn our living through our knowledge and by selling services. Work and home life boundaries are more indistinct, with mobile communications, laptop computers, faxes and the home office bringing work into the home and extending working into the weekend. British Telecom announced in 1999 that they expect about 10 per cent of their workforce to work from home initially, with that number progressively increasing. The pressure of work life also seems to increase. There is now more uncertainty, anxiety and stress, with the roles of parents and partners under constant review, adding societal pressures to fast-changing working activity. These external pressures will influence the kinds of HR policies and practices that can be adopted to fit the business and the HR strategy together

There are also internal pressures for change. These derive from cost pressures and the characteristics of the internal labour market, for example, age profiles, labour turnover amongst strategically important groups, succession plans, and the need to develop a competitive capability for the future. Programmes of activity may well be required to meet these needs – such as organization development and management development policies, employee relations strategies and reward strategies. Some of these will be of a longer-term nature and may necessitate, therefore, adopting policies for which there is no immediate business need.

Overall strategic approaches

Human resource strategies may be understood as objectives, or as processes. Human resource objectives include the development of capability within the company, in order to give the business a competitive advantage. These could be described as broad, overall strategic human resource aims. Human resource strategies which seek to put in place processes, are 'ways of working' akin to the old ideas of 'stratagems' or ploys to achieve particular ends, rather than the ends themselves. For example, we can conceive of organizational cultural strategies that aim to set up a style of working in support of certain values.

In the resource-based view of HR strategy, managers seek to gain a competitive advantage through the quality of the people employed. Since their competitors are also adopting this approach, just following the normal professional disciplines in HRM is not enough to secure an advantage. The basic requirement to trade in most industries now is a well-trained workforce, flexible and responsive to customer demands. These basic policies Purcell (1999) describes as the 'table stakes' – the price necessary for entering and trading in the market, but not a sufficient differentiator for a long-term competitive advantage.

Sustaining competitive advantage requires a unique set of competencies that should be a combination of rare and inimitable skills and knowledge, with organizational systems and distinctive organizational routines. Such elements as the speed of response to the customer, the brand image, the quality of the product or service and the relationship marketing approach are the constituent parts of the competitive strategy, into which the HRM component of competency recruitment and development, motivation and retention, innovation and problem-solving are embedded. Long-term success is an outcome of the whole organizational posture, of which HRM is an integral part.

The ways in which HRM seeks to contribute to organizational performance are through organizational design and OD approaches, through HR systems, programmes and policies and through cost control; leveraging higher output or performance from existing assets. The extent to which HRM achieves these contributions is the extent to which the function can be said to be effective.

We have already discussed organization design and OD. Organization development programmes seek to bring the social sciences to bear on problems of organizational change, and to incorporate the culture change, value-driven activities we described with the example of British Aerospace.

Job design or redesign is a more departmental-level initiative where, with the aid of HR and new technology, jobs are redesigned to become more motivational and where the needs of work groups are incorporated. High-performance work teams are increasingly run as problem-solving groups, engaged in a form of collaborative enquiry, learning as they progress with an open, expressive, type of supervision, and group norms about learning, quality and commitment. Jobs are more fluid and susceptible to change according to the advocates of this approach. Competency hierarchies need to be designed to accommodate these flexibilities, and to encourage the acquisition of new skills.

Already from the above, it is clear that HR programmes and policies are necessary to support OD and job redesign, and therefore that the approaches we discuss here are complementary to each other. The field of employee and management development is now clearly associated with all forms of change and flexibility. Competency frameworks that underpin HR policies in areas such as recruitment, development, appraisal and reward, together with 360-degree feedback mechanisms to monitor progress, provide a comprehensive system for linking HR activities with the organization strategy, by recruiting and developing the strategically relevant competencies into the organization. This can be shown as a virtuous circle of best practice (Figure 22.3).

We can see from this diagram that business strategy is influenced by HR activity. Human resource strategy is not just about implementing strategic plans, but also, through the development of capability, helps to shape those plans by creating new opportunities for what is possible.

The definition of 'best practice' has absorbed many hours of research time. What is argued here is that the organization needs an HR function which selects the *appropriate* best practices from those which are known to be available for the issue in question. This means not following fads and fashions but, rather, analysing carefully what is needed, before introducing new policies.

Research including that reported in this book, has revealed the benefits of approaches which are mostly outcomes. The choice of which particular techniques or policy will produce the outcome is dependent upon circumstances. Tyson and Doherty (1999) developed a model of best practice based on the desired outcomes, at three levels: strategic, operational and process. The way of delivering the outcomes is a matter for debate and choice, according to business needs.

Figure 22.3 Best practice virtuous circle

The model of best practice

In conducting the HR audits as part of the HR Awards 1998 we utilized a model of best practice which sought to establish the approach taken by the organization, and the value of that approach in terms of organizational effectiveness and efficiency. We define 'effectiveness' as the extent to which the members of the HR department and the HR policies give effect to the organization's objectives. 'Efficiency' is defined as achieving these objectives in as cost-effective a way as possible, achieved through constant monitoring of costs and benefits where these can be calculated. Following the criteria found in both the Investors in People and the European Foundation for Quality Management (EFQM), we have taken the position that HRM should help to deliver organizational performance objectives through HR programmes and policies. The consensus on HRM argues that, whatever the model in use, HR activities should be integrated with line management, and that there should be integration within the policies to give coherence, this being the best way to deliver effectiveness and efficiency. We were also concerned that HRM has to work at three different levels – the strategic level, the operational level and at a broad business process level – if it is to influence the whole organization. The model we developed was as follows.

Strategic level

1 HR strategy is seen to fit to the business or organization strategy.
2 HR strategy is designed to deliver against business objectives.
3 Policies are designed to give effect to the strategy.
4 Programmes that bring together a range of policies are integrated with the production/service delivery system.
5 HR function is seen and understood as integral to the main team responsible for the major change processes.

Operational level

1 Competencies are defined as strategically important attributes that give a competitive advantage. These should have been created from within the organization by research into successful performance and an analysis of future staffing needs, both qualitatively and quantitatively.
2 Sourcing strategies are created which seek out these competencies within labour markets and bring them successfully and efficiently into the organization.
3 Employment contracts are formed which are attractive and competitive for the strategically important groups of employees and are appropriate for retention.
4 Employee development needs are met as part of the needs of the business, for all levels. This includes the development of the appropriate competencies, training and promotional systems that also deliver the quality and quantity of people needed in a fair and open manner.
5 Appraisal and performance management systems are connected to organizational objectives and to personal development.
6 Reward management systems are devised which deliver against corporate objectives in terms of motivation, recognition and retention.
7 OD techniques in fields such as organization design and job design are routinely accessed from within the HR function by senior line managers.

Process level

1 Relationships are managed in such a way that there is perceived fairness, and so that employees are involved collectively and individually in those decisions which affect their work.
2 Recognition is given to the different stakeholder relationships (which may include customers and suppliers) and the management approach espoused is inculcated through an appropriate organization culture.
3 Measures are taken which succeed in developing employee creativity and innovation.
4 There is an organization-wide approach to learning and to change management.
5 There are communication systems and processes which facilitate and maintain channels between employees and management in a two-way process (up and down the organizational hierarchy) and interdepartmentally.
6 An overall approach is taken which places the well-being of employees at the centre of organizational life, with preventive measures in place to avoid or ameliorate physical and mental ill health, and which recognizes the significance of home/work life balance.

According to this model, all three levels of HRM should be apparent in an organization: to support strategic objectives, to deliver policies effectively and efficiently and, at the process level, to represent a way of working which is consistent with the organization's espoused values and style.

Cost control, leveraging more from existing assets is another legitimate broad strategic approach, which is important for organizations competing largely on a basis of price. For example, HR functions working to reduce absenteeism can contribute to the bottom line. According to the Institute of Employment Studies the cost of absence to employers in the UK is £11 billion per year. Survey evidence from Gee (1999) showed that absence incidence relates to the size of the organization. The average employee absence for all organization sizes is 6.9 days absence per year (ranging from 5.0 days average absence per employee per year for organizations with less than 100 employees, to 10.0 days per year for organizations employing over 1000 people). Absence rates have been increasing in the period 1996–9, with colds, minor ailments and stress as the main causes.

Other areas where HR might contribute include participating with line management in examining the value added in each process, as part of a campaign to simplify and to re-engineer work practices, and to improve productivity by redesigning work flow and jobs.

As a part of their role to reduce transaction costs, non-employment solutions may be considered by the HR director. These include franchise, outsource and insource work arrangements. Human resource managers have been introducing and extending various forms of flexibility: contract, time, locational and task as fruitful cost-effective solutions to business needs, for some time. Contract flexibility strategies (for example, using casual workers), location flexibility (for example, home workers and telecommuters), time flexibility (for example, annual hours schemes) and task flexibility (for example, multiskilling) are now commonly used throughout Europe (Brewster, 1996).

The idea of the flexible firm, first proposed by Atkinson, suggested that whilst there are many flexible employment options available, firms may wish to combine these with a more stable core of permanent employees, who have strategically important roles (Figure 22.4).

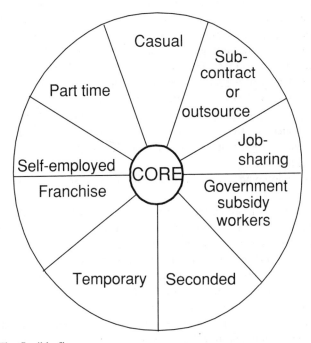

Figure 22.4 The flexible firm

These contractual relationships were described by Tyson (1995) as the 'soft' and 'hard' contract following the ideas of Oliver Williamson:

Soft contract (the core)	*Hard contract (segments of the circle)*
'Clan' culture	Emphasis on transaction costs
Manage by vision and values	Non-employment options used
Horizontal flexibility	Service agreements between departments
Long-term socialization	Emphasis on immediate job performance
Development	Performance-based pay (Taylorism)

The need to fit the HR strategy to the business strategy implies that there would be different contractual relationships, according to the basis on which the company competes:

- Cost minimization/price competition = hard contract
- Quality of product or service = soft contract
- Innovation competition = mixed contract (e.g. soft for core, hard for rest).

Some evidence for these relationships between competitive strategy and the HR policies used was found in research by Schuler and Jackson (1987) in the mid-1980s in the USA. One difficulty with the linkage is that the basis for competition may vary between products, or services and over-time, whereas HR strategy will change more slowly.

Stakeholder models

Frameworks for bringing the business and the HR strategy together were discussed in Chapter 6. Simple frameworks such as lists of business objectives, and the HR implications (expressed as programmes of work, with key performance indicators [KPIs] milestones, and outcome performance measures) are sufficient. There are more elaborate models such as the EFQM's framework, which is used in a quality competition, with points awarded by peer group assessors, resulting in Europe-wide winners. This recognizes that there are different but interlinked groups of people involved in strategy achievement – including suppliers, customers, shareholders as well as employees.

Stakeholder models of HR strategy show the KPIs for each stakeholder in regard to each HR objective or programme as illustrated by the example from a large retail mail-order business (Figure 22.5).

Stakeholders are looming in organizational thinking for several reasons:

1 Shareholder power is more apparent because of the free movement of capital and through their non-executive director representatives on boards and the growing demand for remuneration committees to exercise more control over top pay, and for more transparency and disclosure to produce less generous top pay wards. The spate of mergers, acquisitions and divestments also means shareholders are becoming more sensitive to business strategy. Public sector shareholders, the taxpayers, are even more likely to be concerned about strategy.

2 We commented earlier on the trend for organizations to seek to form trading networks with their suppliers and the recognition of stakeholder relationships as a